Memory, Identity, Community

SUNY Series in the Philosophy of the Social Sciences
Lenore Langsdorf, editor

Memory, Identity, Community

The Idea of Narrative in the Human Sciences

edited by
Lewis P. Hinchman
Sandra K. Hinchman

STATE UNIVERSITY OF NEW YORK PRESS

Published by
State University of New York Press, Albany

© 1997 State University of New York

For information, address the State University of New York Press,
State University Plaza, Albany, NY 12246

Production by Christine Lynch
Marketing by Nancy Farrell

Library of Congress Cataloging-in-Publication Data

Memory, identity, community : the idea of narrative in the human
    sciences / edited by Lewis P. Hinchman and Sandra K. Hinchman.
        p.   cm. — (SUNY series in the philosophy of the social
    sciences)
    Includes bibliographical references and index.
    ISBN 0-7914-3323-4 (alk. paper). -- ISBN 0-7914-3324-2 (pbk. :
alk. paper)
    1. Social sciences--Methodology.   2. Social sciences--Philosophy.
3. Narration (Rhetoric)   I. Hinchman, Sandra, 1950–   .
II. Series.
H61.M4895   1997
300—DC20   96–8702
                                                              CIP

To our son, Bryce Kelley Hinchman,
and all children who love stories

Contents

Preface   ix

Acknowledgments   xi

Introduction   xiii

Part I: Memory   1

1. Narrative and the Real World: An Argument for Continuity   7
   DAVID CARR

2. The Narrative Quality of Experience   26
   STEPHEN CRITES

3. "History with the Politics Left Out"   51
   GERTRUDE HIMMELFARB

4. Storytelling in Criminal Trials: A Model of Social Judgment   72
   W. LANCE BENNETT

5. Human Evolution as Narrative   104
   MISIA LANDAU

Part II: Identity   119

6. The Language of the Self   125
   ANTHONY PAUL KERBY

7. Art, Narrative, and Human Nature   143
   DAVID NOVITZ

8. Narratives of the Self   161
   KENNETH J. GERGEN and MARY M. GERGEN

9. The Genesis of Chronic Illness: Narrative Reconstruction   185
   GARETH WILLIAMS

10. Empowering Women: Self, Autonomy, and Responsibility   213
    BARBARA ROWLAND-SERDAR and PEREGRINE SCHWARTZ-SHEA

Part III. Community 235

11. The Virtues, the Unity of a Human Life,
and the Concept of a Tradition 241
ALASDAIR MACINTYRE

12. Ethnography as Narrative 264
EDWARD M. BRUNER

13. Storytelling and Political Theory 281
PHILIP ABBOTT

14. Narration, Reason, and Community 307
WALTER R. FISHER

15. Postmodern Environmental Ethics:
Ethics as Bioregional Narrative 328
JIM CHENEY

Bibliography 351

Contributors 379

Index 383

Preface

Our intention in this book is to illustrate the ways in which "narrative" has been used as an organizing concept in the human sciences over the last few decades. The volume is premised on the notion that a paradigm shift is occurring, one that leads away from nomological models and toward a more humanistic language and approach, in which narratives are central. Such a shift is evident in many fields of inquiry, including philosophy, history, sociology, anthropology, psychology, education, religion, law, political science, speech and communications, environmental studies, and gender studies. To organize this vast literature, we utilized the categories of memory, community, and identity, which correspond roughly to the three basic elements of narrative: plot, setting, and character.

Partly in order to preserve quality as we ventured outside our own field of political theory, we limited ourselves to articles that had been previously published, and had thus undergone a peer review process. Perhaps the most important task in compiling an anthology is to decide upon principles of selection. In this case, we settled on three: the broad representation of disciplines and of ideological positions; the intellectual power of the contributions and their accessibility to non-specialists; and the likelihood that interested readers would not discover certain pieces on their own.

At times, these principles conflicted, forcing us to choose (for example) between quality and disciplinary representation. In general, we favored essays drawn from journals over chapters contained in books, and we assumed that the works of "big names" in the field of narrative studies—thinkers such as Hannah Arendt, Hayden White, Paul Ricouer, Clifford Geertz, Jean-Francois Lyotard, Roland Barthes, James Hillman, Victor Turner, and so forth—would either be already suffciently familiar to readers of this volume, or easy enough to track down in libraries, as to require no further exposure. We permitted ourselves to make an exception for the singularly influential work of the philosopher Alasdair MacIntyre, which is cited in many of the articles that we chose to include. Once we selected an article for inclusion, we had to decide which of our organizing categories—memory, identity, or community—best suited it, which proved difficult, since the articles typically addressed more than one of these topics. One thing we did not worry about unduly was the fact that all the articles we selected were published prior to 1993; the reader can rest assured that narrative has not waned in importance since then (as the bibliography attests), and that we have detected no major shifts in the way the concept is being utilized in the literature.

Cost, alas, was also a factor in determining which articles to include, and we must thank our universities for helping to defray permissions fees, and several copyright holders for generously reducing their fees to manageable levels. We gratefully acknowledge, too, the assistance of numerous colleagues at Clarkson and St. Lawrence, notably Phil Lewin, John Serio, and David Craig, in referring us to sources that we might otherwise have missed. Special appreciation goes to our secretaries, Sheila Murphy and Linda Snyder, for their help in preparing correspondence for this project, and to Sylvia Haq of Clarkson's Educational Resources Center, who provided useful bibliographic assistance.

Acknowledgments

We are grateful to a number of individuals and publishers for granting us permission to use material from the following sources.

Philip Abbott, "Storytelling as Political Theory," *Soundings: An Interdisciplinary Journal*, vol. 74, no. 3/4 (Fall–Winter, 1991), pp. 369–97, © 1991 by *Soundings*. Reprinted by permission of the publisher.

W. Lance Bennett, "Storytelling in Criminal Trials: A Model of Social Judgment," *Quarterly Journal of Speech*, vol. 64 (1978), pp. 1–22, © 1978 by Speech Communication Association. Reprinted by permission of the publisher.

Edward M. Bruner, "Ethnography as Narrative," *The Anthropology of Experience*, edited by Victor Turner and Edward M. Bruner (Chicago: University of Illinois Press, 1986), pp. 139–55, © 1986 by the University of Illinois Press. Reprinted by permission of the publisher.

David Carr, "Narrative and the Real World: An Argument for Continuity," *History and Theory*, vol. 25, no. 2 (1986), pp. 117–31, © 1986 by *History and Theory*. Reprinted by permission of *History and Theory*.

Jim Cheney, "Postmodern Environmental Ethics: Ethics as Bioregional Narrative," *Environmental Ethics*, vol. 11, no. 2 (1989), pp. 117–34, © 1987 by *Environmental Ethics*. Reprinted by permission of the publisher.

Stephen Crites, "The Narrative Quality of Experience," *Journal of the American Academy of Religion*, vol. LIX, no. 3 (1971), pp. 291–311, © 1971 by the American Academy of Religion. Reprinted by permission of Scholars Press.

Walter S. Fisher, "Narration, Reason, and Community," *Writing the Social Text: Poetics and Politics in the Social Sciences*, edited by Richard Harvey Brown (New York: Aldine de Gruyter, 1992), © 1992 by Aldine de Gruyter, a division of Walter de Gruyter, Inc. Reprinted by permission of the publisher.

Kenneth J. Gergen and Mary M. Gergen, "Narratives of the Self," *Studies in Social Identity*, edited by Theodore R. Sarbin and Karl E. Scheibe (New York:

Praeger Publishers, 1983), pp. 254–73, © 1983 by Praeger Publishers. Reprinted by permission of Greenwood Publishing Group, Inc., Westport, Conn.

Gertrude Himmelfarb, "'History with the Politics Left Out,'" *The New History and the Old* (Cambridge: Harvard University Press, 1987), pp. 13–32, © 1984 by *Harper's Magazine*. Reproduced from the April 1984 issue by special permission of *Harper's Magazine.*

Anthony Paul Kerby, "The Language of the Self," *Philosophy Today* (Fall, 1986), pp. 210–23, © 1986 by *Philosophy Today*. Reprinted by permission of *Philosophy Today.*

Misia Landau, "Human Evolution as Narrative," *American Scientist*, vol. 72 (May–June 1984), pp. 262–68, © 1984 by *American Scientist*. Reprinted by permission of the publisher.

Alasdair MacIntyre, "The Virtues, the Unity of a Human Life, and the Concept of a Tradition," *After Virtue* (Notre Dame, Ind.: University of Notre Dame Press, 1981; Second Edition, 1984), pp. 190–209, © 1984 by Alasdair MacIntyre. Reprinted by permission of the University of Notre Dame Press.

David Novitz, "Art, Narrative, and Human Nature," *Philosophy and Literature*, vol. 13, no. 1 (1989), pp. 57–74, © 1989 by The Johns Hopkins University Press. Reprinted by permission of the publisher.

Barbara Rowland-Serdar and Peregrine Schwartz-Shea, "Empowering Women: Self, Autonomy, and Responsibility," *The Western Political Quarterly*, vol. 44, no. 3 (1991), pp. 605–24, © 1991 by *The Western Political Quarterly*. Reprinted by permission of *The Western Political Quarterly.*

Gareth Williams, "The Genesis of Chronic Illness: Narrative Reconstruction," *Sociology of Health and Illness*, vol. 6 (1984), pp. 175–200, © 1984 by Blackwell Publishers. Reprinted by permission of the publisher.

Introduction

TOWARD A DEFINITION OF NARRATIVE

The word "narrative" comes from the Indo-European root "gna," meaning both "to tell" and "to know."[1] But knowledge today, writes Jean-François Lyotard in *The Postmodern Condition*, is no longer principally narrative. In traditional cultures, whose social bonds were created and sustained by custom, narratives could define "what [had] the right to be said and done."[2] And in the more scientific cultures of high modernity, certain "metanarratives," especially the stories of popular emancipation and the speculative unification of all knowledge, continued to furnish legitimacy and social cohesion. By now, however, even these stories have lost credibility.[3] What we often perceive as a loss of meaning amounts, then, to the eclipse of narrative knowledge as such, and its replacement by other forms of cognition, especially technical ones. Correspondingly, it was long the case in many fields of study that "to choose not to tell a story [was] to be more modern."[4] Summing up the *Zeitgeist*'s verdict, one authority declares that "traditional narrative is dead."[5]

Could it be, though, that reports of the death of narrative have been "greatly exaggerated"? The previous two decades have witnessed an unparalleled efflorescence in writings about narrative and efforts to integrate it into a variety of disciplines. Sociologist David Maines announces confidently that in his field, at least, "narrative's moment" has arrived.[6] While it is true that metanarratives on the order of republicanism or Marxism have gone out of fashion for now, narrative seems alive and well on a more modest scale both in the language of everyday life and in relatively formal discourses such as ethnographic studies or philosophical treatises. Indeed, the overwhelming impression one gets from surveying the "narrative turn" in the human sciences today is that, more than ever before, they have assimilated the idiom of literary criticism in which narrative has always played a very big part.[7] The more radical elements even want to claim that *everything* is a story, including even mathematics and scientific theories.[8] If such claims are to be believed, narrative knowledge, far from fading out, bids fair to monopolize *all* other forms of cognition by converting them to forms of storytelling.

The astonishing "comeback" of narrative seems to have diverse and complex causes, the unearthing of which would require an elaborate story in its own right.[9] But the articles collected in this volume suggest that some of the following factors may have been behind it. First, there has been a disenchantment with theories, especially in psychology, that portray the self as a mere "point" acted upon by external forces. Narrative, by contrast, emphasizes the active, self-shaping quality of human thought, the power of stories to create and refashion personal identity.[10] Narrative seems to offer a way out of the reification that "mechanistic" models of human behavior may unwittingly impose.

Second, many of the perspectives that narrativists attack (or caricature?) owe something to the longstanding social-scientific project of elaborating a body of authoritative knowledge, more or less on the order of that which prevails in the natural sciences. This sort of project strikes quite a few of our contributors as mistaken, even repressive and imperialistic, in presuming that there could be one set of indisputable truths available to an abstractly conceived "subject" of knowledge. In this case narrative appears to reaffirm the plurality of stories that different cultures and subcultures may tell about themselves. The "personal narrative" current marshals the diverse, historically concrete stories and experiences recounted by non-elite people against the version of reality allegedly sanctioned by mainstream social science and philosophy. Storytelling becomes for its supporters an act of resistance against a dominant "Cartesian" paradigm of rationality.[11]

Finally, many of the narrative practitioners represented here have complained that traditional methods, particularly quantitative ones, do not allow them to reconstruct social phenomena in their full richness and complexity.[12] Whether one hopes to understand a cockfight in Bali or the verdicts given by American jurors, one may, so they claim, have to trace out the stories that inform the actions and judgments of the people and institutions under study, for the former "connect the mind to the social world."[13] Leaving stories out of account would mean renouncing the best clues about why people act as they do, since there are no uninterpreted data. Every phenomenon social scientists investigate arises out of a web of communication that, in turn, depends largely on personal or social narratives.

All three inducements for narrative renewal mentioned above probably owe something to the influence of phenomenology and hermeneutics in shaping an American tradition of "interpretive" social science.[14] Hans-Georg Gadamer's magisterial *Truth and Method* (published in 1960, and translated into English in 1975), especially, reminded practitioners of the human sciences that the latter are "connected to modes of experience that lie outside science: with the experience of philosophy, of art, and of history itself. These are all modes of experience in which a truth is communicated that cannot be verified by the methodological means proper to science."[15]

To evaluate the arguments developed by the theorists represented here, we need to work out a preliminary definition of narrative as well as to specify what narrative is not (if indeed there is anything it is not!). But difficulties arise almost immediately. Since the authors define narrative in so many different ways, we run the risk of biasing the entire inquiry for or against some of them in virtue of the definition we choose. The simplest expedient may be to locate the lowest common denominator of all definitions, the features of narrative that most theorists presumably would regard as indispensable to the intelligibility of their topic.

One such feature of narratives—or stories, as we may also call them—identifies them as forms of discourse that place events in a sequential order with a clear beginning, middle and end.[16] In other words, a narrative is not just a list, nor is it even a series of case studies or vignettes. Moreover, though here one might encounter a demurral or two, the sequence must "add up" to something; the units so ordered must have an intrinsic, meaningful connection to one another. By this criterion annals and chronicles would not count as full-fledged narratives (or, as Donald Spence terms them, "significant" as opposed to "plain" narratives),[17] because they only tell "what happened" across a stretch of time, without showing the continuities among the events depicted. At least the stronger versions of narrative theory take the next step, claiming that narratives can actually explain, and not merely describe, although the type of explanation they offer would differ from the deductive models standard in natural science.[18]

Accordingly, most narrativists do distinguish between theories and narratives, and some (e.g., Philip Abbott) explore the productive tensions between the two. They usually conceive of theories as attempts to capture and elaborate some timeless, essential reality "behind" the world of human events, whereas narratives undertake the more modest task of organizing and rendering meaningful the experiences of the narrator in that world.[19] Another way to approach the issue would be by specifying the "location" of the thinking self. In theories, the mind is somehow outside of the phenomena to be examined, and is often pictured as solitary. In narrative, there has to be a teller of the story and an audience to hear it, even if the audience should be only the self considered as addressee.[20]

Finally, narrativists recognize that stories do not simply mirror reality; storytelling inevitably involves selectivity, rearranging of elements, redescription, and simplification. So proponents have struggled to find terms adequate to express the way narratives convey what is true about the world. Some equate them with "paradigms"; another prefers to call them "capsule views of reality"; a third, "interpretive devices"; a fourth, "world views."[21] The list of similar terms could be extended. In all of them the common thread is the notion that narrative somehow mediates between self and world, either evoking or simply creating order and meaning. What the world or experience might be like "before" narratives construct and order it, i.e. "in itself," proves to be one of the more controversial issues in the literature on narrative, one to which we shall return shortly. But narrativists concur that stories are more than merely idiosyncratic or purely private ruminations. Narratives have transsubjective truth value, however fuzzily defined it might be. In sum, we propose that narratives (stories) in the human sciences should be defined provisionally as discourses with a clear sequential order that connect events in a meaningful way for a definite audience, and thus offer insights about the world and/or people's experiences of it.

To locate narratives on a continuum would perhaps suggest the following picture (borrowed loosely from Stephen Crites' article in this volume). Below the threshhold of narrative, we have "immediacy" of whatever kind: bare sensations, particular images, disconnected slices of life, "spots of time," all that seems relatively unformed by the active imagination. We might also add literary and historical genres that do not aim to tell a story, but only to offer thematic reflections. Tocqueville's *Democracy in America* has been suggested as an example of this sort of writing.[22] Beyond narrative would range all those forms of thought that try to identify regularities and patterns in the stories we tell about ourselves. Structuralism and (as noted) mainstream social science both treat narrative accounts as only the first stage in the elaboration of an underlying non-narrative reality.[23]

In a sense, then, the narrative approach begins and ends with everyday life: the experiences, speech, purposes, and expectations of agents as they express them in their stories about themselves. Narrative dwells on the "surface" of human affairs, but its proponents believe that that surface is far more interesting and mysterious than its detractors imagine. Nevertheless, the suspicion remains: can narrative really tell us anything we do not already know? Should we really take seriously the stories people tell, when the latter so often appear self-serving, thoughtless, and shallow? The articles collected in this book may offer some concrete evidence to dispel or confirm such doubts. We have arranged them into three categories, identity, memory, and community, based on the following scheme.

Personal identity, the answer to the riddle of "who" people are, takes shape in the stories we tell about ourselves. Such stories may not necessarily be the ones we tell to others or to the public at large; they are the narratives that we construct as we orient our present choices and actions in light of our imagined futures and the version of our own pasts that fits with these projects. These narratives of identity, which we may entitle "first-order narratives,"[24] have particularly interested psychologists and some philosophers, as the specialists most attuned to the phenomena of individual consciousness.

But the narrative approach has stimulated controversy on a different level: the reconstruction of the past, mainly by historians. Traditionally, the writing of history resulted in stories that depicted the adventures of a definite, often collective "subject" (France, the Middle Ages, the Civil War) over a span of time. Again following Carr, we may call these "second-order narratives," since they involve reflections by a (usually) uninvolved spectator upon the doings and stories of participants in the events themselves. Here, as in the first case, we shall find proponents of narrative trying to defend the claim that life—or history—without narrative proves to be chaotic or meaningless.

Finally, narrative has become a favored concept among many practitioners of the human sciences who study collectivities. Individual narratives, and even the historical tales woven by second-order storytellers, figure in the more encompassing process of community-formation and maintenance. The stories that individuals create often strike variations upon a repertoire of socially available narratives that, in turn, legitimize the community and guarantee its continued existence. It is this self-legitimizing and unifying function of narrative which Lyotard invoked in his argument, noted earlier, that knowledge today is no longer principally narrative. We live in an age, he claimed, in which science and social science pretend to renounce storytelling in favor of theory, yet covertly still rely on venerable, discredited meta-narratives that legitimize what they do. Nevertheless, the contributors to our section on community would insist that social solidarity still requires *some* kind of narratives, even if they are less encompassing than the *grands recits* discussed by Lyotard.

We caution that the groupings we suggest—identity, memory, and community—overlap at many points. The authors whose writings are included here (plus many others not included) recognize that these dimensions of narrative mutually influence and reinforce each other. Thus, their inquiries frequently move from first- to second-order narratives and from thence to the communal, collective aspect of story-making. Nevertheless, each of these facets of narrative has its own peculiar problems and debates, which we shall try to highlight briefly.

MEMORY, IDENTITY, AND COMMUNITY

The philosophy and psychology of narrative identity owe much to semiotics, phenomenology, hermeneutics, and postmodernism in every field.[25] The traditional view of the self, which we might conveniently trace back to Descartes, classed the ego as a *res cogitans,* a substance endowed with the power to think and above all to represent a reality different from itself, namely, the *res extensa,* or extended substance, which soon became the domain of the new physics. The Cartesian dichotomy always harbored instability, for it could easily be pushed in either of two directions. One could simply dispense with the ego as a distinctive substance and reduce it to the same "kind of thing" as the remainder of physical reality, treating it as the focal point of external forces acting in lawlike, predictable ways (as in behavioral psychology). Or, one could despair of the power of this thinking substance to represent or "mirror" anything outside of its own categories, and lapse into solipsism. The theorists represented here have hoped to escape from this dilemma altogether by treating personal identity as that which emerges in and through narratives. As Kerby remarks: "the self is not a *thing* in the metaphysical sense of being a substance, residing beneath experience. It is rather . . . a being of semiosis, a sign or symbol functioning within a given semiotic field."[26]

On this interpretation of identity, we continuously create and reinforce our sense of self by linking our present plans, actions, and states to both the future (as "project") and the past, as the already articulated story of our lives to that point. Take, for example, a day in the life of a priest. He may say a Mass, visit the sick, write a letter to his bishop, and conclude his duties by hearing confession. How could any of these activities be rendered meaningful, indeed intelligible, without tacit yet constant reference to the unfolding story of his life, and the much grander story of the Catholic Church? As the Gergens comment, "one's view of self in a given moment is fundamentally nonsensical unless it can be linked in some fashion with his or her past."[27]

From the viewpoint of psychology and other activist, interventionist disciplines, narrative theories of identity have the virtue of making the self seem a "work in progress" that can be "revised" as circumstances require. Such theories put the individual in the position of being author of his or her own story, an active shaper of outcomes, rather than a passive object acted upon by external or internal forces. Of course, the process of narrative therapy is never easy or automatic; it requires the gradual shifting away from self-destructive and harmful stories to ones that build on an individual's happier, more confident and competent experiences. In this regard, the narrative approach has considerable attraction for feminists like Rowland-Serdar and Schwartz-Shea, who seek to "offer a . . . conception of empowerment which explicitly includes development of self . . . We view the process of overcoming dependency as 'reclaiming one's story.'"[28] Some feminists, especially in the "personal narrative" movement referred to previously, also have saluted the narrative approach for its challenge to mainstream epistemology, which privileges "statistical significance, universality, and logical deduction" over "experiential" ways of knowing that are democratically available to all people.[29] By the same token, the narrative approach appeals to sociologists such as Gareth Williams, who wish to illuminate the interplay between experience and story by showing how we "reconstruct" our autobiographies under the influence of deeply disruptive events.

Within the "narrative identity" school, we can distinguish two currents of thought, tokens of unresolved philosophical difficulties that also continue to afflict other narrative categories. To oversimplify a bit, the problem is essentially as follows. When we spin narratives that form our personal identity, are we creating order out of chaos, i.e. out of a manifold of disordered impressions, sensations, memories, and inner states? Or does the narrative self somehow correspond to, or perhaps develop and articulate, a pre-narrative identity that is already there "in itself," antecedent to the narrative that constructs it? This obviously Kantian dilemma splits narrativists down the middle. Many of the founders of the narrative movement, such as Frank Kermode, Hayden White and Louis Mink, have defended the first, "weaker" alternative, as does David Novitz, who claims that identities are constructed like works of art. I must, Novitz continues, "organize in a sequential, developmental, and meaningful way what I take to be the brute data of my life."[30] He assumes, of course, that the "brute data" are *not* inherently sequential, developmental, or meaningful.[31]

Other philosophers of narrative identity—for example, Paul Ricoeur, Jerome Bruner, and Anthony Kerby—would admit that the stories we imagine and tell about ourselves are indeed constructed; we do not just "find" them ready-made. But Kerby insists that life itself has an implicit narrative structure. Or, more precisely, it is a pre- or quasi-narrative, rooted in temporality. The individual, in the course of fashioning an identity, elaborates and develops the temporality of experience into a narrative, rather than *imposing* it upon some chaotic, recalcitrant material: "if life has this implicit narrative structure, so too must the understanding of human lives."[32] We may call this the "strong" theory of narrative identity, insofar as its exponents find narrativity to be anchored in the way the world really is, an expression, if not a mirror, of the way human beings *must* experience themselves (i.e., as temporal). The section on identity thus leaves unresolved the query: is self-narrative nothing but an elaborate, wholly contingent creation of the self, or does it manifest the underlying character of the object (human experience *qua* temporality) that it strives to encompass?

While debates over identity have been dominated by metaphysical and empirical models of the self, memory has always been the "home" of narrative. To be sure, events have sometimes been memorialized in other ways—for example, as annals or chronicles—but unquestionably, history as we know it in the West has been narrative history until fairly recently. Yet, ironically, as the narrative approach has gained ground in many of the human sciences, it has been on the defensive on its home terrain, under siege by the "new" history. To grasp the situation of narrative for memory, we need to ask two distinct questions. First, why did it seem "natural" to write about human events as stories in the first place? Second, what factors have conspired to make the story model of rendering events less plausible today than it used to be?

Both Steven Crites and David Carr argue that "the formal quality of experience through time is inherently narrative . . . Consciousness grasps its objects in an inherently temporal way . . . Without memory . . . experience would have no coherence at all."[33] These writers thus adopt the strong version of narrative identity discussed above. Memory, in other words, does not falsify or distort that which is recollected; it merely casts it into the story pattern that its inherent structure warrants. Carr sets about proving that proposition by means of rebuttals of the contrary positions that various narrativists have presented.

Crites, on the other hand, takes the reader back to the experiences of the members of traditional societies. They always recognized two kinds of stories: sacred tales, the "dwelling places" of consciousness that could not be directly related at all, and mundane tales, which took soundings in the sacred tales and imparted to them, so far as possible, an objective form (we would include here myths, epics, scripture, and so forth). Thus, narrative turns out to pervade the experience and self-understanding even of peoples who do not yet write history in the Western sense. We might hypothesize that the discipline of history proper emerged at a time when mundane stories gained a degree of independence from their sacred prototypes.[34]

Lance Bennett suggests a different way of exhibiting the connection between memory and narrative. His article on the function of storytelling among jurors argues that the latter, lacking formal training in legal procedures and reasoning, resort to stories as interpretive devices. Through storytelling we can "translate our impressions of a distant event into a form that will allow a listener in an immediate situation to grasp its significance."[35] Specifically, stories deploy the familiar narrative elements of scene, act, agent, agency, and purpose to reconstruct the past in such a way that jurors can choose the most plausible among several different proposed versions of what happened. So, we might suggest, storytelling is the common person's logic, a practical vademecum in a domain of complex and arcane legal principles. Narrative, as Jerome Bruner has put it, is "ancient and universal"; the "capacity to tell and understand stories," Donald Polkinghorne adds, appears at "an early stage of individual and cultural development."[36] In highly differentiated, specialized spheres such as science and law, narrative may indeed be in decline, but it seems to have survived virtually unscathed in the world of everyday life as a way to represent and organize memory.

History, for which time and memory have long been paramount, thus seems far more than a contingent, arbitrary construction. It has in the background deep-seated cognitive principles: the perception of sacred time and its "translation" into mundane stories that we find in many traditional societies, and the interpretation of the past, in practical-political contexts, by means of alternative narratives. In the latter case, we find an explicit link between the writing of history and the procedures for investigating a crime and generating hypotheses about who did what and why. R. G. Collingwood, in *The Idea of History*, studied just such a connection, proposing that historians acted in much the same way as criminologists do (or, we would add, like

Bennett's jurors), arranging and organizing the past in alternative scenarios, choosing the most likely one as the best explanation.[37]

Gertrude Himmelfarb's influential essay on historiography (reprinted here) would classify the kind of history Collingwood had in mind as the "old history," essentially political in subject matter and narrative in form. It is precisely this older, narrative history that has come under attack from several different quarters, including psychohistory as well as the Annales school founded by Fernand Braudel. These currents of "new" history have in common a penchant for analytic studies and a high regard for the contributions that the social sciences, especially psychology, demography, and economics, can make to the study of the past. Himmelfarb insinuates that they also share a "horror of the event": an aversion to treating the past as in some sense the product of conscious, purposive action, the outcome of collective efforts to achieve some identifiable goal such as liberty, constitutional government, or whatever.[38] Instead, they want to move beyond the apparently purposive level of events to the underlying causes that have shaped the past—ones that narratives supposedly cannot touch.

In light of what has already been said about identity, we are clearly confronting a new version of the previous claim that human life is not "really" narrative at all, that stories only impose a factitious order and sense on data that cannot, in themselves, support any such meaning. And again in response, the proponent of a "strong" narrative theory would want to insist on the isonomy of first- and second-order narratives. If people experience their lives as stories, then why shouldn't historians, or anyone who hopes to memorialize human affairs, adapt their methods to the kind of object they are studying? Himmelfarb, Roth, and other proponents of the narrative approach argue that narrative history does not abandon the scientific desideratum of explanation; its explanations are simply different from those that prevail in the nomological sciences. Indeed, even that may not be a bold enough claim. Misia Landau, another contributor to this volume, argues that certain natural sciences, like geology and biology, must perforce adopt something like a narrative understanding of their fields, since they display a temporal, sequential structure analogous to (human) history.[39]

In any case, the narrative theory of memory adds a dimension to our inquiry that needs especially to be emphasized. As historians, social scientists, or (for that matter) prophets and bards weave narratives of the second order—stories that connect the individual mind to the social world—they create artifacts that soon take on a life of their own.

These stories, told and retold, furnish the stock from which individual life narratives can be constructed. In other words, the story of an individual life usually plays off of one or more historically and socially transmitted narratives, which serve as prototypes for the elaboration of personal identity. Narrative theory is thus always implicitly a theory of how communities are formed and maintained, and how individuals are drafted into available social roles.

It would be easy to infer from this communitarian side of narrative theory that it has a bias toward tradition, that it tacitly short-circuits the critical distance that is required for a person to "see through" subtle forms of social control entailed by such stories. And, in fact, some pro-narrative arguments do come close to describing the individual's appropriation of narratives as an uncritical assimilation of self to story. For example, the psychologist Jerome Bruner remarks that "in the end we become the autobiographical narratives by which we 'tell about' our lives . . . We become variants of the culture's canonical forms."[40] Another narrativist, Miller Mair, asserts that stories are "habitations" which so dominate our thinking that we have no other way of knowing the world than through them.[41]

The prevailing view, however, among the writers chosen for our community section is quite different. All of them recognize that people have other ways of knowing than through narrative, and that stories themselves, even the "grand," culturally determining ones, invite debate, contestation, and constant reevaluation in light of new facts and experiences. Certainly, narrative theories of community usually describe social bonds in ways that make them seem more profound and pervasive than would, say, utilitarianism or liberal social contract doctrine. But, as will shortly become apparent, narrative social theory does not much resemble the idea of *Gemeinschaft* common in classical German sociology, or even Durkheim's notion of *conscience collective.* In the section on community, the authors included try to display both the power of narrative to generate a sense of common identity and its potential as a critical, emancipatory instrument.

The philosopher Alasdair MacIntyre advocates a "strong" theory of narrative on both of the levels we have hitherto explored. Narrative is, in his view, constitutive of human identity, not imposed *a posteriori* on a non-narrative thing-in-itself: "stories are lived before being told." Moreover, MacIntyre argues that "narrative history of a certain kind turns out to be the basic and essential genre for the characterization of human actions."[42] These two components, identity and memory, interlock in MacIntyre's theory of community. The story of one's individual life depends on the larger stories of the community to which one belongs. That community, in turn, crystallizes around a stock of common memories revivified in stories. To be sure, one could in principle refuse all of these stories and cast oneself in the role of a "citizen of nowhere," though in practice it is not clear that one could ever really achieve freedom from all available narratives and "invent" oneself from scratch. But, in any case, MacIntyre would find any such freely invented identity to be shallow and empty. People "deform" their present relationships by trying to escape the burdens and opportunities of culturally transmitted stories. A young German who declined all responsibility for the Holocaust, or an American who saw no connection between his or her life and the country's history of slavery, would simply overlook the moral significance of their choices for at least some audiences. The point is that our roles in ongoing stories are not always self-chosen. We are recruited into them by virtue of our membership in the community, and we ignore them at our—and others'—peril.

Nevertheless, the narrative traditions that underlie most communities have enough ambiguity and flexibility that they do not limit members to simply acting out preordained roles. One can always contest and argue about the meaning of stories, and try to reinterpret them so as to change policies and behavior.[43] MacIntyre explicitly rejects the Burkean idea of traditions as fonts of accumulated wisdom somehow superior to abstract reasoning. People probably always think from within some narrative tradition, but that embeddedness in narratives does not preclude reasoning about what they mean and what ought to be done next, as the conflict-laden history of American Constitutional law clearly shows.

Edward Bruner's article on ethnography offers a case in point about how and why narratives change. Within a few generations the story told by anthropologists about Native Americans evolved dramatically: their past, present, and future were all reinterpreted as tales of cultural resistance and renewal rather than tragedies of cultural decline and eventual assimilation. The facts did not precipitate this shift; rather, one might say, it involved a moral debate about a traditional narrative and its consequences for the lives of Native Americans. The dominant story of assimilation had left behind a residue of experiences that did not quite fit; ethnographers gradually worked up those experiences into an alternative story, one that inserted the situation of indigenous peoples into larger American themes of social justice, community identity, and cultural pluralism.

In turn, the new story about Native Americans has helped usher in a renaissance of Indian cultures, languages, and lore.

Walter Fisher and Phillip Abbott also explicitly reject the dominant dichotomy of reason/individualism versus tradition/community. Fisher, a scholar of speech and communications, recognizes the powerful role stories can play in forging social bonds: "communities are co-constituted through communication transactions in which participants co-author a story that has coherence and fidelity for the life that one would lead."[44] But he introduces the notion of "narrative rationality" to counter the easy assumption that one story is as good as another, and that choosing among stories—and thus the sources of communal identity—is a matter of subjective preference. We can debate and negotiate narratives on rational and moral grounds as readily as we can, say, formal theories of justice or utility.[45]

Abbott's article, which examines the uses of narrative in various political theories, suggests that the latter often fall back on narrative to illustrate or clarify their meaning. Some poststructuralists might object that stories do far more than merely "illustrate" theories, that they in fact embody an alternative, non-"Archimedean" or non-foundationalist mode of thought.[46] Although Abbott seems at first to subordinate stories to theories, he too elaborates the various ways in which narratives may work at cross purposes to the intended "point" of the theories. Narrative is not the handmaiden of theory; it may as easily become its foe, since stories are rooted in our everyday life experiences in a way that most theories are not.[47] A "bad" narrative can undermine a theory that at first appears convincing by making us reject the theory or inducing us to attach a different sense to it than the author desired.

In its most radical form, narrative theory is made to seem capable of completely reconstructing communities, putting them on a new foundation. Environmental philosopher Jim Cheney advances such an argument in regard to "bioregionalism." We have come very far from any sort of conservative, common law-guided notion of community here! Narrative is presented as a revolutionary tool capable of reinventing our whole relationship to the land and our place in it. Cheney's article forces us, in fact, to confront directly a question implicit in nearly all of the essays on narrative assembled here, and a good many others as well: does the narrative approach have any inherent political or ethical content? Does it commit us to certain attitudes vis-à-vis the state, social justice, moral obligation and other such themes that go beyond its ostensible aims? We shall try to answer that question next.

THE POLITICS OF NARRATIVE

Until rather recently, narrative theory has been mainly the province of historians and literary critics. And some of the most distinguished among them believe that narrative does indeed carry ethical and political baggage. Hayden White, for example, insists that "every historical narrative has as its latent or manifest purpose the desire to *moralize* the events of which it treats."[48] He seems to think that moralizing reality involves several distinct moves: imparting meaning to happenings that lack it "in themselves"; postulating an underlying subject, the "social system," that continues over time and accumulates experience; giving "closure" to a series of happenings (we avoid the loaded term "event" here)[49] as though they were acts in a drama; and generally providing a foundation for law, legality, legitimacy, and authority. By comparing annals and chronicles to narrative history, White can demonstrate that the latter imports into the reconstruction of the past a penchant for order, coherence, and meaning that those other forms of historiography lacked. Narrative history moralizes the past by presenting it as the unfolding story *of* a subject (a culture, an institution, an idea) that acts and is acted upon. As White reads it, narrative ties in nicely with the modern liberal state and its moral-legal system of authority.

Although its filiations with narrative theory have been complex (more on this to follow), postmodernism's leading intellectuals often seem to share White's doubts about it. Literary critic Robert Scholes, summarizing what he takes to be the postmodernist view, notes that "from this standpoint, traditional narrative structures are perceived as part of a system of psychosocial *dependencies* that inhibit both individual human growth and significant social change . . . Narrativity itself, as we have known it, must be seen as an *opiate* to be renounced in the name of the improvements to come."[50] David Carr, in the essay included here, confirms that one version of the postmodernist stance toward narrative (associated, for example, with Hayden White) has indeed taken a "dark" and "suspicious" turn, accusing narrativity of offering false consolations and "diversions" from reality, and thus allying itself with power and manipulation.[51]

Perhaps this debate over the politics of narrative has taken the course we have described partly because it has focused on the writing of history rather than on the other human sciences. Gertrude Himmelfarb, who clearly wishes to defend the value of the "old," narrative history, agrees with many of the characterizations of it advanced by White. She claims that it is and ought to be predominantly "political," that it should connect a series of events chronologically so as to make them tell a story, and that it should have dramatic movement and literary grace. It is quite proper, she believes, for narrative histories to try to capture the meaning of political events, for history does in fact display "reason"; it is the forum in which freedom is achieved, in which people act autonomously to shape their own destinies.[52]

If narrative history really does have such close affinities with the dominant ideas of reason and freedom in the West, then scholars who reject those ideas have good grounds for mistrusting narrative history as well. Anti-narrativists such as White and Lyotard suspect that narrative history shares many defects with theory (particularly a naive belief in objective knowing and its counterpart, the Cartesian ego)[53] but conceals that complicity by virtue of its supposed immediacy and fidelity to lived experience.

However, some poststructuralist writers, including Lisa Disch, Jim Cheney, Barbara Rowland-Serdar, and Peregrine Schwartz-Shea, would prefer to emphasize the affinities between narrativity and certain aspects of postmodernism. Cheney, for example, reads the import of much postmodern thought as an invitation to eschew "totalizing," "essentializing" language and its ontological complement, the Cartesian self, in favor of a "situated" and "contextualized" story of particular human communities in particular geographic locales. Even many writers who do not specifically identify themselves as postmodernist have been attracted to narrative theory precisely because of its potentially liberating implications for human conduct. David Novitz, for one, depicts an entire "politics of narrative identity" in which various players, especially the state, vie for control of the stories that tend to produce or reinforce our sense of self and thus affect our ideas about what authority is legitimate. Undermining regimes such as those of Nazi Germany or South Africa under apartheid necessarily required a challenge to the stories that sustained them.

The point is that narrative theory, viewed across disciplines in the way we have tried to present it here, has political relevance, but no unambiguous partisan or ideological allegiances. Nevertheless, as we have already adumbrated, the narrative approach to social and psychological reality appeals especially to those who want to stress the efficacy of human agency, the potential for self-transformation, and the embeddedness of human experience in memory, situation, and tradition, however loosely defined. The anti-narrativists prove to be a diverse lot: behavioral psychologists, Annales historians, psychohistorians, logical positivists, and some postmodernists. They seem to share a certain skepticism about human autonomy; that is, they want to treat thought, stories, narrative identity as in a sense epiphenome-nal or illusory.[54] For many of them—and we must be cautious about sweeping generalizations—the practitioner of the human sciences ei-ther ought to be looking for deeper causes of the things people do (op-erant conditioning, demographic trends, or whatever), constructing normative theories that keep ethical/political obligation sharply dis-tinct from empirical research into behavior, or else ought to be un-masking the subtle forms of power involved even in allegedly critical, "oppositional" forms of thought, like narrative.

By contrast, narrative theory seems at home in the world of "prac-tical" affairs as Aristotle understood that term.[55] Theory, for both Plato and Aristotle, required that thinkers distance themselves from the world of human events, taking up a neutral, detached standpoint from which the object of inquiry could be viewed *sub specie aeternitatis*. The theorist's goal was to grasp the unchanging principles that animated and ordered the social world, the sphere in which mutability, opinion, and interests held sway. But the practical person, the citizen or "states-man," needed a way to understand and negotiate his social environ-ment that would be less exact than theory, yet more reliable than guesswork or caprice. The prudent citizen would undoubtedly have drawn on narratives in the course of his deliberations—stories such as the ones told by Homer and the tragic dramatists, histories like Thucy-dides' work on the Peloponnesian War, and the political speeches that the historian memorializes. Lance Bennett's essay on the uses of narra-tive in the courts captures something of the practical, action-guiding quality of stories that we wish to emphasize here.

We note that narratives do not fit very well into the dichotomy of "is" and "ought," science and ethics, that many of the antinarrativists seem to presuppose.[56] People tell stories because they need to know who they are and how to behave in a world that is complex and often dangerous. They want to know whom to trust and who is trying to de-ceive them, why things are done one way and not another. As Gene Outka has pointed out, "our moral lives require narration."[57] Grand theories frequently offer little help in immediate, practical matters, es-pecially when (as in the case of something like Annales historiogra-phy) they do not even take human autonomy and agency seriously.

In any case, we have descried a subtle, but important split in the ranks of narrativists that has a significant bearing on politics in the widest sense. One wing of the narrative movement follows the postmodern trend in mistrusting any sort of "totalization," any effort to shape one's life, identity, or social circumstances into a meaningful whole. We have already mentioned White, Cheney, and Rowland-Serdar and Schwartz-Shea in this context. We might add the names of Laurel Richardson, George Howard, and Hans Kellner to that list of what could perhaps be called anti-foundationalists or pluralists. To them, narrative appeals precisely because it depicts social reality (even the ego) as a collage of stories, perspectives, and values.

A second group, including Kerby, Carr, Crites, MacIntyre, and Edward Bruner, has not abandoned the aspiration toward integral selfhood and community.[58] As Kerby remarks, there is in many of us a "legitimate though often unconscious desire for unification; it is basic to the human project for generating a meaningful co-existence with others."[59] This faction worries about the fragmentation and incoherence of contemporary discourse, and discerns in the narrative approach one means of repairing, or at least better understanding, those ruptures in tradition. The postmodern party tends to take a weak or "antifoundationalist" attitude toward the possible objectivity of narrative, while its more traditional opponents tend to adopt a strong, quasi-essentialist view. In short, the narrative approach still lacks the precision and elegance that would be necessary to bridge the political and cultural fissures of our time; but to imagine that it could ever have done so would probably have been utopian.

Nevertheless, there is something encouraging about the collection of articles here. One finds eminent figures from many disciplines, who could be expected to disagree vehemently about conventional political topics, groping their way toward a common language, a shared story of what it is they are doing. If this anthology can hasten the process, it will have more than served its purpose.

NOTES

1. H. White 1984:1; Mancuso and Sarbin 1986:236. Full citations for this and all subsequent notes are supplied in the bibliography at the end of the book.

2. Lyotard 1984:23.

3. Lyotard 1984:37.

4. Kellner 1987:1; Novak 1975:175.

5. Brown 1980:545.

6. Maines 1993:17.

7. Randall 1984:1; Geertz 1973, 1980; Martin 1986:7; Rosaldo 1989:37; Maines 1993; Sewell 1992; Steinmetz 1992.

8. For example, see Howard 1991:190 and Landau 1984:262.

9. Rosenwald and Ochberg 1992:2,5; Geertz 1980:239; Randall 1984; L. Stone 1981:79–91; Mishler 1995:87–88.

10. Mancuso and Sarbin 1986:241–42.

11. Personal narratives loom large in the work of many social scientists, including Davis and Kennedy 1989; M. Gergen 1990; Vizenour 1986; Cuoto 1993; Rosaldo 1989; Personal Narratives Group 1989; Abrams 1991; Bellah et al. 1985; Buker 1987; Scheppele 1989; Haraway 1988; Massaro 1989; Rowland-Serdar and Schwartz-Shea 1991; and Wagner-Martin 1994.

12. Rosenwald and Ochberg 1992:2; L. Stone 1981:79; Maines 1993.

13. Bennett 1978:6; Geertz 1973; L. Stone 1981:85.

14. Rabinow and Sullivan 1979.

15. Gadamer 1993:xxii.

16. Novitz 1989:61; J. Bruner 1991; Mancuso and Sarbin 1986:246; Himmelfarb 1987:89; Dray 1986:33; Landau 1984:262; Brockelman 1992:102; Hauerwas et al. 1977:28; L. Stone 1981:74; E. Bruner 1986:141.

17. Spence 1982:291.

18. Roth 1989:449–56; Kellner 1987:15; Kaplan 1986:770; Robinson and Hawpe 1986:115; Ricoeur 1984.

19. Rorty 1989:101–7; Novak 1975:175; Mair 1988:133; J. Bruner 1987:17; Mink 1970.

20. Gergen and Gergen 1984:185.

21. See, respectively, Fisher 1992; Bennett 1978; E. Bruner 1986; Kellner 1987.

22. White 1984:2.

23. Ricoeur 1981:281–82.

24. Carr 1986a:131.

25. Kerby 1986:210. Bear in mind, however, that many postmodernists, especially those influenced by Derrida, Foucault, and Lacan, "reject the fundamental need for the individual to adopt a unified, integrated self-identity"; the "self-identical identity" of persons is illusory, if "all meaning is a ceaseless play of difference" (Moi 1985: 7, 9). See also Rudelic 1993.

26. Kerby 1986:216.

27. Gergen and Gergen 1983:255.

28. Rowland-Serdar and Schwartz-Shea 1991:607,612.

29. Abrams 1989:976; Scheppele 1989:2084.

30. Novitz 1989:57.

31. See also Rosenwald and Ochberg 1992:5 and Martin 1986:43.

32. Kerby 1988:236.

33. Crites 1971:294,298.

34. Brooks 1984:xi.

35. Bennett 1978:3.

36. J. Bruner 1987:16; Polkinghorne 1988:112,114.

37. Collingwood 1946:294,298; Bennett and Feldman 1981:41.

38. Himmelfarb 1987:46.

39. See also Harré 1990 and Myers 1990.

40. J. Bruner 1987:15.

41. Mair 1988:125.

42. MacIntyre 1981:197,194.

43. Outka 1980:115.

44. Fisher 1992:214.

45. Hauerwas et al. 1977:30.

46. Disch 1994.

47. See also Mair 1988:133.

48. Mitchell 1981:14.

49. See Mink 1978:147.

50. Cited in Mitchell 1981:206–7.

51. Carr 1986a:120.

52. Himmelfarb 1987:9, 32–33.

53. Disch 1994.

54. Scott 1989:691.

55. Carr 1986a:126–27.

56. Hauerwas et al. 1977:25,30.

57. Outka 1980:114.

58. See Brooks 1984:xii; Novak 1975:175.

59. Kerby 1986:219.

I

Memory

An attribute that may be uniquely human is consciousness of ourselves as temporal beings—beings with a history. Both as individuals and members of various groups, our present existence is powerfully shaped by recollections of the past and anticipations of the future. Narrativists maintain that plot is the main device we use in trying to make sense of this aspect of our lives. As one scholar has put it, there can be "no story without plot."[1] Through narrative emplotment, we organize, integrate, and seek an accommodation with temporality. On this view, emplotment humanizes our experience of time, making its passage meaningful for us.[2] It gives order and direction to events that otherwise might be perceived as random or isolated.[3]

Yet the emplotment process is hardly unproblematical. For example, there may be a significant gap between "historical truth," whose standard is accuracy, and "narrative truth," which is judged on the basis of aesthetic criteria such as "closure, coherence, and rhetorical appeal."[4] Indeed, the realist position, according to which people's "life stories" more or less accurately "mirror events,"[5] has come under attack in many quarters, giving rise to heated debate even among narrativists themselves. Particularly suspect to many in the postmodernist camp is the view that there are megaplots—such as the spread of reason, science, and enlightenment, the growth of "cultural unity," or the "struggle for emancipation"[6]—that can explain the grand sweep of history. A common objection is that such totalizing "master narratives," by imposing a single plot on the historical process, necessarily exclude the stories and experiences of the "other," while artificially privileging the stories of powerful insiders.[7]

Thus, the issues we will grapple with in this section of the book include the following: Is the past something that can be *re*constructed, on the basis of

1

memories, or can it only be *constructed*?[8] To what extent, in other words, is memory itself a reliable guide? Can there be any true stories about the past, or do interpretations as such inherently falsify experience? How, if at all, can we determine whether one plot, one story about the past, is better than others? Is there such a thing as prereflective, prenarrative, unemplotted experience,[9] or does all experience possess at least an implicit narrative structure? Is it valid to say that "where there is no comprehensive story, there is, in some sense, no history"?[10]

David Carr argues in his article that real life shares with fictional and historical texts many of the formal properties of narratives. Drawing primarily upon the phenomenological tradition, Carr refutes the view championed by such thinkers as Ricoeur, Barthes, and White that humans impose narrative form upon their experience, which is itself a jumble of unrelated sensations and events. He posits that we cannot help but perceive experience as structured, however roughly, in a sequence of beginning to middle to end. He further argues that human action is inherently teleological: the processes we initiate derive meaning from the "projected end" that they are intended to achieve. In this sense, narrative order is not an *ex post facto* addition, but an intrinsic part of human action, essential to understanding it. Finally, Carr contends that storytelling has another practical function: through it, we integrate the past, present, and future, and thereby constitute stable, coherent identities on both a personal and communal level. Fictional and historical narratives, as second-order reflections animated (respectively) by an aesthetic or cognitive interest, differ only in degree but not in kind from the "practical" narratives that emerge in real life.

Religion, arguably more than other disciplines in the human sciences, is concerned with the interpretation of texts. Perhaps for this reason, the idea of narrative has assumed a prominent place in this field.[11] In an often-cited 1971 essay, Stephen Crites claims that narrative, like music, is a cultural form reflecting our existence as temporal creatures. Experience, he says (agreeing with Carr), is already an "incipient story," made coherent by memory. While we "live forwards," we "understand backwards."[12] Memory, through which we perceive events in a simple before-and-after sequence, gives rise to "recollection," involving the artful, though by no means arbitrary, transformation of mere chronological sequence into full-blown narratives. Only by virtue of the selective reordering and reconstruction integral to narratives do the concepts of past, present, and future emerge in human consciousness. Crites focuses attention on two types of narratives: sacred stories, which weave music together with plot and define a culture's general manner of relating to the world, and mundane narratives, which transpire within that largely unconscious horizon of style, meaning, and value. Together, these narratives shape and reflect the way a culture interprets temporality. But the temptation to overcome temporality is strong, and Crites speculates that "abstraction" and "contraction" have been modernity's principal anti-narrative strategies.

Prior to the nineteenth century, history was regarded as part of "literature in the broad sense."[13] Its narrative form comprised its chief link with fiction (and with myth). But beginning in the nineteenth century and escalating in the twentieth, with the rise of demographic, cliometric, and economic determinist models, the study of history came to be seen as having more in common with the sciences than the humanities.[14] The historian Gertrude Himmelfarb decries this anti-narrativist tendency in her discipline, which now appears to be reversing itself.[15] In a controversial essay, she attacks the "new history," used as a catch-all term to encompass approaches to the past that reduce it to non-narrative determinants such as demographic data or depth-psychological predispositions. Two things unite specimens of the new history: first, they are unchronological, rejecting narrative as unscientific or old-fashioned, and second, they are focused almost exclusively on social and economic activity, particularly that involving the daily lives of ordinary people. Himmelfarb sees the new history's quotidian, populist aspect and its suspicion of narrative as interrelated. Although professing to have no objection to social history as a supplement to more traditional histories, which centered around the contributions of political and intellectual leaders, she believes that when it dominates the field, the results are unfortunate. A civilization's highest achievements come to appear as mere superstructures designed to maintain elite hegemony, history loses its meaning and coherence, and human beings are shorn of the very attribute that makes them special: their status as rational animals capable of autonomous political choice.

Narrative has crept into legal scholarship through the "law and literature" school,[16] a movement on the academic left which is affiliated with feminism and critical race theory.[17] This school claims that attention to stories, whether real or fictional, humanizes law by promoting empathetic understanding, exposing systematic biases, illustrating the difficulties of interpretation, and providing an antidote to rules and procedures that are rigid, abstract, or indifferent to context and circumstance.[18] The evaluation of different versions of the same event is, indeed, at the heart of legal disputes,[19] a point that W. Lance Bennett effectively brings out. In his article analyzing jury trials, Bennett asks how twelve lay persons having only minimal knowledge of legal conventions and receiving only minimal assistance from various professionals can process the data presented to them and arrive at reasonable verdicts. He answers that jurors are able to perform this task more or less competently because they can draw upon their understanding of stories and how they work in everyday life. Stories, according to Bennett, are forms that allow us to interpret reality by organizing information into plausible sequences and scenarios. Jurors use ordinary narratives as their standard for assessing what goes on in the courtroom when they hear and deliberate on testimony. Specifically, narratives aid jurors in performing three essential cognitive operations: the identification of the occurrence(s) to be explained, the construction of interpretations that weave together all possible relevant facts, and the evaluation of alternative explanations of events for consistency, coherence, and completeness. Although jurors inevitably bring with them predispositions based on their own life experience, their judgments are "objective and fair" to the extent that they remain faithful to the demands of narrative reconstruction.

Lawrence Stone has advanced the claim that anthropology recently supplanted sociology and economics as the human science exerting the most influence on the study of history.[20] Misia Landau's essay, which examines rival hypotheses in the field of anthropology from the standpoint of literary theory, shows that the influence has been reciprocal. Issuing a challenge to positivism, she contends that scientists are essentially storytellers. Her analysis relies mainly on theories of literature and folklore which focus on the "deep structures" that are common to many ostensibly different narratives. Examining accounts of early human development as though they shared the formal properties of fictional texts, Landau uncovers in them a "heroic" plot structure revolving around (1) environmentally-generated crises that put the main character—Paleolithic man—to the test; (2) the character's successful resolution of these crises; and (3) the subsequent growth of hubris within him. She argues, more generally, that attention should be given to the way paleoanthropologists and other scientific researchers utilize narrative constructs such as sequencing, imputations of meaning, critical traditions, and causality in their work.

NOTES

1. Robinson 1981:74.

2. Polkinghorne 1988:1,126,159; Ricoeur 1984, 1985; Rosaldo 1989:135; Brooks 1984:xi; Mink 1978:132.

3. Gergen and Gergen 1988:174.

4. Spence 1982:31–32.

5. Rosenwald and Ochberg 1992:5.

6. Toews 1989:698; Lyotard 1984; White 1973.

7. Scott 1989:680–92.

8. Cohler 1982:211; Spence 1982:35.

9. Brockelman 1992:85; Winson 1990.

10. Baxter 1994:13.

11. Brockelman 1992; Winquist 1986; McFague 1982; Greeley 1994; Hauerwas 1977, 1989; McClendon 1974; Stroup 1981; Simpkinson and Simpkinson 1993; Pellauer 1987; Meilaender 1987; Shea 1978; Wiggins 1975; Tilley 1990; Ford 1989; Goldberg 1989; P. Hall 1994.

12. Crites 1986:165.

13. Martin 1986:71.

14. Martin 1986:71; Sewell 1992; L. Stone 1981; Kellner 1987; Danto 1965; Dray 1986.

15. L. Stone 1981:74–94; Rosaldo 1989:130; Sewell 1992; Steinmetz 1992; Somers 1992; Hart 1992; Harkin 1988; DeMallie 1993; Maynes 1992; Viney and Bousfield 1991; Armstrong and Tennenhouse 1993; Kemp 1986.

16. West 1993; Luban 1989; Abrams 1991; Delgado 1989, 1990; Estrich 1986; Vizenor 1986; Maynard 1988; Massaro 1989. For a critique see Posner 1988.

17. West 1993:11.

18. Scheppele 1989:2080; West 1993:9; Delgado 1989, 1990; Abrams 1991:973; Massaro 1989:2015; Vizenour 1986; La Rue 1995; Jackson 1990.

19. Scheppele 1989:2073; Maynard 1988.

20. L. Stone 1981:86.

1

Narrative and the Real World: An Argument for Continuity

David Carr

What is the relation between a narrative and the events it depicts? This is one of the questions that has been debated by many contributors to the lively interdisciplinary discussion of narrative in recent years.

The debate concerns the truthfulness, in a very broad sense of that term, of narrative accounts. Traditional narrative histories claim to tell us what really happened. Fictional narratives portray events that of course by definition never happened, but they are often said to be true-to-life; that is, to tell us how certain events might have occurred if they had really happened. Some histories may be inaccurate and some stories *invraisemblable*, but nothing in principle prevents such narratives from succeeding at their aim. Indeed, we take certain exemplary cases to have succeeded brilliantly.

But against this common-sense view a strong coalition of philosophers, literary theorists, and historians has risen up of late, declaring it mistaken and naive. Real events simply do not hang together in a narrative way, and if we treat them as if they did we are being *un*true to life. Thus not merely for lack of evidence or of verisimilitude, but in virtue of its very form, any narrative account will present us with a distorted picture of the events it relates. One result for literary theory is a view of narrative fiction which stresses its autonomy and separateness from the real world. One result for the theory of history is skepticism about narrative historical accounts.

I want to argue against this coalition, not so much for the common-sense view as for the deeper and more interesting truth which I

7

think underlies it. Narrative is not merely a possibly successful way of describing events; its structure inheres in the events themselves. Far from being a formal distortion of the events it relates, a narrative account is an extension of one of their primary features. While others argue for the radical discontinuity between narrative and reality, I shall maintain not only their continuity but also their community of form.

Let us look briefly at the discontinuity view before going on to argue against it.

I

In the theory of history one might expect such a view from those, from the positivists to the *Annales* historians, who believe narrative history has always contained elements of fiction that must now be exorcised by a new scientific history. The irony is that skepticism about narrative history should have grown up among those who lavish on it the kind of attention reserved for an object of admiration and affection. Consider the work of Louis Mink. Though he speaks of narrative as a "mode of comprehension" and a "cognitive instrument," and seems at first to defend narrative history against reductionists like Hempel, in the end he comes to a similar conclusion, namely that traditional history is prevented by its very form from realizing its epistemic pretensions. Narrative structure, particularly the closure and configuration given to the sequence of events by a story's beginning, middle, and end, is a structure derived from the act of telling the story, not from the events themselves. In the end the term "narrative history" is an oxymoron: "As historical it claims to represent, through its form, part of the real complexity of the past, but as narrative it is a product of imaginative construction which cannot defend its claim to truth by any accepted procedure of argument or authentication."[1] "Stories are not lived but told," he says. "Life has no beginnings, middles and ends. . . . Narrative qualities are transferred from art to life."[2]

If Mink arrives only reluctantly at such skeptical conclusions, Hayden White embraces them boldly. Like Mink he raises the question of narrative's capacity to *represent*. Inquiring after "The Value of Narrativity in the Representation of Reality" he seems clearly to conclude that in this respect its value is nil. "What wish is enacted, what desire is gratified," he asks, "by the fantasy that *real* events are properly represented when they can be shown to display the formal coherence of a story?"[3] "Does the world really present itself to perception in the form of well-made stories. . . ? Or does it present itself more in the way that the annals and chronicles suggest, either as a mere sequence without beginning or end or as sequences of beginnings that only terminate and never conclude?" For White the answer is clear: "The notion that sequences of real events possess the formal attributes of the stories we tell about imaginary events could only have its origin in wishes, day-dreams, reveries." It is precisely annals and chronicles that offer us the "paradigms of ways that reality offers itself to perception."[4]

Mink and White are led in this skeptical direction in part by their shared belief in the close relation between historical and fictional narratives; and if we look at some of the most influential studies of literary narrative in recent years, we find a similar view of the relation between narrative and the real. It is shared by structuralists and non-structuralists alike. Frank Kermode, in his influential study *The Sense of an Ending*, puts it this way: "In 'making sense' of the world we . . . feel a need . . . to experience that concordance of beginning, middle and end which is the essence of our explanatory fictions. . . ."[5] But such fictions "degenerate," he says, into "myths" whenever we actually believe them or ascribe their narrative properties to the real, that is, "whenever they are not consciously held to be fictive."[6] In his useful presentation of structuralist theories of narrative, Seymour Chatman, also speaking of the beginning-middle-end structure, insists that it applies "to the narrative, to story-events as narrated, rather than to . . . actions themselves, simply because such terms are meaningless in the real world."[7] In this he echoes his mentor, Roland Barthes. In his famous introduction to the structural analysis of narrative, Barthes says that "art knows no static." In other words, in a story everything has its place in a structure while the extraneous has been eliminated; and that in this it differs from "life," in which everything is "scrambled messages" (*communications brouillées*).[8] Thus, like Mink, Barthes raises the old question about the relation between "art" and "life," and arrives at the same conclusion: the one is constitutionally incapable of *representing* the other.

Paul Ricoeur draws together the theory of history and of literature in his *Time and Narrative* to form a complex account of narrative which is supposed to be neutral with respect to the distinction between history and fiction. For Ricoeur, as for White, the problem of representation is of central importance: the key concept in his account is that of *mimesis*, derived from Aristotle's *Poetics*.

By retaining rather than rejecting this concept, Ricoeur's theory seems at first to run counter to the emphasis we have found in others on the *discontinuity* between narrative and the "real world." But in elaborating his complete theory of the mimetic relation he reveals himself to be much closer to Mink, White, and the structuralists than he at first appears. He does not go so far as to say with them that the real world is merely sequential, maintaining instead that it has a "pre-narrative structure" of elements that lend themselves to narrative configuration.[9]

But this prefiguration is not itself narrative structure, and it does not save us from what Ricoeur seems to regard as a sort of constitutional disarray attached to the experience of time, which in itself is "confused, unformed and, at the limit, mute."[10] From a study of Augustine's *Confessions* he concludes that the experience of time is characterized essentially by "discordance." Literature, in narrative form, brings concord to this "aporia" by means of the invention of a plot. Narrative is a "synthesis of the heterogenous" in which disparate elements of the human world—"agents, goals, means, interactions, circumstances, unexpected results, etc."[11]—are brought together and harmonized. Like metaphor, to which Ricoeur has also devoted an important study, narrative is a "semantic innovation" in which something new is brought into the world by means of language.[12] Instead of describing the world it *re*describes it. Metaphor, he says, is the capacity of "seeing-as."[13] Narrative opens us to "the realm of the 'as if'."[14]

So in the end for Ricoeur narrative structure is as separate from the "real world" as it is for the other authors we quoted. Ricoeur echoes Mink, White, et al. when he says, "The ideas of beginning, middle, and end are not taken from experience: they are not traits of real action but effects of poetic ordering."[15] If the role of narrative is to introduce something new into the world, and what it introduces is the synthesis of the heterogeneous, then presumably it attaches to the events of the world a form they do not otherwise have. A story *re*describes the world; in other words, it describes it *as if* it were what presumably, in fact, it is not. [16]

This brief survey of important recent views of narrative shows not only that narrative structure is being considered strictly as a feature of literary and historical *texts*, but also that that structure is regarded as belonging *only* to such texts. The various approaches to the problem of representation place stories or histories on a radically different plane from the real world they profess to depict. Ricoeur's is a fairly benign and approving view. He believes that fictional and historical narratives enlarge reality, expanding our notion of ourselves and of what is possible. Their mimesis is not imitative but creative of reality. Hayden

White seems by contrast to hold a darker, more suspicious view—one which he shares with Barthes and post-structuralists such as Foucault and Deleuze. Narrative not only constitutes an escape, consolation, or diversion from reality; at worst it is an opiate—a distortion imposed from without as an instrument of power and manipulation. In either case narrative is a cultural, literary artifact at odds with the real.[17]

There have been some dissenters, such as the literary critic Barbara Hardy, the historian Peter Munz, and the philosopher Frederick Olafson.[18] Alasdair MacIntyre presents a very different view in *After Virtue*, and I shall have more to say about him later. It is clear, however, that what I have called the discontinuity theory is held by some of the most important people writing about narrative in history and fiction. I would now like to show why I think this view mistaken.

II

My first criticism is that it rests on a serious equivocation. What is it that narrative, on the discontinuity view, is supposed to distort? "Reality" is one of the terms used. But what reality is meant? Sometimes it seems that the "real" world must be the physical world, which is supposed to be random and haphazard, or, alternatively and contradictorily, to be rigorously ordered along causal lines; but in any case it is supposed to be totally indifferent to human concerns. Things just happen in meaningless sequence, like the ticking clock mentioned by Frank Kermode. When asked what it says "we agree that it says *tick-tock*. By this fiction we humanize it. . . . Of course, it is we who provide the fictional difference between the two sounds; *tick* is our word for a physical beginning, *tock* our word for an end."[19]

This ingenious example merely confuses the issue, nonetheless, since it is not primarily physical reality but human reality, including the very activity of "humanizing" physical events, which is portrayed in stories and histories and against which narrative must be measured if we are to judge the validity of the discontinuity view. Can we say of human reality that it is mere sequence, one thing after the other, as White seems to suggest? Here we would do well to recall what some philosophers have shown about our experience of the passage of time. According to Husserl, even the most passive experience involves not only the retention of the just past but also the tacit anticipation, or what he calls protention, of the future. His point is not simply that we have the psychological capacity to project and to remember. His claim is the conceptual one that we cannot even experience anything as happening, as present, except against the background of what it succeeds and what we anticipate will succeed it.[20] Our very capacity to experience, to be aware of what *is*—"reality as it presents itself to experience," in Hayden White's words—spans future and past.

Husserl's analysis of time-experience is in this respect the counterpart of Merleau-Ponty's critique of the notion of sensation in classical empiricism and his claim that the figure-background scheme is basic in spatial perception.[21] He draws on the Gestalt psychologists, who were in turn indebted to Husserl. The supposedly punctual and distinct units of sensation must be grasped as a configuration to be experienced at all. Merleau-Ponty concludes that, far from being basic units of experience, sensations are highly abstract products of analysis. On the basis of Husserl's analysis of time-experience, one would have to say the same of the idea of a "mere" or "pure" sequence of isolated events. It is this that proves to be a fiction, in this case a theoretical fiction: perhaps we can conceive of it, but it is not real for our experience. As we encounter them, even at our most passive, events are charged with the significance they derive from our retentions and protentions.

If this is true of our most passive experience, it is all the more true of our active lives, in which we quite explicitly consult past experience, envisage the future, and view the present as a passage between the two. Whatever we encounter within our experience functions as instrument or obstacle to our plans, expectations, and hopes. Whatever else "life" may be, it is hardly a structureless sequence of isolated events.

It might be objected that structure is not necessarily narrative structure. But is there not a kinship between the means-end structure of action and the beginning-middle-end structure of narrative? In action we are always in the midst of something, caught in the suspense of contingency which is supposed to find its resolution in the completion of our project. To be sure, a narrative unites many actions to form a plot. The resulting whole is often still designated, however, to be an action of larger scale: coming of age, conducting a love affair, or solving a murder. The structure of action, small-scale and large, is common to art and to life.

What can the proponents of the discontinuity view possibly mean, then, when they say that life has no beginnings, middles, and ends? It is not merely that they are forgetting death, as MacIntyre points out,[22] and birth for that matter. They are forgetting all the other less definitive but still important forms of closure and structure to be found along the path from the one to the other. Are they saying that a moment in which, say, an action is inaugurated is no real beginning simply because it has other moments before it, and that after the action is accomplished time (or life) goes on and other things happen? Perhaps they are contrasting this with the absoluteness of the beginning and end of a novel, which begins on page one and ends on the last page with "the end." But surely it is the interrelation of the events portrayed, not the story as a sequence of sentences or utterances, that is relevant here. What I am saying is that the means-end structure of action displays some of the features of the beginning-middle-end structure which the discontinuity view says is absent in real life.

Thus the events of life are anything but a mere sequence: they constitute rather a complex structure of temporal configurations that interlock and receive their definition and their meaning from within action itself. To be sure, the structure of action may not be tidy. Things do not always work out as planned, but this only adds an element of the same contingency and suspense to life that we find in stories. It hardly justifies claiming that ordinary action is a chaos of unrelated items.

There may, however, be a different way of stating the discontinuity view which does not involve the implausible claim that human events have no temporal structure. A story is not just a temporally-organized sequence of events—even one whose structure is that of beginning, middle, and end. To our concept of story belongs not only a progression of events but also a storyteller and an audience to whom the story is told. Perhaps it may be thought that this imparts to the events related in a story a kind of organization that is in principle denied to the events of ordinary action.

Three features of narrative might seem to justify this claim. First, in a good story, to use Barthes' image, all the extraneous noise or static is cut out. That is, we the audience are told by the storyteller just what is necessary to "further the plot." A selection is made of all the events and actions the characters may engage in, and only a small minority finds its way into the story. In life, by contrast, everything is left in; all the static is there.

This first point leads to a second. The selection is possible because the storyteller knows the plot in a way both audience and characters do not (or may not). This knowledge provides the principle for excluding the extraneous. The narrative voice, as Hayden White says,[23] is the voice of authority, especially in relation to the reader or listener. The latter is in a position of voluntary servitude regarding what will be revealed and when. Equally importantly, the narrative voice is an *ironic* voice, at least potentially, since the storyteller knows the real as well as the intended consequences of the characters' actions. This irony is thus embodied primarily in the relation between storyteller and character; but it is related to the audience as well, since their expectations, like the characters', can be rudely disappointed.

The ironic stance of the storyteller can be seen as a function (and this is the third point) of his or her temporal position in relation to the events of the story. Conventionally this is the *ex post* position, the advantage of hindsight shared by the historian and (usually) the teller of fictional stories. As Danto points out, this position permits descriptions of events derived from their relation to later events and thus often closed to participants in the events themselves.[24] This standpoint after the story-events can just as well be seen, in Mink's preferred fashion, as a standpoint *outside* or *above* the events which takes them all in at a glance and sees their interrelation.[25] This apparent freedom from the constraints of time, or at least of following the events, sometimes expresses itself in the disparity between the order of events and the order of their telling. Flashbacks and flashforwards exhibit in no uncertain terms the authority of the narrative voice over both characters and audience.

In sum, the concept of story, as Scholes and Kellogg said, involves not just a sequence of unfolding events but the existence of three distinguishable points of view on those events: those of storyteller, audience, and characters.[26] To be sure, these may seem to coincide in some cases: a story may be told from the viewpoint of a character, or in a character's voice. Here even the audience knows no more or less than the character and all points of view seem identical; but even a first-person account is usually narrated after the fact, and the selection process still depends on the difference in point of view between participant and teller. In any case the very possibility of the disparity between the three points of view is enough to establish this point—that the events, experiences, and actions of a story may have a sense, and thus a principle of organization, which is excluded from the purview of the characters in the story.

As participants and agents in our own lives, according to this view, we are forced to swim with events and take things as they come. We are constrained by the present and denied the authoritative, retrospective point of view of the storyteller. Thus the real difference between "art" and "life" is not organization vs. chaos, but rather the absence in life of that point of view which transforms events into a story by *telling* them. Telling is not just a verbal activity and not just a recounting of events but one informed by a certain kind of superior knowledge.

There is, no doubt, much truth in this analysis, and as an argument for the discontinuity view it is certainly superior to the claim that human events form a meaningless sequence. Nonetheless this argument, like its predecessor, neglects some important features of "real life."

The key to this neglect is a mistaken sense of our being "confined to the present." The present is precisely a point of view or vantage point which opens onto or gives access to future and past. This I take to be the sense of the Husserlian analysis. Even in the relatively passive experience of hearing a melody, to use his example, we do not simply sit and wait for stimuli to hit us. We grasp a configuration extending into the future which gives to each of the sounding notes their sense. Thus present and past figure in our experience as a function of what will be.

The teleological nature of action, of course, lends it the same future-oriented character. Not only do our acts and our movements, present and past, derive their sense from the projected end they serve; our surroundings function as sphere of operations and the objects we encounter figure in our experience in furtherance of (or hindrance to) our purposes. Indeed, in our active lives it could be said that the focus of our attention is not the present but the future—as Heidegger says, not on the tools but on the work to be done.[27] It has been noted by Alfred Schutz that action has, temporally speaking, the quasi-retrospective character which corresponds to the future perfect tense: the elements and phases of an action, though they unfold in time, are viewed from the perspective of their having been completed.[28]

If this is true when we are absorbed in action, it is all the more true of the reflective or deliberative detachment involved—not only in the formulating of projects and plans but also in the constant revision and reassessment required as we go along and are forced to deal with changing circumstances. The essence of deliberative activity is to anticipate the future and lay out the whole action as a unified sequence of steps and stages, interlocking means and ends. In all this it can hardly be said that our concern is limited to the present. Nor can it be said that no selection takes place. To be sure, the noise or static is not eliminated, but it is recognized as static and pushed into the background.

The obvious rejoinder here, of course, is that the future involved in all these cases is only the envisaged or projected future, and that the agent has only a quasi-hindsight, an as-if retrospection at his or her disposal. What is essential to the storyteller's position is the advantage of real hindsight, a real freedom from the constraint of the present assured by occupying a position after, above, or outside the events narrated. The storyteller is situated in that enviable position beyond all the unforeseen circumstances that intrude, all the unintended consequences of our action that plague our days and plans.

Of course this is true; the agent does not occupy a real future with respect to current action. My point is simply that action seems to involve, indeed quite essentially, the adoption of an anticipated future-retrospective point of view on the present. We know we are in the present and that the unforeseen can happen; but the very essence of action is to strive to overcome that limitation by foreseeing as much as possible. It is not only novelists and historians who view events in terms of their relation to later events, to use Danto's formulation of the narrative point of view; we all do it all the time, in everyday life. Action is thus a kind of oscillation between two points of view on the events we are living through and the things we are doing. Not only do we not simply sit back and let things happen to us; for the most part, or at least in large measure, our negotiation with the future is successful. We are, after all, able to act.

What I am saying, then, is that we are constantly striving, with more or less success, to occupy the storytellers' position with respect to our own lives. Lest this be thought merely a far-fetched metaphor, consider how important, in the reflective and deliberative process, is the activity of literally telling, to others and to ourselves, what we are doing. When asked, "What are you doing?" we may be expected to come up with a story, complete with beginning, middle, and end, an accounting or recounting which is description and justification all at once.

The fact that we often need to tell such a story even to ourselves in order to become clear on what we are about brings to light two important things. The first is that such narrative activity, even apart from its social role, is a constitutive part of action, and not just an embellishment, commentary, or other incidental accompaniment. The second is that we sometimes assume, in a sense, the point of view of audience to whom the story is told, even with regard to our own action, as well as the two points of view already mentioned—those of agent or character and of storyteller.

Louis Mink was thus operating with a totally false distinction when he said that stories are not lived but told. They are told in being lived and lived in being told. The actions and sufferings of life can be viewed as a process of telling ourselves stories, listening to those stories, acting them out, or living them through. I am thinking here only of living one's own life, quite apart from both the cooperative and antagonistical social dimension of our action which is even more obviously intertwined with narrative. Sometimes we must change the story to accommodate the events; sometimes we change the events, by acting, to accommodate the story. It is not the case, as Mink seems to suggest, that we first live and act and then afterward, seated around the fire as it were, tell about what we have done, thereby creating something entirely new thanks to a new perspective. The retrospective view of the narrator, with its capacity for seeing the whole in all its irony, is not in irreconcilable opposition to the agent's view but is an extension and refinement of a viewpoint inherent in action itself. Mink and the others are right, of course, to believe that narration constitutes something, creates meaning rather than just reflecting or imitating something that exists independently of it. Narration, nevertheless intertwined as it is with action, does this in the course of life itself—not merely after the fact, at the hands of authors, in the pages of books.

In this sense the narrative activity I am referring to is practical before it becomes cognitive or aesthetic in history and fiction. We can also call it ethical or moral in the broad sense used by Alasdair MacIntyre and derived ultimately from Aristotle. This is to say that narration in our sense is constitutive not only of action and experience but also of the self which acts and experiences. Rather than a merely temporally persisting substance which underlies and supports the changing effects of time, like a thing in relation to its properties, I am the subject of a life-story which is constantly being told and retold in the process of being lived. I am also the principal teller of this tale, and belong as well to the audience to which it is told. The ethical-practical problem of self-identity and self-coherence may be seen as the problem of unifying these three roles. MacIntyre is probably right to attack the ideal of self-*authorship* or authenticity as an idol of modern individualism and self-centeredness.[29] But the problem of coherence cannot always be settled, as he seems to think, by the security of a story laid out in advance by society and its roles. My identity as a self may depend on which story I choose and whether I can make it hang together in the manner of its narrator, if not its author. The idea of life as a meaningless sequence, which we denounced earlier as an inaccurate description, may have significance if regarded as the constant possibility of fragmentation, disintegration, and dissolution which haunts and threatens the self.

III

But what has all this to do with history? We have reproached the discontinuity theory for misunderstanding "human reality," but our sense of this latter term seems tailored, as the conclusion of the previous section indicates, to *individual* experience, action, and existence. Indeed, our recourse to certain phenomenological themes may suggest that what we have said is methodologically tied to a first-person point of view. History, by contrast, deals primarily with social units, and with individuals only to the extent that their lives and actions are important for the society to which they belong. Is the narrative conception of experience, action, and existence developed in the previous section at all relevant to "human reality" in its specifically social forms?

I think it is, and in this section I shall present a brief sketch of how this is so. There is an obvious sense, of course, in which our conception of narrative is social right from the start. The story-telling function, whether metaphorical or literal, is a social activity, and though we spoke of the self as audience to its own narration, the story of one's life and activity is told as much to others as to oneself. On our view the self is itself an interplay of roles, but clearly the individual is constituted in interpersonal transaction as well as intrapersonal reflection. It is one thing to speak of the social construction of the self, however, and another to inquire into the make-up of social entities as such.

To consider this question it is not necessary to take up the attitude of the social scientist or historian observing something from the outside. We are also participants in groups, and our best understanding of their nature may come from a reflection on what it means to participate. What strikes me about social life is the extent to which an individual takes part in experiences and engages in actions whose proper subject is not the individual himself or herself but that of the group. To inhabit a territory, to organize politically and economically for its cultivation and civilization, to experience a natural or human threat and rise to meet it—these are experiences and actions usually not properly attributable to me alone, or to me, you, and the others individually. They belong rather to us: it is not my experience but *ours*, not I who act but *we* who act in concert. To say that *we* build a house is not equivalent to saying that I build a house, and you build a house, and he builds a house, and so on. To be sure, not all linguistic uses of *we* carry this sense of concerted action, division of labor, distributed tasks, and a shared end. In some cases the *we* is just short-hand for a collection of individual actions. But social life does involve certain very important cases in which individuals, by participation, attribute their experiences and acts to a larger subject or agent of which they are a part.

If this is so, it may not be necessary to give up the first-person approach, but only to explore its plural rather than its singular form in order to move from the individual to the social. If we make this move, we find many parallels to our analysis of the individual's experience and action. *We* have an experience in common when *we* grasp a sequence of events as a temporal configuration such that its present phase derives its significance from its relation to a common past and future. To engage in a common action is likewise to constitute a succession of phases articulated as steps and stages, subprojects, means and ends. Social human time, like individual human time, is constructed into configured sequences which make up the events and projects of our common action and experience.

As before, I think the structure of social time can be called a narrative structure, not only because it has the same sort of closure and configuration we found at the individual level, but also because this very structure is again made possible by a kind of reflexivity which is comparable to that of a narrative voice. The temporal sequence must be brought under a prospective-retrospective grasp which gives it its configuration, and lends to its phases their sense of presenting a commonly experienced event or of realizing a common goal. In the case of groups, however, the division of labor, necessary for carrying out common projects, may be characteristic of the narrative structure itself. That is, the interplay of roles—narrator, audience, and character—may here be literally divided among participants in the group. Certain individuals may speak on behalf of, or in the name of, the group, and articulate for the others what "we" are experiencing or doing. The resulting "story" must of course be believed or accepted by the audience to whom it is addressed if its members are to act out or live through as "characters" the story that is told.

In the last section I spoke of the temporal-narrative organization not only of experiences and actions but also of the self who experiences and acts. As the unity of many experiences and actions, the self is constituted as the subject of a life-story. So too with the constitution of certain kinds of groups which outlive particular common experiences and actions to acquire a stable existence over time. Not all groups are of this sort: collections of individuals make up groups simply by sharing objective traits such as location, race, sex, or economic class. But groups of a very special and socially and historically important sort are constituted when individuals regard each other in just such a way that they use the *we* in describing what is happening to them, what they are doing, and who they are. This is, of course, the sort of group for which the word "community" is reserved. In some of the most interesting cases, merely objective traits like sex, race, or class become the basis for the transformation of the one sort of group into the other: individuals recognize that it is *as* a race, sex, or class that they are oppressed or disadvantaged. What is grasped as common experience can be met by common action.

A community in this sense exists by virtue of a story which is articulated and accepted, which typically concerns the group's origins and its destiny, and which interprets what is happening now in the light of these two temporal poles. Nor is the prospect of death irrelevant in such cases, since the group must deal not only with possible external threats of destruction but also with its own centrifugal tendency to fragment. Again we can say that the narrative function is practical before it is cognitive or aesthetic; it renders concerted action possible and also works toward the self-preservation of the subject which acts. Indeed, we must go even further and say that it is literally *constitutive* of the group. As before, narrative is not a description or account of something that already exists independently of it and which it merely helps along. Rather, narration, as the unity of story, storyteller, audience, and protagonist, is what constitutes the community, its activities, and its coherence in the first place.

In this essay I have begun with a discussion of the individual's action, experience, and identity and have proceeded from there to the community, treating the latter as an analogue of the former. Since the story-telling and story-hearing metaphor, as already remarked, is more directly appropriate to the group than to the individual, it could be said that our order might better have been reversed. We might have presented the individual self as a kind of community of tellers, listeners, and characters, fused in their comprehension and execution of a common story. I find this interesting, but it could prove misleading; it is a special kind of story that is relevant here—the autobiographical one in which the issue is the unity and coherence of a subject who is identical with both the teller and the hearer of the story. The unity and coherence of one's own self, with all its attendant problems, is a matter closest to all of us. For this reason it serves as the best point of departure for a comparison designed to cast light on social existence.

Some may feel uncomfortable with this revival of the notion of the collective subject. While the idea that the community is a person "writ large" has strong historical precedents, notably in Plato and Hegel, it is regarded with great suspicion today. Everyone recognizes that in ordinary speech we often attribute personal qualities and activities to groups, but few are willing to grant this more than the status of a *façon de parler*. Even those who favor holism over individualism in debates about the methodology of the social sciences generally give a wide berth to any notion of social subjectivity.[30] It is the individualists who insist on the purposeful, rational, and conscious subject as the key to what goes on in society, but they reserve this conception strictly for the individual person; holists stress the degree to which the individual's behavior is imbedded in non-intentional contexts of a structural and causal sort.

There are no doubt many and very interesting sorts of reasons why the idea of social subjectivity is not taken seriously, especially by the Anglo-Saxon mind, but one reason is doubtless the way this idea has been presented, or is thought to have been presented, by some of its advocates. The well-known caricature of Hegel's philosophy of history has the world spirit single-mindedly pursuing its own career by cunningly exploiting individuals for purposes unknown to them and usually opposed to the ones they themselves pursue. More recently, Sartre envisages the transcendence of the "seriality" of individual existence in the "group-in-fusion," for which the storming of the Bastille serves as the paradigm.[31] Confronted with these cases, Anglo-Saxon individualists cry alarm, since individuals are either unwitting and manipulated dupes or they are swept up in an unruly mob which obliterates their individuality altogether. Viewed with a combination of disapproval and disbelief, these notions are denied any importance or usefulness for the understanding of society and history.

But what I am talking about is really very different from either of those notions, which I agree must be rejected as paradigms. In abandoning and subverting individual subjectivity, these views do not take us from the I to a *we* but merely to a larger-scale I. What I have in mind here fits not the caricature but the genuine insight behind Hegel's notion of *Geist*, which he describes, when he first introduces it in the *Phenomenology*, as "an I that is We, a We that is I."[32] In describing the community of mutual recognition, Hegel insists as much on the plurality as on the subjectivity and agency of the social unit, and the community is not opposed to the individuals who make it up but exists precisely by virtue of their conscious acknowledgment of each other and consequently of it. Hegel also has a very healthy sense of the fragility and riskiness of this sort of community: it is born as a resolution of the conflict among its independent-minded members, and it never really overcomes the internal threat to its cohesion which is posed by their sense of independence. The *Phenomenology* is the account of the resulting drama in many of its possible social and historical variations. This account has a *narrative* structure: a community exists not only as a development, but also through the reflexive grasp of that development, when its members assume the common *we* of mutual recognition.

For all the objections that may be raised against the idea of a plural subject, the fact is that in the sorts of cases I have described, we do say *we* to each other, and we mean something real by it. Moreover, much of our lives and much of what we do is predicated on its reality for us. By stressing our use of language and our sense of participation I hope to make it clear that I am advancing not a straightforward ontological claim about the real existence of such social entities, but rather a reflexive account based on the individuals that compose and constitute them. Furthermore the term "community" as I am using it has a variable application, from the nation-states of modern history to the many economic, linguistic, and ethnic groups that often stand in conflict with them. I do not maintain, as Hegel may have thought or hoped, that such communities fit inside each other in some hierarchical order. Conflict may be inevitable, there may be no *us* without a *them*. As for individuals, obviously many of their personal conflicts may arise from conflicting loyalties to the different communities they may belong to.

To sum up: a community exists where a narrative account exists of a *we* which persists through its experiences and actions. Such an account exists when it gets articulated or formulated—perhaps by only one or a few of the group's members—by reference to the *we* and is accepted or subscribed to by others.

It may be thought that in saying this I have so watered down the idea of a plural subject that it loses its interest. It seems now to exist only as a projection in the minds of individuals, who are the real entities after all in my account. If I have said that the *we* is constituted as the subject of a story in and through the telling of that story, remember that I have said exactly the same thing about the I. If the narrative that constitutes the individual self is at least partly social in origin, then the I owes its narrative existence as much to the We as the We does to the I. Neither the We nor the I is a *physical* reality; but they are not *fictions* either. In their own peculiar senses they are as real as anything we know.

IV

To return to narrative texts as literary artifacts, whether fictional or historical, I have tried to make good on my claim that such narratives must be regarded not as a departure from the structure of the events they depict, much less a distortion or radical transformation of them, but as an extension of their primary features. The *practical* first-order narrative process that constitutes a person or a community can become a second- order narrative whose subject is unchanged but whose interest is primarily cognitive or aesthetic. This change in interest may also bring about a change in content—for example, an historian may tell a story about a community which is very different from the story the community (through its leaders, journalists, and others) tells about itself. The form, nonetheless, remains the same.

Thus I am not claiming that second-order narratives, particularly in history, simply mirror or reproduce the first-order narratives that constitute their subject-matter. Not only can they change and improve on the story; they can also affect the reality they depict—and here I agree with Ricoeur—by enlarging its view of its possibilities. While histories can do this for communities, fictions can do it for individuals. But I disagree that the narrative *form* is what is produced in these literary genres in order to be imposed on a non-narrative reality—it is in envisaging new content, new ways of telling and living stories, and new kinds of stories, that history and fiction can be both truthful and creative in the best sense.[33]

NOTES

1. Louis O. Mink, "Narrative Form as a Cognitive Instrument" in *The Writing of History*, eds. R. H. Canary and H. Kozicki (Madison, 1978), 145.

2. Mink, "History and Fiction as Modes of Comprehension," *New Literary History* 1 (1970), 557f.

3. Hayden White, "The Value of Narrativity in the Representation of Reality," in *On Narrative*, ed. W. J. T. Mitchell (Chicago, 1981), 4.

4. Ibid., 23.

5. Frank Kermode, *The Sense of an Ending: Studies in the Theory of Fiction* (London, 1966), 35f.

6. Ibid., 39.

7. Seymour Chatman, *Story and Discourse—Narrative Structure in Fiction and Film* (Ithaca, 1978), 47.

8. Roland Barthes, "Introduction à l'analyse structurale des récits," *Communication* 8 (1966), 7.

9. Paul Ricoeur, *Temps et récit* (Paris, 1983), I, 113.

10. Ibid., *14*.

11. Ibid., 102.

12. Ibid., 11.

13. Ibid., 13. See Ricoeur's *La Métaphore vive* (Paris, 1975), 305 ff.

14. *Temps et récit*, 101.

15. Ibid., 67.

16. For a more detailed critical account of Ricoeur's book see my review-essay in *History and Theory* 23 (1984), 357–70.

17. In his article, "The Question of Narrative in Contemporary Historical Theory," *History and Theory* 23 (1984), 1–33, White himself gives a much more thorough account of these developments than I have given here. Concerning his presentation, which is otherwise a model of scholarship and synthesis, I have three reservations: modesty apparently prevents the author from documenting his own important role in the developments he describes; he generally approves of the trends I shall be criticizing; and he has not, I believe, properly assessed the position of Ricoeur, perhaps because *Temps et récit* was not available to him.

18. Barbara Hardy, "Towards a Poetics of Fiction: An Approach Through Narrative" in *Novel* (1968), 5f; and *Tellers and Listeners: The Narrative Imagination* (London, 1975); Peter Munz, *The Shapes of Time* (Middletown, 1977); Frederick Olafson, *The Dialectic of Action* (Chicago, 1979). Several German theorists have stressed the continuity of experience and narrative. See Wilhelm Schapp, *In Geschichten Verstrickt* (Wiesbaden, 2nd. ed., 1979); Hermann Lübbe, *Bewusstsein in Geschichten* (Freiburg, 1972); Karlheinz Stierle, "Erfahrung und narrative Form" in *Theorie und Erzählung in der Geschichte*, ed. J. Kocka and T. Nipperdey (Munich, 1979), 85ff.

19. Kermode, 44f.

20. Edmund Husserl, *The Phenomenology of Internal Time-Consciousness*, trans. J. S. Churchill (Bloomington, 1964), 40ff.

21. Maurice Merleau-Ponty, *The Phenomenology of Perception*, trans. C. Smith (New York, 1962), 3ff.

22. Alasdair MacIntyre, *After Virtue* (Notre Dame, 1981), 197.

23. Hayden White, "The Structure of Historical Narrative," *Clio* I (1972), 12ff.

24. Arthur Danto, *Analytical Philosophy of History* (Cambridge, 1965), 143ff.

25. Mink, "History and Fiction as Modes of Comprehension," 557ff.

26. Robert Scholes and Robert Kellogg, *The Nature of Narrative* (New York, 1966), 240ff.

27. Martin Heidegger, *Being and Time,* trans. J. Marcquarrie and E. Robinson (New York, 1962), 99.

28. Alfred Schutz, *The Phenomenology of the Social World,* trans. G. Walsh and F. Lehnert (Evanston, 1967), 61.

29. MacIntyre, 191.

30. See Ernst Gellner, "Explanation in History," in *Modes of Individualism and Collectivism,* ed. J. O'Neill (London, 1973), 251; and Anthony Quinton, "Social Objects" in *Proceedings of the Aristotelian Society* (1975–76), 17.

31. Jean-Paul Sartre, *Critique de la raison dialectique* (Paris, 1960), I, 391ff.

32. G. W. F. Hegel, *Phenomenology of Spirit,* trans. A. V. Miller (Oxford, 1977), 110.

33. The themes in this essay are developed at greater length in my *Time, Narrative, and History* (Bloomington: Indiana University Press, 1986).

2

The Narrative Quality of Experience

Stephen Crites

La narration est toute l'épopée; elle est toute l'historie; elle enveloppe le drame et le sous-entend. —Balzac

The *forms* of cultural expression are not historical accidents. They are not products of culture, much less products of individual choice and contrivance, although actual cultural expressions are to some extent both. The way people speak, dance, build, dream, embellish, is to be sure always culturally particular: it bears the imprint of a time and a place. A people speaks a particular language, not the same as that spoken in another land nor quite the same as that spoken by their fathers, and each person adapts it with some originality to his own use. But the fact that people speak some language is no historical accident. It is a necessary mark of being human, i.e., being capable of having a history. That is also true of other persistent forms of cultural expression. They are the conditions of historical existence; their expressions are molded in the historical process itself into definite *products* of particular cultures.

I do not know how to go about proving any such grandiose thesis. To me, I confess, it seems self-evident, in the sense that once the appropriate distinctions are made it becomes obvious. Be that as it may, I propose here to illustrate the point in relation to storytelling, which I take to be one of the most important cultural expressions. I want to argue that the formal quality of experience through time is inherently narrative.[1]

I introduce this thesis by briefly posing another, to which it is intimately related: The style of action through time is inherently musical.

26

The relation of the two theses can be stated in an equation of positively luminous simplicity: Narrative quality is to experience as musical style is to action. And action and experience interpenetrate. Let us see about that.

We speak of the things we do as having a particular style. There is a style in the way a person writes and speaks. An artist paints in a certain style. A farmer exhibits a style in the way he plows his field; a dealer, in the way he keeps his store and arranges his wares. A man's style is formed by the way he is brought up, by the people among whom he has lived, by his training: by his experience. Westerners have, collectively, a different style from Easterners and Californians. Yet in its details a man's style is idiomorphic—as the ringmaster says, inimitable. What is style?

Suppose I walk with unbroken stride across a room. It is a single complex movement. If I were a dancer I could, perhaps, cross the room at a single leap. But even for a dancer the action involves not only a steady change of position in the space of the room, but a divisible duration. There are variations on a joke about a runner so fast that he can turn and see himself still at the starting line. The point of the joke is that however single and swift a movement is there is always before and after.[2] An action is altogether temporal. Yet it has a unity of form through time, a form revealed only in the action as a whole. That temporal form is what we mean by style. My gait has a particular style— an ungainly one, as it happens, of a sort developed in walking through cornfields. But you could not detect it in a still photograph, because the style is in the movement. The same is true of gestures, mannerisms, the putting together of words, the modulations of the voice in speaking the words. All of these are actions, conscious movements in time, and it is appropriate in each case to speak of their having a particular style.

Why conscious movements? Actions are the movements of bodies, but unlike other movements they are performed by bodies that are both the subjects of experience and purposive agents. It does not occur to us, in common speech, to attribute style to unconscious bodies.[3] Movements must be conscious to have a style. Yet that does not imply that one necessarily attends consciously to these movements or to their style. One may do so, and may even attempt to change or to perfect his style. But he has a style, regardless of whether he ever concerns himself with it. Typically, the style is formed quite unconsciously by an agent intent on the various projects to which he directs his action. I cross the room to look out the window or talk to a friend, not in order to perfect my style of walking. The formation of style is seldom the conscious intent or point of an action, except when someone is deliberately training himself, say, as an artist or an athlete. But it is in any case the inner concomitant of an action, whatever its aim: whatever the product of the action, its style is a by-product, or, as we may say in anticipating our comments on its musicality, it is its accompaniment.

It is no coincidence that musical performance exhibits the formal properties of style generally. The rhythms and melodic lines of music are inherently temporal. We do not hear them all at once, but in a succession of pulses and pitched vibrations; yet we experience them as a unity, a unity through time. The reality of a musical phrase, being inherently temporal, implies the evanescence of all its elements. So it is with style. Its elements, too, are evanescent, yet the style of an action exists in the rhythms and the varying pattern of intensities found in it as a whole. To say that my gait in crossing the room has a style is to say that it expresses certain antic rhythms, that it is a crude kind of dance. Similarly, there is something in the cadences and modulations of a voice in speech that is struggling to become a song. Even this essay, turbid as it is, does, after all, have a style, and if you would have to say that its style is flat compared to your favorite books of poems, I think that in the end you would be indulging in a kind of musical criticism of the two productions.

Style is, of course, musical only in a rudimentary sense. It is not yet music, is so to speak below the threshold of music. Yet there is a definite relation between music and style, and not merely a strained analogy. If style is the form of conscious movement, music is that form purified: To the extent that it becomes conscious art it is purged of any inherent relation to a moving body, except as its mere "instrument." The music itself is pure action, not the movement of any thing but simply movement itself: invisible, light as air, freed from the weight of a body and the confinements of space. It exists in time alone, and is, therefore, experienced in the only way we could experience an altogether temporal reality: as something heard, as sound. It must, to be sure, be produced by a body, by someone singing or someone beating, strumming, blowing an instrument. So it, too, will have a style. Yet in itself, as it sounds forth, it is the aesthetic idealization of style, it is, so to speak, the style of style. In music, style is no longer ancillary to an action with some other aim, but is itself the sole aim of the action.

But style generally, the form of all action, is the source of music, its basis for ordinary life. Because it has its source in an ineluctable feature of human existence, music is one of the universal cultural forms of which we spoke at the outset. It is not an arbitrary contrivance, but is a purified form of the incipient musicality of style itself. People take such satisfaction in music because it answers to a powerful if seldom noticed aspect of everything they do, of every gesture, every footstep, every utterance; answers to it and gives it a purified expression. Courtship, worship, even violent conflict, call forth musical expressions in order to give these activities a certain ideality, a specific ideality rooted in the activities themselves. That is why the music of a culture or subculture has such a vital connection, so revealing yet so hard to define, with its whole style of life. The music of a people, or even a cohesive group, is peculiarly its own. It is the particular musical style that permits a group's life style, its incipient musicality, to express itself in full dance and song. The connection is of course reciprocal: The musical style in turn molds the life style. But it cannot be an altogether alien mold. There is a beautiful paradox in the peculiar intensity with which a person responds to music which is "his own": Even if he has not heard it before it is familiar, as though something is sounding in it that he has always felt in his bones; and yet it is really new. It is his own style, revealed to him at an otherwise unimaginable level of clarity and intensity.

Now I want to suggest that stories have a similar resonance for us. But the comments on the musical style of action are not merely for the sake of establishing an analogy with the narrative quality of experience. Narrative, after all, is the other cultural form capable of expressing coherence through time, though its temporality is not so pure as that of music. Particularly important for our purposes, furthermore, are the kinds of stories that have strong musical overtones, for which verse would be the most appropriate form. So let our comments on style sound quietly and perhaps even musically in the background of what follows.

MUNDANE STORIES AND SACRED STORIES

There are powerful grounds for thinking that narrative form is artifice; that it is simply one of the ways we organize a life of experience that is in itself inchoate. We are being reminded nowadays that stories are fictions after all.[4] Of course there have been many forms of narrative, epic, drama, history, the novel, and so on, and our knowledge of the origins and development of such genres has given us a keen impression of their cultural and historical relativity. Furthermore, among some of the most important modern writers there has occurred a determined reaction against all standard narrative forms, partly on the

grounds that such forms represent a subtle falsification of the immediacies of experience, of the modern experience in particular. Even
writers who retain recognizably narrative forms have experimented
with them freely. The great storytellers of our time as well as those
who refuse to tell stories have made us aware of how much art is involved in all story telling. It no longer appears natural and innocent in
our eyes.

The study of traditional folk cultures has also made us aware that
there is more to narrative form than meets the eye (or the ear), and at
least it raises the question whether that may also be true even for a culture as fragmented, sophisticated, and anti-traditional as ours. For
within the traditional cultures there have been some stories that were
told, especially on festal occasions, that had special resonance. Not
only told but ritually re-enacted, these stories seem to be allusive expressions of stories that cannot be fully and directly told, because they
live, so to speak, in the arms and legs and bellies of the celebrants.
These stories lie too deep in the consciousness of a people to be directly told: they form consciousness rather than being among the objects of which it is directly aware. As such they are intimately related
to what we have called "style," and so it is not surprising that these
stories can hardly be expressed at all without an integral fusion of
music with narrative. Every serious attempt to express them creates
poetry. The expressions admit of great variation in detail, but no variation fully grasps the story within these diverse stories.

We sometimes apply our ambiguous term *myth* to this "story
within the story." But it is not identical with the "myths" or legends
we are able to read in ancient books, although these give us valuable
access to those stories which have so powerfully formed a civilization's sense of itself and its world. We might also call these stories "religious," except that this designation implies modern distinctions between religious forms and secular, artistic, political forms, and these
distinctions are misleading as applied to traditional cultures. Certainly
these mythopoeic stories function quite differently in traditional cultures from the way conscious art does in what we are pleased to call
higher cultures. They are anonymous and communal. None of our in-
dividualized conceptions of authorship are appropriate to them, and
while rich powers of imagination may be expressed in them they are
certainly not perceived as conscious fictions. Such stories, and the
symbolic worlds they project, are not like monuments that men be-
hold, but like dwelling places. People live in them. Yet even though
they are not directly told, even though a culture seems rather to be the

telling than the teller of these stories, their form seems to be narrative. They are moving forms, at once musical and narrative, which inform people's sense of the story of which their own lives are a part, of the moving course of their own action and experience.

I propose, with some misgivings, to call these fundamental narrative forms sacred stories, not so much because gods are commonly celebrated in them, but because men's sense of self and world is created through them. For that matter, only the musical stories that form men's living image of themselves and their world have been found fit to celebrate the powers on which their existence depends. For these are stories that orient the life of people through time, their life time, their individual and corporate experience and their sense of style, to the great powers that establish the reality of their world. So I call them sacred stories, which in their secondary, written expressions may carry the authority of scripture for the people who understand their own stories in relation to them.

The stories that are told, all stories directly seen or heard, I propose to call mundane stories. I am uneasy about that term also, although it is not meant to be in the least deprecatory. It simply implies a theory about the objectified images that fully articulated stories must employ, i.e., about words, scenes, roles, sequences of events within a plot, and other narrative devices: that such images, to be capable of being plausible objects of consciousness, must be placed within that world, that phenomenological *mundus*, which defines the objective horizon of a particular form of consciousness. In order to be told, a story must be set within a world. It may not be an everyday world, i.e., it may be an imaginatively augmented world. But even the most fanciful stories have their proprieties. We speak of a universe of discourse, and this too has its limiting firmament above and below, beyond which nothing can be conceived to happen. Historically there have been a variety of such worlds, correlative to the historical forms of consciousness. The stories of an age or a culture take place within its world. Only in that sense are they necessarily mundane. Here, in some world of consciousness, we find stories composed as works of art as well as the much more modest narrative communications that pass between people in explaining where they have been, why things are as they are, and so on. Set within a world of consciousness, the mundane stories are also among the most important means by which people articulate and clarify their sense of that world. In order to initiate their children in "the ways of the world," parents tell them stories—although in recent times, particularly, the problem has arisen that the children find themselves having to make their way in quite a different world, for which they have to devise quite different kinds of stories than those their parents taught them.

Sacred stories, too, are subject to change, but not by conscious reflection. People do not sit down on a cool afternoon and think themselves up a sacred story. They awaken to a sacred story, and their most significant mundane stories are told in the effort, never fully successful, to articulate it. For the sacred story does not transpire within a conscious world. It forms the very consciousness that projects a total world horizon, and therefore informs the intentions by which actions are projected into that world. The style of these actions dance to its music. One may attempt to name a sacred story, as we shall try to do in our conclusion. But such naming misleads as much as it illuminates, since its meaning is contained—and concealed—in the unutterable cadences and revelations of the story itself. Yet every sacred story is creation story: not merely that one may name creation of world and self as its "theme" but also that the story itself creates a world of consciousness and the self that is oriented to it.

Between sacred and mundane stories there is distinction without separation. From the sublime to the ridiculous, all a people's mundane stories are implicit in its sacred story, and every mundane story takes soundings in the sacred story. But some mundane stories sound out greater depths than others. Even the myths and epics, even the scriptures, are mundane stories. But in these, as well as in some works of literary art, and perhaps even in some merry little tales that seem quite content to play on the surface, the sacred stories resonate. People are able to feel this resonance, because the unutterable stories are those they know best of all.

It is possible for such resonances to sound in poetic productions that seem to defy all traditional forms of story telling. For the surface of conventional narrative forms may have become so smooth and hard that it is necessary to break it in order to let a sacred story sound at all. Such a necessity may signalize that the sacred story is altogether alive, transforming itself in the depths. Break the story to tell a truer story! But there are also darker possibilities in this situation, as we shall see.

THE INNER FORM OF EXPERIENCE:
1. THE CHRONICLE OF MEMORY

Between sacred story and the mundane stories there is a mediating form: the form of the experiencing consciousness itself. For consciousness is molded by the sacred story to which it awakens, and in turn it finds expression in the mundane stories that articulate its sense of reality. But consciousness itself is not a blank. Consciousness has a form of its own, without which no coherent experience at all would be possible.[5] Aside from that formidable inconvenience, it is difficult to see how a consciousness, itself entirely formless, could be the fulcrum that I have suggested it is between sacred and mundane stories. I want further to propose that the form of active consciousness, i.e., the form of its experiencing, is in at least some rudimentary sense narrative. That is why consciousness is able to mediate between the sacred and mundane stories through which it orients itself in a world.[6] A square peg would not fit into a round hole. The stories give qualitative substance to the form of experience because it is itself an incipient story.

That is the central thesis of this essay. Of all the unlikely things that have been said thus far, it perhaps seems the least plausible. In attempting to explain and support it I want to do the usual thing in such straits, and appeal for the help of a favorite teacher. The teacher is Augustine of Hippo. Not that he would necessarily subscribe to my thesis. But being a good teacher, he has helped me find my way to my own notions, and even when I have pursued my own follies he has only given me help when I knew I needed it.

The help in this case is offered in his brooding reflections on memory and time in the tenth and eleventh books of the *Confessions*. Whether or not he succeeded in establishing the subjectivity of time in that famous discussion, whether indeed that is what he was trying to do, I want to invert the problem and suggest that he did succeed in establishing the temporality of the subject. Consciousness grasps its objects in an inherently temporal way, and that temporality is retained in the unity of its experience as a whole.

Augustine ponders the paradox that the future, which does not yet exist, should pass into the past which no longer exists, through a present that is difficult to *conceptualize* as more than a vanishing quasi-mathematical point. The paradox is resolved when past, present, and future are considered to be not necessarily independent metaphysical modalities, but unavoidable modalities of experience in the mind or experiencing consciousness *(anima)*. For consciousness "anticipates and attends and remembers, so that what it anticipates passes through what it attends into what it remembers" (XI:xxviii).[7] We will consider in the next section the highly developed temporality implicit in this threefold function of consciousness. But already in memory alone there is the simple temporality of sequence, of before and after.

Without memory, in fact, experience would have no coherence at all. Consciousness would be locked in a bare, momentary present, i.e., in a disconnected succession of perceptions which it would have no power to relate to one another. It might be argued that that would already imply a temporality of the most elemental sort. It is already significant that experience has, in its present, this sheer momentary quality. But it is memory that bestows the sense of temporal succession as well as the power to abstract coherent unities from this succession of momentary precepts.

In Book X Augustine singles out this capacity of memory for analysis, and also for a kind of awe—Augustine is a thinker for whom awe and close analysis are intensified together:

> Great is this power of memory, excessively great, my God, a vast and infinite interior space: who has plumbed it to the depths? Yet this is a power of my mind and pertains to my nature, so that I myself do not grasp all that I am. (X:viii)

Yet, Augustine muses, people take this prodigy within themselves for granted. Ignoring this interior space, they are amazed by the great dimensions of mountains, oceans, rivers, the orbits of the stars. But greater than the wonder of these external, natural wonders is the simple fact that he himself can speak of these things even though he does not at the moment see them. That is possible because he sees "inwardly in my memory" these things he had once seen outwardly with his eyes—yet it is not the very things themselves that appear in this inner vision: For

> still I did not absorb these things [into myself] in seeing them . . . nor are they themselves attached to me, but their images only, and I know by what sense of the body each was impressed upon me. (X:viii)

Detached from things and lodged in memory, along with inner impressions of feeling and mood, these images are susceptible to the uses of thought and the play of imagination. Called up by the activities of the mind, they can be dismantled and reassembled or combined in original ways. When we do not attend to them they are "submerged and they slide down, as it were, into the remote interior spaces" of memory. But from this "dispersion" they can always be "collected" again by our thought, i.e., literally, by our cogitations. Augustine likes to play on the etymological connection between *cogo*—collect—and *cogito*. (X:xi)

So there is an important distinction between memory and recollection that goes back at least to Augustine. All the sophisticated activities of consciousness literally re-collect the images lodged in memory into new configurations, reordering past experience. But that would be impossible were it not for the much more naive functioning of memory itself, preserving the images drawn from experience. But I venture to suggest that memory does not contain its images quite so "scatteredly and confusedly" as Augustine suggests in the passage cited above. The memory also has its order, not the recollected order formed by thought and imagination, but a simple order of succession. This succession is the order in which the images of actual experience through time have been impressed upon the memory. It constitutes a kind of lasting chronicle, fixed in my memory, of the temporal course of my experience. This chronicle does not need to be recollected strictly, but merely to be recalled: I need only call up again the succession of images which stand waiting in memory in the order in which I experienced them. Of course the recall is not total, the chronicle is not without lacunae. In fact, it is for great stretches quite fragmentary. But what we do succeed in calling up we find differentiated into fairly clear sequence. We are aware of what comes before and what comes after. When we are uncertain, or feel that a crucial scene is missing, we have the sense of "consulting" our memory. The recall is not infallible, but we have the sense that this "consultation" is possible, that the chronicle is "there," in memory, to be consulted, that if we concentrate intensely on our remembering we will be able to recall a sequence of events accurately. I consult my memory in this way, for example, when I mentally retrace my steps in the effort to recall where I may have lost something.

Yet that odd consultation is not strictly an act of recollection. We must consult our memory in order to recollect its images, to reorganize them for the more sophisticated purposes of the mind. But remembering is not yet knowing. Its chronicle is too elemental, too fixed, to be illuminating. Experience is illuminated only by the more subtle processes of recollection. At least in this sense all knowledge is recollection! So is all art, including the art of storytelling. It is an act. It has style. But mere remembering as such has no style, if we could isolate it from the process of recollection that in practice generally accompanies it.

Yet storytelling is not an arbitrary imposition upon remembered experience, altogether alien to its own much simpler form. Images do not exist in memory as atomic units, like photographs in an album, but as transient episodes in an image-stream, cinematic, which I must suspend and from which I must abstract in order to isolate a particular image. The most direct and obvious way of recollecting it is by telling a story, though the story is never simply the tedious and unilluminating recital of the chronicle of memory itself. And, of course, I can manipulate the image-stream in other ways. I can abstract general features and formal elements of it for purposes of theory, or suspend it in order to draw a picture, or splice episodes from it in a way that gives them new significance. I can contemplate a whole segment of the image-stream in a single glance of inner vision, then fragment it so that its elements are left twinkling in isolation like stars—yet even then memory is not shattered. Indeed, I can do such things because the original chronicle, the image stream, is always at hand, needing only to be recalled. I can even measure out its segments into long times and short times, recalling some episodes as having occurred a long time ago, others more recently (a phenomenon that Augustine ponders with great care in XI:xv–xxviii) .[8]

I recall, for example, a sequence from my own memory. In telling it, of course, recollection already intervenes, but I recollect in a way as faithful as possible to the memory itself. I measure out "a long time" and recall an episode from my childhood. I have not thought about it for many years, and yet I find its chronicle in good condition, extremely detailed and in clear sequence. In an impetuous fit of bravado I threw a rock through a garage window. I recall the exact spot on the ground from which I picked up the rock, I recall the wind-up, the pitch, the rock in mid-air, the explosive sound of the impact, the shining spray of glass, the tinkling hail of shards falling on the cement below, the rough, stony texture of the cement. I recall also my inner glee at that moment, and my triumph when a playmate, uncertain at first how to react, looked to me for his cue and then broke into a grin. Now I could cut and splice a bit, passing over hours not so clearly recalled anyway, except that my mood underwent drastic change. Then I recall that moment in the evening when I heard my father's returning footsteps on the porch and my guilty terror reached a visceral maximum the very memory of which wrenches a fat adult belly—for remembering is not simply a process in the head! The details of the scene that ensued are likewise very vivid in my memory.

Now it would be quite possible for me to tell this story very differently. My perspective on it has been changed, partly by the death of my father and the fact that I am now myself the father of children, partly, too, by my reading in the *Confessions* a story about a wanton theft of pears and by some reading in Freud on the rivalry of fathers and sons, and so forth. So I have many insights into this chronicle that

I could not have had at the time its events occurred. Yet the sophisticated new story I might tell about it would be superimposed on the image-stream of the original chronicle. It could not replace the original without obliterating the very materials to be recollected in the new story. Embedded in every sophisticated retelling of such a story is this primitive chronicle preserved in memory. Even conscious fictions presuppose its successive form, even when they artfully reorder it.

THE INNER FORM OF EXPERIENCE:
2. A DRAMATIC TENSION

In the chronicle of memory there is the simple temporality of succession, of duration, of before and after, but not yet the decisive distinction between past, present, and future, that provides the tension of experience and therefore demands the tenses of language. Memory, containing the past, is only one modality of experience, that never exists in isolation from those that are oriented to the present and the future. To understand the relation of the three we may again refer to Augustine.

He points out that past, present, and future cannot be three distinct realities or spheres of being that somehow coexist. Only the present exists.

> But perhaps it might properly be said: there are three times, a present of things past, a present of things present, a present of things future. (XI:xx)

Only the present exists, but it exists only in these tensed modalities. They are inseparably joined in the present itself. Only from the standpoint of present experience could one speak of past and future. The three modalities are correlative to one another, in every moment of experience.

> For these are in the mind as a certain triadic form, and elsewhere I do not see them: the present of things past is memory, the present of things present is direct attention, the present of things future is anticipation. (XI:xx)

I want to suggest that the inner form of any possible experience is determined by the union of these three distinct modalities in every moment of experience. I want further to suggest that the tensed unity of these modalities requires narrative forms both for its expression (mundane stories) and for its own sense of the meaning of its internal coherence (sacred stories). For this tensed unity has already an incipient narrative form.

The chronicle of memory, with its simple successiveness, its before and after, is in actual experience always already taken up into the more sophisticated temporality of tense. If we would attempt to isolate anticipation as we did memory we would again discover a very elemental narrative form. We might call it the scenario of anticipation.[9] I have in mind our guesses and predictions about what may happen, hunches generally formulated in the attempt to lay some plans about our own projected courses of action. Projected action often dominates this modality of experience, though one may simply worry about the future or indulge in euphoric dreams about it. But whether anticipation takes the passive form of dreams, worries, and wishes, or is instrumental in laying plans or making resolutions for projected actions, it seems intuitively clear that we anticipate by framing little stories about how things may fall out. As the term *scenario* implies, these anticipatory stories are very thin and vague as compared with the dense, sharp detail of the chronicle of memory. It is also clear that the course of events generally turns out quite differently from what we had anticipated. But the experience of thwarted expectations, or the comic situation when parties to an encounter come to it with very different scenarios in mind—e.g., she prepared for political discussion, he for romantic rendezvous—simply serve to show that we do orient ourselves to the future by means of such scenarios. Though they are generally vague, they are not altogether formless. However freely our action may improvise upon the scenario, it is never simply random.

Now it is not as though the scenario of anticipation were set alongside the chronicle of memory, as two quite separate stories. Our sense of personal identity depends upon the continuity of experience through time, a continuity bridging even the cleft between remembered past and projected future. Even when it is largely implicit, not vividly self-conscious, our sense of ourselves is in every moment to some extent integrated into a single story. That on the one hand.

On the other hand, the distinction between memory and anticipation is absolute. The present is not merely an indifferent point moving along a single unbroken and undifferentiated line, nor is the temporality of experience such a line. Nor do past and future simply "meet" in the present. Memory and anticipation, the present of things past and the present of things future, are tensed modalities of the present itself. They are the tension of every moment of experience, both united in that present and qualitatively differentiated by it. For precisely in this momentary present which embraces my whole experience, the past remembered is fixed, a chronicle that I can radically reinterpret but cannot reverse or displace: what is done cannot be undone! And within this same present the future is, on the contrary, still fluid, awaiting determination, subject to alternative scenarios.[10] Precisely as modalities of the present of experience, the past remembered is determinate, the future anticipated is indeterminate, and the distinction between them is intuitively clear and absolute.

But how can the present contain such tension, on the one hand unifying, on the other hand absolutely distinguishing its tensed modalities? It can do so because the whole experience, as it is concentrated in a conscious present, has a narrative form. Narrative alone can contain the full temporality of experience in a unity of form. But this incipient story, implicit in the very possibility of experience, must be such that it can absorb both the chronicle of memory and the scenario of anticipation, absorb them within a richer narrative form without effacing the difference between the determinacy of the one and the indeterminacy of the other.

We can define such a narrative form a little more fully by reminding ourselves that the conscious present has a third modality: the present of things present. This *praesens de praesentibus* Augustine designates as *contuitus*—direct attention. True enough, but there is something more. If discussion of the ethereal-seeming objects of memory and anticipation may have tempted us to speak of consciousness itself as if it were an invisibility suspended in a void, mention of its direct present must sharply remind us that consciousness is a function of an altogether bodily life. The conscious present is that of a body impacted in a world and moving, in process, in that world. In this present, action and experience meet. Memory is its depth, the depth of its experience in particular; anticipation is its trajectory, the trajectory of its action in particular. The *praesens de praesentibus* is its full bodily reality.

It is, moreover, the moment of decision within the story as a whole. It is always the *decisive* episode in the story, its moment of crisis between the past remembered and the future anticipated but still undetermined. The *critical* position of this modality gives the story a dramatic character as a whole. And since action and experience join precisely at this decisive and critical juncture in the drama, the whole drama vibrates with the musicality of personal style.

Still, it is a drama of a rudimentary sort. Life is not, after all, a work of art. An artistic drama has a coherence and a fullness of articulation that are never reached by our rudimentary drama. But the drama of experience is the crude original of all high drama. High drama can only contrive the appearance of that crisis which the conscious present actually is. The difference between a fixed past and a future still to be resolved, which in experience is an absolute difference, must be artfully contrived on a stage by actors who know the outcome as well as they know the beginning. The art of drama imitates the life of experience, which is the true drama.

"ONCE UPON A TIME . . . HAPPILY EVER AFTER"

Life also imitates art. The stories people hear and tell, the dramas they see performed, not to speak of the sacred stories that are absorbed without being directly heard or seen, shape in the most profound way the inner story of experience. We imbibe a sense of the meaning of our own baffling dramas from these stories, and this sense of its meaning in turn affects the form of a man's experience and the style of his action. Such cultural forms, both sacred and mundane, are of course socially shared in varying degrees, and so help to link men's inner lives as well as orienting them to a common public world. Both the content and the form of experience are mediated by symbolic systems which we are able to employ simply by virtue of awakening within a particular culture in which those symbolic systems are the common currency. Prevailing narrative forms are among the most important of such symbolic systems. It is not as though a man begins as a purely individual consciousness with the incipient story and musicality of his private experience, and then casts about for a satisfying tale to lend it some higher significance. People awaken to consciousness in a society, with the inner story of experience and its enveloping musicality already infused with cultural forms. The vitalities of experience itself may in turn make a man feel that some of the old stories have a hollow ring and may be the source of originality in the formation of new stories, or even new kinds of stories. But the *way* we remember, anticipate, and even directly perceive, is largely social. A sacred story in particular infuses experience at its root, linking a man's individual consciousness with ultimate powers and also with the inner lives of those with whom he shares a common soil.

There is an entrancing half-truth that has gained wide currency. It is that time itself is a cultural product, e.g., the creation of certain grammatical forms.[11] Presumably we could be rid of it if we played our cards right, say, with a non-western deck. The kernel of truth in this idyllic vision is that particular conceptions of time are indeed imbibed from cultural forms, not only from the structures of a language but from the kinds of stories being told. For the temporality that I have argued is necessary for the very possibility of experience does not of itself imply any particular conception of time. The connections among its episodes or moments is not necessarily, for example, either magical, causal, logical, or teleological. Least of all does it imply any theory regarding the metaphysical status of time. The temporality of lived experience as such, with its inherent tensions and crises, can only, so to speak, raise questions about the reality and meaning of time. For the answers to these questions it must, as it were, turn to the sacred and mundane cultural forms lying at hand. In fact, the answers precede and sometimes preclude the questions! Stories, in particular, infuse the incipient drama of experience with a definite sense of the way its scenes are connected. They reveal to people the kind of drama in which they are engaged, and perhaps its larger meaning. So the fact that there are very different notions of time implicit in the cultural forms of different historical traditions does not contradict the inherent temporality of all possible experience. There is only one absolute limit to that diversity: It is impossible that a culture could offer no interpretation of this temporality at all.

In principle, we can distinguish between the inner drama of experience and the stories through which it achieves coherence. But in any actual case the two so interpenetrate that they form a virtual identity, which, if we may pun a little, is in fact a man's very sense of his own personal identity. The sacred story in particular, with its musical vitality, enables him to give the incipient drama of his experience full dramatic dimensions and allows the incipient musicality of his style to break forth into real dance and song. Hence the powerful inner need for expressive forms, the music played and sung and danced, the stories told and acted, projected within the world of which men are conscious.

So the narrative quality of experience has three dimensions, the sacred story, the mundane stories, and the temporal form of experience itself: three narrative tracks, each constantly reflecting and affecting the course of the others.

And sometimes the tracks cross, causing a burst of light like a comet entering our atmosphere. Such a luminous moment, in which sacred, mundane, and personal are inseparably conjoined, we call *symbolic* in a special sense. Of course, there is a more general sense in which every element in a story is a symbol, an imaginative representation conveying a meaning; but even in that sense the symbol is partly constituted by its position in the story. A story is not a mere assembly of independently defined symbols. Still less is a symbol in the more pregnant sense, e.g., a religious symbol, an atomic capsule of meaning that drops from the heavens or springs from the unconscious in isolated splendor.[12] The cross, or a holy mountain, receives its meaning from the stories in which it appears. Such a symbol imports into any icon or life situation or new story in which it appears, the significance given it in a cycle of mundane stories and also the resonances of a sacred story. The shock of its appearance is like the recurrence in daylight of an episode recalled from dreams. For a religious symbol becomes fully alive to consciousness when sacred story dramatically intersects both an explicit narrative and the course of a man's personal experience. The symbol is precisely that double intersection.

Narrative form, and not the symbol as such, is primitive in experience. But narrative form is by no means innocent. It acknowledges and informs only what is contained in its own ordering of events. Even the most naive tale begins "once upon a time"—a time prior to which there is only darkness, no time so far as the temporality constituted by the story is concerned. That time begins with this "once . . ." and when the tale has run its course there is nothing left. Its characters disappear into a timeless "happily ever after." It is meaningless to ask whether they really do. For they live only within the tensions and crises which constitute the significant time of the story, the narrative "tick-tock,"[13] between the tick of "once upon a time" and the tock of happy resolution. Of course, the resolution may not be happy. We may leave our characters in a state of horror also outside all time and, therefore, pure and unambiguous. This happiness, this horror, are both beyond the possibilities of recognizable human experience. Only narrative form can contain the tensions, the surprises, the disappointments and reversals and achievements of actual, temporal experience. The vague yet unambiguous, uncanny happiness and horror are "beyond." The story itself may, to be sure, contain symbolic accents that refer to such a beyond, e.g., the resurrection, or images of eternal blessedness or torment, or descents into a nether region that is strangely familiar. Such symbolic accents are not necessarily intimations of immortality. Imagination is projected by them beyond any possible experience, and yet the projection itself takes place within the contingencies of experience. It belongs to the story. However deep into the bowels of hell Dante leads us, however high into heaven, it is remarkable how he and his sinners and saints keep our attention fixed on the little disk of earth, that stage on which the drama of men's moral struggles in time is enacted. Far from reducing the significance of this time-bound story in which we are embroiled, such visions of happiness and horror make it all the more portentous. Even in secularized projections beyond the ambiguity of history into social utopia or doomsday, a particular sense of the historical drama itself is implicit. For the meaning of both happiness and horror is derived, even in the uttermost leap of the imagination beyond our story, from our conception of the story itself.

If experience has the narrative quality attributed to it here, not only our self-identity but the empirical and moral cosmos in which we are conscious of living is implicit in our multidimensional story. It therefore becomes evident that a conversion or a social revolution that actually transforms consciousness requires a traumatic change in a man's story. The stories within which he has awakened to consciousness must be undermined, and in the identification of his personal story through a new story both the drama of his experience and his style of action must be reoriented. Conversion is reawakening, a second awakening of consciousness. His style must change steps, he must dance to a new rhythm. Not only his past and future, but the very cosmos in which he lives is strung in a new way.

The point is beautifully made in a passage from the *Protreptikos* of Clement of Alexandria, selections from which, in verse translation, are among the last things we have from the pen of Thomas Merton. Clement, himself a convert to Christianity, is writing at the time Christianity first emerged in a serious way into a classical culture already become decadent. In a passage entitled "The New Song," he retells an old Greek legend but glosses it in a way that gives it a radical new turn. A bard named Eunomos was singing, to his own accompaniment on the lyre, a hymn to the death of the Pythian dragon. Meanwhile, unnoticed by the pagan assembly, another performance is under way.

> Crickets were singing among the leaves all up the mountainside,
>   burning in the sun.
> They were singing, not indeed for the death of the dragon,
>   the dead Pythian, but
> They hymned the all-wise God, in their own mode, far superior
>   to that of Eunomos.
> A harp string breaks on the Locrian.
> A cricket flies down on top of the lyre. She sings on the instrument
>   as though on a branch. The singer, harmonizing with the
>   cricket's tune, goes on without the lost string.
> Not by the song of Eunomos is the cricket moved, as the myth
>   supposes, or as is shown by the bronze statue the Delphians
>   erected, showing

Eunomos with his harp and his companion in the contest!
The cricket flies on her own and sings on her own.

The subversive cricket sings the new song, to Clement old as creation
yet newly come to human lips, of the Christian logos.

See what power the new song has!
From stones, men,
From beasts it has made men.
Those otherwise dead, those without a share in life that is really life
At the mere sound of this song
Have come back to life. . . .
Moreover He has structured the whole universe musically
And the discord of elements He has brought together in an ordered
    symphony
So that the whole Cosmos is for Him in harmony.[14]

MODERNITY AND REVOLUTION:
AN INTEMPERATE CONCLUSION

The form of consciousness to which we apply the name *modernity*
seems to represent a transformation as radical, though of a different
sort, as that celebrated by Clement. Some have even suggested the
emergence of a yet newer sensibility, so new and inchoate that it can
only be designated "postmodern." All this is too close to us to speak of
it with much assurance, but I yield to the temptation to offer some
suggestions that bear on our theme.

I have argued that experience is molded, root and branch, by narrative forms, that its narrative quality is altogether primitive. At the
same time, expression is obviously not limited to storytelling. Mind
and imagination are capable of recollecting the narrative materials of
experience into essentially non-narrative forms. Indeed there seems to
be a powerful inner drive of thought and imagination to overcome the
relentless temporality of experience. One needs more clarity than stories can give us, and also a little rest. The kind of pure spatial articulation we find in painting and sculpture, with all movement suspended,
gratifies this deep need. Also in meditation and in theoretical endeav-
ors we are a little less completely at the mercy of our own temporality.
Traditional myths, stories dominated by timeless archetypes, have
functioned in this way: by taking personal and historical time up into
the archetypal story, they give it a meaning which in the end is timeless, cosmic, absolute.

But an important feature of the modern situation is the employ-ment of quite different strategies for breaking the sense of narrative time. At a very general level, these strategies fall into two opposite and indeed mutually antagonistic types: One is the strategy of abstrac-tion, in which images and qualities are detached from experience to become data for the formation of generalized principles and tech-niques. Such abstraction enables us to give experience a new, non-nar-rative and atemporal coherence. It is an indispensable strategy for con-ducting many of the practical affairs of life in our society; we are all technicians, like it or not. In its more elaborated forms, the strategy of abstraction is the basis for all science. Its importance in the formation of modern institutions can hardly be exaggerated.

But strategies of the other type seem almost equally important in the formation of "modern" consciousness. This other type we may call the strategy of contraction. Here narrative temporality is again frag-mented, not by abstraction to systems of generality, but by the con-striction of attention to dissociated immediacies: to the particular image isolated from the image stream, to isolated sensation, feeling, the flash of the overpowering moment in which the temporal context of that moment is eclipsed and past and future are deliberately blocked out of consciousness. It is commonly assumed that this disso-ciated immediacy is what is concrete and irreducible in experience.

But the sweat and grit of the moment, which some so highly prize, is in fact a contraction of the narrative movement that is really con-crete in experience, as generality is the abstraction from it. The point can perhaps best be made indirectly, by noticing that these two time-defying strategies have projected a distinctively modern version of a dualism in the idea of the self: the dualism of mind and body. We state the matter backwards if we say that something called mind ab-stracts from experience to produce generality, or if we say that "the body" has feelings and sensations. It is the activity of abstracting from the narrative concreteness of experience that leads us to posit the idea of mind as a distinct entity. And it is the concentration of conscious-ness into feeling and sensation that gives rise to the idea of body. Both mind and body are reifications of particular functions that have been wrenched from the concrete temporality of the conscious self. The self is not a composite of mind and body. The self in its concreteness is in-divisible, temporal, and whole, as it is revealed to be in the narrative quality of its experience. Neither disembodied minds nor mindless bodies can appear in stories. There the self is given whole, as an activ-ity in time.

Yet criticism alone cannot dissolve this mind-body dualism. The very fact of its stubborn persistence in our ordinary sense of ourselves, even though we know better (in theory!), testifies to the very great importance in the modern world of the two strategies on which it is based. The power to abstract makes explanation, manipulation, and control possible. On the other hand we seek relief and release in the capacity to contract the flow of time, to dwell in feeling and sensation, in taste, in touch, in the delicious sexual viscosities. So "the mind" dwells in the light, clear, dry, transparent, unmessy. "The body" dwells in the damp privacy of a friendly darkness created by feeling and sensation. In principle, the powers of consciousness to abstract and to contract need no more be in conflict than day and night. But day and night form a rhythm within the continuum of time. If the abstraction and contraction of consciousness were merely temporary suspensions of the narrative quality of experience there would be no crisis.

But the modern world has seen these two strategies played off ever more violently against one another. One could show how the reification of mind and body has killed modern metaphysics by leading it into arid controversies among dualistic, materialistic, and idealistic theories. But this comparatively harmless wrangle among post-Cartesian metaphysicians is only a symptom of the modern bifurcation of experience. Its more sinister expression is practical: the entrapment of educated subcultures in their own abstract constructions, and the violent reaction against this entrapment, a reaction that takes the form of an equally encapsulating constriction of experience into those warm, dark, humid immediacies. One thinks of Faust in his study where everything is so dry that a spark would produce an explosion, and then Faust slavering and mucking about on the Brocken. Against the inhumanly dry and abstract habitations of the spirit that have been erected by technological reason, the cry goes up, born of desperation, to drop out and sink into the warm stream of immediacy. Within the university the reaction and counterreaction have been especially violent in the humanities.

And that is ironical. For the material with which the humanities have traditionally dealt is predominantly narrative. There have been deep conflicts among different kinds of stories and divergent interpretations. Still, the humanities have kept the story alive in the university; and it is precisely the story, with its underlying musicality, that provides generality and immediacy their humanly fruitful functions. So long as the story retains its primary hold on the imagination, the play of immediacy and the illuminating power of abstraction remain in productive tension. But when immediacy and abstract generality are wrenched out of the story altogether, drained of all musicality, the result is something I can only call, with strict theological precision, demonic. Experience becomes demonically possessed by its own abstracting and contracting possibilities, turned alien and hostile to experience itself. When the humanities give up the story, they become alternately seized by desiccated abstractions and scatological immediacies, the light of the mind becoming a blinding and withering glare, the friendly darkness deepening into the chaotic night of nihilism. Ethical authority, which is always a function of a common narrative coherence of life, is overthrown by a naked show of force exercised either in the name of reason or in the name of glandular vitality. Contrary to the cynical theory that violent force is the secret basis of authority, it is in fact always the sign that authority has dissolved.

So much for modernity. Now one speaks, perhaps wistfully, of the emergence of a "postmodern" sensibility. This new sensibility is sometimes called revolutionary," a term that sounds less empty than "postmodern," but is still obscure enough. Certainly it is often discussed in terms of the same dualisms and wearisome strategies of abstraction and contraction that have plagued the "modern" period. Some envision a "revolution" that would consist in extending the control of abstract, technological reason to the whole life of society; maximum manipulation justified on the high moral ground that it would improve behavior—down to the least flicker of an eyelash. Others appear to hope for a society perpetually turned on and flowing with animal juices. The utopia schemed in the crystal palace, or that plotted in the cellar of the underground man: the lure of either of these utopias or any all-purpose combination of them can lead one to nothing more than a variation on an all too familiar refrain. Neither appears to catch the cadences of the new song that I think is struggling to be heard when people speak seriously of revolution.

I think that "revolution" is the name that a postmodern consciousness gives to a new sacred story. I realize that if this essay has ever strayed into the sphere of sober theory, it has with this suggestion abandoned it altogether in favor of testimony. But if we really are talking about a sacred story, what can we do but testify? Certainly the sacred story to which we give this name cannot be directly told. But its resonances can be felt in many of the stories that are being told, in songs being sung, in a renewed resolution to act. The stories being told do not necessarily speak of gods in any traditional sense, yet there seem to be living continuities in this unutterable story with some of the sacred stories of the past. Among those for whom the story is alive there is a revival of ethical authority. For it establishes on a new basis the coherency of social and personal time. It makes it possible to recover a living past, to believe again in the future, to perform acts that have significance for the person who acts. By so doing it restores a human form of experience.

NOTES

1. That is to say that I conceive my undertaking to be phenomenological. It will not, however, be larded with citations from the great German and French phenomenologists. The phenomenology will be homemade.

2. Though not as if, like Zeno's arrow, one passed through a series of quasi-mathematical points in time. The temporality of which we speak is constituted by the movement itself, and not by the (essentially spatial) units of its measure.

3. However poetically we may express our appreciation for, say, the revolutions of the moon, we would not normally attribute style to it, nor even to the "song" of a bird. And while we do speak of the style of a painting, I take it that that is an oblique way of referring to the style of the artist in his act of painting it: the "painting" and not the artifact as such has style. Again, when people are asleep their style slumbers also; "What style!" would be a nice comic caption for a cartoon picturing a woman pointing at her snoring husband.

4. The point is brilliancy argued and elaborated in Frank Kermode, *The Sense of an Ending* (Oxford University Press, 1966). Professor Kermode warns that "If we forget that fictions are fictive we regress to myth. . . ." (p. 41). My argument may well illustrate what he is warning against. I do deny that all narratives are merely fictive, and I go on to deny that myth, or what I call sacred story, is a mere regression from a fiction. But it is ungrateful to single out my disagreements with a book from which I have derived uncommon profit in pondering my theme.

5. As Kant argued in *The Critique of Pure Reason,* though of course reaching quite different conclusions about the constitution of this necessary form. To make at the level of *strenge Wissenschaft* my case that the primary forms of possible experience are narrative, I should also have to follow Kant's lead by providing a transcendental deduction of these incipient narrative forms. But I content myself with the gestures in that direction contained in this and the following section.

6. There is an implicit circularity here that may as well be made explicit, since I am sure to be found out anyway: I appeal to the form of sacred and mundane story to suggest that the structure of experience informed by such

stories must itself be in some sense narrative. But I have not really proven that what I have called sacred story is in any acceptable sense narrative itself, and among the reasons that make me think it is, the most important is that experience has at root a narrative form: Experience can derive a specific sense of its own temporal course in a coherent world only by being informed by a qualifying structure that gives definite contours to its own form. Very well. The points are mutually supportive, i.e., the argument is in the end circular, as any good philosophical argument is. And in the end it has only the explanatory power of this particular circle to commend it.

7. I take responsibility for the translation of extracts from *The Confessions* quoted here.

8. In recognizing the importance of this strange measurement of what no longer exists, Augustine does implicitly acknowledge the primitive order of succession within memory is not simply a vast interior space in which images tumble at random.

9. I have discussed such anticipatory scenarios in some detail in an essay to which the present one is in many ways a sequel: "Myth, Story, History," published in a symposium entitled *Parable, Myth and Language* (Cambridge, Mass.: The Church Society for College Work, 1968), p. 68.

10. The fluidity of the future from the standpoint of consciousness has nothing to do with the truth or falsity of deterministic theories. The point is phenomenological, not metaphysical.

11. This view is usually linked with a lovable primitivism. People who make this link often seize upon the theories of Benjamin Lee Whorf, who had observed, for example, that characteristically western notions of time could not be expressed at all in the language of the Hopi Indians. See "An American Indian Model of the Universe," in the collection of Whorf's writings entitled *Language, Thought, and Reality* (Cambridge, Mass.: M.I.T. Press, 1956). Cf. Richard M. Gale, *The Language of Time* (London: Routlage & Kegan Paul, 1968), pp. 45–48, for a critique of some of the general claims Whorf's observations led him to make. Those who cite Whorf are often less cautious than he is claiming that time is the product of a particular culture, and therefore holding out the possibility that there are or might be peoples blessedly free of the conflicts and traumas of temporal existence.

Far removed from this idyllic vision is the fine work of Georges Poulet, *Studies in Human Time*, trans. by Elliott Coleman (Baltimore: Johns Hopkins University Press, 1956). Poulet points up the radical developments and the subtle modulations in the sense of time within western culture itself, particularly in the works of a succession of important French and American writers.

12. It has been widely assumed that symbols are in some sense primitive in experience, and that myths and other narrative forms are secondary

constructions that assemble the primal symbolic material into stories. That view, for example, in a highly sophisticated form, seems to be an important premise of Paul Ricoeur's fine studies in this field, e.g., *The Symbolism of Evil*, trans. by Emerson Buchanan (New York: Harper & Row, 1967). But such a view seems to presuppose an atomism of experience that I think is quite impossible.

13. Frank Kermode ingeniously treats "tick-tock" as a model of plot, contrasting the organized duration between the "humble genesis" of tick and the "feeble apocalypse" of tock with the "emptiness," the unorganized blank that exists between our perception of "tock" and the next "tick." *The Sense of an Ending*, pp. 44–46.

14. Clement of Alexandria, Selections from *The Protreptikos*, an essay and translation by Thomas Merton (New York: New Directions, 1962), pp. 15–16, 17. It is significant that the early Christian preaching was largely a story-telling mission, offering people a new story, the Christian kerygma, to reorient their sense of the meaning both of historical time and of their own personal lifetime.

3

"History with the Politics Left Out"

Gertrude Himmelfarb

You, the philologist, boast of knowing everything about the furniture and clothing of the Romans and of being more intimate with the quarters, tribes and streets of Rome than with those of your own city. Why this pride? You know no more than did the potter, the cook, the cobbler, the summoner, the auctioneer of Rome. —Giambattista Vico, 1702

When the history of menarche is widely recognized as equal in importance to the history of monarchy, we will have arrived. —Peter Stearns, 1976

A few years ago, in a discussion of recent trends in the writing of history, one young historian proudly described his work as being on the "cutting edge of the discipline." He was writing a study of a New England town toward the end of the eighteenth century, an "in-depth" analysis of the life of its inhabitants: their occupations and earnings, living and working conditions, familial and sexual relations, habits, attitudes, and social institutions. He regretted that he had to confine himself to that one town, but some of his colleagues were doing comparable studies of other towns and their collective efforts would constitute a "total history" of that time and place. I asked him whether his study, or their collective studies, had any bearing on what I, admittedly not a specialist in American history, took to be the most momentous event of that time and place, indeed one of the most momentous events in all of modern history: the founding of the United States of America, the first major republic of modern times. He conceded that from his themes and sources—parish registers, tax rolls, census reports, legal records, polling lists, land titles—he could not "get to," as

51

he said, the founding of the United States. But he denied that this was the crucial event I took it to be. What was crucial were the lives and experiences of the mass of the people. That was the subject of his history; it was the "new history," social history. My rebuttal—that even ordinary people (perhaps most of all ordinary people) had been profoundly affected in the most ordinary aspects of their lives by the founding of the republic, by political events, institutions, and ideas that had created a new polity and with it a new society—seemed to him naive and old-fashioned.

There was, in fact, something anachronistic about this exchange. The "new history"—or rather the new "new history," as distinct from the old "new history" sired by James Harvey Robinson and Charles Beard early in the century—is itself no longer new. If it is dated from the founding of the *Annales* more than half a century ago, it is by now well into middle age. Indeed, it is so firmly entrenched in the profession that while young novitiates flaunt their boldness and originality, they are comfortably enjoying the perquisites of a well-endowed establishment. And some of its leading proponents and practitioners (François Furet and Lawrence Stone) find reason to complain of the excesses and defects of what has become the new orthodoxy.[1]

Nor is the new history as monolithic as the label suggests. It encompasses a variety of subjects and methods, some of which are mutually exclusive. Yet there are characteristics that unite it, and even more that differentiate it from the old history. Thus the new history tends to be analytic rather than narrative, thematic rather than chronological. It relies more upon statistical tables, oral interviews, sociological models, and psychoanalytic theories than upon constitutions, treaties, parliamentary debates, political writings, or party manifestos. Where the old history typically concerns itself with regimes and administrations, legislation and politics, diplomacy and foreign policy, wars and revolutions, the new history focuses on classes and ethnic groups, social problems and institutions, cities and communities, work and play, family and sex, birth and death, childhood and old age, crime and insanity. Where the old features kings, presidents, politicians, leaders, political theorists, the new takes as its subject the "anonymous masses." The old is "history from above," "elitist history," as is now said; the new is "history from below," "populist history."

The new history is by now old enough to have provoked a fair amount of criticism. The analytic approach, it has been said, fails to capture the dynamic movement of history; the quantitative method narrows and trivializes history by confining inquiry to subjects and sources capable of being quantified; psychoanalytic interpretations derive more from *a priori* theories than from empirical evidence; sociological models are too abstract to elucidate specific historical situations; the prevalent ideological bias disposes the historian to identify with his subjects and endow them with his own attitudes and values; the populist mode cannot accommodate those notable individuals whose actions and ideas did, after all, help shape history; and the genre as a whole, in its variety of techniques and approaches, suggests a methodological permissiveness that seems to bear out Carl Becker's famous dictum, "Everyman his own historian."[2] All these criticisms and more have been discussed and debated. But there is another issue that has received less attention and that may be more significant. For the new history is preeminently social history, and as such it makes problematic the kind of history that has been the traditional concern of the historian—political history.

What does it mean to write history that cannot "get to" the founding of the American republic (or the development of the English constitution, or the course of the French Revolution)? What does it mean when this mode of history becomes the dominant mode, when it is practiced not on the periphery of the profession but at the very center, not as an ancillary field but as the main field—indeed, as some social historians insist, as "total" history?[3] What does it imply about one's sense of the past and of the present, about an American past and present devoid of the principles of liberty and right, checks and balances, self-government and good government, which were first enunciated by the founding fathers and incorporated in our Constitution?

It was over fifty years ago, in his *English Social History*—one of the first English works to deal exclusively with social history, and under that label—that G. M. Trevelyan offered the famous definition of social history as "the history of a people with the politics left out." He hastened to add that it was difficult to leave out the politics from history, especially in the case of the English people. All he hoped to do was to "redress the balance," to recover that part of history, the history of daily life, which had been sorely neglected.[4] And he proposed to do so knowing that others were engaged (as he himself had been for most of his professional life) in the writing of conventional, political history. He would have thought it a travesty to redress the balance so far as to reverse it entirely, to make social history the dominant form of history, to have it supplant rather than supplement conventional history.

Trevelyan, after all, like his great-uncle Macaulay, was preeminently a Whig historian, cherishing the political institutions and traditions that had made England the liberal, progressive, enlightened

country that he, like Macaulay, thought it to be. His Whig interpretation of English history, like the Whig mode of writing history—the
"Whig fallacy," as it has been called—has fallen into disrepute.[5] When
Herbert Butterfield exposed that fallacy more than half a century ago,
he meant to caution the historian against the insidious habit of reading history backward, of seeking in the past the sources of those ideas
and institutions we value in the present, thus ignoring the complexi-
ties, contingencies, and particularities that make the past peculiarly,
irrevocably past. But he did not mean to counter a too intrusive pre-
sent-mindedness with a too austere past-mindedness, to deny the
continuity of past and present. If it is unhistorical to permit the present
to determine the past, it is surely as unhistorical to prevent the past
from informing the present. And it is surely unhistorical to belittle or
ignore political ideas and institutions that were agitated and agonized
over sometimes to the point of bloodshed—and have since become our
heritage.

Unlike a Trevelyan or his modern counterpart for whom social
history complements and supplements conventional history, the new
social historian regards social history as the only meaningful kind of
history, even as "total" history. In this sense, it is the new historian
who is truly guilty of the Whig fallacy. For it is he, even more than the
Whig, who permits the present to shape the past, who projects into
the past his own idea of what is real and important. It was once only
the Marxist who regarded politics as the "epiphenomenon" of history,
the "superstructure" or "reflection" of the underlying economic and
social "infrastructure." Today that view of politics has so penetrated
our culture that in this respect it might well be said, "We are all Marxists now." Having failed in so much else—in providing an example of
a communist society that is not tyrannical or authoritarian, in fulfilling Marx's predictions of the pauperization of the proletariat and pro-
letarianization of the petty bourgeoisie, of the collapse of capitalism
and triumph of worldwide revolution—Marxism has succeeded in
this: in demeaning and denigrating political events, institutions, activities, and ideas.

In a sense the new social historian goes even further than the
Marxist. Where the Marxist feels it necessary to prove, or at least assert, a causal relationship between economics and politics, the new
historian may simply ignore the political dimension, making the social
reality so comprehensive and ubiquitous that any form of government, any law or political institution, is automatically perceived as a
form of "social control." Instead of the classic Marxist infrastructure—

the mode of production and the social relations deriving from that mode—the new infrastructure is the daily life of ordinary people: the relations of the sexes as well as of classes, the condition of criminals and the insane as well as of workers and peasants.

For the social historian, however, as for the Marxist, the infrastructure is what the historian thinks it is, not what contemporaries may have judged to be the most significant aspects of their lives and times. Like the Marxist, the social historian finds it all too easy to convict his subjects of "false consciousness," of not understanding their own reality. If he thinks at all about the discrepancy between his account of the past and that of contemporaries, he assumes that he is wiser than they, that the advantages of hindsight and the latest analytic techniques— econometrics, prosopography, psychology, or whatever—give him a more objective, more accurate view of the social reality. His is the "true" consciousness, theirs the "false."

The social historian does this in good conscience because the reality he attributes to the past is the reality he recognizes in the present. If he makes so much of work and play, sex and childhood, it is because these are the things that preoccupy him in his own culture, that he believes to be a more important part of the existential reality than the "merely formal" processes of government and politics. If he interprets the religion of the Victorians as a form of psychic compensation, a sublimation of social distress, an expression of alienation, it is because he cannot credit, for himself or his peers, convictions and experiences that are essentially religious rather than social or psychological. If he puts more credence in local history than in national history, in folk traditions than in political traditions, in oral and informal evidence than in written documents, in popular myths about witchcraft than in theories of statecraft, he is unwittingly telling us more about the political and intellectual culture he himself inhabits than about the culture he is ostensibly describing.

In imposing his own sense of reality on the past, the social historian exhibits all the faults of the Whig interpretation without its redeeming features. However fallacious the Whig assumptions about the origins of civil liberty, constitutional government, and representative institutions, there is nothing fallacious, nothing anachronistic, about attributing to the past a deep concern with political, parliamentary, and constitutional affairs. Social history, in devaluing the political realm, devalues history itself. It makes meaningless those aspects of the past which serious and influential contemporaries thought most meaningful. It makes meaningless not only the struggle over political

authority but the very idea of legitimate political authority, of political rule that is not merely a euphemism for "social control," of rights
and liberties that are not (as Jeremy Bentham thought them) "ficti-
tious entities," of principles and practices that do not merely reflect
(as Antonio Gramsci would have it) the "hegemony" of the ruling
class. The social historian who professes to write a comprehensive,
"total" history of England or America while leaving the politics out
(again, I am not speaking of the historian for whom social history is a
supplement to political history) is engaged in a far more radical reinterpretation of history than even he may suspect.

The truly radical effect of the new enterprise is to devalue not only political history but reason itself, reason in history and politics—the idea
that political institutions are, at least in part, the product of a rational,
conscious, deliberate attempt to organize public life so as to promote
the public weal and the good life. In this respect the social historian is
only following the example of his colleague the political scientist, who
sees politics as essentially a game, with politicians jockeying for position, power, and the perquisites of office, playing upon the interests,
passions, and prejudices of their constituents. This political process is
presumed to be rational on the part of politicians only with respect to
the means of attaining and retaining power, not the ends of power;
and rational on the part of electors only with respect to the satisfaction
of their particular interests, not the public interest. (The language of
political science is itself suggestive: "politicians" rather than "states-
men," "constituencies" or "voters" rather than "citizens.")
    On those occasions when the social historian applies himself to
politics, it is this conception of politics that shapes his research.[6] Thus
he quantifies the economic interests and class status of members of
Parliament and their constituents; or psychoanalyzes the motives and
behavior of those who seek power and those who install them in
power; or describes the relationship of rulers and ruled in terms of
"hegemony" and "deference"; or sees in the bureaucracy and "administrative momentum" the explanation of laws and policies; or looks in
smoke-filled rooms and the corridors of power for the secrets of political decisions. He does everything, in short, except utilize the kind of
sources—constitutions, laws, judicial decisions, debates, commen-
taries, treatises—which might suggest a rationality and deliberation
that were not self-serving, that were directed to the ends rather than
the means of power, that embodied some conception of the national
interest and public welfare. The social historian finds precisely these

sources suspect, as if formal documents are less trustworthy than private communications, as if forethought and deliberation imply Machiavellian attempts to conceal the truth, as if the ephemera of the moment (a casual remark or a hasty note) are more revealing than considered reflection and judgment, as if interests are more real than ideas and passion more compelling than reason.

In his inaugural lecture at Cambridge University in 1968, the eminent historian Geoffrey Elton commented on the title of his new chair.

> The chair is the chair of English Constitutional History. Now I chose that title myself, and I don't think I could have chosen worse, could I? I damned myself twice over. English Constitutional History, in the present climate of opinion. *One* adjective might have been forgiven. Perhaps Chinese Constitutional History would have been all right. Perhaps English Social History would have been wonderful. But no, I will pick them both: English Constitutional History.[7]

Elton, whose *Tudor Revolution in Government*, published in 1953, was itself something of a revolution in Tudor history and whom no one can accuse of being a stodgy old historian, went on to explain why he chose that outlandish title.

> The purpose of constitutional history is to study government, the manner in which men, having formed themselves into societies, then arrange for the orderly existence, through time, and in space, of those societies. It is therefore, like every other form of history, a form of social history, a form of the history of society. But it takes particular note of the question of government. It is concerned with what is done to make that society into a properly structured, continuously living body, so that what goes wrong can be put right, so that the political action of which that society is capable can be efficiently and effectively conducted. Machinery, yes. But also thought, the doctrine, the teaching, the conventional notions. What does the society think its government is, how does it treat it, what does it do to amend it? What forms of change are possible, what reforms, and so on and so forth.[8]

Constitutional history, Elton argued, is central to the understanding of the past because it represents the efforts of a people to organize and govern itself as rationally and effectively as it can. But it is also central to the historical enterprise, because it represents the efforts of the historian to discover as best he can the objective truth about the past—to discover it, moreover, in those written documents that are the objective evidence of the past and thus the principal resource of the historian trying to reconstruct the past as objectively as he can. Those documents have to be interpreted and reinterpreted, amplified and supplemented by other kinds of evidence; but they cannot be denied, falsified, or ignored. And as those documents are the bequest of the past to the historian, so they are also the bequest of the past to the present.

> Therefore, from the point of view both of the continuous work of historical research and from the point of view of teaching history, and from the point of view of conveying to the world and to the future a sense of the past and an understanding of the past, the study of government maintains, to my mind its primacy. It can be most fully explicated, it can be most thoroughly described, it can be most clearly understood, it leaves fewer absolutely open questions, it can instruct in the use of reason better than anything else.[9]

"It can instruct in the use of reason"—that is the heart of the matter. No one knows better than Elton the degree to which politics, in the past as in the present, consists in the struggle for money, power, privilege, position. But he also understands that part of the political process consists in the attempt to restrain these self-serving motives, to create out of them, or to impose upon them, a structure of government that will serve society as a whole. The historian has many tasks, but his main task is "the creation of a right mind, and a right reason." "To discover the truth as best he can, to convey that truth as truthfully as he can, in order both to make the truth known and to enable man, by learning and knowing the truth, to distinguish the right from the wrong reason"—this, Elton assures us, is the "simple" task of the historian.[10]

A great deal is at stake in this simple task, nothing less than the restoration of reason to history. This is not Hegel's Reason, a transcendental spirit or idea infusing history, but a more mundane, pragmatic reason. It is the reason reflected in the rational ordering and organization of society by means of laws, constitutions, and political institutions; and the reason implied in the rational activity of the historian seeking to discover and transmit the truth about that society, so that later generations may be instructed about the past that is part of their own present and that they, in turn, will bequeath to future generations. The title of Elton's address, "The Future of the Past," is deliberately ambiguous: it is the future of history, as well as of the past, that is at issue.

When Elton delivered that lecture in the late sixties, he could not have foreseen the present state of the discipline. Or perhaps he did foresee it and was being as canny about the future as he was about the past. In any event, his remarks are today more pertinent than ever. For it is not only political history that the social historian denies or belittles. It is reason itself: the reason embodied in the polity, in the constitutions and laws that permit men to order their affairs in a rational manner—or, on occasion, in an irrational manner, which other men perceive as such and rationally, often heroically, struggle against. It is the reason transmitted to the present by way of constitutions and laws, which themselves specify the means for their amendment and reform. And it is the reason inherent in the historical enterprise itself, in the search for an objective truth that always eludes the individual historian but that always (or so it was once thought) informs and inspires his work.

This rationality is now consciously denied or unconsciously undermined by every form of the new history: by social history positing an infrastructure that supposedly goes deeper than mere political arrangements and is not amenable to reason or will; by anthropological history exploring such nonrational aspects of society as mating customs and eating habits; by psychoanalytic history dwelling upon the irrational, unconscious aspects of individual and collective behavior; by structuralist history emphasizing the long-term ecological "structures" and medium-term economic and social "conjunctures" at the expense of short-term politics and individuals; by *mentalité* history giving greater credence to popular belief than to the "elitist" ideas of philosophers; by oral history relying on verbal reminiscences rather than written documents; by *engagé* history priding itself on advocacy rather than mere analysis; by populist history seeking to recover not only the lives of ordinary people but intimate feelings that tend to be inaccessible and unknowable; by the new history of every description asking questions of the past which the past did not ask of itself, for which the evidence is sparse and unreliable and to which the answers are necessarily speculative, subjective, and dubious.

Again I must say—I cannot repeat it too often—that it is neither the subjects nor the methods of social history that are at issue but their dominance, which itself reflects the assumption, increasingly common in the profession, that these subjects and methods represent a higher form of history, more real and significant, more elemental and essential, than the old history. About this tendency there is no question: one need only look at the programs of the annual meetings of the American Historical Association, or at the newer historical journals, or at applications for grants, or at the titles of recent and prospective dissertations. If the process is not even more advanced, it is because the old generation of historians has not yet died out (although many have become converts to the new history) and because some among the younger generation have resisted the allure of the new even at risk to their careers.

It is tempting to think of this as a passing fad, one of those paroxysms of enthusiasm to which universities are so prone. Unfortunately universities have a way of institutionalizing such fads: it is called the tenure system. By now a generation of new historians—or several generations as these are calculated in academia—are tenured professors busily producing students in their image. For many young (and no longer so young) professors, and even more graduate students, social history is the only kind of history they know, certainly the only kind they respect. Rather than being a fad, it more nearly resembles a revolution in the discipline. One recalls the revolution in education ushered in by the progressive school three quarters of a century ago, and in philosophy by the analytic school half a century ago, both of which still dominate their disciplines (although they are now beginning to come under attack). This is not to say that social history is or will become the only mode of history. Political, constitutional, diplomatic, and intellectual history will survive, but not in the mainstream of historical studies; they will be on the periphery, as social history once was.

In America this revolution has already filtered down from graduate programs to undergraduate schools and even high schools. A recent documentary-essay question on the College Board Advanced Placement examination in American history was "How and why did the lives and status of Northern middle-class women change between 1776 and 1876?"—a question described in the bulletin of the American Historical Association as a "mainline topic."[11] A similar question on the European history examination dealt with methods of child rearing in England from the sixteenth through the eighteenth centuries.[12] Again, the point is not the propriety of such questions but their prominence. These examinations send out signals to high schools throughout the country telling them what kind of history should be taught if their students are to compete successfully for admission to college; in effect, they establish something very like a national curriculum. And given the limited time available for the study of history in our high schools, the new subjects do not merely supplement the old; they inevitably supplant them.

The practitioners of social history will say, And about time too. Why should not women and children supplant kings and politicians? Why should not the way ordinary people lived, loved, worked, and died take precedence over the way they were governed? Such a reordering of priorities would be eminently reasonable and humane—were it nor for the cost of that enterprise, a cost borne precisely by those ordinary people about whom these historians are most solicitous. If ordinary people are being "rescued from oblivion," as has been said, by the new "history from below," they are also being demeaned, deprived of that aspect of their lives which elevated them above the ordinary, which brought them into relationship with something larger than their daily lives, which made them feel part of the polity even when they were not represented in it, and which made them fight so hard for representation precisely because they themselves attached so much importance to their political status.

When Macaulay prepared his readers for the famous third chapter of his *History of England*—the chapter describing "the history of the people as well as the history of the government," the conditions of life and work, the state of manners, morals, and culture—he said that he would "cheerfully bear the reproach of having descended below the dignity of history."[13] But it never occurred to him to go so far below the dignity of history as to dwell on the history of the people to the exclusion of, or even at the expense of, the history of the government. Still less did it occur to him to impugn the dignity of the people by dwelling on the least dignified aspects of their history. A recent book entitled *A Mad People's History of Madness*, consisting in extracts from writings by the mad, was hailed by one reviewer as "a welcome contribution to history from below."[14] It is only a matter of time before other critics will fault it for being insufficiently "from below," for including such eminences as the medieval mystic Margery Kempe instead of the truly lowly, anonymous madmen (and mad women, one must now hasten to add) in Bedlam and Bellevue.

For Macaulay the "dignity of history"—what an archaic ring that now has—was tantamount to the meaning of history. If political events, institutions, and ideas loom so large in his history, it *is* because he saw them as shaping and defining the past, giving form and meaning to the past as contemporaries experienced it, and to the story of the past as the historian tries to reconstruct it. From a different perspective some Marxists have taken exception to a mode of history that deprives the past of the meaning they find in it. Thus Elizabeth Fox-Genovese and Eugene Genovese have charged that social history, by romanticizing the ordinary life of ordinary people, denies the theory of immiseration that is the Marxist impulse for revolution and, by focusing upon daily life at the expense of politics, obfuscates the class struggle that is, finally, a political struggle, a struggle for power. Against this privatization and depoliticization of history, they cite Engels' *Origins of the Family, Private Property, and the State,* whose very title calls attention to the "decisive political terrain of historical process." Like Lenin attacking the "Left deviationists" for objectively playing into the hands of the counterrevolutionaries, the Genoveses rebuke those "ex-Marxists, ex-new Leftists, and ex-Communists" who perpetrate a "bourgeois swindle" by dwelling upon the daily lives of people instead of the class struggle.[15]

One can sympathize with the Marxist who finds that social history, once his ally, has turned against him, not deliberately but unwittingly, by distracting attention from the revolutionary struggle. One can also sympathize with the social historian who, for all his radical sympathies, finds Marxism inadequate or irrelevant in explaining the ordinary lives of ordinary people, to say nothing of the abnormal lives of deviants, criminals, and the insane. And one may forgive the conventional historian if he takes *Schadenfreude* in finding each of them exposing the weaknesses of the other, thus confirming what he has long said: that it is as much a distortion of history to ignore politics as to make the class struggle the determining fact of history.

After several decades of the new history, we can better appreciate what we are in danger of losing if we abandon the old. We will lose not only the unifying theme that has given coherence to history, not only the notable events, individuals, and institutions that have constituted our historical memory and our heritage, not only the narrative that has made history readable and memorable—not only, in short, a meaningful past—but also a conception of man as a rational, political animal. And that loss is even more difficult to sustain, for it involves a radical redefinition of human nature.

An eminent social historian has appealed to Aristotle for the ultimate vindication of his enterprise: "There is no better definition of human nature than Aristotle's, translated as he understood it: 'Man is a social animal'."[16] What Aristotle said, of course, is "Man is by nature a political animal."[17] It is not in the "household" or in the "village," Aristotle said, but only in the "polls" that man is truly human, decisively different from "bees or any other gregarious animals." The latter, after all, also inhabit households and villages (societies, as we would now say); they also eat, play, copulate, rear their young, provide sustenance for themselves (and, often, for their families), have social relations, and develop social structures. What they do not have is a polity, a government of laws and institutions by means of which—and only by means of which, Aristotle believed—man consciously, rationally tries to establish a just regime and pursue the good life. The social historian, rejecting any such "elitist" idea as the good life, seeking only to understand any life, indeed regarding it as a triumph of the historical imagination to explore the lowest depths of life, to probe the unconscious, unreflective, irrational aspects of life, denies that man is the distinctive, indeed unique, animal Aristotle thought him to be—a rational animal, which is to say, a political animal.

POSTSCRIPT

When this essay was first published in *Harper's* in April 1984, it provoked even more controversy than I had expected. The editors solicited comments from some historians, and others volunteered their opinions, which ranged from effusive praise to unprintable vituperation. But it was not until I received the first batch of letters addressed to me privately, some commending my courage in saying publicly what they thought but had not dared say, others denouncing my ignorance, arrogance, and bigotry, that I realized just how sensitive a nerve I had struck.

Because most of my critics seem to think that I am pronouncing an interdiction on all of social history, I have borrowed one of their techniques and performed a simple arithmetic calculation. I find that in the course of the paper I said, no fewer than *seven* times, that my objections are not to social history as such but to its claims of dominance, superiority, even "totality"—not to social history as it may complement or supplement traditional history but to that which would supplant it. But no amount of repetition seems to avail. Indeed, some of those who charged me with seeking to abolish social history expressed just that claim of superiority, that contempt for all other forms of history, which confirms exactly the point I was making.

The most moving letters I received were from graduate students relating their experiences with professors (including some eminent historians) who refused to approve or supervise dissertations on such "archaic" and "elitist" subjects as political and intellectual history. One of the students in my own seminar, when urged to expand his paper into a dissertation, told me that the professor within whose province that subject would fall warned him that a political and intellectual biography of the kind he was interested in was "old hat," that it would never be published and would hinder his career.

I am not persuaded, therefore, by Lawrence Stone, who took me to task for "flogging a dead or dying horse," citing his own prediction in 1979 that "social historians were beginning to turn back to more traditional modes of historical writing." While it is true, as I said in my article, that some historians have become uneasy with the "new orthodoxy," their misgivings are not reflected in the profession as a whole. Stone himself has had occasion more recently to repeat his criticisms, including the charge that the new history has erred in ignoring the political dimension of history.[18] And his own conception of a "new old history" departs so little from the conventional new history that it does not address the issues I have raised.

Other historians who have warned against the new history have done so precisely because they are troubled by its dominance in the profession. In his presidential address to the American Historical Association in 1982, Gordon Craig described the prevailing attitude toward political history in general, and diplomatic history in particular, as varying "between condescension and antipathy." He pointed out that in the preceding half-dozen annual meetings of the association, the subject of international affairs averaged 5 sessions out of 128.[19] An analysis of more recent programs would show an even greater disproportion; and the few sessions ostensibly on political and diplomatic history are more often exercises in social history in the guise of political and diplomatic history. One of Stone's own colleagues, also a social historian, provides evidence to the same effect (although not in a critical spirit). Analyzing the history courses offered at eight American universities between 1948 and 1978, Robert Darnton finds that the number of courses in political history fell in proportion to the total number of courses offered, while the number in social history rose precipitously.[20]

Responding to my point about the filtering down of social history to the high schools, as demonstrated in the documentary-essay questions on Advanced Placement examinations, one historian who helped make up the examinations assured me that the questions reflected no such bias, that they were merely intended to test the ability of students to use source materials and to think logically and critically about historical facts, assumptions, and deductions. Yet a recent account of the "intellectual origins and impact" of the documentary-essay question, published in the American Historical Association newsletter, more than confirms my charge. This evidence is all the more telling because it comes from someone who fully approves both of social history and of the examinations.

> Overall, many AP American History teachers were involved with the "new" history, and some of the most committed members of this group served on the Committee of Examiners in AP American History where they shared their enthusiasm for these reforms with the college members of the committee. The individual most responsible for the development and introduction of the DBQ [documentary-based question] was Reverend Giles Hayes of the Delbarton School in Morristown, New Jersey. Reverend Hayes had a strong awareness and commitment to the "new" history of the 1960s, while being deeply influenced by the same era's inquiry movement.

This article also supports my claim that the examinations "send out signals" to high schools about the kind of history that should be taught and thus "establish something very like a national curriculum."

> The committee was aware that the DBQ advocated a change from past procedures and norms, and they pondered the implications of such an approach. Some members wondered if the test should be an agent of curriculum change or continue as a measurement of the content and skills of existing college-level American history courses. As noted, DBQ supporters such as Reverend Hayes believed the AP program should be on the "cutting edge" of curricular reform, and this view eventually prevailed as the committee endorsed the DBQ.[21]

It is not surprising to find the same filtering-down process occurring in France, the home of the new history, but it is curious to observe the dismay of the Socialist government when confronted with the practical effects of a social history that is otherwise so congenial to them. In August 1983 a cabinet meeting discussed a recent survey showing that only a third of the children entering secondary schools could give the date of the French Revolution "The deficiency of teaching history," François Mitterand declared, "has become a national danger."[22] Since then there has been much talk, among the parties of the Left as well as of the Right, about the need to restore some sense of political and narrative history, with an emphasis on notable individuals and within a framework of nationality. Even a few Annalistes are beginning to have second thoughts. Marc Ferro, codirector of the *Annales* and director of studies in the social sciences at the École Pratique des Hautes Etudes, described the widespread practice in France of teaching history by having schoolchildren compile "single-street histories" of their own neighborhoods, thus showing them how to use documents and to question supposed facts rather than merely memorize dates and events. The result, he concluded, is that sometimes "children no longer know any history."[23]

That it is not only children who "no longer know any history" because they do not know any political history is occasionally conceded by other social historians. The American historian I quoted, who confessed that he could not "get to" the founding of the United States, has his confreres abroad. The eminent Annaliste François Furet has commented on the neglect of "one of the most classic areas of historiography," the French Revolution—classic because it inevitably calls for narrative treatment and also because it establishes "politics as the fountainhead and instrument of freedom." Yet this subject was "virtually absent," he found, from both the prewar and postwar sets of the *Annales*, "as if this locus classicus of national history were precisely the special preserve of the 'other' history."[24] Eric Hobsbawm too has pointed to "a possible weakness of the *Annales* approach, namely its difficulty in coping with what you call the great formative political events in a country's history: the Risorgimento in Italy, or indeed the French Revolution in France."[25]

Some critics took me to task for criticizing the practice of "asking questions of the past which the past did not ask of itself." Historians they argue, habitually ask such questions. So they do and so they should. But my stricture, I made it clear, has to do with asking those questions "for which the evidence is sparse and unreliable and to which the answers are necessarily speculative, subjective, and dubious." I would obviously not object to questions for which the evidence is available and reliable—and, perhaps more important, which do not presuppose or predetermine the answers, which do not impose upon contemporaries the assumptions, values, and concerns of the historian. A typical example has just come to hand. A high-school history teacher, who chairs the Test Development Committee of the College Board's Advanced Placement European History section, describes an exercise to develop students' comprehension of material that might otherwise seem "opaque."

> One possible exercise assembles students representing nineteenth-century German Liberals, Conservatives, Catholics, Socialists, and Feminists with Chancellor Bismarck. Representatives from each discussion group "confront" Bismarck, expressing their approval or disapproval of his policies and confessing whether they have "sold out" to him.[26]

One does not know which is the greater historical distortion: the idea that Feminists represent a nineteenth-century German group on the order of Liberals, Conservatives, Catholics, and Socialists, or the image of these groups "confronting" Bismarck and confessing whether they have "sold out" to him.

Since Carl Degler is one of the critics who made this point, it may be fitting to cite an article he wrote many years ago, which impressed me then and continues to persuade me. The historian, he wrote, is guided less by "covering laws" that are presumed to be true in all times and places than by "participant-sources"—that is, contemporary evidence. Thus the historian might think it plausible that the American Revolution was caused by high taxes or the navigation laws, but if he finds no evidence for that in the contemporary literature he has to abandon the thesis; conversely, if he finds other reasons given at the time he has to take them seriously, however strange they may seem to him. "The careful historian," Degler concluded, "tries to think as his subjects did, and within their system of values."[27]

Another critic asks, "Have not the vast majority of people in the past thought that where they lived and how they made a living, who they married, and what happened to their children rather more 'basic and significant' than who won the last election?" He rebukes me for thinking that "yet another study of the intricacies of John C. Calhoun's political thought is far more valuable than an analysis of the family life of the four million slaves of the antebellum South." I would agree that an analysis of the family life of the four million slaves would be valuable (if it were more reliable and less speculative and tendentious than are many such studies), but not if it means being so contemptuous of "yet another study" of Calhoun—whose ideas and influence were, as it happens, of considerable significance for the lives of those four million slaves. Nor do I think it a sign of respect for "the vast majority of people" to suppose that they are less interested in "who won the last election" (or who won the last war?) than, perhaps, a Harvard professor who manages to be interested in national politics without neglecting his home, career, and family. This critic, it seems to me, is exhibiting a truly elitist bias—and a truly un-historical one, considering the fact that so many "ordinary" people have been passionately concerned with political, ideological, and religious causes, often to the extent of sacrificing livelihood and even life.

I am also criticized for failing to appreciate the irrationality in history. "Nietzsche, Freud, and Kafka, and, more recently, Richard Hofstadter," I am reminded, "had made clear to everyone that human beings and the politics they practice are hardly guided only by reason." But I never suggested they are guided "only" by reason. Nor did Aristotle (without benefit of Nietzsche, Freud, Kafka, or Hofstadter). Aristotle's "political animal" had all the passions, impulses, interests, feelings, desires—and, yes, irrationality—known to modern man; but he was also presumed to be endowed with a "reason" that made him a human being rather than merely an animal. Nor did Aristotle (and nor did I) claim that politics is entirely a rational activity—only that it is that in part, and that that part is a vital and essential ingredient of political life.

There is even more involved in the idea of rationality than I ventured to suggest in my essay. For rationality is the precondition of freedom, of the free exercise of individual will. To the extent to which the political realm is more conducive to rational choice, compared with the social realm which is governed by material and economic concerns, it is in politics that the potentiality for freedom lies. This explains why social history tends to be more deterministic than political history, and why political history finds a natural ally in intellectual history. Herbert Butterfield, for all his criticism of Whig history, understood this well. "Over and above the structure of politics," he wrote in his critique of Lewis Namier, "we must have a political history that is set out in narrative form—an account of adult human beings, taking a hand in their fates and fortunes, pulling at the story in the direction they want to carry it, and making decisions of their own."[28] But perhaps my critics will be better disposed to the argument when it is made by one of their own. In urging his colleagues to reconsider the Annaliste aversion to political history, François Furet points to the intimate connection between political history and the idea of freedom:

> Thus, too, political history is primarily a narrative of human freedom as seen through change and progress. Although political history does describe the framework, that is, the constraints within which men act, its major function is to describe the thoughts, choices, and actions of men— primarily of great men. Politics is the quintessential realm

of chance, and so of freedom. It gives history the structure of a novel, except that its plot must be composed of authentic facts verified according to the rules of evidence; and this history is indeed the true novel of nations.[29]

NOTES

1. François Furet, "Introduction," In *the Workshop of History*, trans. Jonathan Mandelbaum (Chicago, 1984 [originally published 1981]); Lawrence Stone, "The Revival of Narrative: Reflections on a New Old History" (1979), reprinted in idem, *The Past and the Present* (London, 1981).

2. Carl L. Becker, *Everyman His Own Historian: Essays on History and Politics* (Chicago, 1966 [1st ed., New York, 1935]).

3. Emmanuel Le Roy Ladurie, *The Peasants of Languedoc*, trans. John Day (Urbana, 1974 [1st ed., 1966]), p. 8; Peter Steams, "Coming of Age," *Journal of Social History*, Winter 1976, p. 246; idem, "The New Social History: An Overview," in *Ordinary People and Everyday Life: Perspectives on the New Social History*, ed. James B. Gardner and George Rollie Adams (Nashville, 1983), p. 7; Furet, "Introduction," p. 56; Traian Stoianovich, *French Historical Method: The Annales Paradigm* (Ithaca, 1976), pp. 102ff.; Herve Coutau-Begarie, *Le phénomène "Nouvelle Histoire": stratégie et idéologie des nouveaux historiens* (Paris, 1983), pp. 92ff. One Annaliste, Pierre Vilar, concludes his discussion of Marxist history by observing that it too, like all "true history," must become "new history" and thus "total history." "Any 'new' history which has no ambition to be total in its scope is a history that is obsolete before it even begins." Vilar, "Constructing Marxist History," in *Constructing the Past: Essays in Historical Methodology*, ed. Jacques Le Goff and Pierre Nora (Cambridge, 1985), p. 80.

4. G. M. Trevelyan, *English Social History* (New York, 1941), p. vii.

5. Herbert Butterfield, *The Whig Interpretation of History* (London, 1931).

6. See, for example, Jacques Le Goff, "Is Politics Still the Backbone of History?" *Daedalus*, Winter 1971; Allan G. Bogue, "The New Political History in the 1970s," in *The Past Before Us: Contemporary Historical Writing in the United States*, ed. Michael Kammen (Ithaca, 1980); Samuel P. Hays, "Politics and Social History: Toward a New Synthesis," in Gardner and Adams, *Ordinary People and Everyday Life*; J. Morgan Kousser, "Restoring Politics to Political History," *Journal of Interdisciplinary History*, Spring 1982, and comments on this article by Paul F. Bourke and Donald A. DeBats in the same journal, Winter 1985; Philip R. Vandermeer, "The New Political History: Progress and Prospects," in *International Handbook of Historical Studies: Contemporary Research and Theory*, ed. Georg S. Iggers and Harold T. Parker (Westport, 1979); Alan Brinkley, "Writing the History of Contemporary America: Dilemmas and Challenges," *Daedalus*, Summer 1984; "Political History in the 1980s," in *The*

New History: The 1980s and Beyond, ed. Theodore K. Rabb and Robert I. Rotberg (Princeton, 1982).

One Annaliste has gone so far as to call for a "return to politics." But he then goes on to define the new political history as incorporating political economics, political geography, political science, political sociology, and political ethnography. See Jacques Julliard, "La politique," in Le Goffand Nora, *Faire de l'histoire* (Paris, 1974), II, 227–50. Even David Potter's tribute to Roy Nichols for the "rehabilitation of political history" has something of this character, the rehabilitation involving the denigration of traditional or conventional history, as narrow, superficial, desiccated—"a miscellany of chronology punctuated with anecdote." See "Roy F. Nichols and the Rehabilitation of American Political History" (1971), in *History and American Society: Essays of David M. Potter,* ed. Don E. Fehrenbacher (New York, 1973), pp. 194, 206–7.

7. G. R. Elton, *The Future of the Past* (Cambridge, 1968), p. 4.

8. Ibid., pp. 24–25.

9. Ibid., p. 27.

10. Ibid., p. 22.

11. College Board Examination, 1981; *Perspectives*, January 1982, p. 12.

12. In 1985 the documentary question on the European examination dealt with juvenile offenders in Britain in the nineteenth century.

13. T. R. Macaulay, *Works*, ed. Lady Trevelyan (London, 1875), I, 3. On the "dignity of history," see also Lord Bolingbroke, *Letters on the Study and Use of History* (New York, 1970 [1st ed., 1738]), I, 159 (letter 5).

14. Review by Roy Porter, in *New Society*, July 15, 1982, p. 110.

15. Elizabeth Fox-Genovese and Eugene D. Genovese, "The Political Crisis of Social History: A Marxian Perspective," *Journal of Social History*, Winter 1976, pp. 213–15. For a similar criticism of social history from a Socialist perspective see Tony Judt, "A Clown in Regal Purple: Social History and the Historians," *History Workshop: A Journal of Socialist Historians*, Spring 1979.

16. H. J. Perkin, "Social History," in *Approaches to History*, ed. H. P. R. Finberg (London, 1962), p. 81.

17. Aristotle, *Politics*, bk. I, chap. 2. The historian who mistranslated Aristotle is in good company. Hannah Arendt, who in her own work tried to restore a sense of the importance of political life, traced the perversion of Aristotle's dictum to Seneca and Thomas Aquinas, and hence to modernity. See her *Human Condition* (Chicago, 1958), p. 23.

18. Lawrence Stone, luncheon talk, American Historical Association con-

vention, December 1982; idem, *Newsletter*, American Council of Learned Societies, Winter-Spring 1985, pp. 18–19.

19. Gordon A. Craig, "The Historian and the Study of International Relations," *American Historical Review*, February 1983, p. 2.

20. Robert Darnton, "Intellectual and Cultural History," in Kammen, *The Past Before Us*, pp. 350–51.

21. Michael S. Henry, "The Intellectual Origins and Impact of the Document-Based Question," *Perspectives*, February 1986, pp. 15–16.

22. *The Economist*, September 24, 1983.

23. Marc Ferro, *The Use and Abuse of History; or, How the Past Is Taught* (London, 1984), pp. 239–40.

24. Furet, "Introduction," p. 11.

25. Eric Hobsbawm, report of conference on "The Impact of the *Annales* School on the Social Sciences," *Review*, Winter-Spring 1978, p. 65.

26. Mildred Alpern, "AP European History for Able Sophomores," *Perspectives*, December 1985, p. 16.

27. Carl Degler, in *Philosophy and History*, ed. Sidney Hook (New York, 1963), pp. 205–11.

28. Herbert Butterfield, *George III and the Historians* (London, 1957), p. 206.

29. Furet, "Introduction," p. 9.

4

Storytelling in Criminal Trials:
a Model of Social Judgment

W. Lance Bennett

The criminal trial is a setting in which ordinary people process vast amounts of information and make sophisticated judgments in the face of competing rhetorical appeals. The actors in a trial must communicate effectively with one another even though many of the rules governing speech and action in the situation are foreign to the central participants—the witnesses and the jurors. Moreover, the judgments jurors make about the information presented in trials must conform to complex legal and social standards of justice. In spite of these informational, situational, and social demands on communication and judgment, jurors produce verdicts with the aid of little formal training or guidance. This suggests that participants must rely on some basic everyday communicational form to cut through the formal symbolism and procedures of trials. Evidence suggests that storytelling is the everyday communicational practice that is used to organize information, to transmit understandings among participants, and to guide the judgments of jurors.

Storytelling is probably the most common form of discourse used to provide accounts of social behavior and human events. Stories engage widely shared cognitive routines that virtually any member of society can use to make elegant judgments about a described behavior or situation. The use of stories allows people to communicate effectively even when they must process vast amounts of information in a setting that provides few cues to guide or simplify the task. The study of storytelling as the basis of communication in criminal trials may provide answers to a number of important questions about justice: How are average persons equipped to make the judgments required of jurors in trials? How is effective communication possible within the complex world of the courtroom? To what extent are jurors' judgments related to the "facts" of the alleged crime? How do the communication and judgment practices in the courtroom affect the nature and limits of the rhetorical reconstruction of these facts? What is the connection between the judgment practices employed by jurors and the social and legal standards of justice to which the jurors' interpretation of a case must conform? The development of a model of storytelling and judgment in a particular setting, the courtroom, also provides a basis for exploring more general patterns in the relations among communicational forms, cognitive processes, social structures, and the nature of social activities in other settings.

STORYTELLING IN COMMUNICATIONAL, COGNITIVE, AND SOCIAL PERSPECTIVE

Analyzing a communicational practice in a social setting requires exploration of the relations among the form of communication, the particular cognitive operations that it may engage, and the distinctive features of the social activity that may depend on these cognitive routines. Different social activities probably require different sorts of thinking and reasoning. Particular forms of communication may facilitate particular styles of thought. This implies that certain approaches to the study of communication may yield general models of communication, thought, and social action. It is not surprising that the structure of everyday communication can reveal a great deal about the nature of thought and the practical meanings of social action. However, few efforts have been made to explore these relationships in systematic fashion.[1]

Most of our knowledge in this area stems from the study of communication-cognition linkages. For example, linguists have demonstrated clear connections between ordinary language utterances and the deep cognitive structures that account for their production and interpretation. Although less work has been done on other forms of communication, growing evidence suggests that such forms of everyday discourse as stories, dialogues, and interrogations may yield important insights into difficult cognitive problems of information processing and interpretation. Research in cognitive psychology, information processing, and artificial intelligence is coming to terms with the fact that mundane interpretation is an extraordinarily elegant process. We routinely make sound judgments based on imperfect information. We are able to call upon broad background knowledge in these judgments. We can retrieve this information quickly, and with due consideration to the rapidly shifting definitions of ongoing situations. Two important breakthroughs in cognitive theory suggest that we should look to everyday communicational forms as sources of cognitive models. First, a growing consensus holds that almost all interpretation depends on the use of a small set of information organizing crevices that, variously, have been called "supersets,"[2] "membership categorization devices,"[3] "contexts" and "intercontextual links,"[4] "frames,"[5] and "themes."[6] Second, almost any interpretation requires making rapid connections among (1) these organizing devices; (2) the information at hand; (3) the background information required to fill out the information at hand; and (4) the definition of the social context in which the interpretation will be used. Together, these two factors imply that the ways in which we transmit information must facilitate these connections and mirror the structure of cognition.

The assumption behind this growing conclusion that there is a parallel between cognitive structure and everyday communicational forms is a simple one. If information organizing categories were not connected directly to common-sense knowledge and to ongoing situations, our interpretations would be both slow and quite unreal. Inferences might follow from abstract organizing rules, but the practical results would seldom make sense in social context. This was a typical problem with early cognitive models that failed to take into account the interface between thought and the social and communicational stimuli that must be incorporated in practical thinking. For example, the Abelson and Reich model of ideological reasoning considered only the relationship between the central themes of a belief system and the raw information that it processed (i.e., this model ignored such things as the communicational format, the social context, background information, and common sense).[7] Their model was capable of making some sensible judgments, but it also generated many amusing, and almost schizophrenic, patterns of reasoning. For example, the computer that was programmed with the model reasoned that since radical students had thrown eggs at Richard Nixon in Latin America, Fidel Castro might be expected to throw eggs at Taiwan. In a later attempt to accommodate the commonsense links between information and cognition, Abelson concluded:

The system anticipated continual hostile provocation by Communist actors against vulnerable Free World targets, since that was a key presumption in its master belief. It was, however, innocent of the logistics of egg throwing and of the relative vulnerability of persons versus islands as egg targets (as well as many other low-level facts), so that it often emitted output statements foolishly out of touch with physical reality. Being fanatically ideological is quite different from being schizophrenically disoriented. A convincing simulation of the cognitive system of an ideologue must combine a solid concrete knowledge base with its highly subjective interpretations of the deeper motives and meanings lying behind simple events.[8]

We are still a long way from identifying all the forms of everyday discourse that connect the mind to the social world. However, the story form is clearly one of the most pervasive and powerful agencies of social and psychological organization. Stories are among our most basic units of communication; they permit us to translate our impressions of a distant event into a form that will allow a listener in an immediate situation to grasp its significance. The story form also aids the listener in drawing certain conclusions about the interpretation: Is it plausible? Is it more plausible than some other interpretation? Is it humorous? Is it ironic? Does it fit with some prominent theme in my relationship with the storyteller or in our immediate interaction? Have I had an experience like this that I could recount to indicate my comprehension of, or agreement with, the point of the story? In short, stories are powerful means of transmitting precise interpretations of distant and complex events to people who either did not witness those events or who did not grasp them from the storyteller's perspective.

The inferential power of stories is evidenced by the comparatively small number of facts needed to transmit an adequate impression in story form of most events or experiences. Other measures of the capacity of stories to engage powerful cognitive processes are the routine practices of listeners in completing fragmentary accounts and repairing poorly told stories. Still another indicator of the powerful cognitive processes engaged by stories is the ease with which listeners can "cross reference" a story against both the ongoing themes in an interaction and analogous experiences or information the listener may have stored in forms suitable for storytelling.

In light of these features, it should be no surprise that stories are a central factor in the communication and interaction processes of many familiar situations. For example, the stories that politicians tell make particular versions of the behind-the-scenes political world available to the public.[9] In another setting, stories constitute the basis for structuring and evaluating welfare cases.[10] They also can provide a common basis for everyday legal and administrative reasoning between public agents and their clients.[11] In the discussion that follows, I will develop a model of stories as interpretive devices. Illustration for the model is provided by examples that show how stories organize the kinds of judgments that jurors make in criminal trials. Before presenting this model, I will describe the general role of stories in social justice processes.

STORIES AND SOCIAL JUSTICE

Disputes that mobilize some sort of adjudication procedure are centered around different claims about the significance of some past interaction between the parties involved. These claims are presented to an adjudicator who was not party to the dispute. This person (judge) or group (jury) must evaluate the claims and, based on this evaluation, suggest or impose some remedy for the grievance. The natural response of disputants under these circumstances is to tell their respective stories to the adjudicator. It is worth noting that the behavior in question in such incidents could be described or recounted in forms other than stories. However, the story is the only communicational form that places a problematic action in an informational context that constrains a unique and rhetorically defensible interpretation for it. Even when the procedure for settling a dispute does not allow free-form storytelling from the disputants, stories will still be used in some fashion to organize the understandings among the participants. For example, the rules of evidence and testimony in criminal trials place some obvious limits on story-telling behavior. Despite this, important story-telling episodes emerge during direct examination and during the opening and closing remarks of the lawyers. An especially interesting point is that even when evidence is introduced in the often disjointed "question-answer" format in a trial, the key elements generally will be abstracted by jurors and arranged in story form during deliberation.[12]

This basic story-telling format for adjudication applies whether the dispute involves one child accusing another of "not playing fair" in a game, or whether it involves an adult labeling the actions of an assailant as "attempted murder." From earliest childhood on, we (at least most of us) are encouraged to explain our side of things in a story form that organizes relevant information in the service of a defensible definition for the disputed action. These story-telling skills progress as our everyday experiences with disputes and various forms of adjudication increase. As a result of this socialization process, we learn, among other things, to play all the key roles in adjudication: plaintiff, defendant, and adjudicator. It is the common story-telling element to these roles that allows ordinary people to present and hear evidence in formal trials with remarkable skill. Without this common communications bond most of the lay participants in a trial would become lost in the maze of arcane rules and practices that comprise the liturgy of the court. Indeed, it is highly improbable that the lay participants in a trial (or in almost any sort of adjudication) communicate in terms of cues or routines that they learn after they enter the situation.[13] They must organize their implicit communications in keeping with the obligatory rituals and identifying symbolism of the setting. The forthcoming model describes the basic elements in this communication-cognition process.[14] The model is illustrated with a variety of criminal cases.

A MODEL OF JUDGMENT AND AN APPLICATION TO TRIAL JUSTICE

Stories organize information in ways that help the listener to perform three interpretive operations. First, the interpreter must be able to locate the central action, the key behavior around which the point of the story will be drawn. Second, the interpreter must construct inferences about the relationships among the surrounding elements in the story that impinge on the central action. The connections among this cast of supporting symbols literally create the interpretive context for the action or behavior at the center of the story. Finally, the network of symbolic connections drawn around the central action in a story must be tested for internal consistency and descriptive adequacy or completeness. This simply means that the interpreter must determine whether the various inferences that make up a general interpretation for a story are both mutually compatible (in light of what is known about similar episodes in the real world) and sufficiently specified to yield an unequivocal interpretation. These three cognitive operations comprise the model of judgment that will be developed in this section. Before I describe how stories are geared structurally to these operations, it may be useful to work through a hypothetical example of how these operations enter into the judgments of persons serving as jurors:

Suppose that we have been selected to serve as jurors for a murder trial. The state opens its case by announcing that a woman has been killed. The police found her body in bed. They had been called by her husband, who, according to his story, became alarmed when his efforts to awaken his sleeping wife had failed that morning. The coroner's autopsy determined that the cause of death was poisoning. The poison had been administered the evening before. There was no evidence of any third party in the home that evening, nor was there any known motive that would account for the involvement of an outside party in the incident. There was, however, a motive for the husband. He had been named as the beneficiary in a large insurance policy taken out shortly before the woman's death. The prosecutor concludes his statement by telling us that the state will prove that the defendant killed his wife in order to receive the insurance money. Even though the central action in the incident has not yet been specified, we know already how to recognize it. We know that the central action will be some behavior that could have caused the death (e.g., the wife might have taken an overdose of sleeping pills or the husband might have poisoned her bedtime cocoa). It is this behavior that must be interpreted in order to determine whether the death was suicide, accident, or homicide. Somehow from the sketchy story presented in the opening remarks of the prosecutor we have developed criteria for separating the central action out of all the other actions described in the forthcoming testimony. This is the first cognitive operation facilitated by stories.

The state then produces three witnesses who offer accounts that fit into the general story told by the prosecutor. First, the detective assigned to the case testifies that he had been called to the scene by police officers already present at the home. He questioned a man who identified himself as the husband of the deceased. The man said he had been the only person with the woman during the past twenty-four hours. That man is in the courtroom today. He is the defendant. The detective goes on to say that when he asked the man about the existence of any insurance policies on the deceased, he became visibly nervous. The defense lawyer objects to this speculation about the accused's nervousness, and the judge orders it stricken from the record. The next prosecution witness is the coroner. He testifies that he performed an autopsy and determined the cause of death to be a massive dose of strychnine. Finally, an insurance agent takes the stand and describes an incident that occurred a week prior to the death. The defendant came to the agent's office and made arrangements to purchase a large policy on his wife. The woman did not accompany her husband to the office. The man took the policy with him and returned several days later with her signature. The policy named the defendant as beneficiary.

At this point the state rests its case. Suppose that the defense does not put on a case, but simply argues that the state has failed to prove that the defendant had anything to do with the woman's death. The defense lawyer tells us that the prosecution's case is based on the flimsiest of circumstantial evidence. He also tells us that the prosecutor has not even shown how the woman was killed, let alone whether the defendant was involved in any way. What would we do?

Even though the central action has not been defined formally, we probably have already made some connections among isolated elements that surround the as-yet unspecified central action in the prosecutor's story. For example, from all possible associations that could be made to establish relationships between the two actors in the story, we have probably selected "marriage" and "insurance." We connect the actors in the story with the categories "husband-wife" and "beneficiary-insured." The connection "husband-wife" gives us access to general empirical knowledge about that sort of relationship. We may use that knowledge to establish other connections. For example, we may see significance between the actors as husband and wife and the fact that they were at home alone on the evening in question. We might even infer from these connections that the sort of intimacy characterized by this relationship could have provided many opportunities for such a crime to be committed while they were alone in each other's presence. The connection between "insured" and "beneficiary" might take us along another generalized path to the act in question. For example, we know that beneficiaries collect money from policies upon the death of the insured. The policy in this case was large. The beneficiary would stand to gain great wealth from the woman's death. The beneficiary was the husband. Perhaps he had a motive. The connections shown in Figure 4.1 may now exist in our minds. These inferences are the result of the second general cognitive operation facilitated by story structure.

The inferences established thus far among the elements surrounding the central action in the story do have a certain appeal. However, the defense response to this case is credible also. None of the actions contained in the prosecution story really qualifies as a good central action. We simply do not have a description of an action committed by the husband that could be called "murderous" in the context of the inferences already established; there are still too many gaps in the story to establish a tight causal sequence leading necessarily to a murderous act. How do we know that the inferences drawn thus far, although internally consistent, are nevertheless incomplete from the standpoint of establishing a clear interpretation for the incident? We can know these

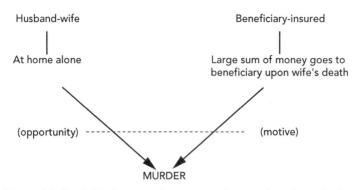

Figure 4.1. Partial inferences about a murder case based on the first two cognitive operations of the story-telling model.

things only if the story structure parallels some general cognitive model of the systematic relations among analogous elements in real world situations. This third cognitive operation allows us to know whether the inferences drawn from a story are consistent with familiar other situations. It also helps us determine if the inferences are complete or systematic enough to yield a clear interpretation for the story. Finally, if the story is judged incomplete, this cognitive operation provides us with knowledge about what is missing.

In this case, it is obvious what is missing. Either we need information about the action that directly induced the poison into the victim's body, or we need to establish a sequence of actions that would leave no doubt about the description of that action. Imagine that the prosecution had called another witness. This person, a neighbor of the defendant, testifies that he was watching television on the night of the death. He went to the kitchen during a commercial and noticed a light in the defendant's garage as he passed a window. Thinking that something might be amiss, he went to a window that provided a better view of the garage. He saw the defendant emerge from the garage carrying a box of rodent poison. The defendant then went into the house. The prosecutor now recalls the detective to the stand. The detective testifies that the police crime lab analyzed a sample of ashes from the fireplace of the home and found abnormal amounts of strychnine along with other elements commonly found in rodent poison. The coroner then resumes the stand to testify that the woman ingested some hot chocolate shortly before retiring and that such a drink would disguise the flavor of the poison.

These additional elements of the story would allow—perhaps even compel—most of us to infer that the husband poisoned the wife's bedtime drink and then destroyed the evidence in the fireplace. These connections between the husband and the probable means of death tighten our inference that the death was probably not attributable to accident, suicide, or some outside party. They also strengthen the conclusion that the husband was responsible for the act that killed his wife, and the circumstances indicate that he probably intended to kill her. We now have a more adequate explanation for the incident—an explanation that offers a clear interpretation for the central action in question in the trial. This explanation was formed by working back and forth between isolated connections among story symbols and the way these symbols fit into our generalized story model of social life.

Although the interpretation diagrammed in Figure 4.2 may not satisfy everyone beyond a reasonable doubt, it will come much closer to doing so than the first version of the story. The point that emerges from this exercise is that we know implicitly how to connect relevant symbols in a story and how to systematize and interpret their bearing on the action that lies at the center of the story. Through this procedure we distinguish the central action in the story from the peripheral

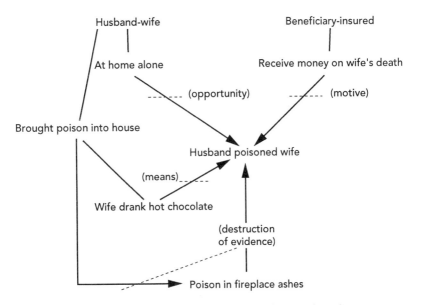

Figure 4.2. Competed inferences about a murder case based on storytelling model.

actions, and we either assign a clear interpretation to it or we determine that the information presented in the story is insufficient to warrant a confident judgment. We now can examine the cognitive operations that underlie these judgments about stories.

IDENTIFYING THE CENTRAL ACTION

The first operation is the isolation of the central action in the story. The most obvious characteristic of stories is that they build interpretations around social behaviors. They tell us, in effect, "Here is a potentially problematic action that becomes quite sensible within this set of circumstances." We know that acts and situations are not static; they develop together and shape one another. Stories "develop" the relations among acts, actors, and situation from some point at which the action and the situation might have had multiple definitional possibilities to a point at which a dominant central action clearly establishes a significance for the situation and vice versa. This is what is often called the "point" of the story.

The listener's recognition of a central action and its development depends on various "bookkeeping" devices in stories. These regularities in story form organize information and enable a listener to make initial judgments about the story. For example, verb tense and pronoun usages in conjunction with common-sense understandings about action sequences provide for the serial development of action in stories. These usage rules include the consistency conventions pertaining to verb, noun, and pronoun references that help keep track of actors, actions, and relationships among actors. For example, we are constrained to introduce nouns in conjunction with pronoun references, and we must flag those references that could index more than one noun. Pronoun-verb usages help to clarify the point of view from which the action is being described. In short, these conventions help establish what happened, to whom, and when. The linear development of action simplifies information organization and aids the identification of a central action and critical junctures in its development.[15] Newmark and Bloomfield illustrate how sequencing alone can distinguish (1) a story from (2) a nonsensical collection of utterances:

(1) Yesterday I was in this bar. The funniest thing happened. A lady walked in and asked for the manager in a loud voice. Well, he came over and asked what the trouble was. All she said was, "You Satan," and then she hit him over the head with her wet umbrella.

(2) All she said was, "You Satan," and then she hit him over the head with her wet umbrella. Well, he came over and asked what the trouble was. A lady walked in and asked for the manager in a loud voice. The funniest thing happened. Yesterday I was in this bar.[16]

The disruption of underlying usage conventions, and not the mere reversal of the time frame, makes the second paragraph incoherent. As long as the usage conventions are observed, the underlying sequential organization in a story will prevail even if it is told with the aid of various plot devices such as "flashback," "flashforward," and multiple points of view. The rules that govern the telling and interpretation of stories permit the basic story to be recovered even from the thickest maze of plot devices.[17]

Another example of a "bookkeeping" device in stories is the obligatory use of causal events or time lapses to move the action through time and through stages of significance. For example, disjointed time references in the absence of causal explanations make this an inadequate story: "Last week George went to Buffalo where he met, for the first time, Sally, his wife of ten years." However, the insertion of a causal qualifier can repair the time warp and create an adequate story: "George and Sally had been pen pals for years. Although their occupations kept them apart, they became married in an unusual ceremony by correspondence. Last week, George went to Buffalo where he met, for the first time, Sally, his wife of ten years."

These and other story devices help the listener keep track of sequencing, climax, point of view, the emergence of new situational and behavioral factors, and possible changes in the relations between action and setting. These constraints on information in stories aid listeners in making their first essential judgment in the process of interpretation. By establishing consistent patterns of relationship between actions and situations, listeners can make calculated guesses about which actions in a story should be interpreted with reference to which specified conventions. These points are illustrated by Propp in his analysis of folktales. He argues that grammar-like conventions in storytelling alert the listener to connections between actions and scenic elements. The overall pattern of connections is organized around a central action that governs the point of the story. However, Propp did not specify how these structural connections are interpreted or systematized.[18] These operations encompass the next two components of my model.

INTERPRETING THE CENTRAL ACTION

After the listener has identified a candidate for a central action in a story, the relations between the action and the surrounding situational elements must be established. The point of the story emerges from these relations. This phase of the interpretation process relies on the second general structural characteristic of stories. As mentioned above, the grammatical, temporal, and causal regularities in story form set up obvious connections among pairs or clusters of symbols in a story. These structural connections guide the process of substantive interpretation. For example, in the simple story, "The baby cried. The mommy picked it up," we know that the significance of the action depends on the relationships among the actors who are connected by the verbs and pronoun usages. A different sort of "picking-up" may occur if the "mommy" is the baby's mother, or someone else's mother, or a kidnapper disguised as a mother. The point is that the story structure sets up connections among various symbol groups in a story. Symbols that are connected in this way become the subjects of a search for some mutual relevance or relationship that is consistent with the probable central action of the story. These isolated interpretations, in turn, further establish the precise relationship between the key action and its surroundings. In other words, there is a sort of "symbolic triangulation" at work in which certain symbols are placed in structural proximity, their mutual relationship is established in light of the central action, and these relationships, in turn, clarify the general significance of the central action.

This system of connections and constraints in stories guides the listener's use of the vast store of background knowledge described by Abelson, and mentioned earlier, as necessary for sensible interpretation. The inferences that fill in the framework of connections among story symbols are based on five generic types of social understanding: empirical knowledge, language categorization, logical operations, norms, and aesthetic criteria. As the following overview indicates, each of these generic grounds for social knowledge can serve as a powerful means of drawing inferences around a story's central action.

Empirical Connections

In many cases an empirical understanding may provide the key connection in an interpretation. In the hypothetical poisoning case, we determined beyond a reasonable doubt that the victim was poisoned and that the cause of death was rodent poison mixed with hot chocolate. In other words, we know that the act was murder and we know how it was done. A chain of circumstances led us to believe that the husband committed the action. However, imagine that the next door neighbor had testified that his vantage point on the night of the crime allowed him to see more than just the garage door; he also saw into the house. After the defendant entered the house he went to the kitchen. He made a hot drink in a mug and added some of the rodent poison to it. He disappeared from the kitchen and reappeared a few moments later in the upstairs bedroom. He gave the mug to the woman in bed and sat beside her as she drank it. This empirical connection between surrounding story elements and a clearly specified central action removes all doubt from the case.

Empirical connections often become important in cases that turn on a conflict between the accounts of the defendant and the only eye witness. The interpretation of these cases may depend on locating subtle inconsistencies in the empirical connections of the two contending stories. These empirical inconsistencies may include the co-occurrence of improbable or impossible events, incorrect statements about causality, distorted connections between time and action, or the unexplained transformation of key scenic or behavioral symbols.

Consider an empirical understanding that became important to the interpretation of the central action in a larceny case.[19] We know that it can happen that a car being driven down a street can stop, the driver can slide over into the passenger's seat, and a waiting pedestrian can take the driver's place and drive off. This familiar scenario was important to the defendant's story, but a gap in the order of events in the scenario inhibited empirical connections that would have favored the defendant's interpretation. An eye witness identified the defendant as the man who put a stolen stereo set in a hiding place across the street from her house. The man then ran around the corner, and she went to call the police. The defendant later took the stand and said that he had been at the scene but that he wasn't the man who hid the stereo set. He was just walking along when he saw another guy from the neighborhood (he thought his name was "J - - -") carrying a stereo set. Suddenly a police car making its rounds came into sight and the man put the stereo in a nearby garbage can and ran off. What, then, happened to the defendant? He claimed that he hid under a nearby porch until the excitement died down. He had a prior arrest record and did not want to get involved in this matter. What became of the man who ran off? Why wasn't he found anywhere in the neighborhood later? According to the defendant, as he pointed to a diagram of the scene, "a car came by here. The guy instead of getting into a car, he got right under the wheel and drove away."

He left something out here. Did the car come to a stop? Did the driver slide over so "J - - -" could drive the car? Was there a driver? The judge (who ruled on the case) took note of these problems in the defendant's account of this otherwise familiar situation. Among the reasons cited for finding the defendant guilty was the following:

> I believe I understood also that your testimony was that when you came out from under the D - - - house you saw J - - - I think further north on the same block emerge running from between some houses and jump into that car, into the driver's seat. That struck me as being unusual, that a man who was running from a burglary would jump into the driver's seat of a car that was moving and waiting for him.

This suggests a listener's maxim in situations, such as adjudications, that require empirical judgments to be made about accounts: *Descriptions are taken literally. Terms that would have to be changed in order to produce a sensible version of an incident are regarded as problematic. They become possible indicators of "made up" versions of reality.*

Language Categorization Connections

Language categories are among the most powerful means of establishing relationships among symbols in stories. Most symbols belong to multiple categories of possible usage. We can narrow the categorical relationship between symbols by locating the set of categories that could include the connected symbolic terms, and then determine the category that best explains the usage in the story context. In his excellent discussion of categorization, Sacks analyzed the simple child's story, "The baby cried. The mommy picked it up."[20] Sacks claimed that virtually all hearers of this story will understand that the mommy is the mommy of the baby. This is because, of all the categories that could have been used to connect the symbols ("family," "stage of life," "sex," etc.), the category that makes most sense in the context of the story is "family." Consequently we understand that the two actors are related even though we have not been instructed explicitly to hear this. Sacks drew from this another "hearer's maxim" in interpretation: *If a categorization permits the hearer (I prefer "listener") to draw a clear and sensible inference about the connection between the categorized symbols, the listener will make that categorical connection.*[21]

A categorization can become the key link in establishing a chain of connections to the central action in a story. An example of this emerged during the testimony in a burglary trial in our sample of cases. The defendant's mother was called to testify as a witness for the prosecution. She was asked if she knew the whereabouts of her son on the day of the crime. She said that she did not know what he was doing. The prosecutor then asked her if she hadn't agreed to sign a statement shortly after the burglary that clearly implicated her son in the crime, but refused to sign the statement after her son talked her out of it. The woman replied that she thought the statement in question was in reference to a friend of hers, a Mr. P - - -, who had been arrested about the same time as her son. She said the statement seemed to fit what she knew about that incident and she was about to sign it when her son arrived at the prosecutor's office, read the statement, and pointed out to her that the statement was about him and not about Mr. P - - -. Since the woman didn't know anything about her son's case, she couldn't sign the statement.

This is a fascinating categorization problem. Did the woman refuse to sign the statement at the last moment in order to protect her son, or was it, as she claimed, a response to discovering that the statement was about the wrong person? In order to make this judgment about the central action, we must rely on our knowledge about categorization and we must also make a categorization. First, we use our knowledge about categorization to determine whether a person who knew two "arrested persons" (category) would identify (categorize) the wrong one of these persons in a prosecutor's statement. We know implicitly that categorization allows us to make both subtle distinctions and powerful generalizations about the world. It is not likely that a person who knew the details of two categorically similar incidents (arrests) would fail to distinguish between them when hearing an account of one of them. This would be similar to knowing that mothers and their babies belong to the category "family," but not knowing that they can be distinguished according to other sorts of categories (size, age, behavior, etc.). Yet this failure to make distinctions is what the woman claimed in response to the prosecutor's questions:

Q: Did I read you a statement after I interviewed you?

A: Yes . . .

Q: Did I ask you if it was true, if it was correct?

A: Yes. I said that because I thought it was Mr. P - - -. I am trying to tell you that now.

Q: You told me the statement was correct that I read you?

A: Yes. I was mistaken.

        *   *   *

Q: And didn't your son appear at my office door at that time and walk you down to the bathroom?

A: Yes. I had the wrong thing—I was talking about the wrong date.

Q: Your son told you that—

A: When he got arrested—when Mr. P - - - got arrested. It was Mr. P - - -.

Q: Is that what your son told you?

A: That's what I found out today. I didn't know.

        *   *   *

Q: Didn't your son object to your signing it?

A: Because I had the wrong date. If I had the right date, he would have let me sign it.

        *   *   *

Q: How did he know the statement was not accurate?

A: He heard me say what time it was and what date. That's why he stopped me. He said "You're talking about Mr. P - - - there." I didn't know.

If we decide that this failure to categorize properly was unlikely under the circumstances, we probably buttress this conclusion by basing it on a categorization that we have made about the actors involved. Our judgment that the key actors in the situation are mother and son is more than incidental. We understand that the "family" category is the appropriate one to use even though many other categories could be invoked to describe the relationship between the actors (age, sex, race, religion, etc.). Thinking of the characters in the story as mother and son increases the chance of considering that mothers often act to protect their children when they are in trouble. This empirical knowledge can be called up more directly through the category "family" than through such categories as age, sex, or religion.

Consider, in this light, the prosecutor's repeated references in his questions to the woman's "son": "And didn't your *son* appear . . ." "Didn't your *son* object . . ." The prosecutor did not refer to the male actor in the story as "the man," "the defendant," "the accused," "the person who came to the door," or "Mr. Smith." These references would have been awkward in the context of the story; they would have strained against connections in the story that would establish the most obvious interpretation for the story's main action (the woman's refusal to sign the statement against her son). It makes sense to combine what we know about the relationship between the actors in the story in order to draw the inference that the mother probably refused to sign the statement in order to protect her son. From this we draw a second "listener's maxim" regarding categorization to complement the one already suggested by Sacks: *To the extent that doubts (or choices) may exist as to the categorical relationship between two story symbols, the interpreter will make the categorization that sets up the most obvious chain of connections between the symbols and the story's central action.*

Logical Connections

When we combine empirical understandings with particular categorical operations, we produce "logic" in the everyday sense. This everyday logic is to be distinguished from "formal" logic that may utilize artificial (non-natural language) symbols and arbitrarily given rules of relationship among these symbols. The logic of ordinary discourse is based on the rules that govern everyday language usage (grammar and semantics) and the rules of empirical relationship that we know to hold in the everyday world. If, for example, we hear a story that begins "We were waiting in the parking lot for our contact to deliver the drugs and a car drove up," we also hear, among other things, that the engine of the car was running. Categorizing a car's action as "driving" presumes a variety of constituent (empirical and categorical) actions: engine running, wheels turning, etc. This categorization also makes it possible to establish empirical connections to a number of "variables": speed, distance, etc. We know these things by virtue of the set of symbols included by the categorical connection between "car" and "driving" and the invariant empirical relationships that connect these symbols. Thus, to modify our definition of everyday logic, we can say that a logical connection depends on categorizing two symbols such that some invariant empirical properties always accompany the categorization.

It happens that this apparently trivial example of a car and its engine became an issue in a narcotics case in our sample. The arresting officer testified that the defendant had driven to the scene of the arranged "buy" in the car containing the drugs. The defense attempted to weaken the connections between the actors, the agency, and the scene. For some curious reason the lawyer questioned the connection between the car and the scene of the crime. Actually, the tactic employed here was to test the credibility of the witness. Such efforts generally fail when they are aimed, as in this case, at unproblematic logical features of the witness's story:

Q: Was the motor of the Gremlin running?

A: I would assume so.

Q: Detective, I don't want you to assume anything that you don't have a fresh recollection of. Do you recall whether it was running or not?

A: I can't answer that question without assuming that it was.

Q: Well, maybe we can approach it another way. Why do you assume that it was running?

A: Because it drove up alongside.

To think other than this would be absurd. We know that a car cannot be "driving" and at the same time not have its engine running. We do understand, logically, that a car can be "coasting" or "rolling" and not have its engine running. However, this sort of recategorization would not make sense within the story.

Normative Connections

Categorizations and logical chains of inference can be supported by, or even based upon, normative understandings about excusable and inexcusable behavior in certain circumstances. Such normative understandings played a key role in establishing and testing the chain of connections leading to the jury's interpretations in the Federal bank robbery trial of Patricia Hearst. The defendant had been an earlier kidnap victim of the group that staged the robbery. However, the defendant entered the bank with her former abductors. Both sides agreed that she was carrying a gun. What did this behavior mean? Was she a willful participant? Had she so changed as to identify herself with her former adversaries? If so, her acts conformed to the definition of robbery that was given to the jury. Or, on the other hand, had she been forced or coerced to participate in the robbery? Was she afraid for her life? If so, she was to be held less responsible for her actions. This is a normative judgment. It is also a case in which an initial categorization helps to establish the basis for the application of normative understandings about her actions.

Both sides agreed that the defendant had been kidnapped earlier by the other accused robbers. The question was whether or not this categorical relationship still existed at the time of the robbery. The prosecution suggested that by the time of the bank robbery, the former victim had become a willing and loyal member of the group that had staged her abduction. Therefore, loyalty, and not threat or coercion, accounted for her participation in the robbery. The defense, however, sought to establish that the relationships that existed between the defendant and the other accused robbers sustained the categorization "kidnapping" throughout the relationship. The defendant took the stand and testified to numerous instances of physical abuse inflicted by her abductors. Surely, the defense argued, these episodes justified the conclusion that her participation in the robbery was secured through physical coercion and, therefore, entitled her to be excused for her acts. However, the prosecution proceeded to introduce other empirical connections into the relationship between the actors in the story. For example, the defendant stood regular guard watches while her "abductors" slept. She also went jogging alone during her period of "captivity." Once she became trapped while trying to climb a bluff near a beach. Two policemen assisted her. She did not inform them of her "plight." Finally, she waited alone in a getaway car (with the keys in the ignition) while two of her "abductors" robbed a store. The defendant even fired shots into the store to aid the escape. These incidents redefined the relationships among the actors from "adversaries" to "comrades." This redefinition relied on a powerful norm: If one is in a relationship against one's will, opportunities to escape the relationship should be acted upon. This set of connections led the jury to the inference that the defendant acted in accord with her conscience while participating in the robbery. This relationship between normative and categorical understandings might have changed had the defense presented a different case. Suppose that the defense had argued that the relationship between kidnappers and victim was more one of "mind control" than "physical coercion." The kidnappers had effectively brainwashed their hapless victim. A new norm would emerge here as a basis for other categorical and empirical connections: Persons who have been brainwashed should not be held accountable for their subsequent behavior. This understanding could have provided consistent connections for the defendant's numerous failures to escape her captors.[22]

This example suggests in graphic terms that issues of truth or fact in our adjudication (and social judgment) processes are intimately tied to the symbolization of accounts and the ways in which the symbolizations fit into the story model. *This means that in some instances perfectly true accounts will be disbelieved due to improper symbolization or structurally inadequate presentations. Conversely, false accounts may be believed due to the skillful juxtaposition of internally consistent symbols.* I will return to this point shortly. For immediate purposes, however, this example also illustrates the complementary use of multiple social understandings (empirical, categorical, normative) to build a solid interpretation.

Aesthetic Connections

Some symbolizations invite us to make connections among objects of reference that go beyond mere empirical, normative, categorical, or logical understandings. Some symbolic relationships seem somehow more perfect, familiar, pleasing, or satisfying than others. These relationships may become targets for emotional release or personal identification. Other symbolizations may elicit connections that seem strange, awkward, unfamiliar, or even repulsive. We may invest negative feelings in these understandings. Both of these kinds of connections are in the realm of aesthetics—relationships among symbols based on emotionally arousing ascriptive characteristics.

That jurors are bombarded by lawyers with invitations to stereotype defendants, victims, and witnesses is obvious. These invitations are, in effect, pressures for jurors to make connections that are, perhaps, too satisfying, too familiar, or too pleasing—connections that may be stronger than the facts, norms, or logic of the matter would suggest. Consider, for example, the defense lawyer's efforts to create an unsavory picture of the victim in a robbery case. It was established that the victim worked as a commercial fisherman. He had been at sea for several months, and he was celebrating his homecoming with his niece and his daughter on the night he was robbed. The celebration was unplanned. The two women had come from another city to visit the man. They went to the boat where he lived. He was not there. They began checking local taverns and found him in one of them. From there the party moved from bar to bar until the man's wallet was stolen as the threesome was in transit between bars. These are the facts of the victim's whereabouts that evening. However, the phrasing of the following sequence of questions on cross-examination would suggest that the defense tried to characterize the victim in terms that might elicit more than obvious or immediate empirical, normative, logical, or categorical connections to other elements in the story:

Q: Now, if you just wanted to socialize with these two relatives of
    yours, wouldn't it have been easier to go to their home and socialize

as opposed to drinking; wouldn't it have been easier to go to one of their houses rather than to the N - - - Tavern, the B - - - Tavern, and the E - - - Club for a period of some five hours?

Q: But you did your socializing in bars and taverns?

Q: Did they just show up at the N - - - Tavern?

Q: And you happened to be there?

Q: Just a coincidence?

Q: You happened to be up at the N - - - Tavern when your daughter and niece were there?

Q: No plans were made?

Q: They just showed up and came in from Sea-Tac and just showed up at the N - - - Tavern where you were?

Such attempts to stereotype defendants, victims, or the circumstances surrounding the crime enable listeners to add or change connections in a story when no informational grounds for such operations exist. For example, the above attempt to characterize the victim of a robbery as an unsavory individual (whose family reunions are conducted in bars and taverns) might make it easy to impose the normative judgment that people of that sort may deserve what happens to them. Had the defense been able to introduce any evidence that the victim had provoked or tempted the defendant, the jury might have relied heavily on these aesthetic judgments about the victim in reaching its verdict.

EVALUATING THE INTERPRETATION

The story form facilitates more than the identification of a central action and the connection of relevant symbols in support of an interpretation. The listener must be able to refine constantly the conception of the central action and to compare it against emerging alternative interpretations for the point of the story. More importantly, the listener must be able to know implicitly when enough connections have been established to make a consistent and confident interpretation. Related to this, the interpreter also must know what particular bits of information would be needed to complete a story if it is found lacking. These interpretive capabilities associated with storytelling indicate that stories must engage some general cognitive models of social action against which particular networks of story connections can be judged for completeness, consistency, and ambiguity.

An obvious candidate for this third cognitive component of the story model is Burke's "pentad" of social action elements.[23] According to Burke, we systematize information about social action in terms of basic relations among scene, act, agent, agency, and purpose. This social "frame" gives us a ready standard against which to compare an emerging interpretation, and through which to identify quickly any connection that appears to deviate from the empirical, categorical, etc., ratios ordinarily associated with the comparison frame. This idea of general frames of reference within which interpretations can be crystallized, tested, and rearranged has become a central construct in cognitive sociology[24] and cognitive psychology.[25] Frames are thought to impose generic attributes on specific data. This accounts for the great speed, flexibility, and information capacity of ordinary interpretation; frames make it unnecessary to reconstruct images that already have been assembled and stored in memory. The appeal of Burke's scheme is that it actually specifies the structure of the frames we apply to social interpretation. Data from trials in our sample suggests that Burke's model makes a good deal of sense. The basic elements of scene, act, agent, agency, and purpose seem to operate as "super categories" into which multiple connections among symbols can be collapsed, and through which quick access can be obtained to alternative symbolizations.

The use of implicit ratios among elements in Burke's frame to generate and test alternative patterns of connections among story symbols is particularly obvious in the consistency tests that are applied by lawyers and jurors to emerging interpretations of stories. In a complex trial, isolated connections among story symbols often make sense, but the overall pattern of connections may be inconsistent. An example of this came up in a narcotics trial. At one point in the development of the case, the central question boiled down to whether the defendant had been duped into driving the car containing the narcotics to the scene of the drug sale, or whether he was in league with the person who arranged the sale. It was an uncontested fact that the defendant met the drug dealer in a bar before the sale. The defendant, however, claimed that he knew the dealer only slightly and certainly not well enough to know that he was a dealer. The defendant explained his presence in the bar by saying that his car had broken down nearby and he was trying to figure out how to get home to pick up his tools. The other fellow walked in about that time and offered the defendant the loan of his car if the defendant would drop him off at a nearby shopping center (the scene of the deal) and return for him later. It was upon his return that the defendant was arrested.

This explanation gave the defendant a plausible purpose for acting as the driver of the car (which was the agency for his action). How was he to know that there were drugs in a car that he had borrowed? However, these favorable connections between "agent-purpose" and "agent-agency" were later shown to be inconsistent with another symbol added to the story when the prosecutor cross-examined the defendant. It turned out that the bar in which the defendant encountered the drug dealer was only a few blocks from his home. Why, the prosecutor asked, didn't he just walk home to get his tools instead of going to such elaborate lengths and wasting so much time? Suddenly, when we consider this scenic element, the formerly consistent connections become inconsistent:

$$\text{agent} \text{ - - - } \text{purpose} \text{ - - } / \text{ - } / \text{ - scene}$$
$$\text{agent} \text{ - - - } \text{agency} \text{ - - } / \text{ - } / \text{ - scene}$$

In this fashion, the basic structure of a story can trigger a large number of structural permutations with which to test the consistency of connections which, if taken in pairs, might seem perfectly consistent.

STORIES, JUDGMENTS, AND REALITY

This model of stories and social judgment explains how ordinary persons can make sophisticated judgments about complex information—even in situations, such as the courtroom, in which there are few familiar formal cues to guide the process. The model also suggests how basic social judgment processes can be accommodated within the symbolic frameworks of different situations. For example, in the courtroom jurors must understand that their judgments satisfy standards of "reasonable doubt." They must try to withhold final judgments until "all the evidence is in." They must try to be "fair." They must try to be "objective."[26] These dimensions of interpretation are stipulated within the foreign context of a trial, yet the basis for this knowledge must be part of the juror's everyday equipment for living. A solution to this problem is suggested by the story model: The cognitive operations made possible by placing evidence into a story framework provide implicit measures of these justice criteria. For example, the constant juxtaposition of story connections within a broader generic social frame allows the juror to know whether an inference is based on a set of connections that are internally consistent and that yield no other interpretations. This, in a nutshell, is our everyday measure of "doubt." In a like manner, the assessment for story completeness tells the juror whether more information of a particular sort would yield a better interpretation. The very process of building an interpretation by work-ing back and forth among the three cognitive operations and testing the result both against the other side's story and against the standard contained in the generic frames of reference is what we mean ordinar-ily by being objective and fair.

Does all of this mean that jurors' judgments (and most other social judgments as well) are based on doubtless and objective pictures of what "really" happened? Not at all. At every stage of the storytelling-interpretation process, both storytellers and interpreters make choices about how to symbolize a story element, what connections to set up among these elements, and what frames of reference to apply. In this sense, a story is a reconstruction of an event in light of the teller's ini-tial perception and immediate judgments about the audience, the in-terests that appear to be at stake, and, perhaps most importantly, what has gone before in the situation in which the story is presented. Like-wise, the jurors' judgment depends on all of these factors, in addition to their basic interpretive capabilities (command of language, general knowledge, etc.), assessment of the situation, and perception of the in-tentions of the storyteller.

This should not be construed to mean that the reconstruction of re-ality in the interpretation process is exclusively of a rhetorical nature. The rhetorical aspect is but one component of the more general dispo-sition that all of us share to make past events fit coherently into the symbolic constraints of present situations. So powerful is this disposi-tion toward continuity in reality that even memory itself seems to be anchored as much in the present as in the past.[27] In short, when we talk about the "objectivity" of judgments in trials and in other social settings, we are referring to reconstructions of past events that become satisfactorily objective only insofar as they cohere within immediate situations. There are two implications of this. One is obvious. The other is not so obvious.

First, as Schutz[28] and, more recently, Garfinkel[29] have demon-strated so convincingly, all of our social judgments and understand-ings are tied inextricably to the social contexts in which they are made. Meaningful discourse and interaction require the construction and use in situations of "relevance structures," "worlds in common," or "taken for granted knowledge." This simply means that versions of past events are symbolized in light of the definitions and relationships that prevail in ongoing situations. This is true even of courtrooms.

Second, this perspective suggests something interesting about the nature of justice. In light of commonsense understandings about justice in this society, it is remarkable that we are now in a position to suggest that the representations on which verdicts are based may have little to do with what "really" happened in a dispute. After all, justice processes are allegedly designed for the impartial determination of issues of fact. The perspective developed here indicates that adjudicators, like most other story audiences, judge the plausibility of a story according to certain structural relations among chosen symbols, not according to direct perception of the actual events in question. Although documentary evidence exists to support some symbolizations in a story, both the teller and the interpreter of a story *always* have some margin of control over the definition of certain key symbols. Therefore, stories are judged in terms of a combination of the documentary or "empirical" warrants for symbols and the internal structural relations among the collection of symbols presented in the story. In other words, we judge stories according to a dual standard of "Did it happen that way?" and "Could it have happened that way?" In no case can "empirical" standards alone produce a completely adequate judgment, and there are cases for which structural characteristics alone are far and away the critical elements in determining the truth of a story.

This means that, within certain limits, disputants have some escape from the reality of their dispute. This presumes a special way of thinking about reality. It is based on the premise (indeed, the primitive understanding) that reality itself can be misleading, illusory, or unjust. This perspective on reality also implies that we understand (again, at a very primitive level) that symbolization, communication, and interpretation are prime moving forces in social life. Although these "creative" processes construct the reality in which we live, they also are fallible, subject to misuse, and capable of presenting false images to participants in situations. In short, we recognize that we can become victims of our own symbols and our own communication processes. In light of this it would seem that one of the basic provisions of our justice processes is a measure of protection from the brute facts of a matter. Justice is done, in this sense, when we are not held accountable for the errors in communication or the arbitrary circumstances that can result from ambiguities in symbolic processes.

These relationships among communication, reality, and justice may account for the popularity of the recurring theme of "victimage by circumstance" in films, novels, and news stories. It is curious that we are so inclined to identify with victims of circumstance and to agonize with their plights. Why does this theme never seem to exhaust possible plots and expressions? How is it that even though we "know" that the defendant in the courtroom melodrama and the suspect in the murder mystery will be proved innocent, we can be engrossed by the story and surprised and relieved by its ending? I cannot hope to answer such complex questions here, but the idea that we share a primitive understanding about communication and reality sheds some light on the subject. We may become absorbed in these familiar episodes in fiction and in everyday life because they contain a tension—indeed, a troubling contradiction—between how things ought to work out (justice) and how, as a result of symbolic usage and communcational practice, things (can) work out differently (circumstance). As beings whose fates often hinge on how we communicate in situations, we understand all too well that configurations of events, actions, and information can seem compelling and substantial; yet a slight shift in perspective, the addition of a bit of new information or the recombination of bits of old information, can reveal, suddenly, a new reality.

In this light it is, perhaps, not so surprising that we would weight our justice processes in favor of a margin of escape from circumstances—circumstances that lead to behaviors that are misconstrued, to imputed motives that are not intended, or to accusations that are well-meaning but false. The importance of stories in this context is that they are capsule versions of reality. They literally pick up an incident and set it down in another social context. In the process of this transition, the data can be selected, the historical frame can be specified, the situational factors can be redefined, and "missing observations" can be inferred. In short, a situation can be re-presented in a form consistent with an actor's perspective and interests both during and after the incident.

Although this framework on communication and the nature of justice is still only a rough one, it illustrates an important use of communication analysis. All too often we reject the notion that communication practices can be the frame within which generic social processes (such as justice routines) develop and change. This is because our common sense tells us that communication is something that happens within (i.e., is contained by) a situational framework. This is true in one sense, but it is equally true that the structure and dynamics of social reality from which all social processes derive are communicational in nature.

The theoretical development of this perspective must go hand in hand with further research. The preceding discussion suggests several directions for additional exploration. The most obvious next step would entail testing the propositions contained in the above discussion about the effects of story structure on interpretation and judgment. For example, it would be useful to know the impact of rhetorical strategies (redefinitions, recategorizations, the introduction of facts, etc.) employed at different junctures in the development of a story. We might examine the impact of the use of such rhetorical moves as they vary in structural distance from the central action of a story. Another obvious area of investigation has to do with the effects of structural variation in stories on different types of judgments. For example, there is support in the above argument for the hypothesis that judgments about the truth status of a story depend heavily on structural properties affecting the clarity of the central action, the consistency of surrounding inferences, and the completeness of the set of inferential connections.

There also are numerous investigations that would clarify further the specific question of the role of storytelling in justice processes. For example, it would be useful to observe how jurors employ stories in their deliberations. This would entail several specific concerns. It would be interesting to document the merger of individual versions of a case into the general account of the crime on which the verdict rests. Perhaps even more could be learned from the documentation of deliberations in which a common story about the incident is not produced. These investigations might be supplemented with interviews to determine what elements of cases were more or less critical to each person's interpretation.

Two lines of research have been proposed here. One deals with stories as general interpretive devices. The second examines stories as they operate within a particular social context. Each approach should enhance the other. These lines of inquiry, when taken together, may yield some important clues about how we structure our social reality, and how, through communication processes, these structuring principles organize and give meaning to everyday social experiences.

ACKNOWLEDGMENTS

The author would like to thank Martha Feldman for her tactful advice on how to make sense of the first draft of this essay. The work of the late Harvey Sachs also has been a source of many insights. The present research was supported by a grant from the Graduate School Research Fund, University of Washington.

NOTES

1. Some promising steps in this direction have emerged from work in the fields of ethnomethodology, cognitive sociology, and cognitive anthropology. See, among others, Basil Bernstein, *Class, Codes, and Control* (New York: Schocken, 1971); Aaron V. Cicourel, *Cognitive Sociology* (Baltimore: Penguin, 1973); Mary Douglas, *Natural Symbols,* 2nd. ed. (London: Barrie & Jenkins, 1973); William Labov, "Rules for Ritual Insults," in *Studies in Social Interaction,* ed. David Sudnow (New York: Free Press, 1972), pp. 120–69; Roy Turner, "Words, Utterance, and Activities," in *Under,* ed. Jack D. Douglas (Chicago: Aldine, 1910), pp. 169–87; and Victor Turner, *Dramas, Fields, and Metaphors: Symbolic Actions in Human Society* (Ithaca: Cornell University Press, 1974).

2. Allan M. Collins and M. Ross Quillian, "Retrieval Time from Semantic Memory," *Journal of Verbal Learning and Verbal Behavior,* 8 (1969), 240-47.

3. Harvey Sacks, "On the Analyzability of Stories by Children," in *Directions in Sociolinguistics: The Ethnography of Communications,* ed. John T. Grumperz and Dell Hymes (New York: Holt, Rinehart and Winston, 1972), pp. 325–45.

4. Roger C. Schank, "The Structure of Episodes in Memory," in *Representation and Understanding: Studies in Cognitive Science,* ed. Daniel G. Bobrow and Allan Collins (New York: Academic Press, 1975), pp. 237–72.

5. Marvin Minsky, "A Framework for Representing Knowledge," in *The Psychology of Computer Vision,* ed. Patrick Henry Winston (New York: McGraw-Hill, 1975), pp. 211–77. See, also, Benjamin J. Kuipers, "A Frame for Frames," in Bobrow and Collins, pp. 151–84; and Terry Winograd, "Frame Representations and the Declarative/Procedural Controversy," in Bobrow and Collins, pp. 185–210.

6. Robert P. Abelson, "Concepts for Representing Mundane Reality in Plans," in Bobrow and Collins, pp. 273–309.

7. Robert P. Abelson and C. M. Reich, "Implicational Molecules: A Method for Extracting Meaning from Input Sentences," *Proceedings of the First International Joint Conference on Artificial Intelligence,* ed. Donald E. Walker and Lewis M. Norton (Bedford, Mass.: Mitre Corp., 1969), pp. 641–45.

8. Abelson, pp. 274–75.

9. W. Lance Bennett, "Political Scenarios and the Nature of Politics," *Philosophy and Rhetoric,* 8 (1975), 23–42.

10. Don H. Zimmerman, "Record-Keeping and the Intake Process in a Public Welfare Agency," in *On Record: Files and Dossiers in American Life,* ed. Stanton Wheeler (New York: Russell Sage Foundation, 1969), pp. 319–54.

11. Michael Moerman, "The Use of Precedent in Natural Conversation: A Study in Practical Legal Reasoning," *Semiotica*, 9 (1973), 193–218.

12. Evidence for this point is contained in the numerous accounts of jurors about their experiences during trials. See, for example, Stephen G. Chaberski, "Inside the New York Panther Trial," *Civil Liberties Review*, 1, No. 1 (1973), 111–55; Edwin Kennebeck, *Juror Number Four* (New York: Norton, 1973); and Mary Timothy, *Jury Woman* (Palo Alto, Ca.: The Emty Press, 1974). These observations are documented further in W. Lance Bennett and Martha S. Feldman, *Reconstructing Reality in the Courtroom: Justice and Judgment in American Culture* (New Brunswick, N.J.: Rutgers University Press, 1981).

13. Garfinkel has observed that jurors must operate on the basis of skills they possess prior to becoming a juror. He underscored this point with the remark that "A person is 95 per cent juror before he comes near the court." See Harold Garfinkel, "Some Rules of Correct Decision Making the Jurors Respect" in his *Studies in Ethnomethodology* (Englewood Cliffs, N.J.: Prentice-Hall, 1967), p. 110.

14. It should be noted here that the forthcoming characteristics of stories include only those properties that are directly relevant to the interpretation process. Other models of stories have addressed the underlying "grammar structure" necessary to construct and to recognize stories. See, for example, B. N. Colby, "A Partial Grammar of Eskimo Folktales," *American Anthropologist*, 75 (1973), 645–62; V. Propp, *Morphology of the Folktale*, 2nd ed. (Austin: University of Texas Press, 1968); and David E. Rumelhart, "Notes on a Schema for Stories," in Bobrow and Collins, pp. 211–36.

15. On the importance of linear and causal coding for interpretation, see Schank, pp. 241–54.

16. Leonard Newmark and Morton W. Bloomfield, A *Linguistic Introduction to the History of English* (New York: Alfred A. Knopf, 1963), pp. 70–71.

17. Plot devices must be distinguished from basic interpretive structure in stories. Plot techniques may thoroughly rearrange the sequence of events in a story, but the basic rules for interpreting a story allow the listener to recombine the information in familiar and more readily accessible form. In this way, a storyteller can use plot techniques to distort, or otherwise call attention to, particular features of the incident, yet still produce an interpretable account. In cases when the plot techniques seem to render the underlying story unrecoverable, it is unlikely that an adequate story has been told at all. Although I apply this maxim to nonfiction stories, a good illustration of it comes from the realm of fiction. The literary genre that critics have termed "postmodern fiction" creates special interpretive problems for readers and critics alike. These problems result from plot-story ambiguities. For example, Alain Robbe-Grillet's works *In the Labyrinth* and *Plan for a Revolution in New York*

contain detailed accounts of realistic situations in which scenes and characters are continuous, time appears to progress, and actions seem to be building toward some climax. Despite these appearances, coherent simple stories cannot be recovered from the plot mazes of these novels. This is because the actions and situations do not build toward a mutually defining relationship, not because the plots are too complex. For an analysis of this phenomenon, see Bruce Morrissette, "Post-Modern Generative Fiction: Novel and Film," *Critical Inquiry*, 2 (Winter 1975), 253–62. Indeed, if an account conforms to basic story rules, it is virtually impossible to complicate the plot to a degree that would foil a careful listener. For example, a "traditional novel" such as *Tristram Shandy* is open to coherent interpretation despite a maddening array of plot distractions. In his analysis of *Tristram Shandy*, Shklovsky provides a succinct summary of the general point here: "The idea of *plot* is too often confused with the description of events—with what I propose provisionally to call the *story.*" See Victor Shklovsky, "Sterne's *Tristram Shandy*: Stylistic Commentary," in *Russian Formalist Criticism: Four Essays*, trans. L. T. Lemon and Marion J. Reis (Lincoln: University of Nebraska Press, 1965), p. 57.

18. In Propp's scheme the significance of a story is a function of the relationship between the central action and the developing situation. Although he doesn't specify how these "functions" are calculated, he uses the term in an analytical sense: *"Function is understood as an act of a character, defined from the point of view of its significance for the course of the action"* (p. 21).

19. References to actual trials are based on data gathered through observation and/or transcription of a sample of approximately 100 trials held at the Superior Court for the State of Washington, King County, Seattle. The data were gathered with Martha S. Feldman and appear in more detail in Bennett and Feldman, *Reconstructing Reality in the Courtroom*. Even though trials are public record, a concern about any further stigmatization of the criminal defendants in these cases underlies my decision not to reveal either the names of participants or the titles of the cases.

20. Sacks, pp. 330–40.

21. A more technical discussion of Sack's general point can be found in John D. Bransford and Nancy S. McCarrell, "A Sketch of a Cognitive Approach to Comprehension: Some Thoughts About Understanding What It Means to Comprehend," in *Cognition and the Symbolic Processes*, ed. Walter B. Weimer and David S. Palermo (Hillsdale, N.J.: Lawrence Erlbaum, 1974), pp. 210–20. Their discussion contains many excellent illustrations.

22. Why wasn't this categorization and its related normative connection suggested by the defense? The defense attorney apparently rejected a "brainwashing" defense on grounds that the issues involved were too complex for most jurors to grasp. (See any United States news magazine for the weeks of

2-22-76, 3-1-76, or 3-8-76.) Although his reasoning seems dubious in retrospect, the lawyer was correct in assuming that the jurors could understand a relationship of "coercion" between people. The category "coercion" did lead jurors to the unequivocal application of empirical and normative understandings to the case. However, when considered in terms of story structure, there were serious inconsistencies among the connections. These inconsistencies, when compared to a consistent prosecution account, led the jury to determine beyond a reasonable doubt that the defendant had participated in a willful theft of property by means of force.

23. See Kenneth Burke, *Permanence & Change*, 2nd rev. ed. (Los Altos, Ca.: Hermes, 1954), and *A Grammar of Motives* (1945; rpt. Berkeley: University of California Press, 1969).

24. See, for example, Erving Goffman, *Frame Analysis* (Cambridge: Harvard University Press, 1974).

25. See, for example, Minsky and, also, Kuipers. This is not to imply that "frame theory" dominates cognitive theory. However, the best evidence against frame theories seems to come from research on physical, not social, perception and judgment. See, for example, William M. Mace, "Ecologically Stimulating Cognitive Psychology: Gibsonian Perspectives," in Weimer and Palermo, pp. 137–64; and M. T. Turvey, "Constructive Theory, Perceptual Systems, and Tacit Knowledge," in Weimer and Palermo, pp. 165–80.

26. See Garfinkel, "Some Rules," for a list of the formal attributes that jurors attach to their decisions.

27. The idea that judgments and recollections are often liberal reconstructions of real events has had a long history in philosophy and psychology. Among the classical statements is Jerome S. Bruner's 1957 essay, "Going Beyond the Information Given," reprinted in *Beyond the Information Given: Studies in the Psychology of Knowing*, ed. Jeremy M. Anglin (New York: Norton, 1973), pp. 218–38. The constructionist perspective is gaining increasing prominence in current theories of memory. See, for example, Elizabeth Loftus "Reconstructing Memory: The Incredible Eyewitness," *Psychology Today*, Dec. 1974, pp. 116–19; Elizabeth F. Loftus and John C. Palmer, "Reconstruction of Automobile Destruction: An Example of the Interaction Between Language and Memory," *Journal of Verbal Learning and Verbal Behavior*, 13 (1974), 585–89, and Elizabeth F. Loftus, "Leading Questions and the Eyewitness Report," *Cognitive Psychology*, 7 (1975), 560–72.

28. See Alfred Schutz, *Collected Papers, I and* II, ed. Maurice Natanson (The Hague: Martinus Nijhoff, 1967), passim; and *The Phenomenology of the Social World*, trans. George Walsh and Frederick Lehnert (Evanston: Northwestern University Press, 1967), pp. 97–138.

29. Garfinkel, Ch. 1.

5

Human Evolution as Narrative

Misia Landau

Scientists are generally aware of the influence of theory on observation. Seldom do they recognize, however, that many scientific theories are essentially narratives. The growth of a plant, the progress of a disease, the formation of a beach, the evolution of an organism—any set of events that can be arranged in a sequence and related can also be narrated. This is true even of a scientific experiment. Indeed, many laboratory reports, with their sections labeled "methods," "results," and "conclusions," bear at least a superficial resemblance to a typical narrative, that is, an organized sequence of events with a beginning, a middle, and an end. Whether or not scientists follow such a narrative structure in their work, they do not often recognize the extent to which they use narrative in their thinking and in communicating their ideas. Consequently, they may be unaware of the narrative presuppositions which inform their science.

Students of literature, on the other hand, are so conscious of narrative that some have argued it is storytelling which makes us human. As the poet Matthew Arnold declared in his famous debate with Thomas Henry Huxley, even man's remote ancestor, "the hairy quadruped furnished with a tail and pointed ears, probably arboreal in his habits . . . carried hidden in his nature something destined to develop into a necessity for humane letters."[1] E. M. Forster, the novelist and essayist, located the origin of narrative in the Paleolithic: "Neanderthal man listened to stories, if one may judge by the shape of his skull. The primitive audience was an audience of shock-heads, gaping round the campfire, fatigued with contending against the mammoth or the woolly rhinoceros, and only kept awake by suspense. What would happen next?"[2]

Depicting Neanderthals as gaping shock-heads may appear gauche scientifically, and yet in tracing storytelling to the very roots of human history Forster anticipates one of the latest trends in scholarship in the humanities. So popular is this recent focus on narrative—not only in literary criticism but also in linguistics, anthropology, philosophy, and history—that the French have coined a term for it: "la narratologie."

The central claim of narratology is simply that human beings love to tell stories. "Our need for chronological and causal connection defines and limits all of us—helps to make us what we are."[3] Narrative, then, is a "primary and irreducible form of human comprehension,"[4] a defining characteristic of human intelligence and of the human species. Related to this assumption, though more controversial,[5] is the idea that we have certain basic stories, or deep structures, for organizing our experiences. Each deep structure comes in many versions and in several different modes. For example, the Cinderella story is embedded not just in fairy tales but in novels, films, operas, ballets, and television shows. Some narratologists, stressing the central role of narrative in human experience, would further argue that we have not only different versions of stories but different versions of reality which are shaped by these basic stories.

One scientific discipline that appears open to the importance of narrative is paleoanthropology. Certainly the number of recent articles and books on the subject of bias in the study of fossil man, including one titled *The Myths of Human Evolution*,[6] suggests that paleoanthropologists are aware of the literary aspects of their study. Yet even these authors betray a lingering positivism, implying that more data and increasingly rigorous hypotheses will eliminate for good the subjective element. Few paleoanthropologists have turned to the humanities for a real contribution. Can the humanities tell us anything about science? Can theories of literary criticism illuminate the study of human evolution?

The purpose of this study is to address these questions. Treating specific theories of human evolution as narratives, it will be argued, can shed light not only on paleoanthropology but also on other scientific disciplines. Thus the aim is not to establish narratological theories, nor to develop a theory of scientific logic, but to test heuristically a method of epistemological analysis which, if persuasive, could lead to different ways of doing science. As background, it will be helpful to review the main literary approaches to narrative.

TWO THEORIES OF NARRATIVE

Given the central claim of narratology—that human beings tend to tell stories, even the same stories, in almost everything they do—literary approaches divide along two broad lines, structuralism and hermeneutics. Despite some important theoretical differences, the two approaches converge in many of their basic goals and concepts.[7] For example, both treat literature as a cultural system that is governed by a set of conventions and codes. Criticism thus consists of uncovering and reconstructing the rules and relations that govern literature. The two approaches diverge, however, in how they draw the boundaries of a literary system, and specifically how they delimit the text.

Structuralism defines a text as an autonomous object with a characteristic internal dynamic and treats literary features such as plot, character, and theme much as a systematist treats anatomical characters: as a means of description and classification. Reading a text, like studying an organism, is thus a way of discovering the principles of structure which operate not just for one text but for many.[8] Indeed, a major aim of structuralism is to construct models of the similarities between texts, to describe genres of literature in much the same way that a zoologist describes a new genus.

Hermeneutics proceeds quite differently. Rather than dissect a text to discover general structural principles, the hermeneutic reader subjectively interprets—indeed, animates—a text to find its individual meaning. Again, these differences in approach may be traced to the way the text is defined: whereas structuralists view the text as a complete and finished (though not necessarily isolated) object, in hermeneutics it is regarded as an open system, depending as much on the reader as on the author for definition, and therefore always changing. Hermeneutics thus attempts to show how a text is constructed by its reader. How does one make sense of a text? What are the conditions, rules, and mechanisms that govern reading?

Taken to their extremes, structuralism and hermeneutics may appear to approach the problem of narrative from opposite directions. One focuses on form, the other on meaning; one concentrates on the text, the other looks at the reader; one eschews subjectivity, the other emphasizes personal interpretation. Structuralists may claim that theirs is the more scientific approach, yet scientists themselves are probably more familiar with the hermeneutic brand of criticism, at least with regard to literary works, and possibly even to scientific writing. (Multiple interpretations and ambiguity are no strangers to readers of evolutionary biology, especially in the aftermath of the Darwinian centenary. A book published in 1966, titled *What Darwin*

Really Said, by Farrington, was obviously not the last word on the subject.)[9] Yet even students of hermeneutics would agree that structuralism has an initial advantage. By explicitly restricting itself to relatively
simple models of the formal patterns and principles operating within
a text and from one text to another, structuralism can provide a useful
method for the more ambitious exploration of the different ways in
which people tell stories.

Although there is no single structuralist methodology, attempts to
find formal patterns and principles in literature may all be said to gain
their impetus from a single book, Vladimir Propp's *Morphology of the
Folktale.*[10] This seminal work begins by addressing the problem of how
to classify and describe a large body of literature, namely, a collection
of over one hundred Russian fairy tales. Dissatisfied with traditional
classifications based on "motifs" such as witches, horses, or kidnap-
pings, Propp observes that one of the most common aspects of the
folktale is that it attributes identical actions to different people, animals, and objects. These actions are the constant elements of the tale,
whereas its *dramatis personae* are the variables.

Because they are defined from the point of view of their significance for the course of action as a whole, these invariant actions are
termed "functions." A function cannot be defined apart from its place
in a particular narrative because identical actions can have very different roles in different stories. For example, a hero may build a castle
(the action) to pass a test, to protect himself, or to celebrate his marriage (the functions).

Propp isolates thirty-one consecutive functions in the fairy tale,
each of which can be fulfilled in numerous ways by diverse characters.
Each function thus constitutes a paradigm, a class of items which can
fill the same slot in the story. For example,

a	king	imprisons	the	queen's	lover
	or	or		or	or
	any	any version		any	anything
	villain	of		possessor's	precious
		disappearance			

From the point of view of structuralism, narrative can be represented
as a string of functional slots or paradigms. The significance of Propp's
work, then, is that it provides a method which allows us to describe individual stories as variations on a basic narrative or deep structure.

Not that this method is without its faults. Indeed, its flaws as well
as its virtues have been an impetus to structuralists.[11] With the limitations taken into account, the structuralist method is an attractive and

powerful way to compare narrative texts which appear very different from one another. At the least, it helps in clarifying the common narrative elements in a body of texts. When applied to scientific writing, such an approach can make us aware of a simple fact: scientists tell stories.

NARRATIVES OF HUMAN EVOLUTION

For the purposes of this paper, a structural description of narratives of human evolution will be confined to the work of a specific set of British and American scientists of the early twentieth century: Arthur Keith, Grafton Elliot Smith, Frederick Wood Jones, Henry Fairfield Osborn, and William King Gregory. All were considered authorities on the subject of human evolution, although each had his primary training in another field, the British in medicine (Keith specializing in anatomy, Elliot Smith and his student Wood Jones in neuroanatomy), and the American Osborn and his student Gregory in vertebrate paleontology. Indeed, each was highly prolific on the subject of human evolution, with numerous scientific articles and several books to his name.

Though intended for a wide audience, the books of Keith, Elliot Smith, Wood Jones, Osborn, and Gregory were also seriously read and reviewed by scientists. Rather than mere popularizations or reviews of the literature, they often contained the first clear and complete expression of a scientist's views on human evolution, and are therefore well-suited to structuralist analysis. For their authors, they often held a special place. Keith, for example, worried that his books would too quickly become "period pieces," that each new discovery would put them more out-of-date.[12] In a sense he was right: we can identify the period to which a piece of paleoanthropological writing belongs by the fossils it takes into account. Encountering Piltdown man in Keith's phylogenetic discussions confirms most strikingly his worst fears.

Comparing Keith's discussion of Piltdown to that of Osborn or Gregory raises another issue, however. So variable are the descriptions that the question is not whether we can identify their publication dates but whether we can identify Piltdown. Like the kings and queens of Propp's fairy tales, Piltdown man can play several roles in human evolution, from missing link to the first Englishman.

This ambiguity extends also to descriptions of events in human evolution. Generally speaking, paleoanthropologists have recognized four main episodes: a shift from the trees to the ground (terreustriality), the development of upright posture (bipedalism), the development of the brain, intelligence, and language (encephalization), and the development of technology, morals, and society (civilization). Which episode came first has been an important source of debate; in fact, each of the five authors under discussion here proposes a different sequence, as shown in Figure 5.1.

Such variability in ordering is reflected in the way each event is described. For example, bipedalism is clearly a primary event for Keith. By his account it was a very complicated affair: bones, muscles, lungs, diaphragm, spinal nerves, cerebral cortex, even the vasomotor mechanisms controlling blood distribution are described. None of this is mentioned by Elliot Smith, however; for him, the brain comes first so absolutely that his book *The Evolution of Man*[13] almost gives the impression that our ancestors had no bodies. As with the hero of a fairy tale who fights a battle or slays a dragon to the same end, the human ancestor as seen by Elliot Smith develops a large brain for the same reason that Keith's protohuman becomes bipedal.

From this perspective, there appears to be some underlying agreement about what happens in human evolution. In constructing their theories most paleoanthropologists seem to have in mind a similar narrative pattern, which, for present purposes, can be represented in terms of nine functions. By stringing the functions along an axis and projecting beneath it the five story sequences from Figure 5.1, it is possible to derive—again, as a heuristic—a set of narrative paradigms, which can be seen in Figure 5.2.

Like many myths, the story of human evolution often begins in a state of equilibrium (function 1, the initial situation), where we find the hero leading a relatively safe and untroubled existence, usually in the trees. Though he is still a nonhuman primate—ape, monkey, or prosimian—he is somehow different (function 2, the hero is introduced). Often he is smaller and weaker than the other animals. The idea of development from humble origins is a common feature of myth and folklore; we have only to think of Cinderella or the ugly duckling to find familiar examples. Similarly, the idea of the human ancestor as one of the most helpless and defenseless of creatures is prevalent in accounts of human evolution, including that of Darwin.[14]

Whether by choice or compulsion, the hero is eventually dislodged from his home. This change of situation, function 3, can be linked to either a change in environment or a change in the hero, for example the acquisition of a large brain (Elliot Smith) or upright posture (Keith, Wood Jones). Though the event that is chosen varies, it always precedes and in some way explains the departure of the hero. Function 4 thus marks the first turning point in the story. As suggested

Figure 5.1. Accounts of human evolution usually feature four important episodes: terrestriality, or a shift from the trees to the ground; bipedalism, or the acquisition of upright posture, encephalization, or the development of the brain, intelligence, and language; and civilization, the emergence of technology, morals, and society. The nature of these events and the order in which they are supposed to have occurred varies from one account to another. According to Darwin, human evolution began when our ancestors, leaving the trees, adopted an upright posture. Other British and American scientists, writing in the early part of this century, held varying views, with Keith and Wood Jones considering bipedalism to be the first important stage, Osborn and Gregory designating terrestriality as first, and Elliot Smith holding that the first stage was encephalization. Gregory's scheme is unusual in placing the use of tools before bipedalism.

by the term "departure," this turning point is often depicted as the beginning of a journey or adventure.[15] The sense of a journey is especially strong in the accounts of Keith and Elliot Smith, in which the hero departs by leaving the trees, but it is also conveyed by Darwin, Osborn, and Wood Jones, where bipedalism becomes the means by which the hero "walks away" or "escapes" from his former existence.[16]

Having departed, the hero moves in a new realm where he must survive a series of tests, function 5, imposed either by the environment (in the form of a harsh climate, predators, and so on) or by qualities of his own character. It is by means of these self-imposed tests, entailed by the hero's growing intelligence or upright posture—that is, his burgeoning humanity—that man seems to "make himself." The idea of self-destiny is stronger in some accounts than in others, but is present to an extent in all the narratives studied here. For it is precisely to bring out his special qualities that the hero is tested. Indeed, the tests are specifically designed for that purpose: to bring out the human in the hero.

As in folktales and myths, this transformation depends on a beneficent power or "donor." The appearance of the donor, function 6, is thus crucial to the outcome of the story. As mentioned earlier, the hero initially suffers from some deficiency, usually physical, and it is often in nonphysical form that the donor appears. This contrast between the physical weakness of the hero and the mental strength of the donor is characteristic of many accounts, including that of Darwin. The power of intelligence, defined variously as "discrimination," "plasticity," and "initiative," is also the donor in the accounts of Elliot Smith, Wood Jones, and Osborn.

In the folktale the hero acquires from the donor the use of a magical agent, perhaps a cloak, a sword, or a ring. Similarly, in human evolution the transformation of the hero, function 7, depends on special gifts provided by his intelligence: tools (Osborn), reason (Keith), a moral sense (Darwin). Still he is not finished, for, to prove his humanity, the hero must be tested again, function 8. Like his earlier ordeal, these tests are often imposed by the environment, usually the rigorous climate of Ice-Age Europe. But again, they can be self-imposed, by the very qualities of intelligence which have transformed him. Here, in the narrative of evolution, man's struggle often takes a turn away from nature and toward men. In any case, the function of these tests is to develop civilization and thus to turn the hero into a modern human.

Given that this was the objective right from the beginning of the story, the achievement of humanity may be thought to signify the

Figure 5.2. Although the order of events may vary between paleoanthropological accounts, they tend to fall into a common narrative
structure. This underlying structure can be represented by nine basic
actions or "functions," each of which can be filled in several ways.

hero's final triumph, function 9. Yet there is a final irony, as in many
myths. Again and again we hear how a hero, having accomplished
great deeds, succumbs to pride or hubris and is destroyed. In many
narratives of human evolution there is a similar sense that man may be

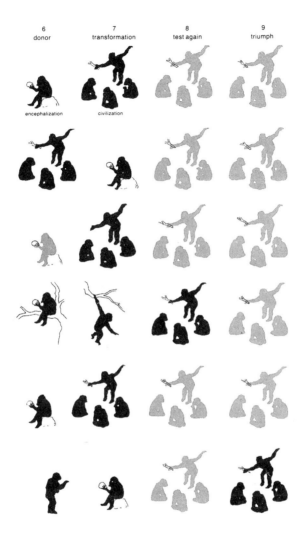

Figure 5.2. *(continued)*
(Events that are latent or continuing from a previous stage are shaded in light gray.) Such a structure can also describe traditional literary forms such as the folktale or hero myth.

doomed, that although civilization evolved as a means of protecting man from nature, it is now his greatest threat. Like many stories, this one draws to a close with the old question of how long man can be successful without succumbing to forces greater than himself.

In one of the most moving passages in *The Descent of Man*, Darwin writes: "Man may be excused for feeling some pride at having risen, though not through his own exertions, to the very summit of the organic scale; and the fact of having thus risen, instead of having been aboriginally placed there, may give him hope for a still higher destiny in the distant future."[17] For Darwin, man's hopes rest with his natural gifts, his "god-like" intellect and moral sense, and his capacity to be humane as well as human.

Oracles of human evolution have not always been so optimistic. "I know no study which is so utterly saddening as that of the evolution of humanity," writes T. H. Huxley in 1889, toward the end of his life. "Man emerges with the marks of his lowly origin strong upon him. He is a brute, only more intelligent than the other brutes, a blind prey to impulses, which as often as not lead him to destruction; a victim to endless illusions, which make his mental existence a terror and a burden, and fill his physical life with barren toil and battle."[18] Redemption was not impossible, however. For Huxley, human salvation lay in science. Though it began to grow dim in his later years, this vision of the revolutionary power of science inspired Huxley's most memorable moments, including his debate with Arnold.

CAN SCIENCE USE LITERARY THEORY?

Many have since written on the relationship between science and the humanities, including Huxley's grandson. In his essay *Literature and Science*, the novelist Aldous Huxley discusses the contribution of science to the literary conception of the nightingale. "And, what makes him sing at night? A passion for the moon, a Baudelairean love of darkness? Not at all. If he sings at intervals during the night it is because, like all the other members of his species, he has the kind of digestive system that makes him want to feed every four or five hours throughout the twenty-four." Illusions dispelled, Huxley is nevertheless optimistic. "To the twentieth-century man of letters this new information about a tradition-hallowed piece of poetic raw material is itself a piece of potentially poetic raw material. To ignore it is an act of literary cowardice. The new facts about nightingales are a challenge from which it would be pusillanimous to shrink."[19]

Thus literature may turn scientific findings into prose or poetry. But can science use literary theory in a similar way? How should scientists respond to the claim that at heart they are, like all human beings, storytellers? One option is to deny it. Fitting theories of human evolution into a common narrative framework does not prove that they are stories, and it may even be argued that theories of human evolution do not actually fit into such a framework. It is worth noting that Propp's study of the fairy tale makes explicit a set of intuitions which he believed to be shared by his readers, "even though we might not be aware of it."[20] Indeed, the success of his model has depended at least in part on the reader's familiarity with fairy tales. In an analysis of paleoanthropological writing, however, appealing to the intuitions of the reader is a rather different proposition. Not everyone will have read the authors discussed here, and, indeed, to many it will appear to run counter to common sense to suggest that scientists tell stories, let alone hero tales. To other readers such a point may appear obvious or even trivial.

But even if it is agreed that scientists tell stories, that is not the most important insight to be gained from a structural analysis. The fitting of theories into a common framework to demonstrate they can fit is not the point of structuralism. On the contrary, it is by examining in what way each theory deviates from the common model that a structuralist analysis may be most fruitful. For example, by comparing the different narrative functions of bipedalism, paleoanthropologists could clarify the ambiguity which surrounds the discussion of this stage in human evolution. Similarly, by comparing the narrative "roles" played by fossils, scientists may become more explicit about the subjective—and often highly imaginative—ways in which they reconstruct human ancestors. Specifying the underlying narrative structure of paleoanthropological accounts would thus provide a basis for comparing conceptual differences between theories.

Still it may be argued that what is true of early twentieth-century theories of human evolution is not true of other scientific theories. Darwin and Huxley saw moral meaning in the study of human evolution, as have many scientists since, and in this sense paleoanthropology could appear to be a special case. Yet this habit of vision has had adherents among other evolutionary biologists.[21] Even the most inhuman species can be viewed symbolically as victors in a struggle with nature. It does not follow, of course, that all evolutionary theories are hero myths or that they have an accessible narrative deep structure. Few theories are likely to be as suitable to structural analysis as those of human evolution. Nevertheless, literary criticism may have something to offer to disciplines other than paleoanthropology. By reminding scientists that they are interpreters of texts as well as of nature, literary criticism can help promote a new and potentially constructive self-consciousness among scientists. (It is here that a hermeneutic approach, with its emphasis on personal interpretation and multiple readings, may be most illuminating.)

With this goal in mind, let us consider three narrative premises commonly found in scientific accounts of the past. One such assumption, often taken for granted, is that history can be seen as a meaningful totality. "No vestige of a beginning, no prospect of an end"—James Hutton's famous aphorism notwithstanding, the search for origins has been a dominant theme in the historical sciences. Behind this search lies the idea that scattered events of the past can be linked with the present in an overall continuous series, a view owing much to the principle of uniformitarianism and to Hutton's conception of the earth as a system of matter in motion. In tracing histories or seeking origins, however, scientists follow a literary principle as well: that a sequence of events should be organized into an intelligible story with a beginning, a middle, and an end.

Another important though rarely stated premise is that history can be seen as a series of critical moments and transitions. Once they are organized into narrative form, individual events that had been conceived of as merely successive often gain additional significance, as "turning points," "crises," or "transitions." This is especially true of Darwinian narratives, which, owing to their emphasis on natural selection, are often cast in terms of transformation through struggle. Events are not inherently crises, however, nor are they transitions; they acquire such value only in relation to other events in a series. The problem is that once events acquire such meaning, they may become associated with moments of crisis or transition found in other kinds of narratives, such as "fall and redemption," or "empire and decline," and thus can take on connotations reaching far beyond their original contexts.

A third narrative presupposition often found in scientific interpretation is that history can be explained by arranging events into a sequence. Selecting events and arranging them sequentially involves considerations of causality as well as of chronology. The question of what happens next often cannot be answered separately from the questions of how and why it happened and how it all turns out. Thus, although scientific explanations may invoke specific laws to account for events (for example, the principles of natural selection, uniformitarianism, or genetics), such explanations must be distinguished from the explanatory effects produced simply by the sequential ordering of events. In other words, the task is to determine whether scientific explanations apparently based on natural laws are actually a function of narrative procedures.

In recognizing that scientific methods depend to an unsuspected degree on narrative procedures, we face further problems. Does working within a narrative form negate the conscious goals and rationales of doing science? This question can be rephrased as: Are narratives testable? One reply is that by specifying a temporal sequence of events, narratives can be used to predict what future investigations will disclose about those events, and thus are open to falsification. The greater the number of events in the temporal sequence, the more testable the narrative.[22] This principle may provide a rule for constructing narratives as well as for choosing among them.

A more basic problem, however, is not whether a particular sequence of events is falsifiable but whether narrative, generally speaking, is an appropriate form of scientific hypothesis. Again, we can rephrase the question to ask whether there is any way to present an evolutionary or historical account that does not involve storytelling. Trying to subvert narrative procedure, as do some contemporary fiction writers, is a possibility, though one requiring great literary ability. Given the difficulty of such an approach and the irreducibly diachronic aspect of history, a more realistic solution may be to treat narratives even more seriously than before. Rather than avoid them, scientists might use them as they are used in literature, as a means of discovery and experimentation. Treating scientific theories as fictions may even be a way of arriving at new theories. As critic Frank Kermode has observed of literary paradigms, "If we cannot break free of them, we must make sense of them."[23] In science, too, telling new stories will require skill as well as imagination.

NOTES

1. A. Huxley, *Literature and Science* (New Haven, Conn.: Leete's Island Books, 1963), p. 2.

2. E. M. Forster, *Aspects of the Novel* (New York: Harcourt Brace Jovanovich, 1954), p. 26.

3. R. Scholes, "Language, Narrative, and Anti-Narrative," *On Narrative,* ed. W. J. T. Mitchell (Chicago: University of Chicago Press, 1981), p. 207.

4. L. Mink, "Narrative Form as a Cognitive Instrument," *The Writing of History: Literary Form and Historical Understanding*, ed. H. Canary and H. Kozicki (Madison, Wisc.: University of Wisconsin Press, 1978), p. 132.

5. B. Herrnstein-Smith, "Narrative Versions, Narrative Theories," *On Narrative*, ed. Mitchell.

6. N. Eldredge and I. Tattersal, *The Myths of Human Evolution* (New York: Columbia University Press, 1982).

7. U. Margolin, "Conclusion: Literary Structuralism and Hermeneutics in

Significant Convergence," *Interpretation of Narrative*, ed. M. J. Valdes and O. J. Miller (Toronto: University of Toronto Press, 1978).

8. J. Culler, *Structural Poetics* (Ithaca, N.Y.: Cornell University Press, 1975).

9. B. Farrington, *What Darwin Really Said* (New York: Schocken Books, 1966).

10. V. Propp, *Morphology of the Folktale* (Austin, Tex.: University of Texas Press, 1925).

11. See R. Scholes, *Structuralism in Literature: An Introduction* (New Haven: Yale University Press, 1984) and Frederic Jameson, *The Prison-House of Language* (New Haven: Yale University Press, 1972).

12. A. Keith, "Man's Posture: Its Evolution and Disorders," *British Medical Journal*, vol. 1 (1923), pp. 451–54, 499–502, 545–48, 587–90, 624–26, 699–72.

13. G. E. Smith, *The Evolution of Man* (Oxford: Oxford University Press, 1924).

14. M. Landau, D. Pilbeam, and A. Richard, "Human Origins a Century After Darwin," *Bioscience*, vol. 32 (1982), pp. 507–12.

15. M. Landau, *The Anthropogenic: Paleoanthropological Writing as a Genre of Literature*, Ph.D. dissertation, Yale University, 1981.

16. C. Darwin, *The Descent of Man, and Selection in Relation to Sex* (London: John Murray, 1871); H. F. Osborn, "The Plateau Habitat of the Pro-Dawn Man," *Science*, vol. 67 (1928), pp. 570–71; and F. W. Jones, *Arboreal Man* (London: Edward Arnold, 1916).

17. Darwin, *Descent of Man*, p. 405.

18. T. E. Huxley, "Agnosticism," *Nineteenth Century*, vol. 24, 1889, pp. 169–94.

19. A. Huxley, *Literature and Science*, p. 117.

20. Propp, *Morphology*, p. 6.

21. S. J. Gould, *Hen's Teeth And Horse's Toes* (New York: W. W. Norton, 1983).

22. T. A. Goudge, *The Ascent of Life* (Toronto: University of Toronto Press, 1961).

23. F. Kermode, *The Sense of an Ending* (Oxford: Oxford University Press, 1967), p. 24.

II

Identity

The nature of selfhood has long been a high-stakes battleground in the human sciences. Narrative theorists approach personal identity in a way that challenges many well-known social, psychological, and philosophical paradigms,[1] such as those which see the self as a bundle of social roles, as the sum of conditioned responses to stimuli, as an entity passing through predictable, crisis-ridden stages of development, or as a pre-formed, ahistorical substratum possessing a more or less stable set of qualities and attributes. Who one is, from the perspective of narrative theory, is inseparable from the way one's personal history unfolds, the *telos* (if any) toward which it builds, and the way that its overall course is emplotted and interpreted by oneself and others. This process of interpretation, which is continuous though not always fully conscious,[2] necessarily utilizes narrative. It transforms life from a mere chronicle of occurrences to a series of sequentially-ordered episodes deriving meaning from their relationship to the entire story that emerges in and through them. Critics have sometimes objected that narrative accounts distort and reify the self by giving it an illusory coherence, unity, and stability. But most narrativists would agree with Stephen Crites' judgment that, in the absence of story, the self "contracts into the thinness of its personal pronoun."[3]

Within this broad consensus among narrativists in regard to personal identity, various rifts and cleavages appear. For example, narrativists disagree about whether some accounts of a person's life can be said to be truer than others and, if so, whether the truth or falsity of a narrative is a matter of consequence for the individual.[4] They disagree over whether individuals can ever be the authors of their stories in any real sense, or only the protagonists.[5] They disagree over whether stories merely "reflect" and "unfold" our inner character, or actively "shape" our identities through the normative and "behav-ioral implications" they contain.[6] They disagree, finally, over whether a story is something we have, something we create and tell, or something we are.[7]

Drawing upon a wealth of poststructuralist scholarship, the philosopher Anthony Paul Kerby argues that the self should not be understood as a meta-physical substance expressing itself in words, deeds, products, and attributes. Instead, the self is constituted pragmatically, through language: specifically, the effort to render experience coherent in story form. Although there is no in-herent psychic need to direct one's gaze upon one's life and fashion it into a narrative, certain situations activate this capacity, issuing in the creation of a character—the narrative subject, or the "I"—moving through an emplotted landscape. According to Kerby, the animating impulse behind autobiography is the individual's desire for meaning, wholeness, and unity. But the form that self-narratives take will be conditioned by culturally available myths, rituals, models, and genres, as well as by the personal narratives of one's cohorts. Kerby contends that the proliferation and fragmentation of narratives in the contemporary world, coupled with our suspicion that narratives ideologically distort reality, serve to complicate the process of crafting a narrative subject.

Building upon Kerby's argument that identity is not pre-given, David Novitz depicts the self as a "cultural object" that, at least in the West, is pro-duced in much the same way as a work of art. For better or worse, our notion of who we are as individuals is shaped by the stories we tell to make sense of the raw materials of our lives. Since personal narratives heavily influence be-havior, it is not a matter of indifference to us what narratives other people construct, or how well these narratives accord with our own. Indeed, all man-ner of psychological disturbances may develop when our narratives are put to the test and found wanting. Not surprisingly, in view of the high stakes in-volved, a "politics of identity" arises, both at the level of the individual and at the level of groups, cultures, and states, in which people do battle over narra-tives or because of narratives. Such battles often represent efforts to legitimize one particular narrative over its possible rivals by establishing its apparent "naturalness," and thereby to confirm one's self-identity and picture of reality.

Within the field of psychology, insights drawn from narrative theory have received wide use in clinical settings,[8] particularly among practitioners influ-enced by Freud and Jung. Narrative therapists have variously described their goal as eliciting patients' life stories, helping patients to construct life stories that are coherent, and encouraging patients to rewrite their life stories by in-terpreting events through a more affirmative or a less distorting lens.[9] But the narrative paradigm has also won adherents among social, cognitive, develop-mental, and depth psychologists[10] and even dream researchers.[11] It seems es-pecially attractive to psychologists inspired by the symbolic interactionism of George Herbert Mead and by the social constructionism of William James, ac-cording to which personal identity is created rather than already present and waiting to be discovered. Kenneth and Mary Gergen, in their contribution, adopt this line of reasoning. Much like Novitz and Kerby, they regard the self as a protean entity that is continually being formed and shaped through narrative. The Gergens specify three main types of self-narratives: the stability narrative, which depicts the individual's situation as unchanging over time; the progressive narrative, which emphasizes a general pattern of improvement; and the regressive narrative, which stresses a trend toward decline. None of these story lines is inherent in any particular course of events; narratives are invented, rather than discovered. Moreover, they should not be understood as solitary constructs or purely personal efforts. The social order has a large stake in people's self-narratives, insofar as they can enhance or inhibit its smooth functioning. Our micronarratives are typically "nested" within, and inseparable from,[12] cultural macronarratives that shape their possible outcomes and meanings. Inevitably, a certain degree of social negotiation is required as individuals struggle to craft personal narratives that are consistent, believable, and flattering, both in their own eyes and those of others. To avoid "ontological abandonment," individuals must work out strategies enabling their self-narratives to dovetail with those of others in their community.

Narrative has had only a marginal influence on economics[13] up until now, but it has exerted a continuing, though never quite mainstream, influence on sociology. That discipline has been dominated, over the last half century, by approaches resting upon the "delegitimation of narrative data."[14] Nevertheless, interest in "life stories" characterized the research of G. H. Mead's "Chicago school" as early as the 1920's and 1930's. Meanwhile, phenomenology (imported from Germany by Edmund Husserl's student, Alfred Schutz) and hermeneutics (as outlined by Wilhelm Dilthey and, later, Hans-Georg Gadamer) began to pose a persistent challenge to formalist and/or quantitative currents of thought in the discipline. Building on this interpretivist tradition, a "new wave" of post-positivist sociologists is rediscovering narrative.[15] A good exemplar is Gareth Williams' article, which describes the process of "narrative reconstruction" occasioned by major life-altering circumstances, such as the onset of debilitating illness.[16] When a hitherto smooth and unproblematical trajectory of life is ruptured, how do people try to explain what happened, and how do they integrate that disturbing new reality into their personal narrative? Williams recounts the narrative reconstructions of three sufferers of rheumatoid arthritis, aiming to show how the diagnosis affected their sense of themselves, their bodies, and the larger world. The diagnosis in each case injected a chaotic element into the patient's life that threatened his or her autobiographical coherence. For life to be seen as having purpose and value again, that coherence must be restored. The case studies presented by Williams illustrate three different attempts at restoring wholeness to a shattered self-narrative: one linking the illness to social injustice and workplace exploitation, another attributing it to psychic stress and the suppression-of-self inflicted upon females, and a third accepting it as part of God's mysterious grand design, a narrative order beyond the human.

In recent decades, the conviction that "the personal is political" has sensitized feminists to narrative.[17] Telling, listening to, and analyzing women's life stories has become important to both feminist political practice and feminist scholarship.[18] Narrative looms particularly large for scholars whose understanding of selfhood challenges the ghostly, abstract, desituated individualism prevalent within the liberal tradition. A key text here is Carol Gilligan's 1982 exploration of moral psychology entitled *In A Different Voice*, which celebrated "feminine" ways of thinking—understood as contextual, empathetic, and rooted in narrative—over more analytical, formalistic, and rule-governed "masculine" approaches. In their article, Barbara Rowland-Serdar and Peregrine Schwartz-Shea argue for a "revitalized" liberal feminism based upon an appreciation of the role of stories in the development of personal identity. The cultural messages internalized by women in liberal societies reinforce their relative powerlessness, dependency, and subordination, and prompt them to seek fulfillment mainly within the private sphere. To combat this destructive process of socialization, women must "reclaim their stories." They can do so by recognizing that life can be understood in narrative terms, by choosing to interpret their histories in ways that give meaning and promote liberation, and by actively directing the way that their stories proceed to unfold. As women ask themselves whether a certain action contributes to the sort of personal narrative they are trying to construct, they become more autonomous, "responding" rather than merely "reacting" to life's challenges and opportunities. This, in turn, works back upon liberal societies, helping to alter some of their most hallowed ideas and practices. In sum, Rowland-Serdar and Schwartz-Shea would endorse Annette Kolodny's assessment that "in altering the images and narrative structures through which we compose the stories of our lives, we may hope to alter the very experiences of those lives as well."[19]

NOTES

1. M. Gergen 1990; Maines 1993.

2. Polkinghorne 1988:150.

3. Crites 1986:171–72.

4. Gergen and Gergen 1984:183; Spence 1982.

5. Arendt 1958:184.

6. Hauerwas et al., 1977:29; Rosaldo 1989:129; Gergen and Gergen 1984:185.

7. Crites 1986; Ricoeur 1986:214; Brockelman 1992:94.

8. Shafer 1976; Hillman 1975, 1979, 1983; Cowley and Springen 1995; Bernstein 1990; Sacks 1987; Trad 1992; Keen 1995; Greenberg 1995.

9. Martin 1986:77; Polkinghorne 1988:178; Russell 1993; J. Smith 1992; Sacks 1987; Aftel 1995; Sarbin 1995.

10. Sarbin 1986; Wyatt 1986; Spence 1982; J. Bruner 1986, 1987, 1991; Howard 1989, 1991; Eagle 1984; Mair 1988; Cohler 1982, 1991; Freeman 1984; Eder 1988; Trad 1991; E. Keen 1986.

11. Cartwright 1992; Hall 1992; Winson 1990.

12. See also Maines 1993:24.

13. West 1993; McCloskey 1990.

14. Maines 1993:26.

15. Bertaux 1981; Richardson 1988, 1990; Lempert 1994; Maines 1992, 1993; Rosenwald and Ochberg 1992; A. Abbott 1992; Antonio 1991; F. Davis 1974; Reed 1989; Bellah et al., 1985; Viney and Bousfield 1991; Polanyi 1989; Rosie 1993; Garro 1994; Stein and Policastro 1984; E. Stone 1988; Van Maanen 1988; Young 1991.

16. Brody 1987; Kleinman 1988; Viney and Bousfield 1991. Many feminists, however, reject this view; see, for example, Moi 1985 and Butler 1990.

17. Maynes 1992; Sewell 1992.

18. West 1993; Estrich 1986; Haraway 1988; Buker 1987; McGoldrick et al. 1982; Lempert 1994; Benstock 1988; Wagner-Martin 1994; Personal Narratives Group 1989; Passerini 1992; Maynes 1992; Richardson 1988; Todd and Fisher 1988; M. Gergen 1990; Hart 1992; Davis and Kennedy 1986; Lanser 1986; Diengott 1988. Brewer (1984:1146) discusses the claim of some contemporary French feminists that "narrative discourse itself is a form that functions to perpetuate" the subordination of women.

19. Rosenwald and Ochberg 1992:141.

6

The Language of the Self

Anthony Paul Kerby

What I want to consider here is the degree to which language structure and usage must be considered if we wish to grasp the nature of that being we term the "self"—the subject that I am, and that others presumably are. Stated in its strongest terms, the view I wish to examine is not simply that the medium of our understanding of the self is language, but the further and more controversial claim that this self is constituted in and through language usage, and more particularly through self-narration.[1]

On this view the self is to be construed not as a pre-linguistic given that merely employs language, but rather as a product of language—what might be called an "implied subject" of narrative utterances. This position, in a somewhat Sartrean fashion, considers the self as a result of discursive praxis rather than as either (a) a substantial entity having ontological priority over praxis, or (b) a self with epistemological priority—an originator of meaning.

I hope to show that the above linguistic position its not as alien as one might at first think with respect to our common sense or everyday views; that it can plausibly arrive at the same conclusions as common sense but, and this is important, via a route that dispenses with the problematic and onto-theo-logically tinged baggage which common sense is prone to employ when asked to account for itself. It is, I think, fairly common to find accounts of the self falling back on theological or poetic manners of speech, both of which commonly contain either implicit or explicit metaphysical assumptions.

This is not to say that such assumptions are to be eradicated as

125

unfortunate mystifications of the subject at hand; it is rather that much can be said concerning the nature of the self that is simply bypassed or overlooked in such descriptions. We should be reminded here of William James' conclusions in *The Principles of Psychology* concerning the onto-theo-logical view. James maintains, for example, that while the existence of a soul-substance cannot be disproven it is nevertheless unnecessary for giving an account of the phenomenal nature of the self.[2] I am basically in agreement with this view.

I would also not want to say that persons are therefore reducible to what I call the self, for surely it is the person (embodied subject) who speaks and acts, and it is the person who makes statements concerning his or her self. But although I accept this common usage, it is still a question of determining what legitimates its use and what its primary content is. I hope to show that our concept of person is itself significantly dependent upon the notion of self and language that I have outlined.

My general philosophical approach, while phenomenological in inspiration, can also be seen as at once hermeneutic and semiological. Both disciplines stress the thoroughgoing importance of language for any consideration of the nature of mankind. In the hermeneutical work of Paul Ricoeur, to whom my own work is particularly indebted, there is a strong emphasis on the mediating function of language in our quest for self-interpretation and self-understanding. In his recent writings, particularly the three volumes of *Temps et Récit*, Ricoeur has especially emphasized the role of narrative language in this quest.

Semiotics, on the other hand, though less "humanistic" in its initial intentions, offers valuable insights into the seemingly inextricable unity of human beings with the realm of sign systems. An extreme example of this view can be found in Charles Sanders Peirce, who stands as a father figure for twentieth-century semiotics: "man is a sign . . . my language is the sum total of myself."[3] Modern semioticians have generally been more hesitant in their characterization of the human subject.[4] I shall have occasion to mention other figures that fall more or less within this somewhat broad category of semiotics.

I see these and other trends in postmodern philosophy, including thinkers in the Anglo-American tradition, as pointing to a much needed revision of our traditional philosophy of mind and philosophy of the human subject generally. Indeed, much of what I have to say about the self in light of language will in turn imply similar conclusions concerning the nature of mind.

The problems of mind, self, and language that I have indicated are by no means indigenous to philosophy; this is where the literary side of both hermeneutics and semiotics becomes evident. Contemporary literary criticism (especially under the influence of Derrida, Roland Barthes, and others) and contemporary literature (from Beckett to Calvino) show a marked turn toward the problematizing of the human subject. Much can be learned, I think, from a broadening of our philosophical horizon to include insights from these other disciplines.

• • •

With this general goal in mind I would like to begin, somewhat critically, with a brief look at what common sense might reply to the narrative position.

I am sure that many people might resent being reduced to the status of some narrated being, to an implied subject of discourse (your own and other's). Somehow this position offends a basic intuition we have of ourselves and other people. After all, how many of us actually set about composing an autobiography, or spend hours and days mulling over "Where do we come from? What are we? Where are we going?" It would appear that the "death of the author" so prevalent in poststructural literary criticism here finds a central place in what was traditionally called philosophy of mind: parallel to the text attaining its autonomy from the authorial consciousness, we have speech or conversation set up as the very locus for the production of a human subject and not vice versa.

I have already quoted Peirce in the above respect, but other authors are readily available. Consider Barthes, from his essay "The Death of the Authors":

> Linguistically, the author is never more than the instance writing, just as 'I' is nothing other than the instance saying 'I': language knows a 'subject', not a person, and this subject, empty outside the very enunciation which defines it, suffices to make language 'hold together', suffices, that is to say, to exhaust it.[5]

A similar view is given by the linguist Emile Benveniste: "Then, what does 'I' refer to? To something very peculiar which is exclusively linguistic . . . the basis of subjectivity is in the exercise of language."[6]

Behind these two views lies a conception of language that grants it a considerable degree of autonomy from the speaking person. It is more the case that language forms the human subject than the other way round. Language becomes the field in and through which the subject is constituted *qua* human subject. It is this strange and elusive interface of subject and language that will be the major theme of my investigations.

One might well wonder, when confronted with a narrative view of self, what has happened to the traditional (and still prevalent) manner of approaching this topic. Am I a bundle of sensations? What, if anything, forms the unity of a person? Is it the body, or memory, and what of the brain? Is mind an epiphenomenon of brain activity? And then there is the celebrated hypothetical jargon of the analytical philosophers—suppose the brain of a peasant were swapped for that of the king, etc., etc.?

Such discussions are conspicuous by their absence from much of the narrative literature (and from the modern European traditions generally), and perhaps, before we enter what has been called the "prison house of language," we have good reason to question this lack of reference to such extra-linguistic considerations. In order better to situate the narrative position, let me take my critical introduction a step further.

The self or subject is one of those types of beings of which one might say, with Augustine: "Sure I know what it is, as long as you don't ask me to explain it." Indeed, we live as though who we are today coincides with who we were yesterday, and perhaps with who we were five years ago or more. We seem to have no trouble with identity over time, for as Dilthey has said: "The knowledge of the course of one's life is as real as experience itself." Not, of course, that it is therefore easily understood, or even grasped in a comprehensive manner.

Experience comes to one not in discrete instances, but as part of an ongoing life, my life. It was Merleau-Ponty, in the *Phenomenology of Perception*, who stressed that "now" is not atomistic but variable, depending on one's perspective—it is equally "this moment," "this day," "this year," and "this life." Experience is in this sense overdetermined, it has an ever unfolding richness before our reflective grasp . . . we can never say enough about it. In more Husserlian terms we can say that it has expansive internal and external horizons. And there is a sense in which it is correct to say that we are this richness, this expanse. It is perhaps this insight that especially makes us question a narratological view of the self.

Apart from language usage, we also have a vivid pictorial and emotional life—surely, one might say, this is more ourselves than the mere story about this life. Even from the narratological viewpoint I do not think we can deny that pre-narrative experience has a "sense" to it. Emotions not only have a cognitive value, but also, and perhaps rightly, serve to define the person having them. Memories appear to bring back past moments and episodes to us, and our bodies serve as an anchor point of continued identity.

Plans, short term and long, also constitute more or less stable structures within which we act, and coupled with these are fairly regular sequences of expectations and fulfillments (or frustrations). It is such structures that give experience a sense of unity and directedness, and it is for this reason that many of us do not need to narrate ourselves explicitly. A sense of identity and of meaningful existence, no matter how vague in actual content, may be adequately filled at this pre-autobiographical stage. We are at most only part-time Montaignes. We tend to narrate ourselves only when the situation calls for it. Perhaps a dilemma calls for a reassessment of our project, or a lover asks for our history, or maybe we are in psychotherapy (and perhaps these stories will be strikingly different). If we do not narrate ourselves in order to understand who we are, it is because this second-order reflection is not necessarily required for everyday praxis.

One may, then, feel so well acquainted with oneself, and others, that one does not feel the need to raise strictly biographical questions. This is backed up by the phenomenological insight that the past is not simply behind oneself but informs or is a constitutive factor of the present. We do not need to continually reformulate or consciously remember our initial rationale or desires to continue meaningfully a present action to its conclusion; this could even be counter-productive.

Now, given what I have said so far, we might well wonder where the narrative subject fits in. If "I" am supposedly nothing but the implied subject of an on-going narration, does this not go against what I have just outlined? Perhaps not, provided that we look a little more closely into the matter.

At the level of everyday reality our narratives most certainly have little of the consistency or coherence of full-blown autobiographies or stories. In fact, I am not even sure that the majority of people have too great a desire or need to know who they are. Coupled with this is the fact that rather than living their lives with a central meaning-giving thread, many people tend to live, to borrow a term from Deleuze, a "rhizomatic" life, a life of partitions and segments: home life separated from work; appearing in different personae with different people; performing one act while thinking of another, etc., etc. We tend to live a somewhat schizophrenic existence.

It may be that a prime factor in tying these disparities together is simply the framework of objective or clock time to which they are submitted. We seem to live at the intersection of a cosmic and a subjective time, where now one and now the other gains prominence for us.[7] But there is also the fact that we categorize things and people, i.e., we use proper names as though to stabilize the person so named, to fix their essence, as it were. We say, "this is John," and thereby create a feeling of unity concerning the person so named. We say "I" not with the express intention of creating a purely narrative subject, but rather to evoke and refer substantially to a subject prior to action—"I speak," "he looks this way," and so on, without seeing the ambiguities of this move. As Nietzsche put it: "the separation of the 'deed' from the doer . . . this ancient mythology established the belief in cause and effect after it had found a firm form in the functions of language and grammar."[8] In this manner we unwittingly generate the problematic, metaphysically tinged subject which the narrative theory repudiates, a subject, Derrida has said, that is indeed implicit in our inherited logocentric languages.

Thus, when Descartes discovered his first principle, the *ego cogito*, he was led to assert thereby that the "I" spoken of existed, in some sense, prior to the pronouncement, outside the discourse (and outside the *Discourse on Method*). We end up, following Nietzsche's reasoning, with the well-known Cartesian substantial dualism. The same criticism can perhaps be applied to Husserl's transcendental ego (as some have interpreted it): rather than being some atemporal spiritual entity, we have here the product of a certain concrete philosophical enterprise (I could also say "philosophical narrative"—philosophy is after all literature), and it is to be found only in and through this and similar narratives as their correlative linguistic or signified subject. As Elizabeth Bruss has said: "Subjectivity takes shape by and in its language rather than using language as a 'vehicle' to express its own transcendent being."[9] It is the reification and mystification of this subject that a narrative or semiotic approach seeks to avoid with its emphasis on the subject of discourse, the linguistic subject.

But let us go back to the naive life of the human subject and see just how much narrating is in fact implicit in it. The literary critic Barbara Hardy offers the following thought-provoking list of narrative instances:

> We dream in narrative, daydream in narrative, remember, anticipate, hope, despair, believe, doubt, plan, revise, criticize, gossip, learn, hate, and love by narrative.[10]

Much of our emotional life, for example, is bound up with the way we narrate experiences. It would be difficult to imagine someone experiencing guilt, joy, or anxiety without having cognizance of the stories to which these are the responses. Narrative, I want to claim, is not a simple description but rather an interpretation—it is an important way in which our lives are understood.

We might turn to Charles Taylor in this latter respect.[11] Many feelings or emotions are, he says, self-referential in that they arise from a certain articulated awareness of one's life-situation. As the various imports on this linguistic level of description change so do the correlative feelings. An inflicted pain, for example, tends to be felt as painful no matter what we say, but that this leads to the further feeling of anxiety, say, or indignation toward one's assailant will very much depend upon one's articulation of the meaning the event has in its broader context. As the interpretation changes so will the attendant feeling; one could forseeably experience pity rather than indignation.

In another respect, Taylor points out that language also serves to shape our feelings as we further attempt to clarify and understand them. One's initial fascination over someone may turn, for example, into admiration as one articulates the importance the other has for oneself. And we are aware, from Freud and Sartre, how our original narratives are very often reformulated in favor of less reprehensible or less painful re-tellings; in one case we have repression, in the other bad faith.

Turning now to memories, it is not at all clear how they can serve as the basis of personal identity, or even become "personal," unless they are themselves united by a narrating reflection or, as Ricoeur would say, by emplotment, and thereby contextualized. With memory, however, this very often begins at a passive pre-linguistic level— a recollection or reverie that comes upon one like a silent movie, a picture-consciousness.

In *The Thread of Life*, Richard Wollheim factually describes recollection and imagination (what he calls "iconic mental states") in terms of a theatrical analogy using narrative as the central key. There is, he says, an internal dramatist bringing together events into sequence, an internal actor representing these events to oneself, and an internal audience affected by the iconic narrative, be it cognitively, emotionally, or otherwise. For Wollheim these are three moments or aspects necessary for an understanding of iconic states, states which are crucial to the way in which the past exercises an influence over the present . . . we draw upon them when in the present we try to predict, or anticipate, or control, the future.[12]

We find a similar tripartite division in a semiotic context, deriving from Benveniste, in the organization of discourse into three subjects:[13] the *speaking subject* or material agent of discourse; the *subject of speech* or purely linguistic subject of the discourse, designated by personal pronouns; and the *spoken subject* or subject produced through or by the discourse as a result of its effect on a receiver. Thus, for example, in the case of self-narration, of the past, the speaking subject is myself *qua* language user and repository of images (and hence conditioned and restricted by that language, by tradition, and by past experience). This narrative then sets up a subject of speech, the character signified by the pronoun "I" and involved in a certain narrated life-situation. What then makes this narrative personally historical or autobiographical is that I correlatively become the spoken subject of the narrative—just as a spectator might identify with some character in a play or film. Of course, this third aspect may be thwarted, the identification may not occur, or it occurs when in fact the subject of speech is a pure fiction, or lie, with no direct relation to one's actual memories or prior narratives. We find here a useful model for discussing certain psychological disorders relating to personal identity and personality, and also a model of reader/text interaction.

For structuralism (and its later developments into literary theory), semiotics, and narrative theory, it is the subject of speech that has been especially emphasized. Indeed, it is here that the stories we tell of ourselves appear in public space, and hence where the linguistic subject is itself constituted—not, of course, out of thin air but on the basis of the speaking subject (including the body and its habitualities). But rather than leaving this subject of speech floating in linguistic space, which is the sense one gets, say, from Benveniste, we must recognize that the third phase, the spoken subject, brings us back again to the body. It is here, I think, that common sense or the naive description of the self I initially offered is satisfied.

This third phase parallels that in William James where he says that the "spiritual self" is ascribed to the body, more particularly to the head and throat regions.[14] The body is, in my terminology, both the *site of narration* and also the normal *site of ascription* for the subject of a personal narrative. This reflexivity is particularly clear when we listen to another person's words and constantly refer the narrated subject, the subject of speech, back to the site of enunciation (the other's body). The crucial point is that this mediated reflexivity (a form of predication) yields a distinctly human body, a body with a "subjective" history, a meaning, and therefore with a "soul"—it yields a person.

We see from this account that the self is not a thing in the metaphysical sense of being a substance, residing beneath experience. It is rather, as C. S. Peirce has claimed (against Descartes), a being of semiosis, a sign or symbol functioning within a given semiotic field, the broad field of self-referring utterances.[15] And like all signs this one is also external, spoken, implying that it requires recognition by another person from a similar linguistic tradition and background—even if this other is oneself, for we are both tellers and listeners. G. H. Mead has made some interesting observations in this respect:

> I know of no other form of behavior than the linguistic in which the individual is an object to himself, and, as far as I can see, the individual is not a self in the reflective sense unless he is an object to himself. It is this fact that gives a critical importance to communication . . .[16]

It is especially important here not to confuse self-consciousness with the unmediated conscious awareness, say, of pains or organic feelings arising directly from the body. As Mead goes on to say:

> The physiological conception or theory of consciousness is by itself inadequate; it requires supplementation from the socio-psychological point of view. The taking or feeling of the attitude of the other toward yourself is what constitutes self-consciousness, and not mere organic sensations of which the individual is aware and which he experiences.[17]

We have already encountered this distinction in Taylor's recognition of self-referential feelings as opposed to those which are experienced without the mediation of interpretation. The latter experiences we may share with other animals, whereas the former are indigenous to a socio-cultural and hence linguistic being. As Taylor says, "our subject referring feelings are the basis of our understanding of what it is to be human."[18] Such feelings are also, I would claim along with Mead, the product of attaining a vision of oneself from the point of view of other persons. For example, one feels cowardly in light of those one has let down, even if this other is oneself. It would probably be true to say that without this reflective socializing break from self-embeddedness to the other, we would lack these important feelings and also what we call our humanness.

The self, then, comes to itself in and through the other—both the other person that responds to me, and the other that I become in my own self-reflection. In this respect, Lacan's mirror stage presents a prototypical example of the generation of the "I," and what is also important, as we shall see later, of an "I" which is in some sense always other. The psychoanalyst Roy Schafer carries this self-reflexivity up to the narrative level. Parallels to the above semiotic position should be clear:

> We are forever telling stories about ourselves . . . In saying that we also tell them to *ourselves,* however, we are enclosing one story within another. This is the story that there is a self to tell something to, a someone else serving as audience who is oneself or one's self.[19]

It should be clear that with respect to the subject of speech it need not be our own speaking which brings this subject into being; TV, literature, and film, for example, may play a considerable role. Here we find yet another major source of narrativization in the everyday world, ready-made narratives and formats which may influence us considerably. The spoken subject is in this regard quite a chameleon, only too eager to identify with a new subject of speech and to relinquish much of the role which it previously played.[20]

The relinquishment or distanciation of the self that can occur with, say, reading, shows very well the importance of external signs or language in self-constitution. Given that self-referential feelings arise out of an interpretive framework, to follow Taylor, it should be evident that much of the value of literary works (particularly novels) derives from their articulation and clarification of just why a character undergoes the joys and torments she or he is characterized by. Such an explication not only allows us important access to those feelings, but also provides a conceptual and pictorial framework that is usefully carried over to our personal lives with their own problems and mysteries. As Ricoeur has said:

> What would we know of love and hate, of moral feelings and, in general, of all that we call the SELF if these had not been brought to language and articulated by literature?[21]

We might also turn to Proust for a confirmation of this view:

For the space of an hour he (the novelist) sets free within us all the joys and sorrows in the world, only a few of which we should have to spend years of our actual life in getting to know, and the keenest . . . of which would never have been revealed to us because the slow course of their development stops our perception of them.[22]

In our ordinary lives, then, our self-narratives are greatly enhanced, albeit vicariously, through the narratives and categories of others, particularly those others whose life-work has been the experience and expression of life's vicissitudes and structures. And no matter to what past epoch we go there are always such narratives: myths serving to consolidate individual lives, individual selves, by providing a framework for their orientation, comprehension, and development.

In his work *Time and Narrative*, Paul Ricoeur states that

time becomes human time to the extent that it is organized after the manner of a narrative, narrative, in turn, is meaningful to the extent that it portrays the features of temporal experience.[23]

It is in narrating or in being narrated that we acquire our sense of communal historical being and situatedness—something that seems to be demanded by our very existence. Why this demand exists is that we are, as Taylor says, language animals, we are committed to meaning and articulation: ". . . we already have incorporated into our language an interpretation of what is really important."[24] Thus our unarticulated feelings, for example, are experienced by us precisely as questions to be explicated.

There is, we might say, a desire to express the sense of our unformed lives, which is also a desire for ourselves and for others. This is perhaps the basic drive behind all truly artistic expression, where it is not limited to verbal employment alone but appeals back, say, to the iconic or visual narratives of Wollheim, which may be especially addressed to the modalities of our sensuous experience of the world.

We experience in the narratives that surround us not only, as Roland Barthes has said, "the pleasure of the text," but also, following Ricoeur, the pleasure of recognition: "To make a plot is already to make the intelligible spring from the accidental, the universal from the singular, the necessary or probable from the episodic."[25] In primitive and in smaller societies such narratives have fairly fixed and precise structures, even to the point of temporally determining the individual by specific "rites of passage." Such ritualist narratives are of course still found in many religions, and also as a framework for much of our literature. For many people in the contemporary world, however, there is a considerable fragmentation of narrative and hence a problematization of individual existence; we come under the sway of various and often contradictory authorities, and also have open to us a rich but extremely varied media network. The problem today of achieving unity and coherence is not simply caused by repression, but also by proliferation and the loss of tradition this brings about.

As much of postmodern philosophy tells us, there is no Ur-text, no origin, and no unquestionable telos (even that of unification). Consciousness becomes, as for Lacan, *méconnaissance,* and the individual, already de-centered, seeks closure in vain. Narratives, we are told, when believed in, become a falsifying imposition on life, perpetrated by the ruling ideology; one that needs to be exposed for what it is, for example, via disclosing historical discontinuities in the manner of Foucault or via the anarchistic deconstructive enterprise of the Derrideans. But as the literary critic Peter Brooks has remarked: "For all the widely publicized non-narrative or anti-narrative forms of thought that are supposed to characterize our times . . . we remain more determined by narratives than we might wish to believe."[26] Even in its most extreme case, e.g., Beckett's *The Unnamable,* we find an overturning not so much of narrative activity itself as of narrative genres and traditional content. The questioning or problematizing of narrative, then, does not simply do away with narrative but serves rather to situate it, much as the questioning of the authorial subject does not eliminate the author but, as Foucault has stressed, results in overcoming naiveté by insisting upon a relocation of the authorial function.

It indeed appears that once the metaphysical view of man's essence has been deconstructed, and along with it the idealisms of teleology and utopia, then the narrative view of self leaves us prey, to use a simple phrase, to the company that we keep. But despite the above problematic and the admonishments of thinkers like Deleuze and Guattari, there is still, I believe, the legitimate though often unconscious desire for unification; it is basic to the human project for generating a meaningful co-existence with others. Postmodern fiction is especially concerned with this paradox—inscribing and then challenging humanistic certainties.

Narrative unity should be conceived not as a metaphysical goal but rather as a pragmatic one. We attempt not to discover the truth of ourselves (as though there were any such beast) but to find, to quote Wallace Stevens, "what will suffice." And that this must be continually revised is just part and parcel of the story or stories we are in. It is a question of plotting the course of our diversities, discerning, to follow Nietzsche, a style common to our various roles, a style that develops in much the same way as the body develops its motor habitualities.

In his important texts on the literary work of art, Roman Ingarden speaks of what he calls the "idea" of the work—that more or less comprehensive unity we carry away with us when our reading has made us sufficiently familiar with the text.[27] It is this "idea" which allows us to classify the work, as a whole, as of a certain type and as gravitating around a certain problematic. I think that this notion of an idea applies equally well to the lives of persons, for no matter how diverse a life may be, there tends always to be that "unity of a *Geschichte*" of which Husserl spoke in his *Cartesian Meditations*. A similar view is found in Benveniste where he says of subjectivity that it is "the psychic unity that transcends the totality of the actual experiences it assembles . . ."[28] The prior chapters of our lives inform and determine the possibilities of later ones. Not that this "idea" fully determines the closure of a life, for we well know that a text has many possible endings. It is just that, as Aristotle noted, whatever one occurs should, after the fact, be quite plausible given the prior events.

I think that we can very usefully cash this notion of idea out in terms of one's character or personality. In this respect the various views of personality types, as found say in Eduard Spranger, Jung, and also Max Scheler, tie into a narrative account of the self. It would be a failing on the part of the narratological view if it could not accommodate such important insights from its predecessors. A narrative theory of the self could be profitably developed in this direction, beginning with a further clarification of the various terms crucial to the discussion: I, self, subject, character, personality, and of course, person. Along with these the various discursive fields within which they occur: the legal, the scientific, the psychological, the religious, the everyday social realm, and the person's own interior monologue.

Before concluding, I would like to offer a few remarks on what I earlier referred to, with reference to Lacan, as the otherness of the self, for this is, I think, a central point in the whole discussion of narrative constitution and the deconstruction of metaphysics. Derrida's somewhat notorious critique of presence can be adapted in our present discussion to a deconstruction of self-presence, that is of a self transparent to itself in a fulfilling intuition, an unmediated presence to oneself. With the loss of such a self, such a presence, there are only "traces," signs that we are wont to trace back to a substantial origin, to a ghost in the machine.

If one accepts Derrida's position, as stated above, then we are committed either to the loss of self or to the self as in some sense other. Of these two positions I think only the second is a live hypothesis. As I previously mentioned, postmodern theory has not served to completely dissolve the self, it has only displaced or decentered it (while also allowing for fracture and division). The persistence of the subject is, I think, guaranteed by language itself. Writes Benveniste: "personal pronouns are never missing from among the signs of a language, no matter what its type, epoch, or region may be. A language without the expression of person cannot be imagined."[29]

As I insisted above, this linguistic subject is at one remove from the site of narration: the speaking subject with its libidinal drives, its heredity, and sedimented beliefs. If the speaking subject is a subject of semiosis, a material subject of signifying activity, then it ascends to selfhood only via the products of its activity—as the self of its own narrative enterprises. This constituted self must initially stand in the position of other, much as a cultural product stands external to its maker. But to think that this "other" is simply the expression of a prior and more ontologically basic self would be a return not only to a reductive foundationalism but also to some form of epistemological circle and narcissistically duplicating subject.

We must view language, at least where the self is concerned, as a development of experience rather than mirroring of it. To put this another way, we cannot simply infer a constitutive subject from a constituted one. Even for Husserl the ego, interestingly enough, always ends up (and perhaps begins) at the object pole as a noematic correlate, as an ego known. Parallel to its important claim that science has surreptitiously substituted a mathematicized world for the real one, Husserlian phenomenology tends to promote an equally surreptitious substitution of a subject or ego as origin meaning rather than as an effect of it.

The self as other, and I mean as subject of speech, is eminently public, occurring in writing as well as speech, and in gestures as well as the various forms of art—all of which can attain autonomy from the actual speaking/acting human subject. It is here that structuralism begins and ends, but where, as Ricoeur has stressed, hermeneutics continues, with its movement of self-appropriation and personal enrichment. This latter, however, is simply the experience of the other as intimate to oneself. This means that one may become, through participation, the spoken subject of the discourse (no matter what origin it has). As Proust has written: "In reality every reader is, while he is reading, the reader of his own self,"[30] thus backing up the hermeneutic claim that all understanding is a form of self-understanding.

We are bound to a hermeneutic reflexivity. We come to ourselves only via external signs—what Dilthey called the "objective mind." This means that the developing self cannot be adequately conceived within the framework of propositional reference, but only through a hermeneutical or productive reference. As Taylor has said:

> [Man] cannot be understood simply as an object among objects, for his life incorporates an interpretation, an expression of what cannot exist unexpressed, because the self that is to be interpreted is essentially that of a being who self-interprets.[31]

This in turn results, to borrow a phrase from David Carroll, from the "desire to solidify and unify the traces constituting experience"[32]—a desire that may never reach fulfillment.

I would not want to say that such traces, such potential meanings, need attain to a solely linguistic expression. *Qua* speaking subject we are, as I have said, a subject of semiosis, where semiosis includes and goes beyond our ordinary definition of language. This is to say that we are a living body of gestures and articulations that exist in extensive inter-action with other acting bodies and the products of semiosis—speech, texts, artworks, and meaningful action generally. Our notion of self will depend upon our reflective grasp of, and participation in, this network of social communication and praxis. Of course, we are actually traveling here in a circular motion, for the spoken subject now adds to the possibilities of the speaking subject and directs it in the generation of new significations for communication and appropriation. But this is, after all, none other than the dynamic framework within which personal development takes place.

By way of a conclusion I would like to offer a diagram outlining, though crudely, what I see to be the results of this narrative and semiological position (see Figure 6.1).

The circle of expression and participation is mediated through what I call "desire," which is founded on the state of mind (*Befindlichkeit*, to borrow a term from Heidegger) of the spoken subject (addressee). Desire activates the semiotic body into speech and gesture, thereby creating an order of signification, which is very often public. From the point of view of a receiver, the signification contains an authorial function, the "implied author" (which is usually attributed to a "speaker"), and may contain, depending on its genre, various

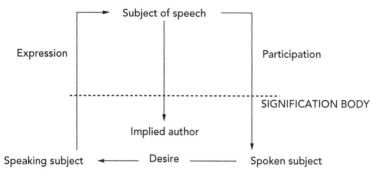

Figure 6.1. The Semiotic Subject

subjects of speech. The receiver may participate in the meaning of the signification, via a form of identification, and therefore enter into the circle vicariously. For self-narrating individuals, a reflective break is usually required if they wish to understand themselves as another might view them; otherwise the immediacy of "listening" to "speaking" carries them automatically forward in the circle to further articulations.

•   •   •

If, after all this and perhaps in spite of it, one still wishes to claim that something like an unmediated awareness of self is more or less continually given to oneself, I would say that this is either a merely formal "I," serving, no doubt, some unifying function, but an "I" that still needs to be given "substance" or made accountable for itself.[33] Or, this self is what might be termed the feeling of subjectivity, the "I am" experience. But what is this, if it is not simply the continually felt possibility or anticipation of expression—of possible speech, gesture, and action?

ACKNOWLEDGMENTS

This essay was presented as a paper at the Conference on Contemporary Issues in Phenomenology and Existentialism held at McGill University in Montreal on November 11–12, 1985.

NOTES

1. Various strains of this narrative position are to be found in contemporary philosophy, especially in French postmodernism (Ricoeur, Derrida, Foucault, Deleuze, etc.), but also in such thinkers as Alasdair MacIntyre and

Charles Taylor. The theme is also prevalent in contemporary literary theory (arising especially from Benveniste), and can also be found in psychoanalytical theory (Jacques Lacan, Roy Schafer, and Donald Spence).

2. William James, *The Principles of Psychology* (Cambridge: Harvard University Press, 1983). "My final conclusion, then, about the substantial Soul is that it explains nothing and guarantees nothing." p. 331.

3. Quoted by Umberto Eco, *A Theory of Semiotics* (Bloomington: Indiana University Press, 1976), p. 316.

4. For example, Eco, *A Theory of Semiotics*, p. 317: "What is behind, before or after, outside or *too much* inside the methodological 'subject' . . . might be tremendously important. Unfortunately it seems to me—at this stage—beyond the semiotic threshold." But see Kaja Silverman's *The Subject of Semiotics* (New York: Oxford University Press, 1983) for a significant overview of this area.

5. Roland Barthes, *Image-Music-Text*, trans. Stephen Heath (New York: Hill and Wang, 1977), p. 145.

6. Emile Benveniste, *Problems in General Linguistics,* trans. Mary Meek (Coral Gables: University of Miami Press, 1971), p. 226.

7. An important analysis of the various senses of time can be found in Alfred Schutz, "On Multiple Realities" in *Collected Papers 1: The Problem of Social Reality* (The Hague: Martinus Nijhoff, 1982).

8. Friedrich Nietzsche, *The Will To Power,* trans. Walter Kaufman (New York: Vintage Books, 1968), p. 631.

9. Elizabeth Bruss, "Eye for I: Making and Unmaking Autobiography in Film" in *Autobiography Essays Theoretical and Critical,* ed. James Olney (Princeton: Princeton University Press, 1980), p. 298.

10. Barbara Hardy, "Towards a Poetics of Fiction: An Approach through Narrative," *Novel 2* (1968):5.

11. Charles Taylor, *Human Agency and Language: Philosophical Papers,* vol. I (Cambridge: Cambridge University Press, 1985). See chap. 2, "Self-Interpreting Animals."

12. Richard Wollheim, *The Thread of Life* (Cambridge: Harvard University Press, 1984), p. 62.

13. See Silverman. *The Subject of Semiotics*, especially pp. 43ff.

14. William James, *The Principles of Psychology* (Cambridge: Harvard University Press, 1983). See chap. X, "The Consciousness of Self."

15. For a useful account of Peirce's position, see Milton Singer, *Man's Glassy Essence* (Bloomington: Indiana University Press, 1984).

16. George Herbert Mead, *Mind, Self, and Society* (Chicago: The University of Chicago Press, 1962), p. 142.

17. Ibid., pp. 171–72.

18. Taylor, *Human Agency and Language*, p. 76.

19. Roy Schafer, "Narration in the Psychoanalytical Dialogue" in *On Narrative*, ed. W. J. T. Mitchell (Chicago: University of Chicago Press, 1981), p. 31. Such role playing is of course particularly evident in a theatrical context where the actor must assume the guise and habits of different characters. This mimetic behavior can be viewed as an amplification of what normally occurs in our lives. For a consideration of this theme see Bruce Wilshire's *Role Playing and Identity: The Limits of Theatre as Metaphor* (Bloomington: Indiana University Press, 1982).

21. Paul Ricoeur, *Hermeneutics and the Human Sciences* (Cambridge: Cambridge University Press, 1983), p. 143.

22. Marcel Proust, *Remembrance of Things Past, vol. I: Swann's Way,* trans. Scott Moncrieff (New York: Random House, 1934), p. 65.

23. Paul Ricoeur, *Time and Narrative,* trans. K. McLaughlin and D. Pellauer (Chicago: The University of Chicago Press, 1984), p. 3.

24. Taylor, *Human Agency and Language*, p. 74.

25. Ricoeur, *Time and Narrative*, p. 41.

26. Peter Brooks, *Reading for the Plot: Design and Intention in Narrative* (New York: Vintage Books, 1985), p. 7.

27. Roman Ingarden, *The Literary Works of Art: An Investigation on the Borderlines of Ontology, Logic, and Theory of Literature,* trans. George Grabowicz (Evanston: Northwestern University Press, 1973). See especially chap. 10.

28. Benveniste, *Problems in General Linguistics*, p. 221.

29. Ibid. p. 225.

30. Proust, *Remembrance of Things Past, vol. II*, pp. 1031–32.

31. Taylor, *Human Agency and Language*, p. 75.

32. David Carroll, *The Subject in Question: The Languages of Theory and the Strategies of Fiction* (Chicago: The University of Chicago Press, 1982), p. 116.

33. I have no quarrel with Kant that the "I" is more or less continually given, and must always be possible; it is when we go beyond this formalism that the problems I have tried to deal with begin to arise.

7

Art, Narrative, and Human Nature

David Novitz

Whenever we speak about ourselves, of the sort of people that we and others are, we lapse almost inadvertently into the idiom of both the visual and the literary arts. It is not just that we have "images," "pictures," and "views" of ourselves which are more or less "balanced," "colorful," or "unified," but that we also have "stories and "narratives" to tell about our lives which both shape and convey our sense of self.

There is something curious about the fact that the language of art finds such a ready niche in discussions about ourselves. After all, it is not as if we are works of art; and yet it seems that there is no other nonartistic phenomenon which provides such a comfortable haven for the idiom of the literary and the visual arts. It is here, too, that the language of art most obviously enters the arena of political skullduggery. We nod conspiratorially when we learn that there is another and very different "story" to be told about an acquaintance; and we spend much time trying to displace the "images" and "pictures" that some people project of themselves.

This invites a range of questions, for it suggests that the arts are more intimately connected with one's sense of self, one's individual identity, than we might have supposed.[1] It suggests, too, that the arts play a political, perhaps even a subversive, role in our lives. My aim in this article is to explore these claims, and in so doing to defend the view not just that the literary and visual arts sometimes influence our sense of self, and with it our idea of human nature, but also—and more significantly—that our individual identities and ideals of personhood are constructs produced in much the way that works of art are produced.

Furthermore, I shall argue that, like works of art in general, the identities that we assume are politically significant and fall prey to all manner of political intrigue.

I

The interest that you and others have in the sort of person I am is, for the most part, a moral interest. You want, among other things, to know how I have behaved in the past and how I am likely to behave in the future. If, in your opinion, I am not the sort of person I ought to be, and if, still worse, I do not appear to see myself for what I am, you may attempt to modify my sense of self. This is what my mother does, when in the Platonic and Judeo-Christian tradition, she exhorts me to "take a good look at yourself." But such an exhortation is problematic, for it is not at all clear what I could hope to learn about the sort of person that I am just by looking at myself.

What, then, would I see were I to follow my mother's advice? This, of course, is not a question which demands recourse to mirrors. Nor is it a question about the size of my neck or my ample girth. It is, as I have said, a question about the sort of person I am, about my nature as a human being. It does not explicitly invite a general account of human nature, although in discussing the sort of answer that such a question deserves, we will, I believe, learn a good deal about the concept of human nature.

A first and obvious point to make in answering the question is that when I take a good look at myself, I do not *see* very much at all. Nor do I really *look* at myself. The reason is obvious. There is more to my person than the body I stand up in. I am not talking of souls, but I am talking, among other things, of my past actions, aspirations, jealousies, fears, beliefs, expectations, values, knowledge, neuroses, and obsessions. These, we are inclined to say, are just the sorts of considerations that we take into account when we want to know, say, what sort of person Mikhail Gorbachev is. Presumably then, they are the sorts of considerations which will have to be taken into account when I want to know what sort of a person I am. So, whatever else I do when I take a good look at myself, I will have to consider a goodly number of those actions, passions, aspirations, psychological states, and the rest that can properly be attributed to me.

These are not things that the eye can discern. The vast majority of my actions and passions are long since past; my beliefs, although indirectly visible, have evaporated or else changed with time; my values have shifted; my neuroses have waxed and waned almost with the phases of the moon. Even if I could capture this with a hypothetical inner eye, through some sort of wide-angle introspection which gathers together in one broad sweep images of all these items, I should still have to make sense of this bewildering array of bits and pieces before I could claim to know what sort of person I am. All that wide-angle introspection would achieve, if such a thing were possible, would be knowledge of a motley collection of disconnected items; and a collection of this sort cannot of itself afford a coherent idea of one's personhood.

But, of course, wide-angle introspection never occurs. It is not as if all of my past is readily found neatly encoded in pictorial form against the back wall of my mind. If I really do look, using the only eyes that I have, I see some of the things in front of me. The ideal, therefore, of discovering the "objective truth" about myself through introspection is simply unattainable. When in this context I am described as "introspecting," I do little other than try to remember and recall the sorts of things that I have done and felt. The process is an active one, and not as empiricists would have, the passive, visual registering of our inner states. What we recall depends in large measure on the sorts of questions we ask, and these, in turn, depend on our purposes in asking them: purposes which do not spring out of thin air, but are, in their turn, shaped by a variety of social influences.

It is clear from this that however else we explain the notion of a self-image, we cannot construe it as a purely visual image: a static "snapshot," passively imprinted on the mind. True enough, my identity as an individual may in part be shaped by certain visual images (including, of course, actual snapshots in the family album), but these do not *tell* me what sort of person I am. Like pictures, visual images have to be used in certain ways if they are to tell us something specific about a subject, for, as I have argued elsewhere, we need to distinguish what a picture depicts or is of, from the illocutionary acts which it is, or can be, used to perform.[2] On my view, it is only in specific contexts, and only if they are used towards a certain communicative end, that pictures or visual images *tell* us anything specific.

II

The many facts that I recall about myself will have to be organized in one way or another before they can help me understand what sort of person I am. Put differently, one could say that I will have to mold the discrete events of my life into something more pregnant than annals or a chronicle or a list of past events. More specifically, I will need to organize in a sequential, developmental, and meaningful way what I take to be the brute data of my life. To do this is just to construct a narrative or a story about my life; a story which, although nonfictional, is in some measure the product of certain creative or fanciful imaginings. For although my story purports to be about certain real-life events, and so is nonfictional, the way in which I relate and organize my memories of these events, and what I treat as marginal or central to my life, can be more or less imaginative.

The stories that people tell about their lives are of considerable importance to us, for there is an intimate connection between the ways in which people construe themselves and the ways in which they are likely to behave. To take but one example, we all know that it is never enough merely to tell ourselves and others of our lives of kindness and bravery if we do not also contrive *to show* that we are worthy of these epithets. And this must involve behaving in certain ways. Because of this, it is tempting to construe the lives we lead on a dramatic model . . . as if our life-narratives furnish the scripts which are to be enacted on "the stage of life." This imagery is familiar enough, and has been around since well before Shakespeare. It is to be found in Machiavelli's *The Prince,* and much more recently in Freud, G. H. Mead, Erving Goffman, and Richard Wollheim.[3] Although I do not propose to explore these versions of the model here, in one way or another they all suggest that how we view and think of ourselves strongly influences our behavior.[4] It is because of this that we are often concerned enough to challenge the stories that people tell about themselves. We urge them to think again, and in giving them reasons for doing so, we attempt to subvert their sense of self. There is an intricate political process at work here: what I should like to call the politics of narrative identity whereby we assert and maintain our own interests not just by advancing a particular view of ourselves, but by undermining the views that others advance of themselves. Stories and counter-stories are told; history is written, subverted, and rewritten. And in this game of strategy, those who have the last word also have considerable power over those who do not.

But do we really need to tell stories about ourselves, or about episodes in our lives, in order to develop a coherent sense of self? It has recently become fashionable to suppose that the self is and has to be a narrative construct, but very little is ever done to argue the case.[5] Why, for instance, shouldn't I develop my sense of self, not by telling a story, but by pointing to the causal connections between certain events in my life? The story form, after all, can distort what actually happened, the order and the importance of what happened, so that what we need (someone might argue) is something less imaginative, less fanciful, more descriptive and more accurate, if I am really to know what sort of person I am.

What this sort of objection overlooks is the fact that reports of causal sequences, like annals, lists, and photographs, do not of themselves afford special significance to any of the events in our lives. They fail to tell us which events are central and formative, and which marginal to the persons we are. Since I can have a coherent, non-fragmented sense of self only if I regard some of the events in, and facts about, my life as more prominent than others, and since reports of causal sequences, like lists or annals, do not afford the requisite prominence to any particular fact or event, they cannot furnish me with a unified sense of self. It is left to narrative to do the job, for it is the only variety of discourse which selectively mentions real or imaginary events, orders them in a developmental or sequential way (the plot), so that the whole discourse (and the sequence of events which it mentions) eventually acquires a significance, usually a moral significance, from the way in which its parts are related to one another (closure). It is because of this that narrative alone gives us the freedom to select and arrange the events of our lives in ways which afford them what we believe to be their proper significance. Without narrative, there simply is no way of emphasizing some events, marginalizing others, *and* at the same time relating all in a significant whole. Certainly, if one were to chronicle the recalled events of one's life, some would achieve greater significance than others, but because chronicles do not, by definition, achieve closure, it would not be possible to impart significance to one's life as a whole. In short, it would not be possible to extract from a chronicle, or any variety of discourse other than narrative, a coherent and unified sense of self.

Part of our fascination with narrative is its flexibility. It can take indefinitely many forms, and so allows its authors considerable scope for their own inventiveness. There are, in consequence, many literary devices which authors invent and introduce into their texts in order to heighten the effect of their stories: devices which make their narratives altogether more plausible, accessible, interesting, and exciting. It is well known, for instance, that a narrative enjoys its own so-called "narrative time," which has to be distinguished from the real time within which the narrative is told. By manipulating narrative time, one can amplify both the affective and cognitive impact of the story. One can "telescope" time, thereby bringing salient events in the narrative "closer together" and forcing them on the attention of an audience. One can make events appear timeless and universally true, or one can so stretch time that each tiny event within the narrative assumes an importance it would otherwise have lacked. Still more, through flashbacks and what are now called "foreflashes,"[6] the manipulation of time allows the narrator an omniscience denied to ordinary mortals. But to see this is only to hint at the powers of narrative. It is not at all to explain how it exercises them. What it does help explain is the attractiveness of the narrative form to those of us who wish to see and present ourselves favorably.

There is another reason why we find life-narrative attractive. It is this. The comprehension of narratives invariably demands the imaginative participation of those who attend to them. While I am not sure that David Hume is right when he says that human beings are naturally empathic, it does seem clear that most people desire and need the empathy of others. Stories about ourselves, in which we figure as central subjects, and to which others attend imaginatively, invite the sort of empathy we most desire.[7]

So, despite the objections, there really are compelling reasons for reverting to life-narratives, to stories about myself, in order to explain the sort of person I am. Chief among these, of course, is the fact that narrative plays an essential role in the development of a unified individual identity. I do not, of course, wish to suggest that we all enjoy such an identity. We do not. Most of us have, at best, a fragmented and changing view of self. We see ourselves successively in different, sometimes incompatible, ways, and we do so, on my view, because we are inclined to tell more than one story about ourselves. This, however, does nothing to affect the fact that narrative is integrally involved in our search for a coherent self-image.

The demand for such coherence seems to me to be historically and culturally specific, and is by no means a feature of all societies. It certainly is a feature of the society that we inhabit, and seems to have taken root in the Greek, Jewish, and Christian injunction to "know thyself." The day of judgment, it would seem, looms large in our lives, and demands a single, unified view of self: a flawless whole which determines our direction in the afterlife. It is no part of my purpose to discuss the desirability of this demand, or of our attempts, in its wake, to develop a unified or coherent view of self. What is clear, however, is that we find it difficult to develop such a view, and that the demand for it may itself be psychologically damaging. For all that, though, it seems plain that the demand for a single and unified view of self is frequently encountered, and it seems plain, too, that in order to develop it, we are forced to rely on plain storytelling: on narrative. For, as we have already seen, the stories that we tell about ourselves impart meaning, purpose, and formal unity to our lives; they give them some or other structure or point (what I have called "closure"). The point might, indeed, be negative. It could turn out, according to the story I tell, that mine is a wasted life; but it could equally turn out that mine is a life of charity and service.

For the most part, people have little difficulty in constructing and telling stories about themselves. They may be too modest or too shy to do so, but if pressed, most people can tell you, in incipient story form, what they think of themselves. It might simply be a statement of the form "I'm a loser." This, of course, is an abridged version of a much longer story which, if told, would relate recalled events in sad and self-diminishing ways. People seldom spell these stories out at length. The self-absorbed and the articulate do, but for the most part our life-narratives are reduced to pat formulae in terms of which we habitually see ourselves. The important point, though, is that people do seem, in ways yet to be specified, to carry with them a view, most often several incompatible views, of themselves: organizational principles, or, as I shall call them, narrative structures according to which, given the inclination, they can construct a full-fledged narrative about themselves. Of course, it is not as if these people will normally settle down for an evening and tell you the complete story of their lives. Most often, they tell stories about parts of, or events in, their lives, and they do so in ways which afford insight into their character.

That we all entertain such narratives, and that they shape our view of self, emerges most clearly when we reflect on the phenomenon sometimes referred to as agent-regret.[8] As a young student at Oxford, Alfred misphrased a question during a seminar at Merton Street and was guilty of a minor howler. There were ripples of laughter, but the drift of the question was grasped easily enough, and an answer given. Now, some decades later, Alfred still feels profound discomfort when he recalls the event. He regrets the howler, and he continues to regret it even though no harm came of it. Alfred was not thought the worse because of it; nor was he declared unemployable. The people present have long since forgotten his question, the howler, and the laughter it occasioned. In fact, Alfred is now a famous and well-paid philosopher. But the howler still continues to rankle, and he regrets it now almost as much as he did then. Why should this be?

On my view, Alfred regrets it because the error is not part of the story he would like to be able to tell of himself: it sits uneasily with his self-image. Alfred is disposed to think of himself as an articulate, intelligent, and fluent philosopher: a stimulating and penetrating thinker to whom people like to listen. Howlers, no matter how minor, have no place in this story. His regret, it seems, is not a moral, but an aesthetic response to what he now regards as a blemished image, a sullied narrative.

One could, of course, say that Alfred's pride was bruised, and hope to explain his regret in this way. If so, it is thought, there would be no need to appeal to narrative identity and the like in explaining this instance of agent-regret. But appeals to pride explain too little, for it is not clear how we are meant to account for human pride. On my view, pride must itself be explained in terms of the stories we prefer to tell about ourselves—in terms, that is, of the ways in which we select and organize the recalled events of our lives and to think of ourselves. It is the desire to protect and retain a particular view of myself—a view which is bred of the life-narrative or history or story I tell of myself—which best helps explain the regrets, stubbornness, and arrogance so characteristic of human pride.

It would seem from this that in one form or another we all carry with us narratives which help furnish us with ways of thinking about ourselves. People are disposed to think of themselves as chaste, pious, devout, humble, and all that this implies; and they would prefer to select and organize the events of their past, and so tell the stories either of their lives, or of episodes and stages in their lives, in terms of these structures.

It is wrong, of course, to treat these ways of thinking about ourselves, these character sketches, as full-blown narratives. They clearly are not. They do, however, express an integral part of narrative. They are narrative structures, for they are the expression of the organizational principles around which detailed narratives can be constructed. They are abstract and truncated narratives. Still more, as I have said, they are narratives of which we are not constantly aware. It is not as if they are perpetually before the mind's eye or ear, bouncing around in one's head, so to speak. Rather, they should be thought of as dispositions to select, relate, and think of the events of one's life in specific ways. This is not to say that we cannot articulate these principles or the detailed stories which they subtend. We can and we do.

III

Our narrative identities are neither God-given nor innate, but are painstakingly acquired as we grow, develop, and interact with the people around us. Our identities may, of course, be based on past experience, but such experience, we have seen, is too complicated, amorphous and anomalous (even if accurately recalled) to admit of a coherent self-image. Most often, I have stressed, life-narratives, and the identities to which they give rise, are imaginative constructs which people adopt, and in terms of which they select and order past events in their lives. However, not all of these constructs are the products of the individual's own imaginings. They may be borrowed from other sources; most obviously, I suppose, from television, the cinema, theatre, and novels. Sometimes, as we shall see, they are not merely borrowed but actively imposed on us by others.

More important for the moment, however, is the fact that the view that we take of ourselves, our narrative identity, is the source of our self-esteem. Those who have reasonably high levels of self-esteem, perhaps because they are disposed to think of themselves as efficient or intelligent, will tend to be guided both in what they attempt, and, as a result, in what they achieve, by their sense of self. They are more likely to undertake demanding tasks than those who suffer an impoverished identity. In this important sense, one's self-image or identity is action-guiding. As a result, any construal of one's actions which challenges one's sense of self, which suggests, say, that one is less than efficient or intelligent, has the potential to inhibit one's behavior and will be the cause of some consternation. People whose self-image is challenged in this way will generally defend themselves against such accusations—either by regarding, say, their inefficiency as momentary and untypical, or else by denying the charge altogether and by attempting to explain it away.

People are generally obliged, for reasons of their own psychological well being, to defend themselves in this way. For any successful attack on an individual's self-image will induce a crisis of confidence, a measure of trauma, depression, and, on occasions, neurosis. It is in order to avoid such crises in our lives and the dislocations and upheavals that they produce, that we protect ourselves by clinging stubbornly to our identity even at the cost of denying the obvious. Sometimes, moreover, rather than risk this sort of upset, we embrace life-narratives which seriously underestimate our capacities and capabilities, leaving us with very little to live up to. These observations, of course, have more to do with empirical psychology than they have to do with traditional philosophy.

The fact that life-narratives tend to guide and regulate our behavior is of the greatest social significance. They are responsible not only for many of the achievements in our society, but also for the many underachievers. The notion of narrative identity also helps explain why people are often immune to reason and rational argument. Individuals

are sometimes confronted by sound arguments which tend to undermine important aspects of their self-image, and so pose the threat of
personal confusion, upheaval, and crisis. Thus, for instance, people
who think of themselves as devout, pious, and obedient, and who
think favorably of themselves on this account, will not generally be
persuaded by an argument—no matter how strong it is—which
demonstrates the incoherence of the traditional concept of God. For
whatever else our narrative identity does, it helps determine what we
consider to be important. Hence a few contradictions and non se-
quiturs may be considered utterly inconsequential by those who see
themselves as primarily devout and obedient theists. On my view,
only those people who think of themselves as fundamentally rational
will take seriously the accusation of irrationality. To accuse such people of intellectual pride is to attack their individual identity or self-
image. It is an attempt to replace it with a self-image more conducive
to the interests of those who are embarrassed by rational argument,
and who regard it as a threat to their identity.

By now it should be clear that narrative identities are of crucial importance not just for the individuals who bear them, but also for the
societies in which they live. How we see ourselves affects what we regard as important, and this, in turn, must affect how we behave towards others. This, as I said earlier, is why the view that you take of
yourself becomes of profound concern to me. I simply cannot afford,
for reasons of my own well being and safety, to allow you to think of
yourself as ruthless, devious, and violent; as powerless or deprived
relative to myself; or as belonging to a race, religion, or civilization superior to my own. If you do think of yourself in any of these ways, and
if I am sufficiently perturbed by this, I will attempt to subvert your
self-image and to replace it with an identity more conducive both to
my interests and to what I perceive as the interests of the society as a
whole.

The process is quintessentially political and occurs at a variety of
levels. At one level it involves a straightforward interchange between
individuals. People try, in ways Goffmanesque, to project particular
views or impressions of themselves. They see themselves, and project
themselves, as efficient, friendly, and so on; and through a variety of
subtle and complex strategies (which involve both *telling* and *showing*)
they may successfully impart this view of themselves to others. If,
however, one is threatened by a particular narrative identity, the political process takes a different turn, and, as we have just seen, attempts
are made to undermine and replace the projected identity. This can

occur in different ways. It might involve persuading some third party that a certain person should not be "taken at face value" and that there is a "different story to be told." Alternatively, it could involve persuading the people themselves that their self-images, their narrative identities, are inaccurate, and that they should see themselves differently.

There is a second, macroscopic, level at which the politics of identity is pursued. The State invariably assumes a proprietorial interest in our individual identities, and is concerned to see them develop in certain ways rather than others. Schools, the media, and religion are only some of the institutions which are used to convey narrative structures in terms of which we are encouraged to see ourselves. They offer ideals of personhood—whether in history lessons, deportment manuals, or popular magazines. Still more, there are Boards of Censors appointed by the State which discourage or proscribe certain narratives: which ban films that portray sadomasochism as a virtue, or that denigrate certain racial or religious groups. They do this precisely because those who are dominant within the State often wish to prevent people from adopting damaging or potentially dangerous narrative identities. They neither want people to be cruel, nor (one hopes) do they want them to feel inferior on account of their race or religion.

Not every State is equally magnanimous, and history tells of those which have fostered entirely pernicious narrative identities. Germans and white South Africans have at various times been encouraged to see themselves as racially superior and to interpret their lives and their rights accordingly. To challenge such narrative structures is, of course, to act politically; so that the politics of narrative identity can easily reach into the core of State politics. It can alter relations of production within the State by altering the passive acquiescence of those who are exploited by it. It seems correct to say that the Black Consciousness movement of the 1970s recognized a good deal of this, and initiated its struggle for liberation at the level of narrative identity.

IV

The message here is not just that our narrative identities are intimately involved in the political process, but also that the facts of my personal existence, the brute data of my life, do not themselves tell, or compel us to tell, any *one* story about myself. In the process of political self-definition it is often in my interest to suggest that the facts of my life "speak for themselves"; that what I say reflects, is shaped and constrained by, what actually happened; that I am not simply telling a story. As Hayden White points out, the narrative element of my personal history is an embarrassment, and I suppress it by pretending that the events of my life cohere in a way which tells their own story.[9] Alternatively, when the embarrassment is overwhelming and the narrative element unmistakable, I will explicitly acknowledge and so defuse it by saying things like: "Of course, this is just *my* version of what happened," or "I *think* I'm being accurate," or "This is how *I* see it." The story takes a different twist at this point, for I now tell it in a way which is designed to demonstrate the narrator's sincerity.

We have seen, of course, that the views that we take of ourselves are constructs, and are invented rather than discovered. At first sight it would seem that we invent these ourselves. After all, we know that we often dream about the sort of people we would like to be: rich, glamorous, dashing, brave, and so on. But individuals do not simply pluck these visions out of the air. They are suggested to us in many different ways by the societies in which we live. Our parents, teachers, priests, and friends all play a role in our socialization, and in so doing they impart values and instill ideals. It is in the light of these that we prefer to imagine ourselves as ruthless and tough rather than sensitive and caring, fearless rather than circumspect. This process of suggestion is also facilitated by the novels we read, and by the films and plays we see. In the light of these we sometimes imagine ourselves in certain ways: as a latter-day Robin Hood, as a sagacious Mr. Knightley, as a soulful and unhappy Maggie Tulliver.[10]

Most often, however, because we already subscribe to certain socially instilled ideals and values, we creatively combine aspects of real and fictional people with selected facts about our past, and in so doing create our narrative identities. But this is not always the case. At times our identities are given to us, and we become the beneficiaries, victims, or playthings of the narratives that others create and push in our direction. J. M. Synge's *The Playboy of the Western World* provides a fictional example of this phenomenon, but it occurs as well among actual people in the world that we inhabit. People do have greatness thrust upon them. In being treated as folk heroes, they think of themselves as folk heroes, arrange the details of their lives, and begin to act accordingly. They internalize the role of judge, doctor, academic, or priest, and begin to think of themselves in the sometimes sterile ways suggested by the institutions to which they belong.

For the most part, whenever people wish to have their narrative identities praised and taken seriously, they try to project them normatively. In such a case, it is not just that I want you to accept the image that I project of myself as truthful and worthwhile, but that I want this image to be accepted as a standard in terms of which to judge others and interpret their behavior. I do not only create a story about myself, but I try to ensure that the story either is, or will become, part of the canon of stories in terms of which to assess other human beings. If, as happened in the sixties, I were to think of myself as a child of peace, a flower child, and if this turns out to be socially unacceptable, I will try in sundry ways—perhaps by forming group movements and by developing ideological arguments and publishing them—to get others to see my identity as desirable. And this, of course, is precisely what happened not only in the sixties, but among those in the eighties who sought to legitimize a homosexual identity and formed the Gay Pride Movement.

It seems clear from this that we can change people's ideas about what constitutes a normal, decent, or natural human being by bringing them to accept and respect the stories we tell about ourselves. Consequently, what we think of as natural in human beings becomes highly variable, depending more on social values and the consequent acceptability of certain narrative identities than on the brute facts and physical substance of our lives.

It is not just that we can change one another's ideas about what is natural in human behavior, but that in changing these ideas we can change our behavior. Human beings are notoriously suggestible and can be brought to think of themselves and construe their lives in indefinitely many ways. This is important because, as I have stressed, people will be kind and charitable if they can be brought to think of themselves as kind and charitable. Alternatively, they will be aggressive and competitive if they are made to think of themselves in these ways. In the light of this, it seems that to say of human beings that they are *naturally* kind, *naturally* competitive, or *naturally* heterosexual is to try to lend normative status or "legitimacy" to particular ways of construing our lives, thereby encouraging certain forms of behavior. We do so by appealing (sometimes tacitly, sometimes explicitly) to the authority of science, attempting thereby to reify our narrative constructions not just by calling them "natural" but by trying to locate their source in our biology.

It is not just that we can change people's ideas about what constitutes a proper, decent, normal, and natural human being by "selling" particular narratives about ourselves, but it is also true that these narratives (or narrative structures) acquire their legitimacy and normative role from the society that accepts them. For the most part, of course, such acceptance will depend on prevailing notions of what is or is not true. If the narrative in question is not considered true, it will usually be rejected. But this need not be the case, for there are societies and subcultures (such as gangs) in which people are encouraged to adopt narrative identities which are known not to fit the facts of their lives. This, of course, suggests that it is the social acceptability of a narrative identity, and not the truth of the narrative that constitutes it, that determines what we regard as natural, worthy, or excellent in human behavior. What is praised as noble or as natural in one society may be condemned as brutal or unnatural in another. There is nothing new about this; nor, I think, need it introduce a moral relativism.

Although I cannot defend the claim here, I do want to insist that there are facts of the matter, and that nonfictional life-narratives may be shown to be true or false by appeal to them. It is particularly important to see that the facts in terms of which we assess a given life-narrative may be known independently of any specific history or story. It seems plain that I can learn that people desire food or that a motor accident occurred at 5:10 P.M. on 25 June, without believing or inventing a specific story which somehow informs my experience. If I am right there is no good reason for denying the existence of so-called prenarrative facts, or for insisting (in a way reminiscent of the post-structuralists) that all experience and knowledge must be mediated by, or derived from, narrative.[11] Not all explanations are narratives, nor are all theories, descriptions, lists, annals, or chronicles. To suppose that they are, or to suppose that all experience is bred of narrative, is to so stretch the meaning of this word as to render it blunt and all but useless. To inform someone of a causal sequence (that food nourishes, or that people deprived of water must die of dehydration) is not to tell a *story* in anything but the most extended sense of this word. Narrative identities, as I have explained them, involve stories in a much fuller, more literary, sense, and can be assessed by appeal to the facts of a particular life.

V

I began by observing how easily the idiom of the literary and visual arts filters into our talk about people—more particularly into our talk about the sorts of people that we and others are and ought to be. This, I said, deserves some sort of explanation, for people are not works of art and it is curious that the language of art should apply so readily to them. So far, however, I have tried only to show that we do not discover our individual identities through some sort of inner observation, but that they are narrative constructions which are of considerable importance both for the individuals who bear them and for the societies in which they live. I have stressed as well that having created or adopted narrative structures in terms of which to construe ourselves, we try, through dramatic projection, not just to get others to see ourselves as we would be seen, but to get them to treat our narrative structures and individual identities as norms in terms of which to judge and understand other human beings.

It is time to explain why the language of art applies so readily and literally to our attempts to develop individual identities and ideals of personhood. The reasons, I believe, are plain enough, for by now it should be clear that there are very strong resemblances between our individual identities—how we come by, foster, and legitimize them; and works of art—how we produce, criticize and secure acceptance for them. Like narrative identities, works of art are not discovered, but invented; they are the product of an artist's creative efforts in a particular social context. We know, too, that, as with our individual identities and ideals of parenthood, works of art do not always find acceptance and favor within the community in which they are produced. There are many reasons for this. The most obvious of these is that the works run counter to, and challenge, prevailing artistic standards. But in so doing, of course, they also challenge individual and group interests within the art world, for the very act of ignoring the established canon and all the standards and artistic myths which it subtends, threatens the status of its advocates and apologists. The criticism of works of art thus carries with it the same political dynamics and intrigue that we have found in the criticism of people and ideals of personhood that they favor or project. And just as individual identities or ideals of personhood have broader ramifications within the larger society, so too, of course, do works of art; so that the State often assumes an interest in, and a measure of control over, the production and dissemination of both the popular and the so-called high arts.

These similarities are neither fortuitous nor merely superficial. What we are describing in both cases is the production of cultural objects: objects produced in a social setting in order to meet specific human needs and desires, but which, through the very fact of their production, may prevent the satisfaction of other needs and desires. There is, in consequence, a perceived need on the part of the members of any society to regulate the production of such objects. One might say that they are produced within a certain social framework which attempts always to preserve specific values and interests at the expense of others—although, of course, it will not always be successful in its endeavor to do so. Whenever it fails, new values achieve a degree of prominence, and different interests are served.

This is true of the production of all cultural objects, from ashtrays to insecticides and works of art. However, the similarity between the production of the literary and visual arts on the one hand, and our individual identities and ideals of personhood on the other, is especially strong since, as we have seen, both frequently contain an imaginatively produced narrative core. Still more, both works of art and narrative identities are constructed with a possible audience in mind—in the hope, in each case, of achieving broadly similar effects. For just as we want our narrative identities to be acceptable and worthwhile, marking what is decent, normal, and natural in human beings, so we want our works of art to be accepted as important and valuable: as standards of merit in the art world. We want to become part of their respective canons, and we engage in each case in the same sort of sociopolitical maneuverings in order to achieve this. Then, too, the construction of narrative identities, like that of works of art, is often highly inventive. Both are usually constructed with immaculate care, often with insight and sensitivity, and in a way, moreover, which must alter and contribute to the sorts of people we are.[12] For in creating either, we are brought to explore a range of human values in a way which tests, teases, and adds to our moral and aesthetic understanding.[13]

It is because of these fundamental similarities between the creation of works of art on the one hand and narrative identities on the other, that the language and idiom of the arts applies to each. They are similarities, we have seen, which take root in the fact that both are cultural objects. There is, then, nothing at all surprising about the fact that the same idiom applies to both. One could only find it so if one were to ignore the cultural dimension either of art or of individual identity.

If my observations and arguments have done nothing else, they have enabled us to see that the process which characterizes artistic production is central to the lives we live. This process, we have found, is not the dispensable luxury that we sometimes take it to be; nor is it something that we are free to take or leave as we please. It is, rather, a primeval process whereby we come to make sense both of ourselves and of the world in which we live: a process at the very heart of our existence and social being, and about which a good deal remains to be said.[14]

ACKNOWLEDGMENTS

I am indebted to Rosemary Novitz, Augustine Schutte, David Brooks, Paul Taylor, Sorrel Kerbel, Bernard Harrison, Stewart Candlish, and Denis Dutton for their comments on this article.

NOTES

1. Throughout this article I use the word "identity" in its epistemological not its metaphysical sense to mean the view or sense or beliefs that one has of oneself.

2. See my *Pictures and Their Use in Communication: A Philosophical Essay* (The Hague: Martinus Nijhoff, 1977), chaps. 2, 4, and 5. Cf. Nelson Goodman, "Twisted Tales; or Story, Study and Symphony," in *On Narrative*, ed. W. J. T. Mitchell (Chicago: University of Chicago Press, 1981), pp. 100–1. Goodman clearly believes that pictures can *tell* stories without being used in a specific context to do so. He does not appear to have an argument for this view.

3. See, for example, Sigmund Freud, "The Relation of the Poet to Daydreaming," *Collected Papers*, trans. I. F. Grant Duff (New York: Basic Books, 1959), vol. 4, pp. 173–83; George Herbert Mead, *Mind, Self, and Society*, ed. Charles W. Morris (Chicago: University of Chicago Press, 1934); Erving Goffman, *The Presentation of Self in Everyday Life* (Garden City: Doubleday, 1959); Richard Wollheim, *The Thread of Life* (London: Cambridge University Press, 1984), lecture 3.

4. See Stanford Lyman and Marvin B. Scott, *The Drama of Social Reality* (New York: Oxford University Press, 1975), chap. 5, for a discussion of some versions of the dramatistic model.

5. See, for example, Roy Schafer, "Narration in the Psychoanalytic Dialogue," in *On Narrative*, p. 26, where it is merely submitted that it "makes sense, and it may be a useful project, to present psychoanalysis in narrational terms." Although Paul Ricoeur is adamant in "The Questions of Proof in Freud's Psychoanalytic Writings, in *Hermeneutics and the Human Sciences* (Cambridge: Cambridge University Press, 1983), that the self is a narrative construct, he merely asserts, but does not argue for the view. For more on this, see Anthony Paul Kerby, "The Language of the Self," *Philosophy Today*, 30 (1986): 210–23; and "The Adequacy of Self-Narration: A Hermeneutical Approach," in *Philosophy and Literature* 12 (1988): 232–44.

6. Goodman, "Twisted Tales," p. 106.

7. For a full account of the way in which we empathize with subjects in a story, see my "Fiction and the Growth of Knowledge," *Grazer Philosophische Studien* 19 (1983): 47–68.

8. I am indebted to the late Flint Schier not just for my use of this term, but for drawing my attention to the phenomenon.

9. Hayden White, " The Value of Narrativity in the Representation of Reality," in *On Narrative*, pp. 1–23, especially pp. 18–20.

10. The precise dynamics of this process are explained in my *Knowledge, Fiction, and Imagination* (Philadelphia: Temple University Press, 1987), chaps. 3 and 5.

11. Cf. Kerby, "The Adequacy of Self-Narration."

12. This same point is made in more detail by Michael Krausz, "Art and Its Mythologies," in *Rationality, Relativism, and the Human Sciences*, edited by Richard Burian, Michael Krausz, and Joseph Margolis (The Hague: Martinus Nijhoff, 1987).

13. For a discussion of the way in which the creation and reading of fiction adds to our moral understanding, see my "Fiction and the Growth of Knowledge."

14. The nature and scope of this process, its epistemological role and metaphysical implications, are extensively discussed in my *Knowledge, Fiction, and Imagination*.

8

Narratives of the Self

Kenneth J. Gergen
Mary M. Gergen

Man is always a storyteller! He lives surrounded by his and others' myths.
With them he sees everything in his life, no matter what befalls him. And he
seeks to live his life as though he were telling it. —Sartre

Traditionally inquiry into self-conception has been concerned with states of being, that is, with the individual as a stabilized entity. The research concern has been essentially triadic. It has first entailed the development of a wide variety of measuring instruments designed to tap the structure, content, and evaluative underpinning of the individual's self-conception at a given time. Second, it has focused on various factors that could figure in the determination and alteration of the individual's conception of self. Finally it has been occupied with the effects of a given configuration of self-conception on subsequent activity. Thus, for example, researchers have developed instruments for assessing self-esteem, have examined a range of formative influences, and explored the behavioral implications of possessing various levels of self-esteem. Yet, in spite of the many insights generated in this traditional orientation to self, it is important to recognize its limitations. In doing so, we may become sensitized to significant lacunae in theoretical development. It is just such limitations in the traditional orientation that set the stage for the present undertaking.

Traditional research on self-conception is earmarked by two widely prevailing characteristics: such research tends to be both *mechanistic* and *synchronic*. It is mechanistic in its assumption of an internal structure governed in mechanical fashion by external inputs, and it is synchronic in its concern with the causes and effects of the individual's characterization of him or herself at a given moment. Thus the individual is generally imbued with a structure of self-descriptions (concepts, schemata, prototypes) that remains stabilized until subjected to external influences from the social surroundings. While revealing in certain respects, such orienting assumptions are myopic in others. First, they ignore the individual's capacity to shape actively the configuration of self-conception. They deny the potential of the individual for reflexive reconstruction of self-understanding. Needed then is attention to the ways in which the individual actively constructs his or her view of self, not as a pawn to social inputs, but as a constructive agent in social life. Second, the traditional views fail to appreciate the individual's understanding of him or herself as a historically emerging being. It may be argued that one's view of self in a given moment is fundamentally nonsensical unless it can be linked in some fashion with his or her past. Suddenly and momentarily to see oneself as "fat," "poetic," or "male," for example, might seem mere whimsy unless such concepts could be attached to a temporal context revealing their genesis. How did it come about that such terms are being employed in the present context? The fact that people believe they possess identities fundamentally depends on their capacity to relate fragmentary occurrences across temporal boundaries. The present analysis, specifically concerned with the individual's active construction of personal history, is thus *reflexive* and *diachronic*. It is concerned with states of active becoming as opposed to passive being.

We shall employ the term "self-narrative" to refer to the individual's account of the relationship among self-relevant events across time. In developing a self-narrative the individual attempts to establish coherent connections among life events.[1] Rather than seeing one's life as simply "one damned thing after another," the individual attempts to understand life events as systematically related. They are rendered intelligible by locating them in a sequence or "unfolding process."[2] One's present identity is thus not a sudden and mysterious event, but a sensible result of a life story. As Bettelheim has argued,[3] such creations of narrative order may be essential in giving one's life a sense of meaning and direction.[4]

It is the purpose of the present essay to open consideration of the manner in which people construct narratives for the self. Our analysis is divided into two parts. First we shall consider narrative forms, in both their temporal and dramatic aspects. The attempt in this case will be to develop a means of characterizing forms of narrative. Using this analysis as grounding we can turn to the relationship of self-narratives to social interaction. Although self-narratives are possessed by individuals, their genesis and sustenance may be viewed as fundamentally social. The function of differing narrative forms along with their construction in social interaction will be of particular concern.

Before embarking on this analysis a word must be said about the relationship between the concept of self-narrative and related theoretical notions. In particular, the concept of self-narrative bears an affinity with a variety of constructs falling generally within the domains of rule-role and dramaturgical theory. However, there are significant distinctions. The concepts of rule,[5] role prescription,[6] interaction ritual,[7] and scripts[8] have all been employed in dealing with the psychological basis for sequences of action across time. Further, in each case, theorists have generally assumed an autonomous base for human action. In these respects, such terms are similar to the concept of self-narrative. However, unlike the latter concept, theorists in each of these cases have tended to assign governing or directive functions to the various structures. That is, the individual is said to consult or interrogate the relevant rule, role prescription, ritual understanding, or script for indications of proper or appropriate conduct. The individual thus carries with him or her a psychological template relevant to interaction sequences, and assesses the propriety of his or her behavior in accord with the template. In contrast, we view the self-narrative as possessing no inherent directive capabilities. Rather, it may be viewed as a construction undergoing continuous alteration as interaction progresses. The individual in this case does not consult the narrative for information.[9] Rather, the self-narrative is a linguistic implement constructed and reconstructed by people in relationships, and employed in relationships to sustain, enhance, or impede various actions. In this sense, self-narratives function much as histories within the society more generally. Histories do not in themselves have directive capacities. They are symbolic systems used for such social purposes as justification, criticism, and social solidification.

DIMENSIONS OF NARRATIVE FORM

Man, in a word, has no nature; what he has is . . . history.
—Ortega y Gasset

To argue that individuals attempt to knit their life events into coherent sequences is to open the door to a variety of interesting and important issues. What functions do self-narratives play in the life of the individual; can self-narratives be distinguished in terms of their functional as opposed to dysfunctional capacities; what are the origins of self-narratives; and what relationship do such narratives bear to social life more generally? Inquiry into such issues depends importantly on the existence of a differentiated vocabulary of narrative form. Without distinctions among narrative forms, theoretical explorations of these various issues may remain shallow or constrained. Although a full elaboration of narrative form is beyond the scope of this essay, our later discussion of the social context of narrative will benefit from consideration of two major aspects of form: the temporal and the dramatic.

TEMPORAL FORM IN SELF-NARRATIVE

One essential aspect of narrative is the capacity to generate directionality among events; that is, to structure the events in such a way that they move over time in an orderly way toward a given end.[10] Our initial question concerning this temporal aspect of narrative concerns that of variations in form. On what grounds can one distinguish among forms of temporal sequence? There are few available resources on which to draw in answering this question. The most extensive accounts of variations in narrative form are found in the analysis of drama and literature. In his analysis of mythical forms, for example, Northrup Frye[11] argues that there are four basic forms of narrative, each of which is rooted in the human experience with nature and most particularly with the evolution of the seasons. Thus, the experience of spring and the uprising of nature gives rise to the comedy. In the classic tradition comedy typically involves a challenge or threat, which is overcome to yield a happy ending. A comedy need not be humorous. It is, rather, similar to what is now popularly called a melodrama. Problematic situations develop and are overcome. In contrast, the free and calm of summer days give inspiration to the romance as a dramatic form. The romance in this case consists of a series of episodes in which the major protagonist experiences challenges or threats and in each case emerges victorious. The romance need not be concerned with attraction between people. During the autumn, when one experiences the contrast between the life of summer and the death of coming winter, the tragic form is born; and in winter, with one's increasing awareness of unrealized expectancies and the death of dreams, irony and satire become relevant expressive forms.

Joseph Campbell's analysis of primitive myth is helpful.[12] As he proposes, there is one central "monomyth" from which a myriad of variations have been drawn in primitive mythology. The monomyth, rooted in unconscious psychodynamics, concerns the hero who has been able to overcome personal and historical limitations to reach a transcendent understanding of the human condition. For Campbell, heroic narratives in their many local guises serve vital functions of psychic education. For our purposes, we see that the monomyth carries a form similar to that of the comedy-melodrama. That is, negative events (trials, terrors, tribulations) are followed by a positive outcome (enlightenment).

These discussions enable us to shift to a more abstract perspective. What is common to the sequential shift we find in the tragedy, the comedy-melodrama, the romantic saga, and the monomyth are shifts in the evaluative character of events over time. Essentially, we seem to be confronted with alterations in a primary dimension of human experience, the evaluative.[13] That is, in linking experiences the dramatist appears to establish directionality along a good-bad dimension. Or, as Alasdair MacIntyre has put it, "Narrative requires an evaluative framework in which good or bad character helps to produce unfortunate or happy outcomes."[14] Do such alterations have a counterpart in the person's attempt to understand his or her cross-time trajectory? It would appear so, as attested to by such common queries as: "Am I improving?" "Is my life happier now?" "Are my abilities declining?" "Am I maintaining the high standards I once committed myself to?" or "Am I growing as a person?" To answer such questions the individual selects discrete incidents or images occurring across time and links them through evaluative comparison.[15]

Given what appears to be a fundamental means of generating coherence and direction over time, we can proceed more formally to consider the problem of narrative types. At the most rudimentary level we may isolate three forms of narrative. The first may be described as a stability narrative, that is, a narrative that links incidents, images, or concepts in such a way that the individual remains essentially unchanged with respect to evaluative position. As depicted in Figure 8.1, we also see that the stability narrative could be struck at any level along the evaluative continuum. At the upper end of the continuum the individual might conclude, for example, "I am still as attractive as I used to be," or at the lower end, "I continue to be haunted by feelings of failure." As can also be seen, each of these narrative summaries possesses inherent implications for the future. That is, they furnish an indication or anticipation of forthcoming events. In the former case the

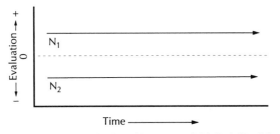

Figure 8.1. Positive (N_1) and Negative (N_2) Stability Narratives

individual might conclude that he or she will continue to be attractive for the foreseeable future and, in the latter, that feelings of failure will persist regardless of circumstance.

This rudimentary narrative may be contrasted with two others of similar simplicity. The individual may link together experiences in such a way that either increments or decrements characterize movement along the evaluative dimension over time. In the former case we may speak of *progressive,* and in the latter *regressive,* narratives (see Figure 8.2). For example, the individual might be engaged in a progressive narrative with the surmise, "I am really learning to overcome my shyness and be more open and friendly with people," or a regressive narrative with the thought, "I can't seem to control the events in my life anymore." Directionality is also implied in each of these narratives with the former anticipating further increments and the latter further decrements.

As should be clear, these three narrative forms, stability, progressive, and regressive, exhaust the fundamental options for the direction of movement in evaluative space. As such they may be considered rudimentary bases for other more complex variants. Theoretically one

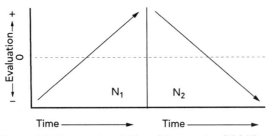

Figure 8.2. Progressive (N_1) and Regressive (N_2) Narratives

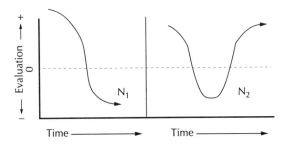

Figure 8.3. Tragic (N_1) and Comedy-Melodrama (N_2) Narratives

may envision a potential infinity of variations on these rudimentary forms. However, for reasons of social utility, aesthetic desirability, and cognitive capability, the culture may limit itself to a truncated repertoire of possibilities. Among this limited set we may place the tragic narrative, which in the present framework would adopt the structure depicted in Figure 8.3. The tragedy, in this sense, would tell the story of the rapid downfall of one who had achieved high position. A progressive narrative is thus followed by a rapid regressive narrative. In this sense, comedy-melodrama is the reverse of the tragedy: A regressive narrative is followed by a progressive narrative. Life events become increasingly problematic until the denouement, whereupon happiness is rapidly restored to the major protagonists. Further, if a progressive narrative is followed by a stability narrative (see Figure 8.4), we have what is commonly known as the happily-ever-after myth, which is widely adopted in traditional courtship. And we also recognize the romantic saga as a series of progressive-regressive

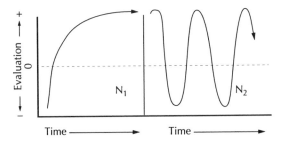

Figure 8.4. "Happily-Ever-After" (N_1) and
Romantic Saga (N_2) Narratives

phases. In this case, for example, the individual may see his or her past as a continuous array of battles against the powers of darkness.

Before considering a second aspect of narrative form, two matters deserve brief attention. First, as should be apparent from this discussion, narrative forms are in no way to be construed as objective reflections of one's personal life. The individual should be able to use virtually any form to account for his or her life history. Particular narratives may be implied by the manner in which one evaluates the events entering into the narrative construction. However, events themselves do not contain inherent valuational properties. Such properties must be attributed, and the attributions are contained within the particular constructions one makes of the events. Whether any given event is good or bad depends on the framework one employs for understanding, and the potential array of frameworks for rendering events intelligible is without apparent limit.[16]

Second, although many illustrations of these narrative forms can be found in the arts, this is not simultaneously to accept the enticing but problematic view that life accounts are merely reconstituted forms of art. To be sure, from children's fairy tales to television serials, from primitive religious myths to the most sophisticated novel, the narratives outlined thus far recur with great regularity. And, one can scarcely imagine that those who are frequently exposed to such forms could remain unaffected by them. Bettelheim's[17] analysis of the profound effects of fairy tales in the life of the developing child is quite compelling in this respect. Yet, at the same time such forms are not necessarily the inventions of autonomous storytellers, witch doctors, or literary craftsmen. Such individuals are also members of their culture and can scarcely remain unaffected by the narrative forms that are already imbedded therein.[18] Life and art are thus interdependent. However, that similar narrative forms may be found over many historical periods and differing contexts suggests that their fundamental genesis may be furnished by the requisites of human interaction. We shall return to this issue in treating the social utility of narrative forms.

DRAMATIC ENGAGEMENT IN NARRATIVE FORM

We now see how coherence among events may be produced through evaluative contrasts. However, we have said little about one of the most phenomenologically salient aspects of narrative form: the capacity to create feelings of drama or emotion. We may refer to this aspect of narrative form in terms of dramatic engagement. In the same way that theatrical productions vary in their capacity to arouse and compel an audience, so may the individual's selection of narrative vary in its capacity to generate or reduce dramatic tension in one's life. How are we to understand the elements giving rise to these variations in emotional engagement? Of course, dramatic engagement cannot be separated entirely from the content of a given narrative. Yet, segmented events in themselves appear limited in their capacity to sustain engagement. For example, a film depicting the continuous, random juxtaposition of startling events (a gunshot, a sword waving, a horse jumping a wall, a low-flying aircraft) would soon produce tedium. It is the relationship among events, not the events themselves, that seems chiefly responsible for sustaining dramatic engagement, and a theory of narrative form is essentially concerned with such relationships. What characteristics of narrative form are necessary, then, to generate dramatic engagement?

At this preliminary juncture, one must again look at the dramatic arts as a source of insight. In this case, it is of initial interest that one can scarcely locate a theatrical exemplar of the three rudimentary narratives proposed above. A drama in which all events were evaluatively equivalent (stability narrative) would scarcely be considered drama. Further, a steady but moderate enhancement (progressive) or decrement (regressive narrative) in a protagonist's life conditions would also seem to produce ennui. At the same time, it is also interesting to observe that the tragic narrative depicted in Figure 8.3 bears a strong resemblance to the simpler, but unarousing, regressive narrative (Figure 8.2). How does the tragic narrative, with its consistently powerful dramatic impact, differ from the more rudimentary regressive narrative? Two characteristics seem particularly significant. First, we note that the relative decline in events is far less rapid in the prototypical regressive narrative than it is in the case of the tragic narrative. Whereas the former is characterized by moderate decline over time, the latter organizes events in such a way that decline is precipitous. In this light one may conjecture that the rapidity with which events deteriorate in such classic tragedies as *Antigone, Oedipus Rex,* and *Romeo and Juliet* may be essential to their dramatic impact. More generally, it may be suggested that the rate of change, or more formally the acceleration of the narrative slope, constitutes one of the chief components of what is here termed dramatic engagement.

A second major component is also suggested by the contrast between the regressive and the tragic narratives. In the former case (see

Figure 8.2) there is unidirectionality in the slope line whereas in the tragic narrative (Figure 8.3) we find a progressive narrative (sometimes implied) followed by a regressive narrative. It would appear to be this "turn of events," or more precisely the change in the evaluative relationship among events, that contributes to a high degree of dramatic engagement. It is when the individual who has attained high goals, has reached the apex of ecstasy, or has at last discovered life's guiding principle, is brought low that drama is created. In more formal terms, the alteration in narrative slope may be considered a second major component of dramatic engagement.

When we consider both alteration in and acceleration of narrative slope as basic components of dramatic engagement, we are led to a more general conclusion. Both of these components are similar in one respect: they point to some aspect of phenomenal change as a basis of dramatic tension. Acceleration and alteration in slope may be viewed as two realizations of this more fundamental experience.

MACRO-, MICRO- AND MULTIPLES IN NARRATIVE FORM

My characters are conglomerations of past and present stages of civilizations, bits from books and newspapers, scraps of humanity, rags and tatters of fine clothing, patched together as is the human soul.   —Strindberg

Thus far we have attempted to outline a number of rudimentary narrative forms, along with some of their more common derivatives, and to open discussion on differences in dramatic impact. We must now turn our attention more directly to the operation of narrative forms in daily life. This account will have two aspects. In the first instance we may consider the normal capacities with which the individual enters social relationships, and in the second, the function and development of narratives in interpersonal encounters. In inquiring into personal capacities it is important to appreciate the individual's exposure to a milieu of multiple narratives. Normal socialization will typically offer the individual exposure to a wide variety of narrative forms, from the rudimentary to the complex. Thus, the individual typically enters relationships with a potential for employing any of a wide number of forms. In the same way an experienced skier approaches a steep incline with a variety of techniques for effective descent or a teacher confronts a class with a variety of means for effective communication, so the individual can usually construct the relationship among life experiences in a variety of ways. At a minimum, effective socialization should equip the person to interpret life events as constancies, as improvements, or as decrements. And, with little additional training, the individual should develop the capacity to envision his or her life as tragedy, comedy-melodrama, or a romantic epic.

Not only do people enter social relationships with a variety of narratives at their disposal, but, in principle, there are no temporal parameters within which events must be related through narratives. That is, one may attempt to relate events occurring over vast periods of time, or determine the relationship among events within a brief period. One may find it possible to see his or her life as part of an historical movement commencing centuries ago, or as originating in early adolescence. At the same time, the individual may choose to describe as a comedy-melodrama that which has unfolded as friends select their positions at the dinner table. We may use the terms "macro" and "micro" to refer to the hypothetical or idealized ends of the temporal continuum within which events are related. Macronarratives refer to those events spanning broad periods of time while micronarratives relate events within brief durations.[19] The historian typically excels in the macronarrative, while the comedian who relies on sight gags may be the master of the micronarrative.

Given the capacity to relate events within different temporal perspectives, it becomes apparent that people often engage in the construction of nested narratives, or narratives within narratives.[20] Thus, they may come to see themselves as part of a long cultural history but nested within this narrative they may possess an independent account of their development since childhood, and within this account establish a separate portrayal of their life as a professional, or the development of their image within the few preceding moments. A man may view himself as bearing the contemporary standard for a race that has struggled for centuries so that he may live (a progressive narrative), and at the same time see himself as one who was long favored by his parents only to disappoint them with increasing frequency as he grew older (the tragic narrative), and simultaneously see how he managed to rekindle the waning ardor of a woman friend on a given evening (the comedy-melodrama).

The concept of nested narratives raises a variety of interesting issues. To what extent may we anticipate coherence among nested narratives? As Ortega y Gassett has argued in his analysis of historical systems, "the plurality of beliefs on which an individual, or people, or an age is grounded never possesses a completely logical articulation."[21]

Yet, on the basis of the wide range of social psychological work on cognitive consistency, one might anticipate a general tendency for people to strive for consistency among nested narratives. There are also many social advantages to "having one's stories agree." To the extent that consistency among narratives is sought, macronarratives acquire preeminent importance. Such narratives seem to lay the foundations within which other narratives are constructed. One's account of an evening with a friend would not seem to dictate one's account of one's life history; however, one's life history does constitute grounds for understanding the trajectory of the evening. To extrapolate, it may be ventured that those people with an extensive background in the history of their culture or subculture, or with an elaborated sense of their place in history, may possess more coherence among narratives than those with a superficial sense of their historical position. Or, placed in a different light, people from a young culture or nation may experience a greater sense of freedom of momentary action than those from cultures or nations with a long and prominent historical narrative. The former may experience a lesser degree of strain to behave in a way that is coherent with the past.

THE SOCIAL UTILITY OF NARRATIVE FORM

Think of the tools in a tool-box: there is a hammer, pliers, a screw-driver, a rule, a glue-pot, glue, nails and screws. The functions of words are as diverse as the functions of these objects.   —Wittgenstein

Having outlined a range of narrative forms within the common repertoire, we are in a position to inquire more directly into the relationship between self-narratives and social interaction. This analysis can proceed in two parts. First, we can examine the social origins of various narrative forms. We can then turn to the manner in which such narratives are molded within social interaction. In the first case, we have seen that although a variety of narrative forms are potentially available to people, the individual usually relies on a delimited subset.[22] We may advance our understanding of why we do not find an infinity of formulations if we consider functional needs within organized society. The viability of complex social institutions, large or small, benefits from the widespread capability of its members to employ a circumscribed range of narrative forms. This is to argue that a major source for narrative form resides in the social sphere and particularly within the requirements for adequate social functioning.

Consider first the primitive narrative of self-stability. Although generally void of dramatic value, the capacity of people to identify themselves as stable units has vast utility within a culture. One's capacity to act functionally within society depends largely on the degree of its social stability. If others' conduct shifted randomly from one moment to the next, one would be rendered helpless. There would be little way of knowing how to achieve any goal (including sustaining life) that depended on others' actions. Thus, much effort is expended by people in establishing recurring or stabilized patterns of conduct, and ensuring through various sanctions that they are maintained. This broad societal demand for stability of conduct finds its functional counterpart in the ready accessibility of the stability narrative on the personal level. Negotiating social life successfully requires that the individual is capable of making him or herself intelligible as an enduring, integral, or coherent identity. For example, in certain political arenas, it may be of great functional value to present oneself as a "born Southerner, raised in the South, married in the South, and part of its future." Or, on the more personal level, to be able to show how one's love, parental commitment, honesty, moral ideals, and so on have been unfailing over time even when their outward appearances have seemed more variable, may be of exceptional importance in retaining ongoing relations. In most relationships of importance, people wish to know that others "are what they seem," which is to say that certain characteristics are enduring across time. One major means for rendering such assurances is through the construction of stability narratives.

It is important to note at this point a major way in which the present analysis conflicts with more traditional accounts of personal identity. Theorists such as Prescott Lecky, Erik Erikson, Carl Rogers, and Seymour Epstein have all viewed personal identity as something akin to an achieved condition of the mind. The mature individual, on this account, is one who has "found," "crystallized," or "realized" a firm sense of self or personal identity. In general this condition is viewed as a highly positive outcome, and once achieved, variance or inconsistency in one's conduct may be minimized. However, from the present vantage point, the individual does not arrive at a stabilized state of mind. Rather, he or she develops the capacity for understanding him or herself in this manner and to communicate this understanding creditably to others. One does not acquire a state of "true self" but a potential for communicating that such a state is possessed.

This latter position becomes fortified when we turn to the social functions of the progressive narrative. On a general level there would appear not only a pervasive need for stability but also a contrasting need for change. Given that any action has both positive and negative consequences according to some standard, and assuming that positive consequences are to be preferred over negative, it follows that an improved or enhanced quality of any action may be desired. In this way people can see themselves, their world, and their relations as possessing the potential for positive change. They can see their poor condition as subject to alleviation, and life as promising brighter horizons. For many people indeed this hope furnishes a chief motivational source. Careers are selected, sacrifices endured, and many personal pleasures (including one's most intimate relations) are sacrificed in the belief that a progressive narrative can be achieved. And, it is clearly of great functional value to be able to construct such narratives for others. For example, a political leader may wish to argue that although the economy was depressed when he or she took office, it has shown steady improvement. Or, on a personal level, the success of many relationships depends importantly on the ability of the participants to demonstrate how their undesirable characteristics have diminished over time—even if they appear to be continuing undaunted. In effect, the general investment in positive change is best expressed through a narrative that demonstrates the ascending relationship among events over time.

As should be evident from this analysis, one must be prepared in most relationships to render an account of oneself as both inherently stable, and yet, in a state of positive change. Functioning viably in a relationship often depends on one's ability to show that one has always been the same, and will continue to be so, and yet, contrapuntally to show how one is continuing to improve. One must be reliable but demonstrate progress; one must be changing but maintain a stable character. Achieving such diverse ends is primarily a matter of negotiating the meaning of events in relationship to each other. Thus, with sufficient skill, one and the same event may figure in both a stability and a progressive narrative. For example, graduation from medical school may be used as evidence that one has always been intelligent, and at the same time demonstrate that one is on route to high professional status.

Can a case be made for the generalized social value of regressive narratives? Inasmuch as increments of one kind are tantamount to decrements of another, the necessary counterpart of the progressive narrative in the first case is the regressive narrative in the second. In order for one's nation to gain hegemony in world politics, it may be necessary to interpret the power of other nations as declining. An increase in feelings of community safety may depend on one's assessment of a decline in juvenile crime. And, on the more personal level, one's account of self as increasing in maturity of judgment, on the one hand, may entail the contrary perception of a reduction in youthful impetuosity on the other. In effect, regressive narratives are logically tied to the creation of progressive narratives.

One may object to this argument: although regressive narratives serve as the logical inverse of the progressive, they are not genuine regressions according to the evaluative criteria proposed above. That is, regressive relations are derived, but the evaluative connotation in such cases is positive as opposed to negative. Can a case be made for regressive narratives in which the evaluative experience is a negative one? What needs might be served by seeing the world or oneself as in a state of degeneracy? At least one compelling answer to this question is furnished by taking account of the common effects of regressive narratives. In particular, when people are informed of steadily worsening conditions they often attempt to compensate. They strive to offset or reverse the decline through enhanced activity. Through intensification of effort, they attempt to turn a potential tragedy into a comedy. Regressive narratives furnish an important means, then, of motivating people toward achievement of positive ends. This means is employed on a national level when a government demonstrates that the steady decline in the balance of payments can be offset only with a grass-roots commitment to purchasing locally manufactured products. The same technique may be employed by the individual in attempting to bolster his or her enthusiasm for a given product. Otherwise wishing to avoid effortful activity, people goad themselves into action by bringing to mind a regressive narrative.[23]

In sum, we see that the development of certain rudimentary narrative forms is favored by functional needs within the society. Stability narratives are favored by the common desire for the social world to appear orderly and predictable; progressive narratives offer the opportunity for people to see themselves and their environment as capable of improvement; and regressive narratives are not only entailed logically by the development of progressive narratives, but have an important motivational function in their own right. Given a social basis for a variety of narrative forms within the individual's repertoire, we turn finally to the manner in which specific narratives are constructed in ongoing relations.

THE SOCIAL NEGOTIATION OF NARRATIVE

Composition of action as plot . . . depends on the consensual and generative relationships of individuals.   —Burns

Narrative construction can never be entirely a private matter. In the reliance on a symbol system for relating or connecting events, one is engaging in an implicit social act. A concept acquires status as a symbol by virtue of its communicative capacity, that is, its position within a meaning system is shared by at least one other person. A movement of the hand is not a symbol, for example, unless it has the capacity to be understood by at least one other person. Thus, in understanding the relationship among events in one's life, one relies on symbols that inherently imply an audience. Further, not all symbols imply the same audience: personal narratives that have communicative value for certain audiences will be opaque to others. Over and above this definitional linkage of narratives to the social sphere, the social basis of narrative construction is amplified in two additional processes: public realization and articulation. Each will be treated in turn.

As apparent in the preceding discussion of the motivational properties of regressive narratives, narrative constructions frequently have behavioral implications. To maintain that one has always been an honest person (stability narrative) suggests that one will avoid temptation when it is subsequently encountered. To construct one's past in such a way that one has overcome increasingly greater obstacles to achievement (progressive narrative) suggests that one should treat oneself with a certain degree of respect. Or, to see oneself as losing one's abilities because of increasing age (regressive narrative) is to suggest that one should attempt to accomplish less. Most importantly for present purposes, as these behavioral implications are realized in action they become subject to social evaluation. Others can accept or reject such actions; they will find them credible or misleading. And, to the extent that such actions are rejected or found improper, doubt is cast upon the relevant narrative construction. If others express doubt about one's honesty, suggest that one's pride is unmerited, or find one's reduction in activity unwarranted, revisions are invited in the narrative construction relevant to such actions. Thus, as narratives are realized in the public arena, they become subject to social molding.[24]

As the individual's actions encounter varying degrees of approbation, the process of articulation comes to play a preeminent role. That is, it becomes increasingly necessary for the individual to articulate the implicit narrative line in such a way that the actions in question become intelligible and thus acceptable. If faced with others who doubt one's honesty, one can demonstrate how his or her previous actions have been without blemish. Or, one can try to convince others of the validity of the progressive narrative by legitimizing one's pride, or the regressive narrative by justifying one's diminished activities. In effect, whether a given narrative can be maintained depends importantly on the individual's ability to negotiate successfully with others concerning the meaning of events in relationship with each other.[25]

Active negotiation over narrative form is especially invited under circumstances in which the individual is asked to justify his or her behavior, that is, when one has acted disagreeably with respect to common frames of understanding. However, the process of social negotiation need not be solely a public one. People appear generally to avoid the threat of direct negotiation by taking prior account of the public intelligibility of their actions. They select in advance actions that can be justified on the basis of an intelligible or publicly acceptable narrative. In this sense, the bulk of the negotiation process is anticipatory or implicit; it takes place with an imaginary audience prior to the moment of action. People take into account others' perspectives and the likelihood of their actions being accepted prior to acting. In this way, most human interaction proceeds unproblematically.

RECIPROCITY AND GUILT IN NARRATIVE FORMATION

My experience cannot directly become your experience. . . . Yet,
nevertheless, something passes from me to you. . . . This something is not
the experience as experienced, but its meaning. —Ricoeur

The social generation of narrative construction does not terminate with the negotiation process in its implicit and explicit forms. An additional facet of narrative construction throws its interactive basis into vivid relief. Thus far we have spoken of narratives as if solely concerned with the temporal trajectory of the protagonist alone. This conception must now be expanded. The incidents woven into a narrative are not only the actions of the single individual but interactions with others. Others' actions contribute vitally to the events to be linked in narrative sequence. For example, in justifying his continuing honesty, the individual may point to an instance in which another person has tempted him; to illustrate one's achievement may depend on showing how another person was vanquished in a particular competition; in arguing that one has lost capabilities he or she may point to the alacrity with which a younger person performed a particular task. In all cases, the action of the other enters as an integral part of one's own actions. In this sense, narrative constructions typically require a supporting cast. The implications of this fact are broad indeed.[26]

First, in the same manner that the individual feels that he or she has priority in self-definition, others also feel themselves to have primary jurisdiction over the definition of their own actions. Thus, one's understanding of the supporting role played by another cannot easily proceed without the acquiescence of the other. If others are not willing to accede to their assigned parts then one can ill afford to rely on their actions within a narrative. If another fails to see his or her actions as "offering temptation," the actor may be unable to conclude that he or she has displayed honesty; if the other can show how he or she was not really vanquished in a given competition the actor can scarcely use the episode as a stepping stone in a progressive narrative; if the younger person can demonstrate that his or her alacrity was only an apparent one, far overestimating true abilities, then the actor can ill afford to weave the incident into a regressive narrative.

This reliance on others' definition of their actions places the actor in a precarious position. As we have seen, people possess a variety of narrative forms ranging over various periods of time and which stand in various relations to each other in terms of nesting. At the same time members of a supporting cast may choose at any point to reconstruct their actions in opposing ways. Thus, an actor's success in sustaining any given narrative is fundamentally dependent on others' willingness to play out certain parts in relationship to the actor. In Wilhelm Schapp's terms, each of us is knitted into others' historical constructions, as they are into ours.[27]

This delicate interdependence of constructed narratives suggests that a fundamental aspect of social life is a reciprocity in the negotiation of meaning. Because one's narrative constructions can be maintained only so long as others play their proper supporting roles, and in turn because one is required by others to play supporting roles in their constructions, the moment any participant chooses to renege, he or she threatens the array of interdependent constructions. For example, an adolescent may reveal to his mother that he believes she has been a very bad mother, thus potentially destroying her continuing self-narrative as a "good mother." Yet, at the same time, the son risks his mother's reply that she always felt his character was so inferior that he never merited her love. His continuing narrative is thus thrown into jeopardy. A lover may announce that she has begun to feel her male partner no longer interests her as he once did, thus potentially crushing his stability narrative; however, she does so at the peril of his replying that he has long been bored with her, and is happy to be relieved of his lover's role. In such instances, the parties in the relationship each pull out their supporting roles, and the result is a full degeneration of the narratives to which they contribute.[28]

It would appear that most relationships are not under the immediate threat of mutual withdrawal. In part this is because many people are content with existing reciprocity. There is little to gain in abandoning the support roles that, in turn, also serve one's own constructions. However, there are three additional mechanisms that may insulate members of a relationship from quixotic resignations, and the resulting "collapse of reality." Reciprocity is protected first by the incorporation of others' narratives into one's own. That is, the other's self-construction and one's place in the supporting cast are integrated into one's own self-narrative. Thus people do not merely rely on the supporting roles that others play but come to believe in others' beliefs in these roles. One may not only see his or her mate playing a supporting role as "loving helper" in one's upward route to success, but also comes to believe that the other possesses a private narrative in which this role has a major place. The attempt is thus not only to weave into one's own narrative others' actions but their underlying narrative constructions as well. The individual thus shelters his or her own constructions by including within them the constructions of others.[29]

A second means of protecting oneself from ontological abandonment is to engage in an objectification of the relationship thus shifting concern to the history of this emergent entity. Rather than each individual seeing him or herself as an independent entity requiring support, individuals may decide that together they create a new entity—that of the relationship itself. Once objectified ("We have a relationship") the participants can shift to the simpler task of negotiating one narrative rather than two. Rather than concerning themselves with such issues as whether each individually is "growing as a person," for example, they can negotiate about the trajectory of the mutually created relationship. "Is our marriage failing?" "Is the team's desire to win growing stronger?" or "What is happening to the morale of this organization?" are all relevant questions to ask once the relationship has become objectified and the relevant narrative created.[30]

Finally, one cannot underestimate the power of guilt in maintaining reciprocity in narrative construction. Guilt can be invoked when one party of an interdependent unit accuses another of falling short of his or her history, of failing to live up to the narrative that has been agreed upon as objective. The feeling of guilt is the emotional counterpart of perceiving a threat both to one's sense of reality and to the other's continuing support. Thus, such comments as "and all along I thought you were an honest person!" "I have supported you all this time because I thought you had real ambition, but now . . ." or "You said you were my close friend, but no friend could ever . . ." all imply that the accused has failed in playing out a part that was implied by a previous narrative construction. The accused is thus faced with the threat of a joint loss, first of being able to rely on the construction itself (e.g., "I am an honest person, ambitious, a friend . . ."), and second, of relying on the continuation of the supporting cast member. A common reaction to such accusations is *restorative negotiation* in which the accused person attempts to demonstrate the falsity of the accusations. Thus, by employing periodic challenges to the validity of the others' narratives, members of a relationship can ensure that collective or reciprocal agreements are maintained over extended periods of time.[31]

ACKNOWLEDGMENTS

Work on this essay was facilitated by a grant from the National Science Foundation (#7809395) and the working facilities at Heidelberg University so graciously provided by Carl F. Graumen. We wish also to express our appreciation to the following friends whose self-narratives gave us inspiration for this chapter: Winston J. Churchill, Deborah Curtiss, Emil Liebman, Harvey S. Miller, and Dagmar Westrick.

NOTES

1. B. Cohler, "Personal Narrative and Life Course," *Life-Span Development and Behavior*, vol. 4, ed. P. Baltes and O. Brim (New York: Academic Press, 1982), pp. 205–41; M. Kohli, "Biography: Account, Text, and Method," *Biography and Society*, ed. D. Bertaux (Beverly Hills, Calif.: Sage, 1981).

2. J. de Waele and R. Harré, "The Personality of Individuals," *Personality*, ed. R. Harré (Oxford: Blackwell, 1979).

3. B. Bettelheim, *The Uses of Enchantment* (New York: Knopf, 1976).

4. The self-narrative need not be a verbal construction. Although verbalization may be common, a sense of narrative may be imbedded in a more basic experience of fittingness or directionality among events. Dialogue is necessary neither for an appreciation of the propriety with which scenes fit together nor for a sense of mounting tension, climax, and denouement. Similarly, jazz musicians may possess an understanding of how one improvised segment of a piece fits with its immediate antecedents, although analytic tools are incapable of precisely rendering the relationship.

5. R. Harré and P. Secord, *The Explanation of Social Behaviour* (Oxford: Blackwell, 1972).

6. T. Sarbin and V. Allen, "Role Theory," *Handbook of Social Psychology*, 5 vols., ed. G. Lindsey and E. Aronson (Reading, Mass.: Addison Wesley, 1968–1969).

7. E. Goffman, *Frame Analysis* (New York: Harper and Row, 1974).

8. R. Schank and R. Abelson, *Scripts, Plans, Goals, and Understanding* (Hillsdale, N.J.: Lawrence Erlbaum, 1977).

9. Although a full critique of the concepts of role, rule, and script as directive devices is beyond the scope of this essay, it is important to note that they are subject to most of the weaknesses inherent in concepts of mental structure.

10. As Applebee maintains, the mature narrative requires the elaboration of a center or core situation; shifts in sequential events thus clarify, extend, or modify new aspects of the central theme. See A. Applebee, *The Child's Concept of Story* (Chicago: University of Chicago Press, 1978). As illustrated in a variety of developmental studies, the ability to construct narratives of this form does not typically emerge in the child until the age of five to six years. See E. Pitcher and E. Prelinger, *Children Tell Stories: An Analysis of Fantasy* (New York: International Universities Press, 1963); L. Vygotsky, *Thought and Language* (Cambridge, Mass.: MIT Press, 1962).

11. N. Frye, *Anatomy of Criticism* (Princeton, N.J.: Princeton University Press, 1957).

12. J. Campbell, *The Hero with a Thousand Faces* (New York: Meridian, 1956).

13. See C. Gordon, "Self-Conceptions: Configuration in Content," *The Self in Social Interaction*, ed. C. Gordon and K. Gergen (New York: John Wiley, 1968), pp. 115–54; C. Gordon, "Development of Evaluated Role Identities," *Annual Review of Sociology*, vol. 2 (Palo Alto, Calif.: Annual Reviews, 1976), pp. 405–34; C. Osgood, G. Suci, and P. Tannenbaum, *The Measurement of Meaning*

(Urbana, Ill.: University of Illinois Press, 1957); L. Wells and G. Marwell, *Self-Esteem: Its Conceptualization and Measurement* (Beverly Hills, Calif.: Sage Publications, 1976).

14. A. MacIntyre, "Epistemological Crises, Dramatic Narrative, and the Philosophy of Science," *The Monist*, vol. 60 (1977), p. 456.

15. See A. Hankiss, "Ontologies of the Self," *Biography and Society* (Beverly Hills, Calif.: Sage, 1981); W. Labov and J. Waletzky, "Narrative Analysis," *Essays on the Verbal and Visual Arts*, ed. J. Helm (San Francisco: American Ethnological Society, 1967).

16. For amplification, see K. Gergen, "Toward Intellectual Audacity in Social Psychology," *The Development of Social Psychology*, ed. R. Gilmour and S. Duck (New York: Academic Press, 1980).

17. Bettelheim, *Uses of Enchantment*.

18. As Rubin and Wolf demonstrate, for example, children rely on social roles to which they are exposed to develop narrative roles in make-believe. See S. Rubin and D. Wolf, "The Development of Maybe: The Evolution of Social Roles into Narrative Roles," *New Directions for Child Development*, vol. 6 (1979), pp. 15–28.

19. See, for example, Albert and Kessler's analysis of the structure of endings in encounters. S. Albert and S. Kessler, "Ending Social Encounters," *Journal of Experimental Social Psychology*, vol. 14 (1978), pp. 541–53.

20. See also Feldman's analysis of nested identities. S. Feldman, "Nested Identities," *Studies in Symbolic Interaction*, vol. 2, ed. N. Dengin (Greenwich, Conn.: JAI Press, 1979).

21. J. Ortega y Gasset, *History as a System* (New York: Norton, 1941), p. 166.

22. As the present treatment indicates, the facts of one's life do not dictate narrative form; one employs a narrative form to order the interpretation of life events. For a discussion of relativity in constructing events themselves, see K. Gergen, *Toward Transformation in Social Knowledge* (New York: Springer Verlag, 1982).

23. It may also be proposed that regressive narratives can sometimes serve as justificatory devices for inaction. By demonstrating how one has been forced by an unfolding series of events into a poor position, one can continue to enjoy the ease of inactivity (e.g., "I have grown too old to take up skiing"; "I have been through such agonies that I deserve a rest.").

24. As should be evident, the present analysis favors what Sutton-Smith has termed the dialogic account of narrative construction rather than the

monologic orientation. That is, it views narratives as emergents from social rather than intrapsychic processes. Proponents of the dialogic view include A. Levitt, *Storytelling Among School Children: A Folkloristic Interpretation*, unpublished doctoral dissertation, University of Pennsylvania, 1978; J. McDowell, *The Speech Play and Verbal Art of Chicano Children*, unpublished doctoral dissertation, University of Texas, 1975; S. Stewart, *Nonsense: Aspects of Intertextuality in Folklore and Literature*, unpublished doctoral dissertation, University of Pennsylvania, 1978; and K. Watson, *The Rhetoric of Narrative Structure*, unpublished doctoral dissertation, University of Hawaii, 1972. Proponents of the monologic view include J. Mandler and N. Johnson, "Remembrance of Things Parsed," *Cognitive Psychology*, vol. 9 (1977), pp. 111–51; N. Stein, "The Comprehension and Appreciation of Stories: A Developmental Analysis," *The Arts, Cognition, and Basic Skills*, ed. S. Mageda (St. Louis: Cemrel, 1978); and B. Sutton-Smith, "Presentation and Representation in Fictional Narrative," *New Directions for Child Development*, vol. 6 (1979), pp. 53–66.

25. Cf. J. de Waele and R. Harré, "The Personality of Individuals."

26. See also Sarbin's analysis of hypnosis as a process requiring participants to agree to assigned roles in relation to each other. T. Sarbin, "Hypnosis: Metaphorical Encounters of the Fourth Kind," *Semiotica*, vol. 37 (1980), pp. 1–15.

27. W. Schlapp, *Geschichte Verstrickt Zum Sein Von Mensch und Ding* (Wiesbaden, Germany: B. Heymann, 1976).

28. As MacIntyre has described, when intensive support-systems drop away, the resulting "epistemological crisis" must be resolved by developing a new narrative "which enables the agent to understand *both* how he or she could have intelligibly held his or her original beliefs and how he or she could have been so drastically misled by them. The narrative in terms of which he or she first understood and ordered experiences is itself made into the subject of an enlarged narrative." A. MacIntyre, "Epistemological Crises," p. 455.

29. Relevant is Cicourel's concept of "reciprocity of perspectives," referring to the common assumption that each person would have the same experience if they were to change places. Thoroughgoing reciprocity would lead to full mutuality of narrative incorporation. See A. Cicourel, "Generative Semantics and the Structure of Social Interaction," *Proceedings of the Conference on Sociolinguistics: 1969* (Rome: Luigisturzo Institute, 1970).

30. One may not always agree to join another's attempt to objectify a relationship. See, for example, Harré's discussion of the way in which people are often trapped by others' use of the term "we." R. Harré, "The Self in Monodrama," *The Self: Psychological and Philosophical Issues*, ed. T. Mischel (Oxford: Blackwell, 1977). As Ellen Berscheid has pointed out in a personal communication, one essential basis for joining in an objectification of relationship is

trust. One must believe in the others' resources to sustain a given construction of "we" across time and situation. People may also resist joining in the objectification of relationship because they fail to see how the future may enable them to generate a history. If creating narratives gives one's life meaning and direction, then one may limit relationships to those with whom histories may be jointly constructed.

31. For a compelling account of the weaving of narratives within the culture at large (including the scientific culture), along with a discussion of the social bonding capacities of such narratives, see H. Nieburg, "Theory-Tales and Paradigms," *Journal of Mind and Behavior*, vol. 2 (1981), pp. 179–93. Inasmuch as historical accounts typically employ the narrative as an ordering device, inquiry is invited into the societal functions of historiography. See A. Danto, *Analytical Philosophy of History* (Cambridge: Cambridge University Press, 1965); W. Gallie, *Philosophy and the Historical Understanding* (London: Chatto and Windus, 1964); and M. White, *Foundations of Historical Knowledge* (New York: Harper and Row, 1965).

9

The Genesis of Chronic Illness: Narrative Reconstruction

Gareth Williams

We are seated in the living room of a modern, urban council house somewhere in the northwest of England. Bill, the fifty-eight year-old man with whom I have been talking for almost an hour, leans forward. Then, in a strained voice and with a look of exasperated incomprehension on his face, he says: "and your mind's going all the time, you're reflecting . . . 'how the *hell* have I come to be like this?' . . . because it isn't me."

Bill has rheumatoid arthritis (RA), which was first diagnosed eight years ago following two years of intermittent pain and swelling in his joints; a serious heart attack has added to his difficulties. We have never met before. His words indicate the way in which a chronic illness such as RA may assault an individual's sense of identity, and they testify to the limitations of medical science in delivering a satisfactory explanation for the physical and social breakdown to which such an illness can lead.

In the *Collected Reports* on the rheumatic diseases published by the Arthritis and Rheumatism Council, and with a beguiling acknowledgment of the popular image of the scientist as Great Detective, the experts admit their limitations and pronounce RA to be "one of the major medical mysteries of our time."[1] What is striking about Bill's interrogative, however, is that it points to a concern with something more than the cause of his arthritis, and what I would like to do in this paper is to examine the nature of his question, and those of two others, and to consider the significance of the answers they provide. That is to say, I want to elucidate the styles of thought and modes of "cognitive organization"[2] employed by three people suffering from RA in making sense of the arrival of chronic illness in their lives. I will not be claiming that these three cases are "representative" in any statistical sense, but I *do* suggest that they symbolize, portray, and represent something important about the experience of illness. They are powerful, if idiosyncratic, illustrations of typical processes found in more or less elaborate form throughout my study group.

The fieldwork on which this study is based consisted of semi-structured, tape-recorded interviews with thirty people who had been first diagnosed as suffering from RA at least five years prior to my contact with them. The rationale guiding selection of people at this point in their illness was that in pursuing a general interest in what might be called the structured self-image of the chronically sick person it seemed sensible to talk to those who were "seasoned professionals" rather than novices in the difficult business of living with a chronic illness. Four members of my study group were inpatients on rheumatology wards and the rest were outpatient attenders at rheumatology clinics at two hospitals in northwest England. The inpatients were interviewed in a relatively tranquil side room off the busy ward while the outpatients were first approached in the clinic and subsequently interviewed in their own homes. Of the 30 respondents, 19 were women and 11 were men, so my group had proportionately more men than one would expect to find in the general population.[3] Their ages ranged from 26 to 68 years at the time of interview; thirteen being between 26 and 49, eleven between 50 and 64, and six being 65 years of age or over. Twenty-two were married; the rest were a mixture of single, widowed, and divorced or separated.

The interview covered a variety of themes relating to the experience of living with arthritis, and the data were elicited according to a simple checklist of topics. The duration of the interview as a whole and the sequencing of particular topics were influenced more by contingent features of the interview process than by any well-considered plans of my own. Where I had to compete with an obstreperous budgerigar or a boisterous young child, the interviews would likely be short and fragmented. On better days, with a minimum of interruption and an eager and lucid respondent, the interview could last for three or even four hours.

Although my central concepts—*narrative reconstruction* and *genesis*—are, I believe, novel,[4] the issues they are designed to address—how and why people come to see their illness as originating in a certain way, and how people account for the disruption disablement has wrought in their lives—have been the subject of innumerable investigations. Sociological and anthropological research into illness behavior and health beliefs and psychological research into processes of attribution have all, in one way or another, attended to related issues; but there is so much of it! I cannot possibly indicate all my debts, but perhaps the body of work which has had the most influence on this paper is that which examines lay beliefs or folk theories about the causes of specific diseases or illness in general.[5] Although much interesting material has been collected in this line, it has tended to rest content with treating people's casual beliefs as simply that: beliefs about the etiology of illness. However, it seems to me that if, in some fundamental way, an individual is a social and historical agent with a biographical identity (in the fullest sense) and if the prime sociological importance of chronic illness is the "biographical disruption"[6] to which it gives rise, then an individual's account of the origin of that illness in terms of putative causes can perhaps most profitably be read as an attempt to establish points of reference between body, self, and society and to reconstruct a sense of order from the fragmentation produced by chronic illness.

In this essay, therefore, I use my three cases to illustrate the way in which people's beliefs about the cause of their illness needs to be understood as part of the larger interpretive process which I have chosen to call narrative reconstruction. Before looking at the specifics of my analysis, however, I would like to clarify the theoretical concepts which inform it.

THEORETICAL PROLOGUE

The concept of "narrative" does not hold an established theoretical place in any sociological school or tradition. In general speech it is often used, in noun form, as a synonym for "story," "account," or "chronicle." When used as an adjective, as in "narrative history," it typically refers to the process of relating a continuous account of some set of events or processes. When A. J. P. Taylor, for example, refers to himself as a "narrative historian," as he often does, he implies both a concern with telling a good story and also a preference for a common-sense, empirical reading of historical events, unencumbered by any theoretical baggage, be it Marxist, structuralist, or psychoanalytic.

As I see it the term has two aspects: the routine and the reconstructed. In its routine form, it refers to the observations, comments, and asides, the practical consciousness which provides essential accompaniment to the happenings of our daily lives and helps to render them intelligible. In this sense narrative is a process of continuous accounting whereby the mundane incidents and events of daily life are given some kind of plausible order. If "biography" connotes the indeterminate, reciprocal relationships between individuals and their settings or milieux and between those milieux and the history and society in which they are a part,[7] then narrative may be seen as the cognitive correlate of this, commenting upon and affirming the multiform reality of biographical experience as it relates to both self and society.

In his fictional, philosophical chronicle, *The Man Without Qualities*, Robert Musil, speaking through his central character Ulrich, suggests that narrative order is: ". . . the simple order that consists in one's being able to say: 'When that had happened, then this happened.'"

Musil/Ulrich goes on to argue:

> In their basic relation to themselves most people are narrators. They do not like the lyrical, or at best they like it only for moments at a time. And even if a little "because" and "in order that" may get knotted into the thread of life, still they abhor all cogitation that reaches out beyond that. What they like is the orderly sequence of facts because it has the look of a necessity, and by means of the impression that their life has a "course" they manage to feel somehow sheltered in the midst of chaos.[8]

The trouble is that sometimes the "orderly sequence of facts" gets broken up. It cannot be sustained against the chaos and, for a time at least, the life-course is lost. The routine narrative expressing the concerns of the practical consciousness as it attends to the mundane details of daily life is pitched into disarray: a death in the family, serious illness, an unexpected redundancy and so forth. From such a situation narrative may have to be given some radical surgery and reconstructed so as to account for present disruptions. Narrative reconstruction, therefore, represents the workings of the discursive consciousness.[9]

In my interviews, the reason for the conversation and the excuse for the occasion was the fact of the person being ill. In this context, the etiology of the affliction and the narrative history of the illness held a key place in the dialogue. I remarked earlier on the many studies examining lay theories about illness. In one such study comparing the beliefs of cancer and non-cancer patients with regard to the etiology of that disease, the authors suggest:

> The person without cancer can afford to be more dogmatic about cancers and likely to think in stereotypes. The closer he comes to dealing with the disease, the less clear-cut and more complex the explanations may become.[10]

The reason for such complexity, it seems to me, is that the explanations advanced by afflicted individuals have both causal and purposive or functional components. They represent not only explanations for the onset of a given disease, but also acts of interpretation, narrative reconstructions of profound discontinuities in the social processes of their daily lives. The illness is part of their story and as with any story, to borrow from George Orwell, the closer one gets to the scene of events the vaguer it becomes.[11] In some ways narrative reconstruction may be seen to involve a process of remembrance akin to R. G. Collingwood's notion of historical thinking, where:

> Every present has a past of its own, and any imaginative reconstruction of the past aims at reconstructing the past of this present, the present in which the act of imagination is going on, as here and now perceived.[12]

In confronting the experience of chronic illness, then, like any unusual or disturbing experience, Musil's narrative thread—"when that had happened, then this happened"—becomes *questionable*. The individual's narrative has to be reconstructed both in order to understand the illness in terms of past social experience and to reaffirm the impression that life has a course and the self has a purpose or *telos*. It is from this viewpoint that I have read the "causes" to which my respondents refer both as delineations of putative, efficient connections between the "dependent variable (arthritis) and various "independent variables," and also as narratively reconstructed reference points in an unfolding historical relationship between body, self, and society. These reference points may be seen as constituents in the *genesis* of a misfortune within a narrative which imaginatively reconstructs the past so that it has meaning or purpose for the present.[13] In this way narrative reconstruction becomes a framework for teleological explanation.

Given the teleological form of narrative reconstruction, I employ the concept of "genesis" not for stylistic or rhetorical purposes, but in order to liberate myself from the semantic straitjacket imposed by the term "cause" as it has been generally understood since Hume,[14] and so as to establish a connection with the Greek tradition of reflection on the origins of things which attained its apogee in Aristotle's doctrine of the four causes.[15] Robert Nisbet has remarked that the modern consciousness has been, inevitably, so influenced by Roman, Christian, and skeptical thought about causality that it is difficult for us nowadays to tune-in to the Aristotelian schema. Nisbet argues:

> To Aristotle—and to the Greeks generally, I believe,—something different is involved, something that is somewhat less "cause" in our inherited sense of the word than it is a point of reference in a self-contained, developmental process.[16]

In Aristotelian philosophy different levels of causality are conceived within an overall process of becoming which includes an account of ends as well as beginnings and purposes alongside "causes" (in the modern sense). In this regard the "causes" to which my respondents refer are seen, in part, as points of reference within the process of becoming ill, and the genesis, or mode of formation, of the illness constitutes, in a sense, the dominant theme of the account. It is an analytic construct through which the respondent can be seen to situate a variety of causal connections as reference points within a narrative reconstruction of the changing relationships between the self and the world; a world within which the biographical *telos* has been disrupted. In this way Humean "constant conjunctions" are absorbed into an Aristotelian teleology.

The three case studies in this paper illustrate the way in which distinctive narrative forms are reconstructed to answer the question of genesis as it arises in different lives. The first two reformulate an abstract question: "Why do you think you got arthritis?" into substantive questions more suitable for interrogating the genesis-of-illness experience. Bill, as we saw at the start, wants to know "'how the *hell* have I come to be like this?'. . . because it isn't me." In the same vein, Gill wonders: "Where have I got to? There's nothing left of me." The third case is rather different. Betty exemplifies a situation in which both "causal" analysis and narrative reconstruction may be transcended when the *telos* of life is gently enshrouded within a powerful theodicy. She does not need to reformulate my question because: "people say, 'Why you?' Well, why not me? Better me who knows the Lord."

BILL: NARRATIVE RECONSTRUCTION
AS POLITICAL CRITICISM

A significant portion of Bill's working life had been disrupted. In fact, he had had a tough time. He had worked as a skilled machine operator in a paperworks and, shortly before the first appearance of symptoms, was promoted to the position of "charge hand" which entailed his supervising three floors in the factory. It was shortly after assuming his expanded responsibilities as a "working gaffer" that things began to go wrong:

> I was a working gaffer . . . but, you know, they were mostly long
> hours and the end result, in 1972, was every time I had a session like,
> my feet began to swell and my hands began to swell. I couldn't hold
> a pen, I had difficulty getting between machines and difficulty get-
> ting hold of small things.

At this time he also had a massive heart attack and was off work for
five months. A series of blood tests were done by his heart specialist
who then referred him to a rheumatologist, and within the space of a
couple of weeks he was hospitalized. At the time this unpleasant sequence of events was ambiguous and confusing, but over ten years
Bill had become clearer about it:

> I didn't associate it with anything to do with the works at the time,
> but I think it was chemically induced. I worked with a lot of chemi-
> cals, acetone and what have you. We washed our hands in it, we had
> cuts, and we absorbed it. Now, I'll tell you this because it seems to be
> related. The men that I worked with who are all much older than
> me—there was a crew of sixteen and two survived, myself and the
> gaffer that was then—and they all complained of the same thing, you
> know, their hands started to puff up. It seems very odd.

Yes, very odd indeed. If I were simply interested in identifying his central etiological motif no more need be said because the rest of the discussion was essentially a reiteration of this connection. However, in
order to understand the strength of his attachment to this belief, in the
face of highly plausible alternatives, it is necessary to examine how his
view of life has called forth this essential connection between work
and illness.

An important point about narratives, whether they be routine or
reconstructed, is that they are necessarily co-authored.[17] The interview, of course, is itself a particularly clear case of co-authorship, but,
more generally, narratives are bounded by and constructed in relationship with various individual people and organizations. With regard to
illness, any narrative built around it needs to take account of the medical world within which the official definition of that illness has been
specified. Bill described how, following the diagnosis of "rheumatoid
arthritis" resulting from clinical and laboratory investigations, the
doctors disclaimed any interest in his hypothesis about workplace toxicity and pursued alternative hunches:

> I was assured by them [the doctors] that this is what it was, it was
> arthritis. Now, it just got worse, a steady deterioration, and I put it

down that it was from the works. But with different people questioning me at the hospital, delving into the background, my mother had
arthritis, and my little sister, Ruth, she died long before the war,
1936/7, and she had not arthritis, just rheumatism and that naturally
did for her.

From a clinical perspective and, indeed, from a common-sense appreciation of "inheritance," there appeared to be a strong case for accepting an explanation in terms of genetic transmission. Certainly, in
rheumatological circles, genetic and viral hypotheses are those receiving most serious and sustained attention. Why was he not content
with this?

Bill had spent many years in the military services, and had served
eighteen years with the paratroopers completing 211 successful jumps.
Had he suffered any joint trouble during this time?

No, none whatever. This is why I couldn't associate it. All that time
during the war we had a minimum of clothing on, we never went
under shelter, we kipped in holes, slept on the deck—great stuff! You
know, no problems.

What he appeared to be suggesting by reference to his life in the services was two separate but related things. Firstly, given that he had
"no trouble" during a hard life in the services, he could not realisti-
cally entertain any idea of inherited weakness. On more than one occasion he said that *because* of his harsh experiences he "couldn't associate
anything with it" (his arthritis). If there had been some inner predispo-
sition surely it would have become manifest sooner? The second
theme was that the absence of symptoms while he was in the sevices
made it unlikely that those activities *themselves* were responsible for
creating physical vulnerability. It all happened so much later and with
such suddenness.

Bill was never entirely clear about his state of health while in the
services. At a later point in the interview he mentioned that he *had*
had some symptoms at that time, and that parachuting with 60 lb.
packs was a "probable factor" but, in clarification, he remarked that
many of his mates in the services had symptoms of a similar kind
and that it was put down to "fatigue." While conceding that the
tough life with the paratroopers must have had some effect on his
body, he could not square those experiences with the debilitating development of RA: "To see myself as that, and now, from 1956, I can't
accept it, it's not on."

The references to the services, like the account of the workplace, make it clear that, for Bill, the body is defined by its relationship to the world of social action not in isolation from it. The medical model, employing a reduced range of clinically ascertainable factors, has no sensible meaning in the light of his pragmatic perspective. He was never dogmatic in his beliefs, but his pragmatism would not allow him to accept the validity of the medical model which appeared to rest upon an image of biological arbitrariness and caprice:

> I was trying more or less self-analysis—where have I got it from? How has it come? And you talk to different people over all ages and you find that they are at a loss. They don't know, they don't know, nobody knows. And who do we ask? we ask the doctor (who says): "It's just one of them things . . . and there's nothing to be done about it."

At this point there is no indication of the basis for Bill's refusal of medical rationality. All we have is a statement of preference for one explanation, workplace toxics, over others. A little later we returned to the workplace and to the experiences of his fellow workers as he remembered them:

> But thinking back to the way the other blokes were who are now gone, so we can't ask them, and what I remember of them, they more or less came to it in the same manner . . . I wasn't in there with them all the time, I was traveling between floors so l was coming out of it and getting fresh air and washing more frequently than they did. So this is something to do with it.

Bill had mentioned the "odd" coincidence of similar symptoms at the start of the interview, but his thinking had clearly gone beyond a simple observed correlation. Not only, it seems, was there evidence of infinite patterns of symptomatology amongst the workers, but also a differential severity which he explained by reference to the amount of time spent in contact with toxic substances. In the language of classical epidemiology Bill is invoking, unwittingly, the "dose-response criterion," according to which the investigator considers "whether the risk of disease increases commensurately with degree of exposure"[18] and then examines this in relation to characteristics of both host and environment.

It seemed then, that, notwithstanding the doctors' declared lack of interest in Bill's hypothesis, there was *something* happening at the factory:

They just complained, and I noticed their hands were getting puffy,
and that was one of the things, this seemed to be a common factor for
everybody. Their hands started to puff and their shoes busted. And
there was one guy, Joe [. . .], he was a very tall man, walked fairly
rapidly, and he became slower and slower. And he said: "That's it,
I'm out, it's this . . ." He said straight: "It's killing me, I'm getting
out," and it fetched him straight down. And that's where it's stuck, in
the back of my mind. If Joe . . . remembering the way Joe was, a good
walker, he could nip up and down steps, seeing him just shuffling till
he couldn't even get from the lodge to the workshop without coming
through the lift, he just couldn't make the steps. Well I got that way
till I couldn't make the steps, just couldn't make the steps.

This graphic description of the destruction of men by their work adds
little to the facts of the matter. What it does is to shift the quality of the
discussion away from a simple description of illness associations to an
intimation of the sense of revolt which existed among the workers in
their consciousness of the situation.

Bill recognized the pressure to accept the doctors' analysis as legitimate, but in the light of his practical knowledge he felt that their
analysis was inadequate:

But putting it out of my mind, and having spoken to the specialists,
they say: "No way." So you take their word for it. But it seems a bit
. . . thinking in my mind when I go to bed . . . I can't go to sleep
straight away, I have to wait until I get settled and your mind's going
all the time, you're reflecting "How the *hell* have I come to be like
this?," you know, because it isn't me.

Bill has gone some way towards answering the question. He has identified a causal agent which seemed to explain his arthritis as well as
symptoms in others, and he has described the milieu in which the
causal nexus was situated. He has also portrayed a critical consciousness and a feeling of revolt among the workers which helps to explain
his own unswerving attachment to his explanation when faced with a
plausible clinical alternative. But is this observation of work experience also part of a far more pervasive image of the world?

At another point in the interview, echoing his observation of the
workers whose shoes "busted," Bill told me of the experience of his
wife who "busted her back" while working with the local authority
school meals service. How did this happen?

Well, it was ridiculous because there were no men working there, and they had to go into a stock-room and the "veg man" had stacked spud bags which are 56 lb. five high. And it came to a particular day where they had to get one off the top, and she [his wife] was on her own, and she stood on a chair to get one off, and as it came down— up to that point she was a very strong woman—it just pushed her over and she went right down on the table. But she didn't realize at the time just how badly hurt she was. It was a couple of days after, she just couldn't move, she was almost paralyzed.

This episode, as well as providing an analogue with his own experience, has also led to shared involvement in a long struggle with medical and governmental bureaucracy:

She has a pension from [her employers], but the [invalidity] allowance which was taken from me has been stopped for her, and they didn't even have to give it back. It's the usual "cock-up" at the DHSS.

While Bill did not cite his wife's experience as an explicit parallel, these details of his biography, it seems to me, provide the basis for analogical reasoning and are central to an understanding of the explanation he elaborates for his own affliction. Taking these details into account, the narrative reconstruction of his personal experience has expanded into a more general political criticism exposing the illusions and false consciousness purveyed by various representatives of officialdom. Within this act of interpretation, the model of causation which informs his perception of his own illness and his wife's accident is one where the origins of misfortune are seen as direct, immediate, and within the bounds of human agency, but where the sick/injured person is not culpable in the slightest degree. In both episodes the workplace is defined not in terms of neutral tasks and accidental events, but as the locus of exploitative social relations in which workers are the victims of injustice and neglect.

The increasingly political tenor of his discussion of work and illness became even clearer in a section of the interview where Bill discussed issues surrounding his wife's claim for compensation. She was refused compensation, he told me, firstly because there was no witness to her accident, and secondly because the DHSS medical advisor had diagnosed "osteoporosis" (a chronic deterioration in bone strength) antedating her accident. Bill's response to this was un-equivocal:

> I think that "osteoporosis" is a cop-out. Nobody examined her or
> tested her, nobody took any samples from inside her bones. And this
> would be the only way, decalcification of the bones, because she's on
> calcium tablets now. But this only came up to my way of thinking be-
> cause it was a cop-out, so they wouldn't have to pay a great deal of
> compensation. You know, so what the people at the DHSS said was
> that everybody has this, *you* have it, I'm a liar but you've got it. They
> will say so without even examining you.

When issues of diagnosis are removed from the quiet location of the doctor's clinic and situated within the context of a struggle for compensation, the neutrality of the medical task and the objective validity of its procedures are thrown into doubtful relief. Bill recognized that technology and science are ideological, and that medicine can support political bureaucracy in preventing the establishment of social justice.

The tenacity of Bill's attachment to a workplace toxics explanation for the etiology of his own arthritis takes on clearer significance in the light of these other experiences which, together, form a narrative reconstruction of the genesis of illness which carries a highly political image of the social world. Both illness, and the response of professionals to it, suggest a world of power inequality. There was much more in Bill's account that drew upon images of injustice in society. His experience of getting beaten-up by the police was introduced into the interview and recounted at some length and, as a whole, the world was presented as a place where ordinary people are exploited, conned, and manipulated by a range of social "powers," be they doctors, bureaucrats, or the police. However, it is important not to jump the gun. So far, all I have shown is that Bill locates the onset of his arthritis within the workplace, and that other features of his account suggest mistrust and skepticism with regard to the interests and intentions of people in positions of power. What we have to do now is to look further to see if this radical populist image of society *directly* influences his ideas with regard to the genesis of his own illness.

Following the excursions into the subjects of his wife's accident and the incident with the police, we returned to his own illness and disablement, and Bill related more scenes from his working life:

> 'cause there you had extremes of heat, in the tapes section, we were
> doing computer tapes. There was a special section, and that was
> quite hot up there. Your entry and exit was through the fire door, and

there was no air intake, no fresh air from the outside because it had to be at a particular temperature. And even the chemist down there realized that they're like ovens. It's totally enclosed, it's double thick glass, and they always had the damn things shut till we opened them. We said: "Get us a vent in here or we're not running." And he got one in—that's the chairman who is now dead—he got us an intake. But it was too late for them lads. They had been in it all the time and they were much older than me, and I think their age was against them. They had minimum resistance.

Not only, then, was there a sense of revolt amongst individual workers such as Joe, but a collective refusal by a number of workers to continue what they were doing until certain health and safety measures were instigated. It was not clear how long it was from the workers' recognition of detrimental effects to management compliance, but it was certainly too long for some of them. In this way, Bill's particular arthritic symptoms and their origin became absorbed into a public issue, the issue of health and safety at work, and the original question about the causes of his arthritis was transformed into an examination of the power struggle between workers and management.

By situating the cause of his own misfortune in this context and juxtaposing it with the experience of his wife and friends, Bill's narrative reconstruction articulated a nascent political criticism of the way of life in modern society in which the genesis of his own misfortunes and those of others could be understood as the product of malevolent social forces. Bill himself, of course, did not make such extravagant claims on behalf of his own thinking and, with an almost apologetic appreciation of the limitations of biographical evidence, he said:

> I'm just going off the way the other fellows were, that it became too much for them, and they probably had arthritis at one time, of one type or another. Because none of them walked with a proper gait apart from myself at that time.

Nonetheless, if his narrative reconstruction is read as a sort of historically rooted political criticism, his original identification of workplace toxics as the cause of his arthritis can be seen as part of a more complex attempt to define the dynamics of the relationship between illness, the individual, and society. This society is seen as the locus of exploitation, bureaucratic silence, and multiple frauds upon the laity, where personal troubles are also public issues requiring political intervention.

Bill's analysis did not stop at the workplace. In a final statement he located the issue of illness in the workplace in the context of societal power:

> All those other lads, all their dependents got was two and a half years pay. Probably any investigation that the company made into it had been hushed up a bit 'cause the man I worked for at that time, Sir John Smith, and he became a Lord and is now deceased, and Lord Green and Lord Black were into the company and therefore had very powerful knowledge, and they shut two up if they were giving toxics out and killing men you see. 'Cause nothing's happened since . . . nothing's happened since.

The precise extent of the damage incurred by the workers was never made entirely clear (although it is clear enough). Apparently, the company accepted liability and paid compensation, but Bill argued that the full scale of damage and responsibility was hidden within a strategy of non-decision and silence, ultimately controlled by powerful members of the ruling class who wanted to protect their economic and political interests.

The fact that Bill talked of all these things is not necessarily surprising. What is important is that these observations constitute essential reference points in a narrative reconstruction within which the genesis of illness and other misfortunes can be defined and rendered sensible. Within this reconstruction Bill encompassed what had happened to his body, the nature of his social roles, the quality of his immediate milieu, and the structure of power in society. In doing so, he linked his own demise with that of others, transcended the particulars of his own illness, and redefined his personal trouble as a public issue.

GILL: NARRATIVE RECONSTRUCTION AS SOCIAL PSYCHOLOGY

In Bill's long and detailed reconstruction, both discrete causes and biographical genesis were located essentially outside himself. Although his account encompassed social relations, it left out any reference to his identity or self; there was no sense of personal responsibility or even of any socio-psychological involvement in the development of his affliction. Social relations, however, are also the place in which a sense of identity is developed and constrained, nurtured and broken. In this regard the genesis of an illness may be seen in terms of the body's relationship to the self and the self's relationship to the world.

Gill was a middle-aged school teacher living in a wealthy and conservative suburb. She had had RA for approximately five years, and the onset of the disease took place in a twelve-month period which included a number of tragic events. In my interview with her we spent less time discussing the cause of her affliction than had been the case with Bill. Nevertheless, her ideas were interesting and they represent an illuminating form of narrative reconstruction. As with Bill, I simply asked her why she thought she had got arthritis:

> Well, if you live in your own body for a long time, you're a fool if you don't take note of what is happening to it. I think that you can make naive diagnoses which are quite wrong. But I think that at the back of your head, certainly at the back of my head, I have feelings that this is so and that is so, and I'm quite certain that it was stress that precipitated this.

Now, there is nothing unusual about the identification of "stress" as an important etiological factor. Indeed, in my study group stress was one of the most popular factors, particularly among women and, as Allan Young has indicated, the "discourse on stress" is firmly entrenched is modern thinking on illness and disease.[19] However, more often than not the content of "stress" is left unspecified and, indeed, part of its attractiveness is that it can be used to designate anything from excessive noise to bereavement. Gill, however, felt it necessary to specify exactly what she meant by stress, and having suggested that it precipitated her arthritis she went on:

> Not simply the stress of events that happened but the stress perhaps of suppressing myself while I was a mother and wife; not "women's libby" but there comes a time in your life when you think, you know, "where have I got to? There's nothing left of me. "

Gill did not conceptualize stress in terms of external stressors, exogenous agents which impinge upon the body in some arbitrary fashion; rather she saw her illness as the bodily expression of a suppression of herself. However, while it was not simply a question of external stressors, neither was it a question of internal psychological pathology because she saw the stress of events and the suppression of herself as merely components in the social process of being a wife and a mother. It is within this process that the genesis of bodily breakdown finds its meaning. The causal efficacy of certain events could only be understood within a purposive account of the social process of womanhood in which her personal *telos* and sense of identity had become lost.

However, as Gill has implied, within this overall social process there were specific events that were deemed to have a causal import and which are needed to explain why arthritis supervened at this precise moment in her life-course:

> And then on top of that feeling of . . . not really discontent, but rather confusion about identity . . . to have various physical things happen like, you know, my daughter . . . I'm quite certain that the last straw was my husband's illness. So, I'm sure it was stress induced. I think that while my head kept going my body stopped.

The various "physical things" that happened to Gill were a number of life events that followed in sequence in a twelve-month period. Her daughter went away from home in distressing circumstances (which she asked me not to reproduce), her husband became seriously ill, she suffered a rapid onset of RA (from ambulant to bedridden within 36 hours), her sick husband died, her youngest son was killed in a motorcycle accident, and finally, as a consequence, she lost her long-standing belief in God. Thus, within the social process of womanhood, which was itself stressful, aspects of that womanhood which gave meaning and definition to it—her relationships with her husband and daughter—were damaged. Her arthritis developed in the wake of these events only to be followed by the tragic losses of her husband and her youngest son and the obliteration of the cosmological framework that might have helped her come to terms with these losses: "I feel very lost now that I've lost God. I do. I feel that terribly." It was after the death of her son that she lost God, and she was left with: "A big black hole. Nothing." The symbolically reconstituted past revealed in her narrative reconstruction is one of almost total loss: the disappearance of her daughter, the loss of her physical competence, the death of her husband, the destruction of her youngest son, and, not surprisingly perhaps, the death of God. Now, one of the crucial criteria required for the ascertainment of a causal relationship is a clear time-order separating independent and dependent factors. In this regard, the loss of her husband, her son, and God can have no effective relationship to the onset of her arthritis, but they nevertheless lie within the same crucial matrix of social relationships within which her arthritis has arisen, and they thus form an essential component of her narrative reconstruction. They represent critical ruptures which have formed her present ideas about the causal role of other factors antedating the onset of her arthritis.

At this point, Gill has located the cause of her arthritis within a web of stressful events and processes: a genesis arising out of particular features of a woman's relationships in the modern world. It is a recognition of the distorting and constraining tendencies in these relationships that leads her to the question: "Where have I got to? There's nothing left of me," and to develop her narrative reconstruction around this theme of loss of self and confusion about personal identity. Gill is good example of what Alasdair MacIntyre has in mind when he suggests:

> When someone complains—as do some of those who attempt to commit suicide—that his or her life is meaningless, he or she is often and perhaps characteristically complaining that the narrative of their life has become unintelligible to them, that it lacks any point, any movement towards a climax or *telos*.[20]

Gill did not commit suicide; her mind did not admit the problems and kept going, but her body indicated the necessity of rebellion by breaking down. Because her sense of ontological security was so firmly located within the context of conventional social relationships, the disturbance in those relationships led to an intimation of pointlessness, the development of illness, and the obliteration of all metaphysical referent.

What we have so far then is Gill's essentially sociological explanation of why she developed arthritis. But, in the years between onset of the illness and our meeting, Gill had regular contact with the medical profession and its mode of rationality. To forget this is to create an artificial abstraction. The medical model has often been disparaged by sociologists for, on the one hand, reducing the problems of the sick individual to a set of biophysical parameters and, on the other, reifying the concept of disease to a thing-in-itself.[21] In opposition to this, Mike Bury has argued that the medical model is often a useful symbolic resource which can be employed by individuals to mitigate the feelings of guilt and responsibility which often inform their response to illness and to help them maintain some sense of integrity and autonomy in the context of meaninglessness. While Gill developed a sophisticated socio-psychological model to explain her illness, she also understood that, in terms of the way illness became manifest, a general and popularized version of the medical model had a pleasing common-sense plausibility.

> I had quite forgotten until you mentioned the word virus . . . I said myself that I thought stress had precipitated this, but I would not preclude the fact that it might have been a kind of virus, because in

the early stages I did feel as if I had bad "flu". . . Do you remember
when you get like that?

And, of course, I did remember. In this instance, the medical model
provided us with a shared concept and a common understanding. The
sociological model of "womanhood," on the other hand, was not
something which I could possibly have encompassed within my social
experience. But the problem with the influenza analogy is that it
merely describes a sensation from which a viral etiology may be inferred. It does not provide an adequate account of the genesis of her
illness because it fails to locate it within a context of the changing relationship between herself and the social world.

Although Gill was not racked by feelings of guilt about her illness
and did not feel personally responsible, she did have a sense of involvement in what had happened:

It's the old Adam, we've all got to be ill. No . . . well, I don't know,
certainly things like osteoarthrosis, you're bound to get worn out
parts, like cars. . . . Mind you, I sometimes wonder whether arthritis
is self-inflicted . . . not consciously. You know, your own body says,
"right, shut-up, sit down, and do nothing." I feel very strongly about
myself that this happened to me, that one part of my head said, "if
you won't put the brakes on, I will." Because I had had many years of
very hard physical work, you know—washing and ironing and cook-
ing and shopping and carting kids around and carrying babies and
feeding babies and putting babies to bed and cleaning up their sick. It
all sounds again so very self-pitying, but it's fact. Bringing up five
children is hard work. That, and with the stress on top, I'm sure that I
just cut out, I just blew a fuse.

In this passage from my interview with Gill, the final one relevant to
the subject under consideration, the relationship of womanhood, and
specifically motherhood, to illness was reaffirmed and described in the
bold style of someone confident of their position. But some new elements have been introduced which elaborate that original relationship. Gill brought into play two metaphors, one religious and one mechanical, to suggest the inevitability of illness in society. The image of
the Fall from Grace was introduced to account for the ubiquity of illness in human life and then, hesitatingly, wary perhaps of the fatalism
in a religiosity she has lost, she rejected this in favor of the idea of an
obsolescence built into the body-machine where certain kinds of mechanical degeneration are a necessary consequence of the structure
and functioning of the component parts. While both these images fit

nicely into the teleological framework of an Aristotelian world-view, they do not explain the particular manifestation of illness in *her* life at this moment in time. Thus, following this metaphorical addendum, Gill returned to the central motif of her narrative reconstruction. Given the necessity, mechanical or metaphysical, of *some* kind of illness, the genesis of her arthritis was seen to reside in the social processes of stress and hardship which are the result of the role of women in the modern social structure. The notion of arthritis being self-inflicted implies not simply an individual flaw in a psyche brutalized by contingent events, but more the constraints placed upon the self within a social flow of essential activity.

Much of the work that has considered "lay beliefs" about the causes of particular diseases or illness in general has drawn a line between those beliefs which refer to the source of illness as outside the individual and those which see it as coming from within the individual.[22] Gill's account indicates the inadequacy of such an analytic bifurcation. In a crude sense, she located the source of her arthritis outside herself in a variety of events and processes, but the events she cites are precisely those which speak of the complex relationship between her personal *telos* and her roles in modern society. What she was attempting to express, it seems to me, was that illness arises out of our relationship to the social world when personal identity and the social processes within which that identity is defined come into conflict. When the social self is forced to continue its everyday work and where personal revolt is impossible, the body may instigate its own rebellion. This is what Gill means when she refers to her arthritis being self-inflicted but not consciously.

In her illuminating account Gill managed to describe the relative autonomy of the body, the self, and the social world while indicating the way in which they interrelate. If her narrative is read as a simple description of cause and effect processes, it could be easily categorized as a belief model invoking social stress/life events plus (possible) virus, but this would be to violate it. As a narrative reconstruction, Gill's account can be read as an attempt to portray the genesis of illness within a socio-psychological interpretation of the relationships between personal identity and social roles in modern society, given the inevitability of some kind of illness and the ever-present possibility of viral attack. The complexity of her account results less from her concern to identify the causes of her arthritis and more from her need to reaffirm *telos* and to reconstruct a narrative order in the presence of profound disruptions in the biographical processes of daily life.

BETTY: THE TRANSCENDENCE OF CAUSALITY
AND NARRATIVE RECONSTRUCTION

I have indicated that the degree of narrative embellishment or complexity in the process of reconstruction is related to the amount of biographical disruption to which the individual's life has been exposed.
It could be argued, however, that since the amount of biographical
disruption cannot be assessed apart from the actors' accounts of their
perceptions the whole argument becomes circular. There is a horrible
logic to this, and it is something which I cannot properly refute
within the constraints of my present methods. Nonetheless, in partial
mitigation of this objection, I would suggest that it is reasonable, if
not entirely valid, to infer the amount of disruption from certain brute
"facts." Bill's own premature retirement followed by his wife's accident would certainly spell disruption for the home economy of most
working-class families and, in the same vein, it would be difficult to
imagine the tragic chapter of accidents experienced by Gill being accepted by anyone with equanimity. Their narrative reconstructions
were attempts to account for and repair breaks in the social order. I realize that there are all sorts of methodological and epistemological
objections to this but, as I write, there is little else I can say in my own
defense. Instead, I rest content with presenting the experiences of
Betty who, in spite of inability to hold a much-needed job, to wash
and dress herself, and, because of chronic pain, to sleep in the same
bed as her husband, appeared remarkably composed.

There are some situations in which the central meaning of a life is
defined by some transcendent principle—whether or not we accept
the validity of the principle or the authenticity of the proclaimed belief
in it. Where God is a powerful feature of an individual's cosmology
His existence may be adduced not as a cause of the illness, as some
other studies imply,[23] but as good reason why, in matters of illness and
other misfortunes, the believer is not granted automatic exemption.
Where God is the Cause or the Unmoved Mover, the individual may
be liberated from the burdens of narrative reconstruction and causal
analysis and left free to indulge their lyrical sensibility.

Betty was in her early sixties, married, and had worked full-time
and then part-time in a shop until developing disablement made continuation impossible. She had had arthritis for about seven years. Her
life was not a comfortable one, and she had worked, as she put it, "out
of necessity," in order to supplement her husband's low wage, to pay
off the mortgage, and to maintain a base equilibrium in the home

economy. The loss of her wage rendered the future profoundly inse-
cure. I asked her why she thought she got arthritis:

> The Lord's so near, and, you know, people say "why you?" I mean
> this man next door, he's German, and of course he doesn't believe in
> God or anything [sic] and he says to me, "you, my dear, why he
> chose you?" And I said, "Look, I don't question the Lord, I don't ask
> [. . .], He knows why and that's good enough for me." So he says,
> "He's supposed to look after . . ." [and] I said "He is looking after his
> own [. . .], and he does look after me," I said. I could be somewhere
> where I could be sadly neglected [. . .], well, I'm not. I'm getting all
> the best treatment that can be got, and I do thank the Lord that I'm
> born in this country, I'll tell you that.

Instead of simply affirming that her arthritis originated in the
mysterious workings of God's will, Betty tells a story that locates her
attitude to her illness within a framework of justification that has been
called forth on other occasions by non-believers. She suggests that her
personal misfortune can only be approached within an understanding
of the good fortune in other aspects of her life. The goddess Fortuna
faces both ways. The secular search for cause and meaning or what
Alasdair MacIntyre calls the "narrative quest"[24] is redundant because
the cause, meaning, and purpose of all things is pre-ordained by God:

> I've got the wonderful thing of having the Lord in my life. I've got
> such richness, shall I say, such meaning. I've found the meaning of
> life, that's the way I look at it. My meaning is that I've found the joy
> in this life, and therefore for me to go through anything, it doesn't
> matter really, in one way, because I reckon that they are testing
> times. . . . You see, He never says that you won't have these things,
> He doesn't promise us that we won't have them, He doesn't say that.
> But He comes with us through these things and helps us to bear them
> and that's the most marvelous thing of all.

So, for Betty, biographical robustness, narrative order, and the personal *telos* were not actually contingent upon what happened to her in
the profane world. In fact the idea of a separate and vulnerable "personal" *telos* would make little sense in the context of her essential relationship with God's purpose. MacIntyre argues that teleology and unpredictability coexist in human lives and that the intelligibility of an
individual life depends upon the relationship between plans and purposes on the one hand, and constraints and frustrations on the other.

The anxiety to which this might give rise did not exist for Betty because the unpredictability of, say, pain and illness are part of an ulterior teleology.

This kind of interpretation of life and its difficulties is hard to appreciate in the context of a secular society with its mechanical potions of cause and effect. In talking of "God's purpose" as a component in people's understanding of the genesis of illness, it is important to think carefully about what exactly is entailed in the use of such expressions. When Betty talked about God and personal suffering, she did not imply that God's will was an efficient or proximate cause in the development of her arthritis, rather He is the cause of everything and, as such, makes narrative quests unnecessary. Nonetheless, from a sociological viewpoint, Betty's concept of "God" had similarities to Gill's image of "womanhood" and Bill's notion of "work" in that it transcended linear frameworks of cause and effect so as to define a symbolic and practical relationship between the individual, personal misfortune, social milieu, and the life-world. However, although both Gill and Bill went beyond a linear explanation of disease by placing their experiences of illness within, respectively, a socio-psychological and political narrative reconstruction of their relationships to the social world, Betty's "God" implied a principle of meaning that transcends the social world as such. Betty did not have to reconstruct order through narrative because God, existing "outside" both the individual and society, encompasses within His plans what appear to us as biological caprice and senseless biographical disruption. Physical suffering was only important insofar as it signified a feature of her essential relationship to God and so her sense of identity was not unduly threatened by the body's afflictions. The body itself is nothing as was made clear when, elsewhere in the interview, Betty aired her thoughts on donating her body to medical science:

> Your body is dust and that is what it goes to. I mean the spirit goes to the Lord, the part of me that's telling you all that I am and what goes to the Lord.

Although much that Betty said of her material life would suggest profound disruptions in socio-economic circumstances, there was no sense of disruption because her life was part of God's unfolding purpose. Moreover, "God's will" does not imply self-blame where the individual is bad and illness is retribution; at least, there is no direct relationship:

> You see, it's got nothing to do with Man's goodness. It's all to do with
> Christ, all to do with Him being born to save me, to suffer my sins
> and everything I've ever done. I'm made righteous and sanctified by
> the wonder of that cross and that to me is marvelous, that to me is the
> jewel of life [. . .]. You see, there's a beauty about everything and you
> can sort of go through it in this way, you know, talking to the Lord
> and entering into it. He knows all about it. So people say, "why
> you?" Well, why not me? Better me who knows the Lord.

Because she did not see herself as the author of her own narrative
there was nothing for her to reconstruct or explain. For Betty the
course and end of her life were defined outside herself and history:

> And I think that, yes, it's helped me to understand, and even to the
> [point where] it can have a mental depressive [effect] on some peo-
> ple, because if they haven't got the Lord in their lives, of course, it
> must do. You know, "why am I here? why this, that and the other?"
> To me there's an end to it, something the Lord has for it, and He
> knows best what to do. I reckon, you know, that with faith I'll go
> through with this to an extent and that'll be it, and God will say,
> "well, that's it."

The interview with Betty was a particularly difficult one to conduct
because my sociological questions appeared insignificant and redundant in the face of the teleological certainty of her beliefs. When inter-
viewing someone with such a profound sense of meaning, it seemed
almost meaningless to ask whether the illness had damaged her sense
of self-worth or whatever. For Betty, most people live their lives in the
immediacy of personal and material interests. Their lives follow a narrative thread defined by everyday events and happenings and routines, and when major problems occur in their social world, their identity is bound to be threatened, and it is not surprising that they should
become lost and depressed. But for her "there is an end in it" and all
analytic puzzlement and personal doubt evaporate in the glare of
God's purpose.

CONCLUSION

In his study of the Gnau tribe of New Guinea, Gilbert Lewis described
how these people say of some illnesses that they "just come" and how
they say of the sick person that he or she is "sick nothingly." In this
way, sickness may be defined as having no cause or function, and
no intent. He goes on to contrast this situation with that of western

societies where illness is seen as the result of natural processes which we can study by the scientific method. However, recognizing perhaps the bluntness of this viewpoint, Lewis adds a crucial caveat:

> Individual people in our society may not accept it [the scientific view] as fully adequate to account for illness and seek religious and moral reasons for the illnesses of particular people, or even for illness in general; or individuals may feel an obscure and yet deep emotional dissatisfaction with explanation purely in natural terms, but the general view remains.[25]

The cases I have presented show a far more eclectic search than this. It is true that Bill's account, and those of some other respondents, have the same quality of systematic observation and inference that characterizes representations of scientific procedure. Many of their belief models, at least in formal terms, bear a striking resemblance to the multifactorial models of susceptibility/vulnerability/trigger employed in sophisticated medical discourse, and a large number of respondents resembled those women in Mildred Blaxter's study of lay beliefs whose

> general models of causal processes, painstakingly derived from their experience as they saw it, were often scientifically wrong in detail, but were not in principle unscientific.[26]

I have tried to show that there may be more to such "causal" models than at first meets the eye. Although in my interviews I framed the question in terms of "what causes arthritis?" I have shown in the cases presented that this question was explicitly translated into more substantive biographical questions. It was not just that they were "personalizing" the question; they were transforming the meaning of it.

In this light, Lewis appears to be conflating two different levels of analysis—disease and illness, fact and value, science and morality. People may well draw upon some common-sense version of science and the medical model, but when Gill asks: "Where have I got to? There's nothing left of me," she is asking a question that breaks the bounds of traditional scientific discourse and shifts into a complex social psychology and practical morality. Furthermore, developments in science itself have rendered it increasingly distant from the language and perceptions of everyday life while, at the same time, forming part of the secularization of the western mind which has made overarching cosmologies less available and less plausible. As Comaroff and Maguire put it:

> In our society biomedical science and practice may provide satisfactory explanation and resolution for a wide range of afflictions often (but not always) seeming to render more thorough-going metaphysical speculation redundant. But precisely because of its apparent wide applicability in everyday life, particularly in the wake of the decline of overarching cosmological systems, we are especially bereft when we have to face events for which no rational explanation or remedy is forthcoming.[27]

This was written in relation to childhood leukemia where the limits of rational explanation are particularly obvious, and, to paraphrase Turgenev, death may be an old jest but it comes new to everyone.

RA is not a terminal illness, and therefore lacks the existential gravity of leukemia or typhus. Nevertheless, it assaults the taken-for-granted world and requires explanation. Bill and Gill, finding no meaning in the medical view and having no overarching theodicy or cosmology, elaborated reconstructions of their experience in such a way that illness could be given a sensible place within it. These reconstructions bridge the large gap between the clinical reductions and the lost metaphysics. Once you begin to look at causal models as narrative reconstructions of the genesis of illness experience in the historical agent, moral or religious and, indeed, political and sociological factors become central to elucidating illness experience and rendering intelligible the biographical disruption to which it has given rise.

The body is not only an object among other objects in the world, it is also that through which our consciousness reaches out towards and acts upon the world. This is the dual nature of the body referred to by Sartre,[28] and within this duality chronic illness is a rupture in our relationship with that world. However, consciousness is itself biographically framed, so that consciousness of the body and the interpretations of its states and responses will lead us to call upon images of the private and public lives we lead. Narrative reconstruction is an attempt to reconstitute and repair ruptures between body, self, and world by linking-up and interpreting different aspects of biography in order to realign present and past and self with society. In this context, the identification of "causes" creates important reference points in the interface between self and society. My respondents were, perhaps, not so different from the *baladi* women in Evelyn Early's study for whom "The dialectic between the diagnosis and the life situation is crystallized in the illness narrative, where somatic progression and social developments are both documented."[29]

For Bill, illness developed out of a working life, but the significance of work could only be understood by elaborating an image of the kind of society in which that work was situated. His attachment to workplace toxicity as a causal factor could be understood only in terms of his image of society as a place of exploitative relationships and power inequality. In Gill's case, illness was seen to arise out of a way of life in which personal identity had been defined and constrained by essential features of womanhood. The genesis of her illness was located not solely in the person nor outside in the external world, but within the relationships constitutive of social being. For Betty, the genesis of illness was seen to reside in the transcendental realm of God's purpose. This is not to say that God was seen as an efficient cause of her illness but rather that her illness was necessitated and justified by reference to her intrinsic relationship to a suffering God.

These accounts all speak of illness experience at one moment in time. Their pasts were the pasts of those presents in which they were interviewed, and I have no evidence for or against the proposition that the image of the past would have been substantially different in other presents. To test that would require an altogether more sophisticated piece of research. Within the constraints, what I have attempted to demonstrate is that causality needs to be understood in terms of narrative reconstruction, and that both causal analysis and narrative reconstruction may be rendered redundant in the presence of an embracing theodicy. For medical sociologists such an approach suggests caution in attributing particular belief models to individuals out of relation to other aspects of their narrative, and for doctors it could alert them to reasons for the apparent resistance of some patients to clinical explanations.

ACKNOWLEDGMENT

A shorter version of this work was presented at the BSA Medical Sociology Conference, University of Durham, September 1982. This elaboration owes a lot to the advice and criticism of Peter Halfpenny, and to the valuable comments of Philip Wood and the anonymous referees of the journal in which the article was originally published.

NOTES

1. The Arthritis and Rheumatism Council for Research, *Reports on Rheumatic Diseases. Collected Reports 1959–1977,* London: ARC, 1978, p. 6.

2. D. Locker, *Symptoms and Illness: The Cognitive Organization of Disorder,* London: Tavistock, 1981.

3. P. H. S. Wood (ed.), *The Challenge of Arthritis and Rheumatism: A Report on Problems and Progress in Health Care for Rheumatic Disorders,* London: British League Against Rheumatism / Arthritis and Rheumatism Council, 1977.

4. The term "genesis" is used by Claudine Herzlich in her monograph: *Health and Illness: A Socio-Psychological Approach,* London: Academic Press, 1979. Although I employ a somewhat different definition, I have been much influenced by both the style and substance of that excellent book.

5. For example, J. H. Mabry, "Lay concepts of etiology," *Journal of Chronic Diseases and Therapeutics Research,* vol. 17, 1964, pp. 371–86; R. G. Elder, "Social class and lay explanations for the etiology of arthritis," *Journal of Health and Social Behavior,* vol. 14, 1 973, pp. 28–38; M. Linn, B. Linn, and S. Stein, "Beliefs about causes of cancer in cancer patients," *Social Science Medicine,* vol. 16, 1982, pp. 835–39; R. Pill and N. Stott, "Concepts of illness, causation, and responsibility: some preliminary data from a sample of working class mothers," *Social Science Medicine,* vol. 16, 1982, pp. 43–52; M. Blaxter, "The causes of disease: women talking," *Sociology of Health and Illness,* vol. 17, 1983, pp. 59–69.

6. M. Bury, "Chronic illness as biographical disruption," *Sociology of Health and Illness,* vol. 4, no. 2, 1982, pp. 167–82.

7. See P. Berger and B. Berger, *Sociology: A Biographical Approach,* Harmondsworth: Penguin, 1976; C. W. Mills, *The Sociological Imagination,* Harmondsworth: Penguin, 1970; D. Bertaux (ed.), *Biography and Society: The Life History Approach in the Social Sciences,* New York: Sage, 1981.

8. R. Musil, *The Man Without Qualities, Two: The Like of It Now Happens,* London: Picador, 1979, p. 436.

9. The terms "practical consciousness" and "discursive consciousness" are borrowed from: A. Giddens, *Central Problems in Social Theory: Action, Structure and Contradiction in Social Analysis,* London: Macmillan, 1979, p. 5.

10. M. Linn et al., op. cit., p. 838.

11. G. Orwell, "Shooting an elephant," in *Inside the Whale and Other Essays,* Harmondsworth: Penguin, 1962, p. 93.

12. R. G. Collingwood, *The Idea of History,* Oxford: Clarendon Press, 1946, p. 247.

13. This idea of the relationship of past to present is similar to that of G. H. Mead. For a useful exposition see: D. R. Mains, N. M. Sugrue, and M. A. Katovich, "The sociological import of G. H. Mead's theory of the past," *American Sociological Review*, vol. 48, 1983, pp. 161–73.

14. Probably the best version of Hume's ideas on causality and related issues may be found in: David Hume, A *Treatise of Human Nature*, Oxford University Press, 1978. This includes a helpful analytic index by L. A. Selby-Bigge.

15. R. Bambrough, *The Philosophy of Aristotle*, New American Library, Mentor, 1963.

16. R. Nisbet, *Social Change and History: Aspects of the Western Theory of Development*, New York: Oxford University Press, 1969, p. 27.

17. A. MacIntyre, *After Virtue: A Study in Moral Theory*, London: Duckworth, 1981.

18. N. S. Weiss, "Inferring causal relationships: elaboration of the criterion of 'dose response,'" *American Journal of Epidemiology*, vol. 113, no. 5, 1981, pp. 487–90.

19. A. Young, "The discourse on stress and the reproduction of conventional knowledge," *Social Science Medicine*, vol. 14B, 1980, pp. 133–46.

20. A. MacIntyre, op. cit., p. 202.

21. For example, M. Taussig, "Reification and the consciousness of the patient," Social Science Medicine, vol. 14B, 1980, pp. 3–13.

22. For example, R. Elder, op. cit.; R. Pill and N. Stott, op. cit.

23. M. Linn, et al., op. cit.

24. A. MacIntyre, op. cit.

25. G. Lewis, *Knowledge of Illness in Sepik Society*, London: Athlone Press, 1975, p. 197.

26. M. Blaxter, op. cit., p. 68.

27. J. Comaroff and P. Maguire, "Ambiguity and the search for meaning: childhood leukaemia in the modern clinical context," *Social Science Medicine*, vol. 15B, 1981, p. 119.

28. J-P. Sartre, *Sketch for a Theory of the Emotions*, London: Methuen, 1971.

29. E. A. Early, "The logic of well-being: therapeutic narratives in Cairo, Egypt," *Social Science Medicine*, vol. 16, 1982, p. 1496.

10

Empowering Women:
Self, Autonomy, and Responsibility

Barbara Rowland-Serdar
Peregrine Schwartz-Shea

Liberal feminism is under attack from socialist, radical, and essentialist feminists, who argue that liberal feminism cannot advance the feminist cause "save in a very limited sense."[1] As feminists who believe we must struggle against the systemic subordination of women in public and domestic spheres, and as supporters of a liberal civic order structured by the rule of law, constitutionally limited government, private property, and the legal and moral tradition of individualism, we argue that there is a great need for a revitalized liberal feminism. In this article, we redefine a concept central to liberal feminist theory—the concept of empowerment. We explore the foundations of women's powerlessness in the domestic sphere, suggesting that women can move from powerlessness to empowerment by reclaiming the stories of their lives. We argue that this enlarged understanding of empowerment leads us to rethink the core liberal concepts of autonomy and responsibility and to examine the relationship between family processes and empowerment in the liberal society.

EMPOWERMENT BEYOND RIGHTS

For liberal feminists, empowerment has meant extending the options of women beyond the domestic to the public sphere. This focus sought to extend to women certain "rights" which typically were assumed to be granted to males, or at least white males. The vehicle for such empowerment was legal and constitutional action; liberal ideals were to be extended to all individuals. That today we can talk about what is needed to make empowerment for women possible beyond these rights is testimony to the progress women have made in gaining access to previously closed male domains. This is not to deny, and we believe feminists must criticize, the continuing presence of barriers, prejudice, discrimination, and inequality.[2]

But as feminist commentary on the experience of many women in the 1970s and 1980s illustrates, gaining access to equal legal and constitutional rights, and gaining admission to previously male-dominated arenas is not the equivalent of empowerment for women. The "double day" of work which women who have crossed the barriers into the public sphere confront (and which many women confronted before; feminists publicized it) is a vivid example of the ambiguous nature of women's progress. For many women, it appears that one type of subjugation has merely been exchanged for another. Thus some feminists argue that the juggling of child care, outside work, and home work is a new and perhaps more onerous burden, because it is most often individual women who confront these difficulties, with little support from individual male partners or society at large. And the ambivalence of women themselves toward feminism reflects not only confusion about the value of equal opportunity but, in our interpretation, women's doubts about their own power to shape their lives in either the public or domestic arenas.

Liberal feminists have not addressed these doubts and the underlying issues of selfhood and self-definition they reflect. We believe this is due to the absence of theorizing about the self that is characteristic of liberal thought. Non-liberal feminists criticize liberals for building theory around an abstract, isolated view of the self. But it is not clear that liberal feminists hold such views of the self. Liberal feminism advocates political equality and individual liberty; these goals, however, need not be tied to a vision of abstract individualism. Wendell makes the point clearly: "[s]ince liberal ideals of political equality and individual liberty need not be derived from a view of human nature that includes abstract individualism and do not imply such a view, [there is] no reason to attribute a belief in abstract individualism to liberal feminists unless they express such a belief or it is implied by other positions they adopt."[3]

The difficulty with the liberal feminist theory of the self is not in the abstract individualist notion, but in the apparent failure of liberal feminists (along with liberals in general) to address the process by which a secure sense of self is developed. People whose sense of self is secure *are* capable of becoming empowered through choice and the utilization of rights. Liberals have tended to assume ready-made selves for whom a language of rights is second nature. Rather than assume selfhood, we examine how selfhood develops. With an understanding of selfhood, liberal feminism can more fully address the empowerment of women.

We offer a new conception of empowerment which explicitly includes development of self. We define empowerment as a process in which women come to believe in their ability "to construct, and take responsibility for, [their] gendered identity, [their] politics, and [their] choices."[4] Powerlessness, in contrast, we see as the continuing subordination of women to men in public and private spheres, supported by cultural messages of devaluation internalized, in varying degrees, by women. These messages form the basis for women's doubts about their power to shape their lives.

The foundational messages about women's powerlessness which hinder development of an empowered self are transmitted in large part through the family in liberal society. Yet the liberal tradition has had little to say about the role of the family; failure to theorize about the self reflects and is reflected in the dearth of work on the family. The domestic or family sphere has been assumed to be the site of harmonious, private interactions largely irrelevant to politics. Furthermore, women have been viewed typically as subordinate inhabitants of the family sphere. Therefore, women were politically irrelevant as well.[5]

In response to this truncated liberal view, feminists have articulated two deeply opposed positions on women and the family. Early liberal feminists, like many other feminists, at times exhorted women to reject motherhood, parenting, and work in the home in order to lead lives of liberation in the public sphere. The possibility that women did exercise power in their family and personal lives was disregarded; the idea that there was value in the lives of women engaged exclusively in work in the home was largely absent. Recent feminist literature, which Judith Stacey characterizes as "conservative pro-family feminism,"[6] explicitly challenges the devaluation of mothering and work in the home. The values and virtues of these activities are rigorously defended.

We argue for a third position which transcends the limits of liberal theory by drawing from insights of an interdisciplinary feminist scholarship on the family. In particular, we extend these insights to theorize about how certain kinds of family *processes* (messages, rules, and relationships with the family) support cultural prescriptions about the powerlessness of women and hinder the development of self. This article is part of a larger project in which psychological and cultural barriers to empowerment are considered alongside oppressive economic, social, and political structures. Here we move beyond the work of previous liberal feminists, recasting our understanding of empowerment in ways which challenge traditional formulations of liberal theory while respecting liberal values.

POWERLESSNESS AND DEPENDENCY

Before examining family processes, we need to identify more specifically what we mean by cultural prescriptions about the powerlessness of women. Feminists have identified a variety of cultural mechanisms which communicate the "proper" place of women in liberal society.[7] We identify a set of core components communicated by these mechanisms. The more deeply these messages are internalized by female children and believed by women, the more difficult it is for women themselves to envision empowerment.

These cultural messages can be summarized in terms of three beliefs central to the subordination of women to men: (1) the belief that men have the *right* to control women's lives; (2) the belief that men are *essential* for the well-being of women; and (3) the belief that women are *responsible* for the well-being of relationships.[8] Because the belief in legal rights and equal opportunities for women conflicts with the first belief, this is the area in which the most dramatic change has occurred. Yet even as women have obtained more equal rights, the second and third beliefs persist because they fit with the liberal tradition's treatment of women.

These beliefs prevent the empowerment of women for, to the extent that these messages are internalized, women are too busy focusing their energies outside themselves to examine their own needs. These beliefs also indicate a deep-seated confusion about rights and responsibilities as they relate to women, men, and relationships. This confusion reflects the skewed emphasis on public sphere activities typical of liberal societies; women engaging in domestic activities have no right to control their own lives, and their well-being is dependent upon the men who lead "public" lives. And while women are given the difficult task of caring for relationships, that task itself—as a "domestic" activity—is not highly valued or even much discussed by liberal theorists. Empowerment for women involves the process of resolving the conflicts posed by these beliefs in order to develop a sense of self able to make, and take responsibility for, choices affirming their sense of self even when those choices challenge prevailing cultural messages.

How are these conflicts to be resolved? In order to begin addressing that question, we must look at how family systems and processes transmit these beliefs about powerlessness, and the results of that transmission. In this paper we focus on the family structure found in the white, middle-class American family as it arose in the mid-nineteenth century. This family structure has been regarded as "typical" or "traditional" in Anglo American liberal thought. More important, despite its increasing irrelevance to contemporary family structures, this model of the family still affects public policy and legal analysis.[9]

The middle-class American family in the mid-nineteenth century assigned clear roles to husbands and wives. These roles reflected a series of historical changes well documented by feminist scholarship.[10] In keeping with liberal political thought, the primary role of men was to go out into the public realm; women were to play necessary but adjunct roles of serving and nurturing within the home. Women were to serve sexually (by being a desirable sexual object) and to nurture emotionally (by acting as a surrogate mother). In contrast to the instability and change of the competitive work place, women in the home were to provide stability and unconditional loving; women were seen as "passionless"[11] or as "beautiful souls."[12] Their responsibility was unquestioningly and dutifully to nurture men and children, while acknowledging the authority of men within and outside the home. In this setting, the primacy of the emotional needs of men for nurturing is dominant; the exhausting work of raising children is not to interfere with caring for men. The emotional needs of women and children—particularly female children—fade into the background. In return, men fight battles in the public sphere and "bring home the bacon."[13]

What "family messages" are experienced by children in such families and, in particular, by female children? While this is a complex subject, most of the messages revolve around loss of self. The mother figure, dependent and powerless, must exist through her service to others; the father figure distorts his self by an over-investment in work and an under-investment in emotional relationships. *Both* parents lack resources for living full lives. Lacking these resources, and not having received them themselves as children, parents have a difficult time giving respect to a child as "a unique and worthwhile human being."[14] Children come to experience themselves as objects rather than as worthwhile people whose feelings and preferences matter.

As an object, a child is devalued. The experience of devaluation for a female child can be particularly devastating in conjunction with sexualization. Sexualization of female children means the process by which a female child learns that she is a sex *object* and that her sexuality is *the* fundamental aspect of her identity to which men respond. Because the treatment of female children and women as sex objects is so widespread in liberal society, some forms of sexualization of children appear eminently "normal."

We see female children's learning about their sexuality as a continuum, extending from one extremely empowering and supportive end point (where the female child learns about her sexuality and is taught to value it as one among many aspects of her identity) to another profoundly disempowering and devaluing end point (where the practice of incest and molestation teaches the female child that her value comes from involuntarily servicing the sexual needs of powerful male figures). Even on the more supportive end of the continuum, widely accepted, "trivial" cultural norms, such as the importance of appearance and clothing in female children, beauty pageants for very young female children, and "niceness" in "little girls" can give rise to obsessions about eating, body image, and other perfectionistic approaches to appearance. Common practices of flirtation, teasing about sexual attractiveness and the development of breasts, and allusions to the overriding importance of sexual attractiveness move down the continuum toward the extreme of incest.

The dynamics of incest involve the sexualization of women (all women are seen as sexual objects) and the asymmetry of power in familial relations. The notion that males deserve nurturing from females (including sexual nurturing) can be easily extended to female children if female adults are not present, or are incapable of providing what men consider sufficient nurturing, or are incapable of defending female children against the advances of males in the family. Scholarly, as well as more "popular," studies of father-daughter incest provide support for this interpretation of incest as an extreme form of the sexualization of female children.[15] Sociologist David Finkelhor suggests that sexual victimization reflects male supremacy and serves to perpetuate such supremacy through control of female children. Other feminist researchers document the lack of remorse on the part of incest-perpetrating fathers, citing their beliefs that they "had the right to be nurtured and served at home, if not by their wives then by their daughters."[16] Judith Herman believes that "the greater the paternal dominance and authoritarianism in a family . . . the more may violations of the incest 'taboo' be expected."[17]

A female child is "denied choice, intention and the freedom to transform her situation according to her vision"[18] through devaluation *and* sexualization. The experience of having one's needs denied in order to meet the purposes of the adult male, in conjunction with the lack of respect, means that female children do not have the opportunity to feel safe, lovable, accepted, and worthy.[19] Instead they experience a male father figure controlling their lives; they lack the self-acceptance to believe they can love themselves; and they learn that they are responsible for meeting the needs of men with whom they have familial relationships.

Children who do not feel "safe" nor sure of their acceptability live in anxiety and fear which must be managed one way or another. Westkott identifies three coping strategies children may adopt: helpless dependency, domination, and detachment. The predominant strategy adopted by girls[20] is helpless dependency, in large part because it is consistent with the liberal tradition's views on the subordination of women and therefore most likely to be successful at reducing anxiety. Women as children learn to gain love, acceptance, and worth by pleasing, serving, and relating to others in the domestic sphere. Uncertain of their own internal worth, they are externally referenced; helpless dependents develop "a special sensitivity to unconscious signals manifesting the needs of others."[21] For the female child, dependency is a survival mechanism; for women caring for men becomes a means to bolster one's faltering self-esteem.[22]

The beliefs we have identified as constituting the powerlessness of women, then, are passed on to women as children in the family, via the messages about the needs of the father and other males and the corresponding nurturing expected of women, producing—at worst—the helplessly dependent woman. Thus do the cultural messages of earlier times reproduce and perpetuate themselves in succeeding generations. Of course, over time, these cultural messages and family forms have changed. The "traditional" authoritarian family structure has declined while there has been a steady increase in "non-traditional," egalitarian families. Such family structures may attenuate the messages of powerlessness so that fewer women will face helpless dependency as a barrier to empowerment in the future. Overcoming helpless dependency and reclaiming the self remain, at present, a necessary first step toward empowerment.

TOWARD EMPOWERMENT: RECLAIMING THE SELF

We view the process of overcoming dependency as "reclaiming one's story." Reclaiming one's story involves two key steps. The first is to recognize and embrace the concept that one's life can be thought of as an unfolding story. The second is to exercise choice about how that story will unfold in one's adult life. As Hillman puts it, stories are "containers" in the back of the mind for "organizing events into meaningful experiences."[23] The stories we tell are *always* culturally rooted; we find the analogy of a channel of water helpful here. It is as though each person is born into a channel of water, with the water standing for the cultural and familial patterns existing prior to the individual's birth. After birth, and especially as the child moves toward adulthood, the possibility for forging side-channels develops. With reflection, a person may decide to swim upstream, to stay in the middle of the channel and swim downstream, or to navigate a side-channel unused for many years—but it is not possible for the person somehow to create a whole new channel. Thus the stories we tell are variations on themes which we are supplied by virtue of being born into a certain culture and family.

Selfhood for women, then, involves coming to terms with the cultural stories that have shaped their lives. While the past cannot be undone, the chaotic and traumatic events of the past can be woven into a new and more meaningful story. This implies that women are *active* in the process of making meaning, interpreting their past and their current experiences as their understandings of contemporary culture and history change. As Alcoff expresses it, "women can (and do) think about, criticize, and alter discourse and thus, subjectivity can be reconstructed through the processes of reflective practice."[24]

This process of reflection need not imply "pure reason" capable of "transcending" experience—the mind/body dualistic thinking condemned in numerous feminist critiques.[25] Instead, our account of storytelling recognizes the close connection between reflection and daily experience in women's lives. As women's roles in public and private spheres change, and as more women speak and write about their experiences, women have the opportunity to reconsider old messages of devaluation and sexualization. This is not to say that the old messages disappear; rather, new messages are allowed to enter to challenge the old ones. Reclaiming one's story is a conversational process, including internal dialogue as well as discussion with other individuals. The emphasis on process indicates there is no end point at which a new identity is found; but women can achieve "a more communicative form of life—the possibility of conversational reconciling, both in ourselves and with others."[26]

Conversational reconciling is especially problematic for the helplessly dependent woman. The challenge for helplessly dependent women is to bring their powers of reflective assessment to bear on their experience of powerlessness. To do so requires that one be a "female hero" who begins this process by affirming her capacity to change.[27] This simple prescription, is, of course, far from easy to implement but only the woman herself can make the choice to change. Is this a harsh prescription? Westkott answers by offering an illustrative analogy distinguishing between the cause of a problem and its cure:

> "If a tree, because of storms, too little sun, or too poor soil, becomes warped and crooked, you would not call this its essential nature." Nor would you blame it. Like the tree that suffered from unfriendly or indifferent nature, the injured adult has adapted to the deprivation of her past. And, like the tree, the individual is unable to correct past deficiencies: the storms and the soil, as it were, are a matter of recorded history. Yet, unlike the tree, the human being has the capacity to change.[28]

The capacity to change relies upon two choices: first, willingness to accept the devaluation and sexualization of childhood and, second, a willingness to feel the feelings around that knowledge. As Westkott puts it, women must accept that "the self was not loved for who she really was," and then experience the anger, fear, and sadness around that loss. Women can become reconciled to the earlier realities of their lives in order to move on to self-acceptance. "With this felt self-acceptance, the confounding of fear of others and the need for their love and approval loses its base. No longer fearing others, she no longer feels that she must appease them."[29] Helpless dependency is no longer needed.

Overcoming helpless dependency through reclaiming and telling one's story changes a person's own life and the lives of others around that person. The process of storytelling as it relates to women's empowerment also changes liberal society. At the very least, the traditional liberal denial of the relevance of the family sphere for public matters and politics is challenged. As women (and men as well) insist that many family processes are inappropriate for creating empowered individuals, and as they challenge those practices by refusing to perpetuate them in their own families, liberal theorists will find it increasingly difficult to ignore the topic of family and development of self. The process of reclaiming one's story has been made possible as women have acquired equal rights and the opportunities for independence they imply. And, just as the struggle for equal rights for women has undermined the once common belief that men have the right to control women's lives, the struggle for selfhood can undermine other beliefs about the roles of men and women. The extent to which such changes will translate into changes in the political agenda depends, partly, we argue, on women moving on to acquire autonomy and responsibility in their struggle for empowerment.

EMPOWERMENT AND THE AUTONOMOUS SELF

The pursuit of autonomy, which we regard as a core liberal value, has been regarded with suspicion by many feminists. The confusion around the concept is illustrated by the variety of attacks upon it. Recent criticisms include those of essentialist feminists who do not encourage women to develop autonomy, seeing that as a betrayal of female virtues in favor of the male (and liberal) interest in dominating nature. More important are those critics who link autonomy with the alleged liberal feminist project to turn women into entirely "public" persons who, like men, place the pursuit of self-interest above that of nurturing relationships.[30] Kathryn Addelson, for example, emphasizes the association of autonomous activity with public sphere activities,[31] and in a review of contemporary accounts of autonomy, John Christman uses the account of a "housewife" to illustrate the absence of autonomy, not even noting the possibility that such an occupation could be autonomously chosen.[32] The bias that rational, autonomous choice must propel one into the public sphere and, therefore out of the family sphere, is deeply and widely held—but we maintain that that bias need not be retained in a feminist account of autonomy.

We do agree, however, that the Kantian-inspired notion of autonomy as self-government according to the dictates of reason is an extremely limited concept of autonomy. Reason, in the accounts of prominent liberal thinkers from Kant to Rawls, is clearly separated from the natural/emotional/feeling world; therefore, autonomy is separate from them as well. As Alison Jaggar points out, these accounts reveal an underlying belief that "what is especially valuable about human beings is a particular 'mental' capacity."[33] We move in this paper toward a liberal feminist perspective on autonomy consistent with the account of selfhood provided in the previous section.

We argue that autonomy is best regarded as a process characterized by growth of an ability to *respond* to people and situations rather than to *react*. While critical reflection is involved, choosing to respond involves more than rational knowledge of one's self because self-knowledge is more than a matter of simple introspection. As Grimshaw so succinctly states, "the structures of desire, emotion, and fantasy have deep roots in the self which are not necessarily amenable in any simple way to processes of conscious rational argument."[34] Additionally, physiological limitations of the brain,[35] including the tendency to categorize and then reify those categories to simplify decision making, and the habits and routines of daily life make autonomy a struggle. Thus, autonomy must be conceived of not as an "end state," but as a day-to-day struggle; to do otherwise is to romanticize the concept.[36]

The distinction between responding and reacting is especially important for the development of autonomy out of helpless dependency. Reacting means that a woman's choices are structured largely by beliefs, perspectives, and perceptions belonging to others; reacting means that her personal energy is devoted to monitoring those others and making her choices according to what they do, say, or feel. The external referencing we saw as central to dependency is central to reaction.

Responding allows women to act from knowledge of themselves, their values, and their priorities.[37] The concept of autonomy as responding need *not* be rooted in any valuation of rational decision making, nor need it imply self-sufficiency or separation from others.[38] At the same time, responding is not the same unreflective, passionate venting of feelings of rage and worthlessness left from childhood devaluation. Without intellectualizing, distancing, or denying feelings, responding involves accepting, feeling, and reflecting on feelings in order to decide about "how, when, and with whom we want to express them."[39] We argue that feelings always inform decisions; the question is whether to welcome those feelings and see them as part of oneself, choosing—with the knowledge one has of them—how to act or to deny their presence in favor of the myth of the "strong, independent, rational, coherent" and consistent self.[40]

The choice of response is perhaps the most basic psychological freedom, but it is also a heavy and painful burden which most people fear, preferring familiar pain, the pain generated by reacting and remaining stuck in old patterns of powerlessness. Implicit in choice of response is acceptance that there are situations that cannot be changed, and "our part in [our situation] is the only thing we can change."[41] Feminists long ago recognized that "we had to clarify our own needs, define the terms of our own lives, and take action on our own behalf'" because "no one else would do it for us."[42]

While autonomous response is personally freeing, we argue it also has profound and lasting social, cultural, and political effects. Women who respond rather than react are capable of initiating change in both public and private spheres. The process of changing the helplessly dependent personality empowers women to oppose ongoing social practices that disempower women. We quote at length here from Westkott on this point.

> To be released from externalized living banishes dependency on others, which means opposing their controlling or victimizing behavior. . . . This is not to deny the conditions in which women actually are victimized, but only to change the dependent response to these experiences. . . . The sense of being an innocent victim contains a truth, but it also distorts and denies other aspects of reality, including one's own choice and the possibilities for creating change . . . to deconstruct the dependent character structure . . . develop[s] the strength to oppose actual abuse.[43]

Choosing to struggle for autonomy is simultaneously, for women, choosing to struggle against the cultural messages and family processes which have shaped their subordination. Autonomy, the struggle for choice of response, is the bridge between the powerlessness of dependency and the empowerment of self. The autonomous self is capable of taking responsibility for her actions and choices, and it is responsibility which is the last element of empowerment we wish to consider here.

RESPONSIBILITY AND EMPOWERMENT

In the process of reclaiming their stories and choosing to respond rather than to react, women have developed selves capable of responsibility. We understand responsibility to mean accepting the challenge of acting or choosing in a manner consistent with one's sense of selfhood and sense of meaning in the world. Implicit in this idea is the belief that responsible persons make judgments about whether or not their actions and choices contribute positively to the life stories they are constructing. In contrast to responsibility, paternalism "encourages us to cease relying on our ability to judge, hence it encourages the loss of moral agency."[44] Moving through dependency to autonomy allows for the possibility of a self with integrity; paternalistic intervention invades an individual's integrity, clearly reducing autonomy and empowerment.

In keeping with Rosaldo's reminder that feminists ought to avoid opposing "woman" to "man" in "the same way in all contexts,"[45] we argue that paternalistic behaviors should not be associated exclusively with men. Clearly, dependency and powerlessness in women is perpetuated by paternalism but, in turn, helplessly dependent women engage in paternalistic behaviors themselves. Women's paternalism is rarely recognized as such. We argue that the practice of paternalism by women in relationships with men, in particular, not only impedes the full growth of self for women, but similarly cripples the development of self in men. As Tronto argues, "The dearth of caretaking experiences makes privileged males morally deprived."[46] The controversy about women's morality and moral judgment brought to prominence by Carol Gilligan's work, in our reading, provides support for our view that paternalistic behaviors hinder women's empowerment.

In her book, *In a Different Voice*, Gilligan starts out quite carefully and deliberately to describe two distinct "ways of speaking about moral problems."[47] One of these, the "justice perspective," she finds more often in the comments of male subjects; reason and rights dominated in explanations of decision making. The other is a "care perspective" which articulates a morality of care and responsibility. This perspective, which she finds more often in the comments of female subjects, reflects a "self enmeshed in a network of relations to others, and whose moral deliberations aims to maintain these relations."[48] Gilligan is most interested in rethinking prominent views on the development of morality, views which she maintains have relied solely upon male experience.

Gilligan's work has been commented upon extensively[49] and interpreted in a number of ways. Her research has been utilized by essentialist feminists to argue that women's morality is not only different from that of men, but also superior to that of men. It also has been cited to demonstrate that men are indeed more rational and women care more about feelings—interpretations which can be used to justify any number of sexist practices. Even more troubling is the evidence in Gilligan's work of women either forgetting their own needs and rights, or having difficulty affirming their own needs and rights. As Susan Wendell says, "Surely there is now good reason to believe that they forget or avoid this because girls and women are taught that pleasing and taking care of others is what gives them worth."[50] Indeed, for the helplessly dependent self, referencing one's actions to others is firmly entrenched. Westkott is clear about the significance of Gilligan's findings: "this female voice of moral responsibility is an expression of a contradiction of powerless responsibility, a duty to care for others out of subordination to them."[51]

In our interpretation, Gilligan's work reveals the continuing presence in liberal society of the third cultural belief outlined earlier in this paper: that women are responsible for the well-being of relationships. Detachment from such responsibility often occurs as part of an empowering process in which women come to value themselves as worthy individuals, valuable in themselves. It is undeniable that coming to see oneself as a worthy individual "limits one's obligations and responsibilities."[52] The growth of self in women does have implications for their relationships with others; valuing oneself more means that women do their share of emotional work and nurturing—and then refuse to do more. Naomi Scheman reacts with alarm to such a possibility, picturing "a world filled with self-actualizing persons pulling their own strings, capable of guiltlessly saying 'no' to anyone about anything."[53] But a change in the willingness of women to do more than their share of emotional work "appears selfish and uncaring *only if* we assume that men are incapable of responding by taking greater responsibility for their own and their children's nurturance and emotional life, i.e., for doing their share."[54] Here we see the paternalism inherent in women's "caring" for men; this caring, when it takes the form of discerning men's needs and responding to them, not only denies men the integrity of identifying their needs and asking to have them met, but additionally places men in "the position of the peripheral 'other' in the domestic sphere, just as women have been so rendered in the public domain."[55]

Rather than thinking of responsibility in terms of being responsible for others and caring for others' needs, we suggest a language of responsibility *to* self, and *to* others. Responsibility to self involves caring for oneself as a valuable human being and engaging in the struggle for the autonomous self by working through one's own issues and clarifying one's own beliefs and values. This kind of responsibility to self makes possible a new way of thinking about responsibility to others in a nonpaternalistic way. Responsibility to others involves respecting others' integrity and, rather than taking responsibility for others' welfare, encouraging them "to find the strength and skill to take care of themselves."[56] This view of responsibility promotes cooperation between equals and supports the empowerment of others, children included, in relationships and in families.

The tendency to glorify women's nurturing abilities can reify what are historically produced traits. Such glorification encourages women to lose sight of the connection between the care ethic of women and the context of subjugation within which it arose. Lerner comments that the more women are celebrated as nurturers, "the less likely it is that men will identify and utilize their own competence in this arena."[57] Yet as women move into the public realm out of necessity and choice, the need for men to share in nurturing activities is greater than ever.[58] One of Gilligan's other findings, that *both* men and women are capable of responding to *both* justice and care perspectives, is far more supportive of women's empowerment. Empowered selves can choose to care from genuine affection and weigh trade-offs between rights and care from a secure sense of self, rather than from powerlessness.

Empowered individuals—able to nurture and care as well as speak the language of rights—can form genuinely nurturing families which challenge rather than support cultural messages about women's powerlessness. This does not mean erasure of all difference or specialization of tasks; instead we have in mind what Gould terms "mutuality,"[59] where individuals work to empower others while still recognizing and respecting difference. Nor does it mean mythical family harmony; the changes in women's and men's lives that make empowerment and intimacy possible are such fundamental and deep-seated changes that the turmoil they bring is extremely painful. And there is no way around that pain; nor do we minimize the extent to which women, in the quest for empowerment, have born a disproportionate share of the burdens of change.[60] The conservative pro-family feminism Stacey discusses reflects the enormous difficulty and the high costs of confronting sexual politics in the family. Because of the pain and the costs, not all women (and clearly not all men) share the goal of empowering women in the way we describe in this paper. For liberal feminists, and ultimately for all liberals, this vision of empowerment suggests fundamental changes in theorizing about the liberal society.

LIBERALISM AND THE EMPOWERMENT OF WOMEN

Our vision of a revitalized liberal feminism builds on liberal themes of rights, choice, and agency, and then enriches and extends the liberal vision by arguing that certain kinds of family interactions are as essential to the liberal society of empowered individuals as are certain kinds of public institutions. Or, in other words, if liberals retain the goal of respecting individuals and individual choices, the "private" sphere can no longer be ignored or dismissed as irrelevant to politics and beyond the reach of public policy. The liberal's uncritical acceptance of "family harmony" that has justified the patriarchal family[61] and supported a "clean" dichotomy between public and private spheres must be rejected. Liberals must look carefully at broad questions about how family processes shape the development of the self as well as specific questions about the effects of particular public policies.

Valuing the empowerment of individuals requires liberal feminists and all liberals to address at least two key issues: domestic violence and the value placed upon nurturing activities, including parenting, in the liberal society. As the historical and contemporary statistics on family violence attest,[62] the harmonious family has been and is a myth. Serious attention to domestic violence is critical if the promise of liberalism is to be meaningful. This requires recognition that the family is not "naturally private" but a unit "constructed" in myriad ways by public policy (i.e., requiring school attendance, regulation of child labor, immunization laws, contraceptive policies, etc.). The granting of family privacy in a liberal society must be consistent with the protection of individual rights. Such a vision with its emphasis on individual rights has been questioned by those who see a tension between an ethic of caring and a language of rights; some argue that talk of children's rights, in particular, can be hazardous to family intimacy.[63]

We maintain that genuine nurturing flourishes when *all* individuals in the family unit are treated as worthy of respect. But respectful and nurturing relationships do not appear "naturally"; they require acceptance of responsibility for creating such relationships and investment of time, energy, and effort. Yet liberal theorists, and liberal societies, have ignored or discounted the worth of such investment in the domestic sphere. This is most apparent when we look at issues of parenting. Liberals must reassess the assignment of responsibility for relationships to women and simultaneously look at how public and workplace structures can be changed to encourage, or at least allow, investment in parenting activities by men as well as women.

Looking at the empowerment of women in the way we have suggested here, with our emphasis on the processes by which selfhood, autonomy, and responsibility develop, clearly challenges liberals to examine deep-seated and long-standing tenets of liberal society. Such an examination, which we have barely begun here, will be difficult and painful, with far-reaching effects. But as women move toward empowerment by reclaiming and telling their stories, the liberal's denial of the relevance and importance of the private sphere to creating a liberal polity becomes increasingly difficult to sustain. And, finally, as more and more women become empowered, their personal and political choices will require changes in men's lives and in the public policies which structure the liberal society.

NOTES

1. Judith Evans, "Feminist Theory and Political Analysis," *Feminism and Political Theory*, ed. Judith Evans, Jill Hills, Karen Hunt, Elizabeth Meehan, Tessa ten Tusscher, Ursual Vogel, and Georgina Waylen (Beverly Hills, Calif.: Sage, 1986), pp. 103–19.

2. The issues involved in confronting these persistent factors are discussed in, for example, Sanford Dornbusch and Myra Strober, *Feminism, Children, and the New Families* (New York: Guilford Press, 1988).

3. Susan Wendell, "A (Qualified) Defense of Liberal Feminism," *Hypatia*, vol. 2, no. 2 (1987), pp. 65–93.

4. Linda Alcoff, "Cultural Feminism versus Post-Structuralism: The Identity Crisis in Feminist Theory," *Signs*, vol. 13, no. 3 (1988), pp. 405–36.

5. The work of John Stuart Mill (see his *Subjection of Women*) is a notable exception. For examples of scholarly work addressing the assumptions of Western philosophers about women, see Susan Moller Okin, *Women in Western Political Thought* (Princeton, N.J.: Princeton University Press, 1979) and Lorenne Clark and Lynda Lange, eds., *The Sexism of Social and Political Thought* (Toronto: University of Toonto Press, 1979).

6. Judith Stacey, "Are Feminists Afraid to Leave Home? The Challenge of Conservative Pro-Family Feminism," *What Is Feminism?*, ed. Juliet Mitchell and Ann Oakley (Oxford: Basil Blackwell, 1986).

7. Cf. Rosalind Coward, *Female Desires: How They Are Sought, Bought, and Packaged* (New York: Grove Press, 1985).

8. This list is adapted from Thelma Goodrich, Cheryl Rampage, Barbara Ellman, and Kris Halstead, *Feminist Family Therapy* (New York: Horton, 1988); the use to which it is put is entirely our own responsibility.

9. Lyla O'Driscoll, "Toward a New Theory of the Family," *The American Family and the State*, ed. Joseph Peden and Fred Glahe (San Francisco: Pacific Research Institute for Public Policy, 1986), pp. 81–101; David Kirp, Mark Yoduf, and Marlene Strong Franks, *Justice* (Chicago: University of Chicago Press, 1986).

10. Cf. Linda Nicholson, *Gender and History: The Limits of Social Theory in the Age of the Family* (New York: Columbia University Press, 1986); Marcia Westkott, *The Feminist Legacy of Karen Horney* (New Haven, Conn.: Yale University Press, 1986).

11. Nancy Cott, "Passionlessness: An Interpretation of Victorian Sexual Ideology, 1790–1850," *Signs*, vol. 4, no. 2 (1976), pp. 219–36.

12. Jean Bethke Elshtain, *Women and War* (New York: Basic Books, 1987).

13. The persistence of this imagery should not, we believe, be discounted. Consider the following "restaurant reading" from Dan Valentine's *American Essays*, vol. II, on "the wife": "she's a pair of waiting arms for a weary warrior. She repairs frayed banners torn on daily battlefields . . . She cushions defeat . . . and makes victories worthwhile . . . Each morning she stands in the doorway with a smile in her heart and love in her eyes and waves good-bye to the warrior as he sets out for another day to hunt dragons . . . She needs extra endurance and extra insight to match the highs and lows of her husband's ever-changing moods."

14. Westkott, *Feminist Legacy*, p. 82.

15. Important accounts include Susan Forward and Craig Buck, *Betrayal of Innocence: Incest and Its Devastation* (New York: Penguin, 1978); Ellen Bass and Laura Davis, *The Courage to Heal: A Guide for Women Survivors of Child Sexual Abuse* (New York: Harper and Row, 1988); and Judith Herman (with Lisa Hirschman), *Father-Daughter Incest* (Cambridge, Mass.: Harvard University Press, 1981).

16. Cited in Wini Breines and Linda Gordon, "Review Essay: The New Scholarship on Family Violence," *Signs*, vol. 8, no. 3 (1983), pp. 490–531, at p. 527.

17. Cited in ibid, p. 527.

18. Westkott, *Feminist Legacy*, p. 121.

19. Alice Miller, *The Drama of the Gifted Child* (New York: Basic Books, 1981).

20. Boys also may adopt this strategy, particularly in severely anxiety-ridden homes, but more often they use domination and detachment.

21. Westkott, *Feminist Legacy*, p. 137.

22. We do not confuse the "helpless dependent" personality type discussed here with the experience of interdependence which is a universal given of human experience. Nor do we contrast the helpless dependent with an emotionally self-sufficient person, a person having no need for others or a person who is unwilling to care about other people. We wish to emphasize the extent to which helpless dependence is a deeply-rooted psychological reaction to experiences of powerlessness and lack of worth.

23. James Hillman, "A Note on Story," *Parabola: Myth and the Quest for Meaning*, vol. 4, no. 4 (1979), pp. 43–46, at p. 43.

24. Alcoff, "Cultural Feminism," p. 425.

25. For an introduction to feminist debates on these topics, see the varying approaches of Genevive Lloyd, *The Man of Reason: "Male" and "Female" in*

Western Philosophy (Minneapolis: University of Minnesota Press, 1984); Carol McMillan, *Women, Reason, and Nature: Some Philosophical Problems with Feminism* (Princeton: N.J.: University Press, 1982); Janet Richards, *The Skeptical Feminist: A Philosophical Enquiry* (Boston: Routledge and Kegan Paul, 1980); Sherry Ortner, "Is Female to Male as Nature Is to Culture?," *Women, Culture, and Society*, ed. Michelle Rosaldo and Louise Lamphere (Stanford, Calif.: Stanford University Press, 1974), pp. 67–87; and Sandra Harding, "The Instability of the Analytical Categories of Feminist Theory," *Signs*, vol. 11, no. 4 (1986), pp. 645–64.

26. Elisabeth Young-Bruehl, "The Education of Women as Philosophers," *Signs*, vol. 12, no. 2 (1987), pp. 207–21, at p. 219.

27. Westkott, *Feminist Legacy*.

28. Ibid., pp. 200–1.

29. Ibid., p. 213.

30. Jean Bethke Elshtain, *Public Man, Private Woman: Women in Social and Political Thought* (Princeton, N.J.: Princeton University Press, 1981).

31. Kathryn Addelson, "Autonomy and Respect," *Journal of Philosophy*, vol. 84, no. 11 (1987), pp. 628–29, at p. 628.

32. John Christman, "Constructing the Inner Citadel: Recent Work on the Concept of Autonomy," *Ethics*, no. 99 (October, 1988), pp. 109–24.

33. Alison Jaggar, *Feminist Politics and Human Nature* (Totowa, N.J.: Rowman and Allanheld, 1983), p. 28.

34. Jean Grimshaw, *Philosophy and Feminist Thinking* (Minneapolis: University of Minnesota Press, 1986), p. 401.

35. Herbert Simon, "Human Nature in Politics: The Dialogue of Psychology with Political Science," *American Political Science Review*, vol. 79, no. 2 (1985), pp. 293–304.

36. bell hooks, "Feminism: A Movement to End Sex Oppression," *Feminism and Equality*, ed. Anne Phillips (New York: New York University Press, 1987), pp. 62–76, at p. 69.

37. Harriet Lerner, *Women in Therapy*, (New York: Harper and Row, 1988).

38. Thomas Hill, "The Importance of Autonomy," *Women and Moral Theory*, ed. Eva Kittay and Diana Meyers (Totowa, N.J.: Rowman and Littlefield, 1987), pp. 129–38, at p. 135.

39. Lerner, *Women in Therapy*, p. 205.

40. Grimshaw, *Philosophy and Feminist Thinking*, p. 97.

41. Lerner, *Women in Therapy*, p. 208.

42. Ibid.

43. Westkott, *Feminist Legacy*, p. 201.

44. Sara Lucia Hoagland, "Lesbian Ethics: Some thoughts on Power in Our Interactions," *Lesbian Ethics*, vol. 2 (1986), pp. 5–32, at p. 10.

45. Michelle Rosaldo, "The Use and Abuse of Anthropology: Reflections on Feminism and Cross-Cultural Understanding," *Signs*, vol. 5, no. 3 (1980), pp. 389–417 at p. 401.

46. Joan Tronto, "Beyond Gender Differences to a Theory of Care," *Signs*, vol. 12, no. 4 (1987), pp. 644–63 at p. 652.

47. Carol Gilligan, *In a Different Voice: Psychological Theory and Women's Development* (Cambridge, Mass.: Harvard University Press, 1982), p. 1.

48. Kittay and Meyers, *Women and Moral Theory*, p. 10.

49. For a sampling of this commentary, see the special issues of *Ethics*, vol. 92, no. 3 (1982) and *Social Research*, vol. 50, no. 3 (1983) and a symposium in *Signs*, vol. 11, no. 2 (1986).

50. Wendell, "Liberal Feminism," p. 83.

51. Westkott, *Feminist Legacy*, p. 141.

52. Sandra Harding, "The Curious Coincidence of Feminine and African Moralities: Challenges for Feminist Theory," *Women and Moral Theory*, ed. Kittay and Meyers, pp. 296–315, at p. 301.

53. Cited in Grimshaw, *Philosophy and Feminist Thinking*, p. 161.

54. Wendell, "Liberal Feminism," p. 77; emphasis added.

55. Lerner, *Women in Therapy*, p. 242.

56. Wendell, "Liberal Feminism," p. 84.

57. Lerner, *Women in Therapy*, p. 253.

58. Robert Karen, "Becoming Attached," *The Atlantic Monthly* (February, 1990), pp. 35–70.

59. Carol Gould, "Private Rights and Public Virtues: Women, the Family, and Democracy," *Beyond Domination: New Perspectives on Women and Philosophy*, ed. Carol Gould (Totowa, N.J.: Rowman and Allanheld, 1983), pp. 3–18.

60. Stacey, "Are Feminists Afraid," p. 238.

61. O'Driscoll, "Toward a New Theory," p. 92; Okin, *Women in Western Political Thought*, p. 74.

62. Cf. Joyce Gelb, "The Politics of Wife Abuse," *Families, Politics, and Public Policy: A Feminist Dialogue on Women and the State* (New York: Longman, 1983), pp. 250–62.

63. Ferdinand Schoeman, "Rights of Children, Rights of Parents, and the Moral Basis of the Family," *Ethics*, vol. 91, no. 1 (1980), pp. 6–19; Robert Nisbet, *Prejudices: A Philosophical Dictionary* (Cambridge: Harvard University Press, 1982).

III

Community

Neither the crystallization of personal identity nor the attempt to make experience intelligible, discussed previously in this volume, occurs within a social void. These processes are guided and constrained by culture, and narrativists like to emphasize the crucial role that stories play in socializing people into accepted ways of acting, thinking, and perceiving, in fostering group cohesion, and in perpetuating communal traditions. A community's stories offer members a set of canonical symbols, plots, and characters through which they can interpret reality and negotiate—or even create—their world.[1] The culture "speaks to itself" as members replicate these canonical forms in their own lives.[2] Indeed, without the consensus that narratives help to establish, the memories they preserve, and the values and behavior-patterns they transmit, culture would be impossible.[3] As Barthes has observed, "there does not exist, and never has existed, a people without narratives."[4]

Narratives, then, are what constitute community.[5] They explain a group to itself, legitimate its deeds and aspirations, and provide important benchmarks for non-members trying to understand the group's cultural identity. The form and content of a community's preferred narratives reflect its political situation and social structure as these have developed over time. Culture itself, in fact, has been conceptualized as "the story its members tell so as to make sense of all the different pieces of their social life."[6]

Many narrativists recognize that socialization into any narrative order will have its repressive side, and is unlikely to be completely successful. The narratives of the powerful tend to be, by definition, privileged and hegemonic,

235

but there may be room for interpretations that challenge prevailing orthodoxies.[7] "Outgroups" typically create "counterstories," often having an ironic or satiric flavor.[8] Such counterstories may heighten social tensions, energize opposition, or catalyze political and ideological change. Through their ability to foster "communities of memory [and of] hope," they may be effective in preparing individuals for leadership and keeping resistance alive "at the height of repression."[9] In this respect, narratives can contribute to social disequilibrium as well as its opposite, both within and between communities.[10] At bottom, political and cultural conflicts frequently turn on how reality is to be interpreted—on which of the available narrative forms is most appropriate and persuasive.

Certainly, the image of communities guided by intact, well-articulated narratives seems to fit "traditional" societies better than modern ones. Lyotard and others, as discussed previously, have even argued that the age of grand narratives is over.[11] No doubt, many narrativists would concur that culturally shared stories are being progressively hollowed out and debunked by empirical science and critical rationality.[12] And some of these thinkers worry that the decline of narrative will make it more difficult to maintain any sort of social cohesion, since the latter has relied so much on common stories in the past. In times of rapid social change, the "guiding myths developed by previous generations fail to fit the territory."[13] Can we, given the fragmentation and heterogeneous character of contemporary society, hope to create persuasive new narratives of our own? To paraphrase Ricoeur, the fear is that "the end of the era of narrative may come because we no longer have narratives to share."[14] But the more common view, developed already in earlier sections of this volume, has been that narratives will never simply fade away, because they are integral to identity and memory. The writers in the current section on community would all, we think, reject the "end of narrative" argument (which is, of course, *itself* a grand narrative).

The first selection presented below is excerpted from Alasdair MacIntyre's influential work of moral philosophy, *After Virtue*. Hoping to strike a balance between an overly individualistic and an excessively socialized depiction of community, MacIntyre opts for the narrative approach. We are, he claims, "story-telling animals"; the stories that can be woven from our deeds and experiences define, for ourselves and others, who we are. In MacIntyre's view, the notion of purposive behavior lies at the heart of what it means to be a story-telling being. Our individual words and deeds only make sense as elements in a more encompassing set of projects which, in their turn, derive meaning from the purpose (*telos*) that we pursue. Purposes depend not only on our personal situations and predelictions, but also on the stories that our culture makes available as models. Following Aristotle, MacIntyre suggests that we should understand human life as a quest for some good, one that needs socially transmitted virtues for its fulfillment. Story, drama, and plot are thus not merely clever interpretive devices imposed on people's lives; they flow naturally from the more fundamental characteristic of the intelligibility of human action. However, MacIntyre's notion of narrative unity does not imply that any community is or ought to be a closed association defined exclusively by consensus about valid plots, scripts, and characters. Narrative leaves room for differences of opinion about the meaning of the dominant stories in a culture and the virtues requisite to acting them out.

If anthropologists are "the natural anti-scripturalists of the social sciences"[15] because of their discipline's traditional focus on pre-literate cultures and its time-worn method of field research, this proclivity has waned with the declining fortunes of structuralism and functionalism and the rise of hermeneutics.[16] "Distanced, normalizing discourse" dominated the discipline for decades, and classic ethnographers such as Malinowski "literally marginalized narrative."[17] But when the primary aim of anthropology becomes understanding cultures from the inside, in terms of their own stock of meanings and associations, narratives loom larger in importance[18]—as do the inevitable problems of interpretation that accompany them. Edward Bruner, operating within a "social constructivist" paradigm, regards ethnographic scholarship as a form of collaborative storytelling which has no real author. In the "second-order" narratives elaborated by ethnographers, meaning and structure are elicited from a culture's present existence by the way that its relationship to the past and the future are understood. What counts, in other words, is the plotline that imaginatively connects the tenses. Ethnographies, according to Bruner, should not be looked upon as more or less objective extrapolations from the researcher's data. It is actually the other way around: anthropologists gather, approach, and interpret data in light of a narrative that they bring with them into the field, one that inevitably reflects the larger historical situation. Such narratives can shift suddenly and dramatically, as Bruner illustrates with reference to the Native American ethnographic literature, and they condition both what facts, topics, and observations anthropologists deem salient and how they conceive of their role vis-à-vis the culture under scrutiny.

Concern with narrative has come rather belatedly to the various subfields of political science, and although analysts of public policy and social movements have begun to use the category,[19] it has made the greatest impact within political philosophy, where it is traceable above all to the influence of Heidegger's student, Hannah Arendt.[20] Communitarian thinkers such as Charles Taylor and Michael Walzer have been especially partial to narrative, since they stress not the values, interests, and identities that individuals have in atomistic isolation, but rather what people share as members of an on-going civic order.[21] Philip Abbott's article examines the uses and abuses of narratives in political philosophy. Abbott argues that although stories, if well-chosen and coherent, can engage the reader and bring a theory to life, theorists who employ this device do so at significant risk. This is so for several reasons. The story's point may not be completely consistent with what the author seeks to prove; the story may be reinterpretable in a way that challenges the theory; the story may be countered by other stories that call the theory into question; and the story may even spotlight weaknesses in the theory that would not otherwise have been apparent. In short, narrative and theory, while often wedded in particular works of political thought, always coexist uneasily. Still, theorists—at least in politics—have rarely been able to dispense entirely with stories. Perhaps the reason is that politics grows out of practical life, in which narratives are at home, and only becomes theoretical by a leap of abstraction.

In his essay, Walter Fisher—building on the work of such diverse thinkers as Alasdair MacIntyre, Jürgen Habermas, and Richard Rorty—takes note of the discrepancy between the requirements for ideal communication and the realities of existing communities.[22] Inevitably, the sort of communication that actually prevails will fall short of our rhetorical standards, and in consequence the community itself will lose legitimacy in our eyes, appearing to be rooted in ideology and domination rather than dialogue, reason, and consensus. Fisher offers a way around this conundrum by articulating a notion of "narrative rationality." Human beings, in a view he shares with MacIntyre, are story-telling animals. It is narratives, along with the values they prescribe, that form the basis of communities large and small, and thereby define who we are. The potential members of a community are capable of judging such narratives by means of two gauges of rationality: fidelity, or accuracy in representing experience, and coherence, meaning roughly internal harmony, consistency, and believability. We extend or withhold allegiance to communities depending on our rational judgments concerning the narratives on which they are based.

The interdisciplinary field of environmental studies has seen a dawning of interest in narrative.[23] Some thinkers have argued that an important cause of our environmental problems is the loss of stories that once bound people to nature, bringing "personal meaning together with the grandeur and meaning of the universe."[24] Jim Cheney's article, however, takes a different tack. It attempts to reconceptualize ecological ethics in terms of narratives created by the inhabitants of bioregional communities, i.e., communities in which political affiliations follow natural, ecological boundary lines. Writing from a postmodernist perspective, Cheney believes that we should avoid both a totalizing "masculine" discourse and an essentializing "feminine" discourse as we try to fashion an ethic that will help us relate responsibly to the rest of nature. Bioregionally-based narratives can satisfy this requirement, in his view. They are inherently local, contextual, and negotiable, and they help us to define our relations to the land and each other in healthy, respectful, life-affirming ways. They also bear on the problem of identity: a coherent notion of the self must be "a narrative of self-in-place"; it cannot emerge in abstraction from the communities, both human and natural, in which we reside. In order to live well, we need to construct what Cheney calls a "mindscape/landscape" out of which moral obligations can flow.

NOTES

1. J. Bruner 1986:66, 1987:15; Rosenwald and Ochberg 1992:7; Johnstone 1990:76; Polkinghorne 1988:20; Geertz 1973:208–13.

2. Gergen and Gergen 1988:40; J. Bruner 1987:15; Rosenwald and Ochberg 1992:7.

3. Berger and Kellner 1964:3; Kellner 1987:26; Ricoeur 1985:222; Cuoto 1993:76; Maines 1992:366–67; Berry 1988:130.

4. Quoted in Polkinghorne 1992:14. See also Trumpener 1992 and De-Mallie 1993.

5. Keeshig-Tobias 1994:120; Maines 1992:366–67; Katriel and Shenhar 1990; DeMallie 1993.

6. Walzer 1983:319. See also Richardson 1988:201; Howard 1991:187; Polkinghorne 1992:14; Mair 1988:127; J. Bruner 1991:17–21; Geertz 1987:239.

7. Rosaldo 1989:28; Cuoto 1993; MacIntyre 1981:206; Polkinghorne 1988:6; Vizenour 1986; Davis and Kennedy 1986; Brewer 1984:1144; M. Gergen 1990; Trumpener 1992.

8. Delgado 1989:2412,2414; Scheppele 1989; Abrams 1989:972; Cuoto 1993.

9. Cuoto 1993:60, 57. See also Steinmetz 1992; Somers 1992; Hart 1992.

10. Georges 1969:315,325; Turner 1986:34; Davis and Kennedy 1986.

11. Lyotard 1984.

12. Wiggins 1975; Hauerwas et al. 1977:25; Novak 1975:175–76; Crites 1986:162; Berry 1988; Kellner 1987:26.

13. Feinstein 1979:199.

14. Kellner 1987:26.

15. Gellner 1988:21.

16. Gellner 1988; Geertz 1980.

17. Rosaldo 1989:120,37.

18. Geertz 1980, 1973; Georges 1969; DeMallie 1993; Harkin 1988; Vizenor 1986; Sass 1986; Van Maanen 1988.

19. Kaplan 1986; Kling 1993; Roe 1994; Dryzek 1982; W. Lewis 1987.

20. Arendt 1958. For commentary see Disch 1994; Luban 1983; Benhabib 1990. See also Smith 1985.

21. Massaro 1989:2121.

22. Other scholars of speech and communications who have utilized narrative in their work include Polanyi 1989; Bochner and Ellis 1992; Scott 1984; Carey 1989; Labov 1982; Labov and Waletzky 1967; Todorov 1977; Katriel and Shenhar 1990; Tannen 1982; Roeh 1989; and Lewis 1994.

23. B. Taylor 1995; Berry 1988; Snyder 1990; Maines and Bridger 1992; Raglon and Scholtmeijer 1996; and Van Buren 1995.

24. Berry 1988:131.

11

The Virtues, the Unity of a Human Life, and the Concept of a Tradition

Alasdair MacIntyre

Any contemporary attempt to envisage each human life as a whole, as a unity, whose character provides the virtues with an adequate *telos* encounters two different kinds of obstacles, one social and one philosophical. The social obstacles derive from the way in which modernity partitions each human life into a variety of segments, each with its own norms and modes of behavior. So work is divided from leisure, private life from public, the corporate from the personal. So both childhood and old age have been wrenched away from the rest of human life and made over into distinct realms. And all these separations have been achieved so that it is the distinctiveness of each and not the unity of the life of the individual who passes through those parts in terms of which we are taught to think and to feel.

The philosophical obstacles derive from two distinct tendencies, one chiefly, though not only, domesticated in analytical philosophy and one at home in both sociological theory and in existentialism. The former is the tendency to think atomistically about human action and to analyze complex actions and transactions in terms of simple components. Hence the recurrence in more than one context of the notion of "a basic action." That particular actions derive their character as parts of larger wholes is a point of view alien to our dominant ways of thinking and yet one which it is necessary at least to consider if we are to begin to understand how a life may be more than a sequence of individual actions and episodes.

Equally the unity of a human life becomes invisible to us when a sharp separation is made either between the individual and the roles that he or she plays—a separation characteristic not only of Sartre's existentialism, but also of the sociological theory of Ralf Dahrendorf—or between the different role—and quasi-role—enactments of an individual life so that life comes to appear as nothing but a series of unconnected episodes—a liquidation of the self, characteristic of Goffman's sociological theory. Both the Sartrian and the Goffmanesque conceptions of selfhood are highly characteristic of the modes of thought and practice of modernity. It is perhaps therefore unsurprising to realize that the self as thus conceived cannot be envisaged as a bearer of the Aristotelian virtues.

For a self separated from its roles in the Sartrian mode loses that arena of social relationships in which the Aristotelian virtues function if they function at all. The patterns of a virtuous life would fall under those condemnations of conventionality which Sartre put into the mouth of Antoine Roquentin in *La Nausée* and which he uttered in his own person in *L'Etre et le néant*. Indeed the self's refusal of the inauthenticity of conventionalized social relationships becomes what integrity is diminished into in Sartre's account.

At the same time the liquidation of the self into a set of demarcated areas of role-playing allows no scope for the exercise of dispositions which could genuinely be accounted virtues in any sense remotely Aristotelian. For a virtue is not a disposition that makes for success only in some one particular type of situation. What are spoken of as the virtues of a good committee man, or of a good administrator, or of a gambler, or a pool hustler are professional skills professionally deployed in those situations where they can be effective, not virtues. Someone who genuinely possesses a virtue can be expected to manifest it in very different types of situation, many of them situations where the practice of a virtue cannot be expected to be effective in the way that we expect a professional skill to be. Hector exhibited one and the same courage in his parting from Andromache and on the battlefield with Achilles: Eleanor Marx exhibited one and the same compassion in her relationship with her father, in her work with trade unionists, and in her entanglement with Aveling. And the unity of a virtue in someone's life is intelligible only as a characteristic of a unitary life, a life that can be conceived and evaluated as a whole. Each stage in the emergence of the characteristically modern views of the moral judgment was accompanied by a corresponding stage in the emergence of the characteristically modern conceptions of selfhood. In defining the particular premodern concept of the virtues, it has become necessary to say something of the concomitant concept of selfhood, a concept of a self whose unity resides in the unity of a narrative which links birth to life to death as narrative beginning to middle to end.

Such a conception of the self is perhaps less unfamiliar than it may appear at first sight. Just because it has played a key part in the cultures which are historically the predecessors of our own, it would not be surprising if it turned out to be still an unacknowledged presence in many of our ways of thinking and acting. Hence it is not inappropriate to begin by scrutinizing some of our most taken-for-granted, but clearly correct conceptual insights about human actions and selfhood in order to show how natural it is to think of the self in a narrative mode.

It is a conceptual commonplace, both for philosophers and for ordinary agents, that one and the same segment of human behavior may be correctly characterized in a number of different ways. To the question "what is he doing?" the answers may with equal truth and appropriateness be "Digging"; "Gardening"; "Taking exercise"; "Preparing for winter"; or "Pleasing his wife." Some of these answers will characterize the agent's intentions, others unintended consequences of his actions, and of these unintended consequences some may be such that the agent is aware of them and others not. What is important to notice immediately is that any answer to the questions of how we are to understand or to explain a given segment of behavior will presuppose some prior answer to the question of how these different correct answers to the question "What is he doing?" are related to each other. For if someone's primary intention is to put the garden in order before the winter and it is only incidentally the case that in so doing he is taking exercise and pleasing his wife, we have one type of behavior to be explained; but if the agent's primary intention is to please his wife by taking exercise, we have quite another type of behavior to be explained and we will have to look in a different direction for understanding and explanation.

In the first place the episode has been situated in an annual cycle of domestic activity, and the behavior embodies an intention which presupposes a particular type of household-*cum*-garden setting with the peculiar narrative history of that setting in which this segment of behavior now becomes an episode. In the second instance the episode has been situated in the narrative history of a marriage, a very different, even if related, social setting. We cannot, that is to say, characterize behavior independently of intentions, and we cannot characterize intentions independently of the settings which make those intentions intelligible both to agents themselves and to others.

I use the word "setting" here as a relatively inclusive term. A social setting may be an institution, it may be what I have called a practice, or it may be a milieu of some other human kind. But it is central to the notion of a setting as I am going to understand it that a setting has a history, a history within which the histories of individual agents not only are, but have to be, situated, just because without the setting and its changes through time the history of the individual agent and his changes through time will be unintelligible. Of course one and the same piece of behavior may belong to more than one setting. There are at least two different ways in which this may be so.

In my earlier example the agent's activity may be part of the history both of the cycle of household activity and of his marriage, two histories which have happened to intersect. The household may have its own history stretching back through hundreds of years, as do the histories of some European farms, where the farm has had a life of its own, even though different families have in different periods inhabited it; and the marriage will certainly have its own history, a history which itself presupposes that a particular point has been reached in the history of the institution of marriage. If we are to relate some particular segment of behavior in any precise way to an agent's intentions and thus to the settings which that agent inhabits, we shall have to understand in a precise way how the variety of correct characterizations of the agent's behavior relate to each other first by identifying which characteristics refer us to an intention and which do not and then by classifying further the items in both categories.

Where intentions are concerned, we need to know which intention or intentions were primary, that is to say, of which it is the case that, had the agent intended otherwise, he would not have performed that action. Thus if we know that a man is gardening with the self-avowed purposes of healthful exercise and of pleasing his wife, we do not yet know how to understand what he is doing until we know the answer to such questions as whether he would continue gardening if he continued to believe that gardening was healthful exercise, but discovered that his gardening no longer pleased his wife, *and* whether he would continue gardening, if he ceased to believe that gardening was healthful exercise, but continued to believe that it pleased his wife, *and* whether he would continue gardening if he changed his beliefs on both points. That is to say, we need to know both what certain of his beliefs are and which of them are causally effective; and, that is to say, we need to know whether certain contrary-to-fact hypothetical statements are true or false. And until we know this, we shall not know how to characterize correctly what the agent is doing.

Consider another equally trivial example of a set of compatibly correct answers to the question "What is he doing?" "Writing a sentence"; "Finishing his book"; "Contributing to the debate on the theory of action"; "Trying to get tenure." Here the intentions can be ordered in terms of the stretch of time to which reference is made. Each of the shorter-term intentions is, and can only be made, intelligible by reference to some longer-term intentions; and the characterization of the behavior in terms of the longer-term intentions can only be correct if some of the characterizations in terms of shorter-term intentions are also correct. Hence the behavior is only characterized adequately when we know what the longer and longest-term intentions invoked are and how the shorter-term intentions are related to the longer. Once again we are involved in writing a narrative history.

Intentions thus need to be ordered both causally and temporally and both orderings will make references to settings, references already made obliquely by such elementary terms as "gardening," "wife," "book," and "tenure." Moreover the correct identification of the agent's beliefs will be an essential constituent of this task; failure at this point would mean failure in the whole enterprise. (The conclusion may seem obvious; but it already entails one important consequence. There is no such thing as behavior, to be identified prior to and independently of intentions, beliefs, and settings. Hence the project of a science of behavior takes on a mysterious and somewhat *outré* character. It is not that such a science is impossible; but there is nothing for it to be but a science of uninterpreted physical movement such as B. F. Skinner aspires to. It is no part of my task here to examine Skinner's problems; but it is worth noticing that it is not at all clear what a scientific experiment could be, if one were a Skinnerian, since the conception of an experiment is certainly one of intention- and belief-informed behavior. And what would be utterly doomed to failure would be the project of a science of, say, *political* behavior, detached from a study of intentions, beliefs, and settings. It is perhaps worth noting that when the expression "the behavioral sciences" was given its first influential use in a Ford Foundation Report of 1953, the term "behavior" was defined so as to include what were called "such subjective behavior as attitudes, beliefs, expectations, motivations and aspirations" as well as "overt acts." But what the Report's wording seems to imply is that it is cataloguing two distinct sets of items, available for independent study. If the argument so far is correct, then there is only one set of items.)

Consider what the argument so far implies about the interrelationships of the intentional, the social, and the historical. We identify a particular action only by invoking two kinds of context, implicitly if not explicitly. We place the agent's intentions, I have suggested, in causal and temporal order with reference to their role in his or her history; and we also place them with reference to their role in the history of the setting or settings to which they belong. In doing this, in determining what causal efficacy the agent's intentions had in one or more directions, and how his short-term intentions succeeded or failed to be constitutive of long-term intentions, we ourselves write a further part of these histories. Narrative history of a certain kind turns out to be the basic and essential genre for the characterization of human actions.

It is important to be clear how different the standpoint presupposed by the argument so far is from that of those analytical philosophers who have constructed accounts of human actions which make central the notion of "a" human action. A course of human events is then seen as a complex sequence of individual actions, and a natural question is: How do we individuate human actions? Now there are contexts in which such notions are at home. In the recipes of a cookery book for instance actions are individuated in just the way that some analytical philosophers have supposed to be possible of all actions. "Take six eggs. Then break them into a bowl. Add flour, salt, sugar, etc." But the point about such sequences is that each element in them is intelligible as an action only as a-possible-element-in-a-sequence. Moreover even such a sequence requires a context to be intelligible. If in the middle of my lecture on Kant's ethics I suddenly broke six eggs into a bowl and added flour and sugar, proceeding all the while with my Kantian exegesis, I have *not*, simply in virtue of the fact that I was following a sequence prescribed by Fanny Farmer, performed an intelligible action.

To this it might be related that I certainly performed an action or a set of actions, if not an intelligible action. But to this I want to reply that the concept of an intelligible action is a more fundamental concept than that of an action as such. Unintelligible actions are failed candidates for the status of intelligible action; and to lump unintelligible actions and intelligible actions together in a single class of actions and then to characterize action in terms of what items of both sets have in common is to make the mistake of ignoring this. It is also to neglect the central importance of the concept of intelligibility.

The importance of the concept of intelligibility is closely related to the fact that the most basic distinction of all embedded in our discourse and our practice in this area is that between human beings and other beings. Human beings can be held to account for that of which they are the authors; other beings cannot. To identify an occurrence as an action is in the paradigmatic instances to identify it under a type of description which enables us to see that occurrence as flowing intelligibly from a human agent's intentions, motives, passions, and purposes. It is therefore to understand an action as something for which someone is accountable, about which it is always appropriate to ask the agent for an intelligible account. When an occurrence is apparently the intended action of a human agent but none the less we cannot so identify it, we are both intellectually and practically baffled. We do not know how to respond; we do not know how to explain; we do not even know how to characterize minimally as an intelligible action; our distinction between the humanly accountable and the merely natural seems to have broken down. And the kind of bafflement does indeed occur in a number of different kinds of situations when we enter alien cultures or even alien social structures within our own culture, in our encounters with certain types of neurotic or psychotic patients (it is indeed the unintelligibility of such patients' actions that leads to their being treated as patients; actions unintelligible to the agent as well as to everyone else are understood—rightly—as a kind of suffering), but also in everyday situations. Consider an example.

I am standing, waiting for a bus and the young man standing next to me suddenly says: "The name of the common wild duck is *Histrionicus histrionicus histrionicus.*" There is no problem as to the meaning of the sentence he uttered: the problem is, how to answer the question, what was he doing in uttering it? Suppose he just uttered such sentences at random intervals; this would be one possible form of madness. We could render his act of utterance intelligible if one of the following turned out to be true. He has mistaken me for someone who yesterday had approached him in the library and asked: "Do you by any chance know the Latin name of the common wild duck?" *Or* he has just come from a session with his psychotherapist who has urged him to break down his shyness by talking to strangers. "But what shall I say?" "Oh, anything at all." *Or* he is a spy waiting at a prearranged rendezvous and uttering the ill-chosen code sentence which will identify him to his contact. In each case the act of utterance becomes intelligible by finding its place in a narrative.

To this it may be replied that the supplying of a narrative is not necessary to make such an act intelligible. All that is required is that we can identify the relevant type of speech-act (e.g., "He was answering a question") or some purpose served by his utterance (e.g., "He was trying to attract your attention"). But speech-acts and purposes too can be intelligible or unintelligible. Suppose that the man at the bus stop explains his act of utterance by saying "I was answering a question." I reply: "But I never asked you any question to which that could have been the answer." He says. "Oh, I know *that.*" Once again his action becomes unintelligible. And a parallel example could easily be constructed to show that the mere fact that an action serves some purpose of a recognized type is not sufficient to render an action intelligible. Both purposes and speech-acts require contexts.

The most familiar type of context in and by reference to which speech-acts and purposes are rendered intelligible is the conversation. Conversation is so all-pervasive a feature of the human world that it tends to escape philosophical attention. Yet remove conversation from human life and what would be left? Consider then what is involved in following a conversation and finding it intelligible or unintelligible. (To find a conversation intelligible is not the same as to understand it; for a conversation which I overhear may be intelligible, but I may fail to understand it.) If I listen to a conversation between two other people my ability to grasp the thread of the conversation will involve an ability to bring it under one out of a set of descriptions in which the degree and kind of coherence in the conversation is brought out: "a drunken, rambling quarrel"; "a serious intellectual disagreement"; "a tragic misunderstanding of each other"; "a comic, even farcical mis-construal of each other's motives"; "a penetrating interchange of views"; "a struggle to dominate each other"; "a trivial exchange of gossip. "

The use of words such as "tragic," "comic," and "farcical" is not marginal to such evaluations. We allocate conversations to genres, just as we do literary narratives. Indeed a conversation is a dramatic work, even if a very short one, in which the participants are not only the ac-tors, but also the joint authors, working out in agreement or disagree-ment the mode of their production. For it is not just that conversations belong to genres in just the way that plays and novels do; but they have beginnings, middles and endings just as do literary works. They embody reversals and recognitions; they move towards and away from climaxes. There may within a longer conversation be digressions and subplots, indeed digressions within digressions and subplots within subplots.

But if this is true of conversations, it is true also *mutatis mutandis* of battles, chess games, courtships, philosophy seminars, families at the dinner table, businessmen negotiating contracts—that is, of human transactions in general. For conversation, understood widely enough, is the form of human transactions in general. Conversational behavior is not a special sort or aspect of human behavior, even though the forms of language-using and of human life are such that the deeds of others speak for them as much as do their words. For that is possible only because they are the deeds of those who have words.

I am presenting both conversations in particular, then, and human actions in general as enacted narratives. Narrative is not the work of poets, dramatists, and novelists reflecting upon events which had no narrative order before one was imposed by the singer or the writer; narrative form is neither disguise nor decoration. Barbara Hardy has written that "we dream in narrative, daydream in narrative, remember, anticipate, hope, despair, believe, doubt, plan, revise, criticize, construct, gossip, learn, hate and love by narrative" in arguing the same point.[1]

At the beginning of this chapter I argued that in successfully identifying and understanding what someone else is doing we always move towards placing a particular episode in the context of a set of narrative histories, histories both of the individual concerned and of the settings in which they act and suffer. It is now becoming clear that we render the actions of others intelligible in this way because action itself has a basically historical character. It is because we all live out narratives in our lives, and because we understand our own lives in terms of the narratives that we live out, that the form of narrative is appropriate for understanding the actions of others. Stories are lived before they are told—except in the case of fiction.

This has of course been denied in recent debates. Louis O. Mink, quarreling with Barbara Hardy's view, has asserted: "Stories are not lived but told. Life has no beginnings, middles, or ends; there are meetings, but the start of an affair belongs to the story we tell ourselves later, and there are partings, but final partings only in the story. There are hopes, plans, battles, and ideas; but only in retrospective stories are hopes unfulfilled, plans miscarried, battles decisive, and ideas seminal. Only in the story is it America which Columbus discovers and only in the story is the kingdom lost for want of a nail."[2]

What are we to say to this? Certainly we must agree that it is only retrospectively that hopes can be characterized as unfulfilled or battles as decisive and so on. But we so characterize them in life as much as in art. And to someone who says that in life there are no endings, or that final partings take place only in stories, one is tempted to reply, "But have you never heard of death?" Homer did not have to tell the tale of Hector before Andromache could lament unfulfilled hope and final parting. There are countless Hectors and countless Andromaches whose lives embodied the form of their Homeric namesakes, but who never came to the attention of any poet. What is true is that in taking an event as a beginning or an ending we bestow a significance upon it which may be debatable. Did the Roman republic end with the death of Julius Caesar, or at Philippi, or with the founding of the principate? The answer is surely that, like Charles II, it was a long time a-dying; but this answer implies the reality of its ending as much as do any of the former. There is a crucial sense in which the principate of Augustus, or the taking of the oath in the tennis court, or the decision to construct an atomic bomb at Los Alamos constitute beginnings; the peace of 404 B.C., the abolition of the Scottish Parliament, and the battle of Waterloo equally constitute endings; while there are many events which are both endings and beginnings.

As with beginnings, middles, and endings, so also with genres and with the phenomenon of embedding. Consider the question of to what genre the life of Thomas Becket belongs, a question which has to be asked and answered before we can decide how it is to be written. (On Mink's paradoxical view this question could not be asked until *after* the life had been written.) In some of the medieval versions, Thomas's career is presented in terms of the canons of medieval hagiography. In the Icelandic *Thomas Saga* he is presented as a saga hero. In Dom David Knowles's modern biography the story is a tragedy, the tragic relationship of Thomas and Henry II, each of whom satisfies Aristotle's demand that the hero be a great man with a fatal flaw. Now it clearly makes sense to ask who is right, if anyone: the monk William of Canterbury, the author of the saga, or the Cambridge Regius Professor Emeritus? The answer appears to be clearly the last. The true genre of the life is neither hagiography nor saga, but tragedy. So of such modern narrative subjects as the life of Trotsky or that of Lenin, of the history of the Soviet Communist Party or the American presidency, we may also ask: To what genre does their history belong? And this is the same question as: What type of account of their history will be both true and intelligible?

Or consider again how one narrative may be embedded in another. In both plays and novels there are well-known examples: the play within the play in *Hamlet*; Wandering Willie's Tale in *Redgauntlet*;

Aeneas' narrative to Dido in book 2 of the *Aeneid;* and so on. But there are equally well-known examples in real life. Consider again the way in which the career of Becket as archbishop and chancellor is embedded within the reign of Henry II, or the way in which the tragic life of Mary Stuart is embedded in that of Elizabeth I, or the history of the Confederacy within the history of the United States. Someone may discover (or not discover) that he or she is a character in a number of narratives at the same time, some of them embedded in others. Or again, what seemed to be an intelligible narrative in which one was playing a part may be transformed wholly or partly into a story of unintelligible episodes. This last is what happened to Kafka's character K. in both *The Trial* and *The Castle.* (It is no accident that Kafka could not end his novels, for the notion of an ending, like that of a beginning, has its sense only in terms of intelligible narrative.)

I spoke earlier of the agent as not only an actor, but an author. Now I must emphasize that what the agent is able to do and say intelligibly as an actor is deeply affected by the fact that we are never more (and sometimes less) than the co-authors of our own narratives. Only in fantasy do we live what story we please. In life, as both Aristotle and Engels noted, we are always under certain constraints. We enter upon a stage which we did not design and we find ourselves part of an action that was not of our making. Each of us being a main character in his own drama plays subordinate parts in the dramas of others, and each drama constrains the others. In my drama, perhaps, I am Hamlet or Iago or at least the swineherd who may yet become a prince, but to you I am only A Gentleman or at best Second Murderer, while you are my Polonius or my Gravedigger, but your own hero. Each of our dramas exerts constraints on each other's, making the whole different from the parts, but still dramatic.

It is considerations as complex as these which are involved in making the notion of intelligibility the conceptual connecting link between the notion of action and that of narrative. Once we have understood its importance, the claim that the concept of an action is secondary to that of an intelligible action will perhaps appear less bizarre and so too will the claim that the notion of "an" action, while of the highest practical importance, is always a potentially misleading abstraction. An action is a moment in a possible or actual history or in a number of such histories. The notion of a history is as fundamental a notion as the notion of an action. Each requires the other. But I cannot say this without noticing that it is precisely this that Sartre denies—as indeed his whole theory of the self, which captures so well the spirit of modernity, requires that he should. In *La Nausée*, Sartre makes Antoine Roquentin argue not just what Mink argues, that narrative is very different from life, but that to present human life in the form of a narrative is always to falsify it. There are not and there cannot be any true stories. Human life is composed of discrete actions which lead nowhere, which have no order; the storyteller imposes on human events retrospectively an order which they did not have while they were lived. Clearly if Sartre/Roquentin is right—I speak of Sartre/Roquentin to distinguish him from such other well-known characters as Sartre/Heidegger and Sartre/Marx—my central contention must be mistaken. There is none the less an important point of agreement between my thesis and that of Sartre/Roquentin. We agree in identifying the intelligibility of an action with its place in a narrative sequence. Only Sartre/Roquentin takes it that human actions are as such unintelligible occurrences: it is to a realization of the metaphysical implications of this that Roquentin is led in the course of the novel, and the practical effect upon him is to bring to an end his own project of writing an historical biography. This project no longer makes sense. Either he will write what is true or he will write an intelligible history, but the one possibility excludes the other. Is Sartre/Roquentin right?

We can discover what is wrong with Sartre's thesis in either of two ways. One is to ask: what would human actions deprived of any falsifying narrative order be like? Sartre himself never answers this question; it is striking that in order to show that there are no true narratives, he himself writes a narrative, albeit a fictional one. But the only picture that I find myself able to form of human nature *an-sich*, prior to the alleged misinterpretation by narrative is the kind of dislocated sequence which Dr. Johnson offers us in his notes of his travels in France: "There we waited on the ladies—Morville's.—Spain. Country towns all beggars. At Dijon he could not find the way to Orleans.—Cross roads of France very bad.—Five soldiers.—Women.—Soldiers escaped.—The Colonel would not lose five men for the sake of one woman.—The magistrate cannot seize a soldier but by the Colonel's permission, etc., etc."[3] What this suggests is what I take to be true, namely that the characterization of actions allegedly prior to any narrative form being imposed upon them will always turn out to be the presentation of what are plainly the disjointed parts of some possible narrative.

We can also approach the question in another way. What I have called a history is an enacted dramatic narrative in which the characters are also the authors. The characters of course never start literally *ab initio:* they plunge *in medias res,* the beginnings of their story already made for them by what and who has gone before. But when Julian Grenfell or Edward Thomas went off to France in the 1914–18 war they no less enacted a narrative than did Menelaus or Odysseus when *they* went off. The difference between imaginary characters and real ones is not in the narrative form of what they do; it is in the degree of their authorship of that form and of their own deeds. Of course just as they do not begin where they please, they cannot go on exactly as they please either: each character is constrained by the actions of others and by the social settings presupposed in his and their actions, a point forcibly made by Marx in the classical, if not entirely satisfactory, account of human life as enacted dramatic narrative, *The Eighteenth Brumaire of Louis Bonaparte.*

I call Marx's account less than satisfactory partly because he wishes to present a narrative of human social life in a way that will be compatible with a view of that life as law-governed and predictable in a particular way. But it is crucial that at any given point in an enacted dramatic narrative we do not know what will happen next. Unpredictability is required by the narrative structure of human life, and the empirical generalizations and explorations which social scientists discover provide a kind of understanding of human life which is perfectly compatible with that structure.

This unpredictability coexists with a second crucial characteristic of all lived narratives, a certain teleological character. We live out our lives, both individually and in our relationships with each other, in the light of certain conceptions of a possible shared future, a future in which certain possibilities beckon us forward and others repel us, some seem already foreclosed and others perhaps inevitable. There is no present which is not informed by some image of some future and an image of the future which always presents itself in the form of a *telos*—or of a variety of ends or goals—towards which we are either moving or failing to move in the present. Unpredictability and teleology therefore coexist as part of our lives: like characters in a fictional narrative we do not know what will happen next, but none the less our lives have a certain form which projects itself towards our future. Thus the narratives which we live out have both an unpredictable and a partially teleological character. If the narrative of our individual and social lives is to continue intelligibly—and either type of narrative may lapse into unintelligibility—it is always both the case that there are constraints on how the story can continue and that within those constraints there are indefinitely many ways that it can continue.

A central thesis then begins to emerge: man is in his actions and practice, as well as in his fictions, essentially a story-telling animal. He is not essentially, but becomes through his history, a teller of stories that aspire to truth. But the key question for men is not about their own authorship; I can only answer the question "What am I to do?" if I can answer the prior question "Of what story or stories do I find myself a part?" We enter human society, that is, with one or more imputed characters—roles into which we have been drafted—and we have to learn what they are in order to be able to understand how others respond to us and how our responses to them are apt to be construed. It is through hearing stories about wicked stepmothers, lost children, good but misguided kings, wolves that suckle twin boys, youngest sons who receive no inheritance but must make their own way in the world, and eldest sons who waste their inheritance on riotous living and go into exile to live with the swine, that children learn or mislearn both what a child and what a parent is, what the cast of characters may be in the drama into which they have been born and what the ways of the world are. Deprive children of stories and you leave them unscripted, anxious stutterers in their actions as in their words. Hence there is no way to give us an understanding of any society, including our own, except through the stock of stories which constitute its initial dramatic resources. Mythology, in its original sense, is at the heart of things. Vico was right and so was Joyce. And so too of course is that moral tradition from heroic society to its medieval heirs according to which the telling of stories has a key part in educating us into the virtues.

I suggested earlier that "an" action is always an episode in a possible history: I would now like to make a related suggestion about another concept, that of personal identity. Derek Parfit and others have drawn our attention to the contrast between the criteria of strict identity, which is an all-or-nothing matter (*either* the Tichborne claimant *is* the last Tichborne heir; *either* all the properties of the last heir belong to the claimant *or* the claimant is not the heir—Leibniz's Law applies) and the psychological continuities of personality which are a matter of more or less. (Am I the same man at fifty as I was at forty in respect of memory, intellectual powers, critical responses? More or less.) But what is crucial to human beings as characters in enacted narratives is that, possessing only the resources of psychological continuity, we have to be able to respond to the imputation of strict identity. I am forever whatever I have been at any time for others—and I may at any time be called upon to answer for it—no matter how changed I may be now. There is no way of *founding* my identity—or lack of it—on the psychological continuity or discontinuity of the self. The self inhabits a character whose unity is given as the unity of a character. Once again there is a crucial disagreement with empiricist or analytical philosophers on the one hand and with existentialists on the other.

Empiricists, such as Locke or Hume, tried to give an account of personal identity solely in terms of psychological states or events. Analytical philosophers, in so many ways their heirs as well as their critics, have wrestled with the connection between those states and events and strict identity understood in terms of Leibniz's Law. Both have failed to see that a background has been omitted, the lack of which makes the problems insoluble. That background is provided by the concept of a story and of that kind of unity of character which a story requires. Just as a history is not a sequence of actions, but the concept of an action is that of a moment in an actual or possible history abstracted for some purpose from that history, so the characters in a history are not a collection of persons, but the concept of a person is that of a character abstracted from a history.

What the narrative concept of selfhood requires is thus twofold. On the one hand, I am what I may justifiably be taken by others to be in the course of living out a story that runs from my birth to my death; I am the subject of a history that is my own and no one else's, that has its own peculiar meaning. When someone complains—as do some of those who attempt or commit suicide—that his or her life is meaningless, he or she is often and perhaps characteristically complaining that the narrative of their life has become unintelligible to them, that it lacks any point, any movement towards a climax or a *telos*. Hence the point of doing any one thing rather than another at crucial junctures in their lives seems to such a person to have been lost.

To be the subject of a narrative that runs from one's birth to one's death is, I remarked earlier, to be accountable for the actions and experiences which compose a narratable life. It is, that is, to be open to being asked to give a certain kind of account of what one did or what happened to one or what one witnessed at any earlier point in one's life the time at which the question is posed. Of course someone may have forgotten or suffered brain damage or simply not attended sufficiently at the relevant times to be able to give the relevant account. But to say of someone under some one description ("The prisoner of the Chateau d'If") that he is the same person as someone characterized quite differently ("The Count of Monte Cristo") is precisely to say that it makes sense to ask him to give an intelligible narrative account enabling us to understand how he could at different times and different places be one and the same person and yet be so differently characterized. Thus personal identity is just that identity presupposed by the unity of the character which the unity of a narrative requires. Without such unity there would not be subjects of whom stories could be told.

The other aspect of narrative selfhood is correlative: I am not only accountable, I am one who can always ask others for an account, who can put others to the question. I am part of their story, as they are part of mine. The narrative of any one life is part of an interlocking set of narratives. Moreover this asking for and giving of accounts itself plays an important part in constituting narratives. Asking you what you did and why, saying what I did and why, pondering the differences between your account of what I did and my account of what I did, and vice versa, these are essential constituents of all but the very simplest and barest of narratives. Thus without the accountability of the self those trains of events that constitute all but the simplest and barest of narratives could not occur; and without that same accountability narratives would lack that continuity required to make both them and the actions that constitute them intelligible.

It is important to notice that I am not arguing that the concepts of narrative, or of intelligibility, or of accountability are *more* fundamental than that of personal identity. The concepts of narrative, intelligibility, and accountability presuppose the applicability of the concept of personal identity, just as it presupposes their applicability and just as indeed each of these three presupposes the applicability of the two others. The relationship is one of mutual presupposition. It does follow of course that all attempts to elucidate the notion of personal identity independently of and in isolation from the notions of narrative, intelligibility, and accountability are bound to fail. As all such attempts have.

It is now possible to return to the question from which this inquiry into the nature of human action and identity started: In what does the unity of an individual life consist? The answer is that its unity is the unity of a narrative embodied in a single life. To ask "What is the good for me?" is to ask how best I might live out that unity and bring it to completion. To ask "What is the good for man?" is to ask what all answers to the former question must have in common. But now it is important to emphasize that it is the systematic asking of these two questions and the attempt to answer them in deed as well as in word which provide the moral life with its unity. The unity of a human life is the unity of a narrative quest. Quests sometimes fail, are frustrated, abandoned, or dissipated into distractions; and human lives may in all these ways also fail. But the only criteria for success or failure in a human life as a whole are the criteria of success or failure in a narrated or to-be-narrated quest. A quest for what?

Two key features of the medieval conception of a quest need to be recalled. The first is that without some at least partly determinate conception of the final *telos* there could not be any beginning to a quest. Some conception of the good for man is required. Whence is such a conception to be drawn? Precisely from those questions which led us to attempt to transcend that limited conception of the virtues which is available in and through practices. It is in looking for a conception of *the* good which will enable us to order other goods, for a conception of *the* good which will enable us to extend our understanding of the purpose and content of the virtues, for a conception of *the* good which will enable us to understand the place of integrity and constancy in life, that we initially define the kind of life which is a quest for the good. But secondly it is clear the medieval conception of a quest is not at all that of a search for something already adequately characterized, as miners search for gold or geologists for oil. It is in the course of the quest and only through encountering and coping with the various particular harms, dangers, temptations, and distractions which provide any quest with its episodes and incidents that the goal of the quest is finally to be understood. A quest is always an education both as to the character of that which is sought and in self-knowledge.

The virtues therefore are to be understood as those dispositions which will not only sustain practices and enable us to achieve the goods internal to practices, but which will also sustain us in the relevant kind of quest for the good, by enabling us to overcome the harms, dangers, temptations, and distractions which we encounter, and which will furnish us with increasing self-knowledge and increasing knowledge of the good. The catalogue of the virtues will therefore include the virtues required to sustain the kind of households and the kind of political communities in which men and women can seek for the good together and the virtues necessary for philosophical inquiry about the character of the good. We have then arrived at a provisional conclusion about the good life for man: the good life for man is the life spent in seeking the good life for man, and the virtues necessary for the seeking are those which will enable us to understand what more and what else the good life for man is. We have also completed the second stage in our account of the virtues, by situating them in relation to the good life for man and not only in relation to practices. But our inquiry requires a third stage.

For I am never able to seek the good or exercise the virtues only *qua* individual. This is partly because what it is to live the good life concretely varies from circumstance to circumstance even when it is one and the same conception of the good life and one and the same set of virtues which are being embodied in a human life. What the good life is for a fifth-century Athenian general will not be the same as what it was for a medieval nun or a seventeenth-century farmer. But it is not just that different individuals live in different social circumstances; it is also that we all approach our own circumstances as bearers of a particular social identity. I am someone's son or daughter, someone else's cousin or uncle; I am a citizen of this or that city, a member of this or that guild or profession; I belong to this class, that tribe, this nation. Hence what is good for me has to be the good for one who inhabits these roles. As such, I inherit from the past of my family, my city, my tribe, my nation, a variety of debts, inheritances, rightful expectations and obligations. These constitute the given of my life, my moral starting point. This is in part what gives my life its own moral particularity.

This thought is likely to appear alien and even surprising from the standpoint of modern individualism. From the standpoint of individualism I am what I myself choose to be. I can always, if I wish to, put in question what are taken to be the merely contingent social features of my existence. I may biologically be my father's son; but I cannot be held responsible for what he did unless I choose implicitly or explicitly to assume such responsibility. I may legally be a citizen of a certain country; but I cannot be held responsible for what my country does or has done unless I choose implicitly or explicitly to assume such responsibility. Such individualism is expressed by those modern Americans who deny any responsibility for the effects of slavery upon black Americans, saying "I never owned any slaves." It is more subtly the standpoint of those other modern Americans who accept a nicely calculated responsibility for such effects measured precisely by the benefits they themselves as individuals have indirectly received from slavery. In both cases "being an American" is not in itself taken to be part of the moral identity of the individual. And of course there is nothing peculiar to modern Americans in this attitude: the Englishman who says, "*I* never did any wrong to Ireland; why bring up that old history as though it had something to do with *me*?" or the young German who believes that being born after 1945 means that what Nazis did to Jews has no moral relevance to his relationship to his

Jewish contemporaries, exhibit the same attitude, that according to which the self is detachable from its social and historical roles and statuses. And the self so detached is of course a self very much at home in either Sartre's or Goffman's perspective, a self that can have no history. The contrast with the narrative view of the self is clear. For the story of my life is always embedded in the story of those communities from which I derive my identity. I am born with a past; and to try to cut myself off from that past, in the individualist mode, is to deform my present relationships. The possession of an historical identity and the possession of a social identity coincide. Notice that rebellion against my identity is always one possible mode of expressing it.

Notice also that the fact that the self has to find its moral identity in and through its membership in communities such as those of the family, the neighborhood, the city, and the tribe does not entail that the self has to accept the moral *limitations* of the particularity of those forms of community. Without those moral particularities to begin from there would never be anywhere to begin; but it is in moving forward from such particularity that the search for the good, for the universal, consists. Yet particularity can never be simply left behind or obliterated. The notion of escaping from it into a realm of entirely universal maxims which belong to man as such, whether in its eighteenth-century Kantian form or in the presentation of some modern analytical moral philosophies, is an illusion and an illusion with painful consequences. When men and women identify what are in fact their partial and particular causes too easily and too completely with the cause of some universal principle, they usually behave worse than they would otherwise do.

What I am, therefore, is in key part what I inherit, a specific past that is present to some degree in my present. I find myself part of a history and that is generally to say, whether I like it or not, whether I recognize it or not, one of the bearers of a tradition. It was important when I characterized the concept of a practice to notice that practices always have histories and that at any given moment what a practice is depends on a mode of understanding it which has been transmitted often through many generations. And thus, insofar as the virtues sustain the relationships required for practices, they have to sustain relationships to the past—and to the future—as well as in the present. But the traditions through which particular practices are transmitted and reshaped never exist in isolation or larger social traditions. What constitutes such traditions?

We are apt to be misled here by the ideological uses to which the concept of a tradition has been put by conservative political theorists. Characteristically such theorists have followed Burke in contrasting tradition with reason and the stability of tradition with conflict. Both contrasts obfuscate. For all reasoning takes place within the context of some traditional mode of thought, transcending through criticism and invention the limitations of what had hitherto been reasoned in that tradition; this is as true of modern physics as of medieval logic. Moreover, when a tradition is in good order it is always partially constituted by an argument about the goods the pursuit of which gives to that tradition its particular point and purpose.

So when an institution—a university, say, or a farm, or a hospital—is the bearer of a tradition of practice or practices, its common life will be partly, but in a centrally important way, constituted by a continuous argument as to what a university is and ought to be, or what good farming is, or what good medicine is. Traditions, when vital, embody continuities of conflict. Indeed when a tradition becomes Burkean, it is always dying or dead.

The individualism of modernity could of course find no use for the notion of tradition within its own conceptual scheme except as an adversary notion; it therefore all too willingly abandoned it to the Burkeans, who, faithful to Burke's own allegiance, tried to combine adherence in politics to a conception of tradition which would vindicate the oligarchical revolution of property of 1688 and adherence in economics to the doctrine and institutions of the free market. The theoretical incoherence of this mismatch did not deprive it of ideological usefulness. But the outcome has been that modern conservatives are for the most part engaged in conserving only older rather than later versions of liberal individualism. Their own core doctrine is as liberal and as individualist as that of self-avowed liberals.

A living tradition then is an historically extended, socially embodied argument, and an argument precisely in part about the goods which constitute that tradition. Within a tradition the pursuit of goods extends through generations, sometimes through many generations. Hence the individual's search for his or her good is generally and characteristically conducted within a context defined by those traditions of which the individual's life is a part, and this is true both of those goods which are internal to practices and of the goods of a single life. Once again the narrative phenomenon of embedding is crucial: the history of a practice in our time is generally and characteristically embedded in and made intelligible in terms of the larger and longer history of the tradition through which the practice in its present form was conveyed to us; the history of each of our own lives is generally and characteristically embedded in and made intelligible in terms of the larger and longer histories of a number of traditions. I have to say "generally and characteristically" rather than "always," for traditions decay, disintegrate, and disappear. What then sustains and strengthens traditions? What weakens and destroys them?

The answer in key part is: the exercise or the lack of exercise of the relevant virtues. The virtues find their point and purpose not only in sustaining those relationships necessary if the variety of goods internal to practices are to be achieved and not only in sustaining the form of an individual life in which that individual may seek out his or her good as the good of his or her whole life, but also in sustaining those traditions which provide both practices and individual lives with their necessary historical context. Lack of justice, lack of truthfulness, lack of courage, lack of the relevant intellectual virtues—these corrupt traditions, just as they do those institutions and practices which derive their life from the traditions of which they are the contemporary embodiments. To recognize this is of course also to recognize the existence of an additional virtue, one whose importance is perhaps most obvious when it is least present, the virtue of having an adequate sense of the traditions to which one belongs or which confront one. This virtue is not to be confused with any form of conservative antiquarianism; I am not praising those who choose the conventional conservative role of *laudator temporis acti*. It is rather the case that an adequate sense of tradition manifests itself in a grasp of those future possibilities which the past has made available to the present. Living traditions, just because they continue a not-yet-completed narrative, confront a future whose determinate and determinable character, so far as it possesses any, derives from the past.

In practical reasoning the possession of this virtue is not manifested so much in the knowledge of a set of generalizations or maxims which may provide our practical inferences with major premises; its presence or absence rather appears on the kind of capacity for judgment which the agent possesses in knowing how to select among the relevant stack of maxims and how to apply them in particular situations. Cardinal Pole possessed it, Mary Tudor did not; Montrose possessed it, Charles I did not. What Cardinal Pole and the Marquis of Montrose possessed were in fact those virtues which enable their possessors to pursue both their own good and the good of the tradition of which they are the bearers even in situations defined by the necessity of tragic, dilemmatic choice. Such choices, understood in the context of the tradition of the virtues, are very different from those which face the modern adherents of rival and incommensurable moral premises. Wherein does the difference lie?

It has often been suggested—by J. L. Austin, for example—that *either* we can admit the existence of rival and contingently incompatible goods which make incompatible claims to our practical allegiance *or* we can believe in some determinate conception of *the* good life for man, but that these are mutually exclusive alternatives. No one can consistently hold both these views. What this contention is blind to is that there may be better or worse ways for individuals to live through the basic confrontation of good with good. And that to know what the good life for man is may require knowing what are the better and what are the worse ways of living in and through such situations. Nothing *a priori* rules out this possibility; and this suggests that within a view such as Austin's there is concealed an unacknowledged empirical premise about the character of tragic situations.

One way in which the choice between rival goods in a tragic situation differs from the modern choice between incommensurable moral premises is that *both* of the alternative courses of action which confront the individual have to be recognized as leading to some authentic and substantial good. By choosing one I do nothing to diminish or derogate from the claims upon me of the other; and therefore, whatever I do, I shall have left undone what I ought to have done. The tragic protagonist, unlike the moral agent as depicted by Sartre or Hare, is not choosing between allegiance to one moral principle rather than another, nor is he or she deciding upon some principle of priority between moral principles. Hence the "ought" involved has a different meaning and force from that of the "ought" in moral principles understood in a modern way. For the tragic protagonist cannot do everything that he or she ought to do. This "ought," unlike Kant's, does not imply "can." Moreover any attempt to map the logic of such "ought" assertions on to some modal calculus so as to produce a version of deontic logic has to fail.[4]

Yet it is clear that the moral task of the tragic protagonist may be performed better or worse, independently of the choice between alternatives that he or she makes—*ex hypothesi* he or she has no *right* choice to make. The tragic protagonist may behave heroically or unheroically, generously or ungenerously, gracefully or gracelessly, prudently or imprudently. To perform his or her task better rather than worse will be to do both what is better for him or her *qua* individual or *qua* parent or child or *qua* citizen or member of a profession, or perhaps *qua* some or all of these. The existence of tragic dilemmas casts no doubt upon and provides no counter-examples to the thesis that assertions of the form "To do this in this way would be better for x and/or for his or her family, city, or profession" are susceptible of objective truth and falsity, any more than the existence of alternative and contingently incompatible forms of medical treatment casts doubt on the thesis that assertions of the form "To undergo this medical treatment in this way would be better for x and/or his or her family" are susceptible of objective truth and falsity.[5]

The presupposition of this objectivity is of course that we can understand the notion of "good for x" and cognate notions in terms of some conception of the unity of x's life. What is better or worse for x depends upon the character of that intelligible narrative which provides x's life with its unity. Unsurprisingly, it is the lack of any such unifying conception of a human life which underlies modern denials of the factual character of moral judgments and more especially of those judgments which ascribe virtues or vices to individuals.

Every moral philosophy has some particular sociology as its counterpart. What I have tried to spell out is the kind of understanding of social life which the tradition of the virtues requires, a kind of understanding very different from those dominant in the culture of bureaucratic individualism. Within that culture, conceptions of the virtues become marginal and the tradition of the virtues remains central only in the lives of social groups whose existence is on the margin of the central culture. Within the central culture of liberal or bureaucratic individualism new conceptions of the virtues emerge and the concept of a virtue is itself transformed. We shall only understand the tradition of the virtues fully if we understand to what kinds of degeneration it has proved liable.

NOTES

1. Barbara Hardy, "Towards a Poetics of Fiction: An Approach Through Narrative," *Novel*, vol. 2 (1968), pp. 5–14, at p. 5.

2. Louis O. Mink, "History and Fiction as Modes of Comprehension," *Literary History*, vol. I (1970), pp. 541–58, at pp. 557–58.

3. Quoted in Philip Hobsbaum, *A Reader's Guide to Charles Dickens* (New York: Farrar, Straus and Giroux, 1973), p. 32.

4. See, from a very different point of view, Bas C. Van Fraasen, "Values and the Heart's Command," *Journal of Philosophy*, vol. 70 (1973), pp. 5–19.

5. See, from a different point of view, the illuminating discussion in Samuel Guttenplan, "Moral Realism and Moral Dilemmas," *Proceedings of the Aristotelian Society* (1979–80), pp. 61–80.

12

Ethnography as Narrative

Edward M. Bruner

*. . . of all learned discourse, the ethnological seems to come closest to a
Fiction.* —Roland Barthes

My aim here is to take a reflexive view of the production of ethnography; my thesis is that ethnographies are guided by an implicit narrative structure, by a story we tell about the peoples we study. We are familiar with the stories people tell about themselves in life history and psychiatric interviews, in myth and ritual, in history books and Balinese cockfights. I wish to extend this notion to ethnography as discourse, as a genre of storytelling.[1] To develop this position I take as an example ethnological studies of Native American culture change. It is an area in which I have had direct field experience and for which the facts are widely known; also, the subject has occupied a prominent place in the history of American anthropology.

In the 1930s and 1940s the dominant story constructed about Native American culture change saw the present as disorganization, the past as glorious, and the future as assimilation. Now, however, we have a new narrative: the present is viewed as a resistance movement, the past as exploitation, and the future as ethnic resurgence. What is so striking is that the transition from one narrative structure to another occurred rapidly, within a decade after World War II. Equally striking is that there is so little historical continuity between the two dominant stories: one story simply became discredited and the new narrative took over. The theoretical concepts associated with the outmoded story, such as acculturation and assimilation, are used less frequently

264

and another set of terms has become prominent: exploitation, oppression, colonialism, resistance, liberation, independence, nationalism, tribalism, identity, tradition, and ethnicity—the code words of the 1970s.

The transition from a story of acculturation to one of ethnic resurgence is not merely characterized by a change in theoretical concepts on the level of vocabulary—there has also been a shift in the way the ethnography is constructed, on the level of syntax. In the old story the golden age was in the past and the descriptive problem was to reconstruct the old Indian culture, to create a beginning.[2] The end of the narrative, the disappearance of Indian culture, was not problematic— it was assumed—and the middle, the present-day scene, was interpreted in terms of this sense of an ending[3] as progressive breakdown, pathology, and disintegration. In the 1970s story, however, the golden age is in the future, as the indigenous people struggle against exploitation and oppression to preserve their ethnic identity. The ethnographic problematic is now one of documenting resistance and telling how tradition and ethnicity are maintained; or if they are seriously threatened, the anthropologist may even make a political decision to intervene on behalf of the people, or possibly to take steps to help prevent cultural extinction or genocide. In the early development of American anthropology there was definite concern with cultural extinction, but as it was assumed to be inevitable; the aim was to describe Indian cultures before they disappeared, not to facilitate their continuity. In this sense narrative structures provide social roles for the anthropologist as well as for the Indian people. Regarding the latter, from my own experience in 1948 among the Navajo, and starting in 1951 among the Mandan-Hidatsa of the Fort Berthold Reservation, I can testify that we met many Indian informants, particularly older men, who were eager to provide information about the glorious past, whereas now we meet many Indian activists fighting for a better future. In the 1930s narrative it was the past that pervaded the present; in the 1970s narrative, it was the future.

Stories make meaning. They operate at the level of semantics in addition to vocabulary and syntax.[4] Just as a story has a beginning, a middle, and an end, culture change, too, almost by definition, takes the form of a sequence with a past, a present, and a future. Our predicament in ethnographic studies of change is that all we have before us is the present, the contemporary scene, and by one means or another we must situate that present in a time sequence. It would be naive to believe that we anthropologists simply describe the present but reconstruct the past and construct the future, even though we use language that suggests this—for example, when we talk of gathering or collecting the data as if it were like ripe fruit waiting to be picked, or when we talk of our special anthropological methodologies for reconstructing the past, as if the present were not equally constructed. The past, present, and future are not only constructed but connected in a lineal sequence that is defined by systematic if not causal relations. How we depict any one segment of the sequence is related to our conception of the whole, which I choose to think of as a story.

My position may become clearer when contrasted with that of Lévi-Strauss. He writes that "all myths tell a story,"[5] but "instead of reducing the story or myth to a mere narrative [he urges us] to try to discover the scheme of discontinuous oppositions governing its organization."[6] The power of his method of analyzing paradigmatic structures has been amply documented, but we may do equally well to try to discover the syntagmatic structure beyond the surface narrative. Such structures cannot be reduced to metonymy precisely because they are more than relations of contiguity—they are systematically ordered and therein lies their meaning. If classificatory schemes provide a science of the concrete, narrative schemes may provide a science of the imagination. At the very least, a reemphasis on temporality may enable us to deal more directly with change, and thereby to make structural and symbolic studies more dynamic.[7]

Let me illustrate the semantic dimension with the 1930s narrative. Given the master story of a once proud people whose spirit had been broken and who would soon become assimilated into what was then called the "mainstream of American life," all tribes could be located—the acculturated Sioux in one chapter, the more traditional Hopi in an earlier chapter, and the Indians of the East Coast, who were thought to be virtually extinct, in the last chapter. Ethnographers were able to interpret their field experience in terms of how their particular reservation situation fitted into the lineal sequence of the dominant story of the era.

As editor of a volume of seven case studies prepared in the late 1930s, Linton wrote of the San Ildefonso: "Although the old ceremonies are still going on with full apparent vigor . . . it seems probable that the next few years will see a collapse of the esoteric aspects of the culture and a rapid acculturation of the society."[8] And ". . . Ute culture steadily approaches its final resolution in complete assimilation."[9] Of the White Knife Shoshoni he wrote: "There seem to be no internal factors which would prevent their complete Europeanization."[10] "Lastly, everything indicates that the ultimate end of situations of close and continuous firsthand contact is the amalgamation of the societies and cultures involved, although this conclusion may be postponed almost indefinitely . . ."[11] We are told that amalgamation is inevitable but that it may be postponed indefinitely—a neat trick. What is so remarkable is that in not one of the seven cases discussed had complete assimilation occurred, but such a distinguished anthropologist as Ralph Linton assumed that it would, despite evidence to the contrary in the very case studies he was analyzing. Such is the power of a story once it has captured the imagination.

Given this 1930s vision of the future and the convention of reconstructing the "aboriginal" past as an integrated culture, the present could only be interpreted as disintegration, framed as it was by both glorious integrity and eventual disappearance. My aim here is not to review a literature with which we are all familiar, but rather to emphasize that the present is given meaning in terms of that anticipated present we call the future and that former present we call the past.[12] Stories are interpretive devices which give meaning to the present in terms of location in an ordered syntagmatic sequence—the exact opposite of anthropological common sense. As anthropologists, we usually think that we first investigate the present, more or less scientifically, and thereafter reconstruct the past and anticipate the future. In my view, we begin with a narrative that already contains a beginning and an ending, which frame and hence enable us to interpret the present. It is not that we initially have a body of data, the facts, and we then must construct a story or a theory to account for them. Instead, to paraphrase Schafer,[13] the narrative structures we construct are not secondary narratives about data but primary narratives that establish what is to count as data. New narratives yield new vocabulary, syntax, and meaning in our ethnographic accounts; they define what constitute the data of those accounts.

My claim is that one story—past glory, present disorganization, future assimilation—was dominant in the 1930s and a second story—past oppression, present resistance, future resurgence—in the 1970s, but in both cases I refer to dominance in the anthropological literature, in ethnographic discourse, not necessarily in Indian experience. My focus is on our talk about Indians, not on Indian life itself. Our anthropological stories about Indians are representations, not be confused with concrete existence or "real" facts. In other words, life experience is richer than discourse.

Narrative structures organize and give meaning to experience, but there are always feelings and lived experience not fully encompassed by the dominant story. Only after the new narrative becomes dominant is there a reexamination of the past, a rediscovery of old texts, and a recreation of the new heroes of liberation and resistance. The new story articulates what had been only dimly perceived, authenticates previous feelings, legitimizes new actions, and aligns individual consciousness with a larger social movement. What had previously been personal becomes historical: a "model of" is transformed into a "model for."[14] From the perspective of the present we construct a continuous story stressing the continuity of resistance, whereas actually there was a marked discontinuity from the diminution of one narrative to the rise of another. Foucault's notion of strata[15] is relevant here, but more as an archaeology of discourse than an archaeology of epistemological fields. Certainly, there was active Indian resistance in the past, probably more so in expressive culture than in direct political action, in the form of jokes,[16] and in such religious movements as the Ghost Dance, the Sun Dance, and the Native American Church. Retrospectively, we see that there always were expressions of resistance in Indian experience, and there were early formulations of the story of resistance. Nevertheless, we can pinpoint the time when the new narrative became dominant in discourse—with the formation in 1961 of the National Indian Youth Council and the American Indian Chicago Conference,[17] with the publication of the *Indian Historian* in 1964, with the establishment of AIM in 1968, with the publication of Vine Deloria's *Custer Died for Your Sins* in 1969, and with the anthropological writings of Clemmer,[18] Jorgensen,[19] and others.

I am reasonably confident in my identification of the two narrative structures and in the prominence of one in the discourse of the 1930s and of the other in the 1970s. A possible explanation of the two narratives is that the Indian story is resistance and the white story is assimilation—that the two are just the different points of view of the oppressed and the oppressor. I reject this explanation because it is, in effect, only another telling of the resistance story and because I do not believe it is historically accurate. The resistance story was not dominant in Indian discourse until after World War II, and by the early 1950s American anthropologists[20] were questioning Indian assimilation, the myth of the melting pot. Further, both Indian and anthropologist share the same narrative—not that one narrative is Indian and the other white—a fact that subsequently will be made evident.

Another view is offered by Jorgensen,[21] who wrote that the acculturation story is "nonsense" and the resistance story is "truth," so that in effect the movement from one story to the other is seen as an advance in scientific understanding. Jorgensen was simply privileging one of the two stories, but I understand the reasons for his conviction. I have published on the side of ethnicity and against the acculturation-urbanization framework in a series of papers dating back to 1953.[22] I also realize that stories are not ideologically neutral.

Narratives are not only structures of meaning but structures of power as well. The assimilation story has been a mask for oppression; the resistance story is a justification for claims of redress for past exploitation. Both carry policy and political implications. The reasoning in the assimilation narrative is that if Indians are going to disappear anyway, then their land can be leased or sold to whites; in the ethnic resurgence narrative we are told that if Indians are here to stay, tribal resources must be built up. Assimilation is a program for redemption; resistance, for self and ethnic fulfillment. The terms themselves—acculturation, resistance, neocolonialism—are pregnant with meaning. Each narrative uses different images, language, and style. The Indian in the acculturation narrative is romantic, the exotic Other: the resistance Indian is victimized. Stories construct an Indian self; narrative structures are constitutive as well as interpretive.

The two narratives, in my view, are dual aspects of the same phenomenon; one is a counterpoint to the other. There may even be cycles of narratives, for each contains a basic contradiction. The assimilation story leads to outside pressures for change, which thereby generate resistance. The resistance story, in time, will lead to greater security in the people's own culture and identity, making it easier to change more rapidly and thereby facilitate assimilation. In any case, there also was resistance in the 1930s and acculturation in the 1970s, for the dual processes of change and persistence, of acculturation and nationalism, have occurred simultaneously throughout Indian history. My only claim is that different narratives are foregrounded in the discourse of different historical eras.

The key elements in narrative are story, discourse, and telling. The *story is* the abstract sequence of events, systematically related, the syntagmatic structure. *Discourse* is the text in which the story is manifested, the statement in a particular medium such as a novel, myth, lecture, film, conversation, or whatever. *Telling* is the action, the act of narrating, the communicative process that produces the story in discourse. No distinction is made here between telling and showing, as the same story may be recounted or enacted or both.[23]

We may ask whether the "same" story is told in different versions.

as Chatman[24] assumes. If a story is conceived of as an "invariant core,"[25] independent of its presentation, then it becomes a kind of "Platonic ideal form . . . that occupies a highly privileged ontological realm of pure Being within which it unfolds immutably and eternally."[26] The issue is a familiar one to anthropologists. In explaining the distinction between model and behavior, for example, Leach[27] uses a musical analogy: although we may hear an incompetent performance of a Beethoven symphony, we must remember that the real symphony exists as a musical score, as a model, and not in any particular manifestation. My friends in musicology tell me that Leach might well have selected Mahler instead of Beethoven, as Mahler's scores are exceedingly detailed and precise whereas Beethoven's scripts are loosely written and hence subject to more varied interpretation. In any case, Leach's perspective is theoretically paralyzing, as he has no way to take account of experience and no way to discriminate between a flawed performance and structural change. For Leach, every item of behavior, every potential evidence of change, may be explained away as another incompetent performance, leaving the model intact and thereby avoiding the question of determining when the model, or the story, has changed.

Herrnstein-Smith[28] goes too far in the other direction, however, for in her emphasis on the social context of the telling she dispenses with the concept of story. My position is that the story is prior to, but not independent of, the discourse. We abstract the story from discourse, but once abstracted the story serves as a model for future discourse. Each telling depends on the context, the audience, and the conventions of the medium. A retelling is never an exact duplicate of the already told story, for it takes account of previous tellings, the conditions of which are never identical. Thus, diachronically considered, the story is transformed and transformative, its inherent possibilities are explored, as in the unfolding of an art style, and the pure play and delight in its various combinations are made manifest. In his retelling of the story of Beckett, for example, Turner[29] was very sensitive to the dialectic between root metaphor and historical experience; and the same sensitivity is shown by Schafer[30] in his analysis of psychoanalytic dialogue. In ethnography, we need the concept of story to serve as a "model for." To paraphrase Barthes,[31] there is no primary, naive, phenomenal understanding of the field data we later explicate or intellectualize. No ethnographer is truly innocent—we all begin with a narrative in our heads which structures our initial observations in the field.

There is a dialectic between story and experience, but in the production of ethnography we are continually oriented toward the dominant narrative structure. We go to the reservation with a story already in mind, and that story is foregrounded in the final professional product, the published article, chapter, or monograph. If we stray too far from the dominant story in the literature, if we overlook a key reference or fail to mention the work of an important scholar, we are politely corrected by such institutional monitors as thesis committees, foundation review panels, or journal editors. At the beginning and the end the production of ethnography is framed by the dominant story. Most of the time there is a balance to research innovation—the study is new enough to be interesting but familiar enough so that the story remains recognizable. There are those who are ahead of their times— Bateson did publish *Naven* in 1936—but we usually define research with reference to the current narrative and report back our particular variation of that narrative to our colleagues, most of whom already know the plot structure in advance. The process is self-reinforcing and reconfirms everyone's view of the world.[32]

Most interesting is what happens in the middle of the ethnographic research process, in the field, where we find much folk wisdom. Sol Tax used to advise his students to write the first draft of their dissertations before going to the field; another view is that the research proposal does not really matter, since we usually end up studying something different anyway. We can all agree, however, that the field situation initially presents itself as a confusing "galaxy of signifiers."[33] It is alien, even chaotic; there is so much going on, all at once, that the problem becomes one of making sense of it. How do we accomplish this? I am reminded of Abrahams's statement about hijacking: "A common reaction of people involved in airplane hijackings, when asked how they felt and what they did, was 'Oh, everything was familiar to us: we had seen it in the movies already.'"[34] Previous ethnographic texts and the stories they contain are the equivalent of the movies. Narrative structures serve as interpretive guides; they tell us what constitute data, define topics for study, and place a construction on the field situation that transforms it from the alien to the familiar. Even when we are settled in, however, feeling comfortable in our new surroundings, there is still the problem of going back from the lived experience of the field situation to the anthropological literature, to our final destination.

In the field we turn experience into discourse by what I refer to as the three tellings of fieldwork. First we tell the people why we are there, what information we are seeking, and how we intend to use the data. We do this directly, by explaining our project and by our behavior, by the questions we ask, and the activities we attend. As the people respond to our questions, we begin the ethnographic dialogue, the complex interactions and exchanges that lead to the negotiation of the text. In the second telling we take this verbal and visual information and process it, committing it to writing in our field diaries. This transcription is not easy. Every ethnographer is painfully aware of the discrepancy between the richness of the lived field experience and the paucity of the language used to characterize it. There is necessarily a dramatic reduction, condensation, and fragmentation of data. In the third telling the audience consists of our colleagues, who provide feedback as we prepare our materials for publication, and here the story becomes even more prominent. There is, of course, a fourth telling—when other anthropologists read what we have written and summarize it in class lectures and in their own publications. We all retell the same stories, even the very old ones such as the progressive development of culture from the simple to the complex and the diffusion of traits from a center to a periphery. Retellings never cease; there is an infinite reflexivity as we go from experience to discourse to history. Eventually, all experience is filtered out and we end where we began—with the story.

Our ethnographies are coauthored, not simply because informants contribute data to the text, but because, as I suggested earlier, ethnographer and informant come to share the same narratives. The anthropologist and the Indian are unwitting co-conspirators in a dialectical symbolic process. In suggesting that narratives are shared, I acknowledge that the case is obviously stronger for American anthropologists and Native Americans, as they are members of the same larger society. I know that many stories do not apply to culture change, that alternative stories exist simultaneously, that the sharing is not complete, that there are variations of the basic plot, and that individuals manipulate stories. But stories *are* shared. Let me turn now to an example.

In New Mexico and Arizona during the summer of 1980, the tricentennial of the Pueblo Revolt of 1680 was celebrated by a series of events, including a reenactment of the original revolt, feast days at various pueblos, an arts and crafts show, foot races, ceremonials, and a proclamation by the governor of New Mexico. The narrative guiding these events was clearly the current story of resistance and ethnic resurgence, as is evident in the following quote from an article in *New*

Mexico Magazine, based on a document issued by the Eight Northern Indian Pueblos Council: "The Pueblo Revolt of 1680 was the first successful rebellion on American soil. [It] expressed unyielding determination to safeguard ancient traditional beliefs and practices [and] will stand forever as a symbol of encouragement to all oppressed peoples everywhere in search of freedom and self-determination."[35]

The Pueblo Indians are performing our theory; they are enacting the story we tell about them in the pages of our professional journals. We wonder if it is their story or ours. Which is the inside and which the outside view, and what about the distinction between emic and etic? I question these oppositions, just as I question the notion that the Indian story is resistance and the white story is acculturation. My position is that both Indian enactment, the story they tell about themselves, and our theory, the story we tell, are transformations of each other; they are retellings of a narrative derived from the discursive practice of our historical era,[36] instances of never-ceasing reflexivity. The story of exploitation, resistance, and resurgence goes beyond American society, of course. It is an international story that I have heard in Sumatra and in India; it is retold almost daily in debates at the United Nations.

Some scholars make a sharp distinction between the ethnographer as subject and the native peoples as the object of an investigation. To the extent that we see the ethnographer as an outsider looking in, the privileged stranger who can perceive patterns not apparent to those within the system, then we further magnify the separation between anthropologist as subject and indigene as object. We have long recognized that it is difficult to obtain an accurate description of the object, to know the true nature of the outside world. And we have been concerned with the accuracy of our ethnographic accounts, especially when confronted with conflicting interpretations of the same culture (e.g., Redfield and Lewis). The question of what is really out there then emerges. We have recognized a problem with the subject, the anthropologist, but this tends to dissolve into details of personal bias, individual personality traits, and selective perception—after all, we are only human. We also have dealt with subject-object relations in another way, by suggesting that the object of our ethnography is constituted by a Western mode of thought, by our language, and that we have created the category of the native or the concept of the primitive. Said[37] argues, for example, that Orientalists in western Europe have represented and constituted Orientalism as a mechanism of domination.

I wish to offer a different interpretation of subject-object relations. Borrowing from Barthes and Foucault, I take both subject and object as problematic and dissolve the sharp distinction between them; I see both anthropologist and Indian as being caught in the same web, influenced by the same historical forces, and shaped by the dominant narrative structures of our times. In a personal communication Bill Sturtevant remarked that this thesis seems "to undermine the entire enterprise," and his statement deserves to be taken seriously, especially since he has devoted most of his professional life to editing the monumental *Handbook of the American Indian*. Ethnography, as I have described it, does seem less privileged, less the authoritative voice about native peoples. The ethnographer appears not as an individual creative scholar, a knowing subject who discovers, but more as a material body through whom a narrative structure unfolds. If myths have no authors (*à la* Lévi-Strauss), then in the same sense neither do ethnographic texts. Cassirer has argued that when we think we are exploring reality we are merely engaging in a dialogue with our symbolic systems.[38] My point is that both anthropologist and native informant participate in the same symbolic system. Not that our cultures are identical; rather, we share, at least partially, those narratives dealing with intercultural relations and cultural change.

Marx, in that famous first sentence of *The Eighteenth Brumaire*, quoted Hegel to the effect that all the great events of world history occur twice, the first time as tragedy and the second as farce. In a sense, the Pueblo Revolt occurred twice—in 1680 as tragedy, and in 1980, if not as farce then at least as play, as ritual enactment. To look at it another way, the Pueblo Revolt is an example of intertextuality, in that the 1980 text contains or quotes the 1680 text. The 1980 enactment is a story about a story: the production of a text based on another text. What is created in 1980, however, is not the original event but another version of reality, for the meaning of the tricentennial is in the 1980 telling, not in the origin or source. We tend to go back to 1680 to interpret the actions of the first Pueblo revolutionaries and their Spanish conquerors, and this may be important for historical scholarship. But the Pueblo Revolt, for us, is constituted by the contemporary telling based on the contemporary narrative of resistance. Once enacted, of course, the tricentennial reinforces that narrative and revitalizes everyday Pueblo life. I do not see a 300-year continuity to the story of resistance; the peaceful people chose to celebrate a 1680 rebellion at a 1980 tricentennial but not at a 1780 centennial or an 1880 bicentennial. Whether they commemorate the revolt in 2080 remains to be seen—

much depends on the ideological dynamic of the twenty-first century and the narrative structures of that time.

If stories are shared, as I claim, there are many implications for the production of ethnographic accounts. For if the story is in our heads before we arrive at the field site, and if it is already known by the peoples we study, then we enter the ethnographic dialogue with a shared schema. We can fit in the pieces and negotiate the text more readily; we begin the interaction with the structural framework already in place. It is as if our informants know, in advance, the chapter headings of our unwritten dissertations. There is, of course, considerable variability and factionalism within any population, so the task of the anthropologist is to select his or her informants carefully. This we have always done, but I suggest here that the concept of "my favorite informant" may be less a question of personal compatibility than of shared narrative structure. We choose those informants whose narratives are most compatible with our own—just as, I am sure, informants select their favorite anthropologists based on the same criterion of compatibility.

The final question I will raise concerns how narratives, or models, change. If the narrative is transformed with each retelling, then how much transformation can occur before the story is no longer acknowledged as being the same? And where do new stories come from? In part, this is a question of perspective, for we can look back over the various tellings and stress either continuity or discontinuity: continuity, or incremental change, in which the old story is continually modified; or discontinuity or structural change, in which a new story emerges. The first is experienced as evolutionary change and the second as revolutionary, as a rupture in the social fabric.

In the first process, stressing continuity, the telling takes account of the context, previous telling, and the relationship between narrator and audience; thus, the story is modified incrementally. Each retelling starts from the old story and encompasses new conditions, but it is recognized as being the same story. In structural change a new narrative is seen, as in the change from assimilation to resistance, because the old narrative can no longer be stretched to encompass the new events. The key to structural change is a radical shift in the social context. New stories arise when there is a new reality to be explained, when the social arrangements are so different that the old narrative no longer seems adequate.

New narratives do not arise from anthropological field research, as we sometimes tell our graduate students, but from history, from world conditions. The Indian acculturation story was part of the American dream, the expansion of the frontier, the conquest of the wilderness, and the Americanization of immigrants. After World War II the world changed, with the overthrow of colonialism, the emergence of new states, the civil rights movement, and a new conception of equality. Narrative structures changed accordingly.

Before World War II the acculturation story was dominant. Although the resistance story was told, it was not yet prominent in the larger discourse. After World War II the story of oppression, resistance, and ethnic resurgence was told in an increasingly louder voice and applied to many different peoples. As the old story became discredited and was labeled reactionary, the new story was articulated by new organizations, leaders, and prophets. With the early telling of the resistance narrative, new "facts" began to emerge which the acculturation story could not explain. For a time the two stories overlapped, but as the new story achieved dominance, the old story increasingly appeared to contradict common sense. It had lost its explanatory power and credibility.

During the period of competition between the two stories, there was a change in the role of the Indian in discourse. New narratives open up new spaces in discourse that arise precisely from the gaps and silences of the previous era.[39] Let me characterize the difference, although for purposes of emphasis I shall overstate the case. In the past we had the cigar store Indian, the traveling troupe in full ceremonial dress representing the quintessential American Indian, on display at the sideshow at county fairs, carnivals, and rodeos.[40] Indians were mute, like museum specimens, a disappearing breed. It was not that they had nothing to say; rather, they were denied a space in discourse and hence had no power. Now, however, we have a new narrative. Indians march on Washington, become legal experts on water rights, and come to our universities to lecture. They speak directly in the political arena, not just in ritual and expressive domains, and stress such new themes as the value of Indian culture for white society, tribalism and ecology, and how to live in harmony with each other and with nature.

Because of its new role in discourse, the new narrative can be forcefully articulated. It is eventually accepted, not piecemeal, bit-by-bit, but whole, all at once, as a story. It takes time, however, for a new narrative to become dominant. For such change to occur there must be a breakdown of previously accepted understandings, a perception that a once familiar event no longer makes sense, a penetration of the previously taken-for-granted. Stories operate not simply in the realm of the mind, as ideas; to be convincing they also must have a base in experience or social practice. It is the perceived discrepancy between the previously accepted story and the new situation that leads us to discard or question the old narrative; and it is the perceived relevance of the new story to our own life situation that leads to its acceptance. Tricentennial enactments, political conflict, and social dramas play a key role in precipitating the sense of behavioral contradiction that leads to the acceptance of new narratives.

I conclude by noting that narrative structure has an advantage over such related concepts as metaphor or paradigm in that narrative emphasizes order and sequence, in a formal sense, and is more appropriate for the study of change, the life cycle, or any developmental process. Story as model has a remarkable dual aspect—it is both linear and instantaneous. On the one hand, a story is experienced as a sequence, as it is being told or enacted; on the other hand, it is comprehended all at once—before, during, and after the telling. A story is static and dynamic at the same time. And although I have focused on American Indian change in this paper, as an example, I trust the thesis of ethnography as narrative has wider applicability.

Stories give meaning to the present and enable us to see that present as part of a set of relationships involving a constituted past and a future. But narratives change, all stories are partial, all meanings incomplete. There is no fixed meaning in the past, for with each new telling the context varies, the audience differs, the story is modified, and as Gorfain writes, "retellings become foretellings." We continually discover new meanings. All of us, then anthropologists and informants, must accept responsibility for understanding society as told and retold.

ACKNOWLEDGMENTS

Cary Nelson, Claire Farrer, Phyllis Gorfain, Kay Ikeda, Larry Grossberg, Norman Whitten, Nina Baym, William Schroeder, Barbara Babcock, and the members of my Fall 1980 graduate seminar provided generous assistance.

NOTES

1. For similar studies see Hayden White, *Metahistory* (Baltimore: Johns Hopkins University Press, 1973); James Boon, *The Anthropological Romance of Bali* (Cambridge: Cambridge University Press, 1977); Edward Said, *Beginnings* (Baltimore: Johns Hopkins University Press, 1975); and especially Roy Schafer, "Narration in the Psychoanalytic Dialogue," *Critical Inquiry*, vol. 7, no. 1

(1980), pp. 29–54. I am heavily indebted to Michel Foucault, *The Order of Things* (New York: Vintage Books, 1973) and *The History of Sexuality* (New York: Pantheon Books, 1978).

2. Said, *Beginnings*.

3. Frank Kermode, *The Sense of an Ending* (New York: Oxford University Press, 1967).

4. Hayden White, "The Value of Narrativity in the Representation of Reality," *Critical Inquiry*, vol. 7, no. 1 (1980), pp. 5–58, and Victor Turner, "Social Dramas and Stories About Them," *Critical Inquiry*, vol. 7, no. 1 (1980), pp. 141–68.

5. Claude Levi-Strauss, *The Savage Mind* (Chicago: University of Chicago Press, 1966), p. 26.

6. Ibid., p. 136.

7. Work in the field of narratology by French structuralists [Roland Barthes, *S/Z* (New York: Hill and Wang, 1974); Gerard Genette, *Narrative Discourse* (Ithaca, N.Y.: Cornell University Press, 1980)] and the almost simultaneous appearance in 1980 of special issues on narrative in three different journals (*New Literary History, Poetics Today, Critical Inquiry*) testify to the recent interest.

8. Ralph Linton, ed., *Acculturation in Seven American Indian Tribes* (New York: Appleton-Century, 1940), p. 462.

9. Ibid., p. 201.

10. Ibid., p. 118.

11. Ibid., p. 519.

12. Jonathan Culler, "Derrida," *Structuralism and Since: From Lévi-Strauss to Derrida*, ed. John Sturrock (Oxford: Oxford University Press, 1979), pp. 154–80, at p. 162.

13. Schafer, "Psychoanalytic Dialogue," p. 30.

14. Clifford Geertz, *The Interpretation of Cultures* (New York: Basic Books, 1973).

15. Foucault, *Order of Things*.

16. *Keith Basso, Portraits of "The Whiteman"* (Cambridge: Cambridge University Press, 1979).

17. Nancy O. Lurie, "The Voice of the American Indian: Report on the American Indian Chicago Conference," *Current Anthropology*, vol. 2 (1961), pp. 478–500.

18. Richard O. Clemmer, "Truth, Duty, and the Revitalization of Anthropologists: A New Perspective on Cultural Change and Resistance," *Reinventing Anthropology*, ed. Dell Hymes (New York: Random House, 1970), pp. 213–47.

19. Joseph Jorgensen, *The Sun Dance Religion* (Chicago: University of Chicago Press, 1972).

20. E.g., E. Z. Vogt, "The Acculturation of American Indians," *Annals* (Philadelphia: American Academy of Political and Social Science), pp. 137–46, and John Province, "The American Indian in Transition," *American Anthropologist*, vol. 56 (1954), pp. 389–94.

21. Jorgensen, *Sun Dance Religion*, p. ix.

22. Edward M. Bruner, "Assimilation among Fort Berthold Indians," *American Indian*, vol. 6, no. 4 (1953), pp. 21–29; "Urbanization and Ethnic Identity in North Sumatra," *American Anthropologist*, vol. 63 (1961), pp. 508–21; and "The Expression of Ethnicity in Indonesia," *Urban Ethnicity*, ed. Abner Cohen (London: Tavistock, ASA Monograph 12, 1974), pp. 251–80.

23. These definitions are based on Genette, *Narrative Discourse*. In this essay, I have not had space to consider a number of important issues: for example, is storytelling universal, and is narrativity a Western concept? I believe the answer to both questions is yes, but the issues are complicated [see A. L. Becker, "Text-Building, Epistemology, and Aesthetics in Javanese Shadow Theatre," *The Imagination of Reality: Essays in Southeast Asian Coherence Systems*, ed. A. L. Becker and Aram Yengoyan (Norwood, N.J.: Ablex, 1979), pp. 211–43].

24. Seymour Chatman, *Story and Discourse* (Ithaca, N.Y.: Cornell University Press, 1978).

25. Culler, "Derrida," p. 28.

26. Barbara Herrnstein-Smith, "Narrative Versions, Narrative Theories," *Critical Inquiry*, vol. 7, no. 1 (1980), pp. 213–36.

27. Edmund Leach, *Culture and Communication* (New York: Cambridge University Press, 1976), p. 5.

28. Herrnstein-Smith, "Narrative Versions."

29. Victor Turner, *Drama, Fields, and Metaphors* (Ithaca, N.Y.: Cornell University Press, 1974).

30. Schafer, "Psychoanalytic Dialogue."

31. Barthes, *S/Z*, p. 16.

32. Thomas Kuhn, *The Structure of Scientific Revolutions* (Chicago: University of Chicago Press, 1962).

33. Barthes, *S/Z*, p. 16.

34. Roger Abrahams, "Toward an Enactment-Centered Theory of Folklore," *Frontiers of Folklore*, ed. William Bascom (Boulder: Westview Press, 1977), pp. 79–120, at p. 99.

35. Joseph Hill, "The Pueblo Revolt of 1680," *New Mexico Magazine*, vol. 58, no. 6 (1980), pp. 52–54, at p. 54.

36. Foucault, *Order of Things*.

37. Edward Said, *Orientalism* (New York: Vintage Books, 1978).

38. See Lawrence Grossberg, "Language and Theorizing in the Human Sciences," *Studies in Symbolic Interaction*, ed. Norman Denzin, vol. II (Greenwich, Conn.: JAI Press, 1979), pp. 189–231, at p. 201.

39. Foucault, *Order of Things*, p. 207.

40. Margaret Mead, *The Changing Culture of an Indian Tribe* (New York: Columbia University Press, 1932), p. 67.

13

Storytelling and Political Theory

Philip Abbott

In *After Virtue,* Alasdair MacIntyre complains about the absence of storytelling in modern political and moral theory. "Man is in his actions and practice," says MacIntyre, "essentially a story-telling animal." Modern theory by focusing upon the question, "What am I to do?" rather than the question, "Of what story or stories do I find myself a part?" leaves theory dependent upon the development of "impersonal rational arguments," creating insurmountable problems in theoretical incommensurability and leaving us as individuals "unscripted" and, hence, "powerless to detect the disorders of moral thought and practice." In this article I affirm the importance of storytelling but examine the relationship between a political theory and a story, suggesting that narratives nearly always create an internal incommensurability with the theory.

Despite the close connection between political theory and storytelling, there are important tensions between these activities, Whether a story is long or short, whether it is new or a retelling of a widely recognized narrative, whether it is an historical reconstruction or as is more popular today, a hypothetical reconstruction, whether it is a self-contained narrative or only a "sketch" or passing example, its telling represents a departure from a theoretical point even if to return again.[1] A writer takes a chance when he tells a story. There are several reasons for this special relationship between storytelling and theorizing. First, no matter how directly a story is related to a theory or part of a theory, its impact can be challenged by the offering of another story. In a sense, the number of counter-stories is limitless. Second, the story itself is subject to internal challenge. Historical reconstructions are subject to re-interpretations; fictional narratives are subject to alteration. Third, the story itself, like the status of the fact in scientific analysis, is theory embedded in ways independent of or at odds with the writer's own theoretical project. The story may serve to introduce a counter theoretical point on its own terms rather than establish that of the writer. Fourth, since the relationship between the story and the theory is broadly analogical, the "point" of the story must be made to fit the "point" of the theory. In the process of putting a story to a broader use, the writer must engage in a series of actions or be assured that the reader will undertake them. Telling the story commits a writer to this process without the assurance that it will be successful. In light of these tensions, the fit between the story and the theory can never be complete or perfect. Thus, Amy Guttman writes, even as she defends the stories of analytic philosophers, that all such attempts "break down," that at best they provide steps toward resolving theoretical problems, that "they can rarely clinch the case for a particular position."[2]

But while the fit between storytelling and theorizing can at best be described as awkward, it is still possible to speak of a "good" story in political theory. If we can be convinced that the story itself is accurate and coherent, and if it serves basically to support and even enrich the theoretical point, a theory's plausibility can be dramatically enhanced. But the assessment of a good story is so complex that I would like to examine four stories, or, more properly, four sets of stories told by four different political theorists: Locke's story of Jepthah, Judith Thomson's story of a kidnapping by the Society of Music Lovers and her story of people spores, Michael Walzer's stories of the Macy and Strauss brothers, the Conscription Act of 1863, and the invention of the washing machine, and Robert Bellah and his colleagues' autobiographical retelling of the lives of Brian Palmer and Mary Taylor. Since the stories themselves are quite different in theme and structure and each theory is quite different in scope and method, an evaluation can serve as a test and refinement of the four points listed above, and as a basis for determining "good" stories.

JOHN LOCKE'S STORY OF JEPTHAH

Locke's retelling of the events in the *Book of Judges* illustrates the intricate relationship between storytelling and political theory. The story of Jepthah is Locke's focus.[3] He provides a complete narrative in both the *First Treatise* and the *Second Treatise* and returns to cite the story more briefly as an example several more times in both works. Jepthah, the bastard son of a harlot, has been disinherited and exiled by the Gileadites. When the Ammonites threaten war, the elders of Gilead beg Jepthah to be their captain. After reminding the petitioners of his past treatment, Jepthah agrees on the condition that upon victory he shall be their leader. The elders agree, and Jepthah engages in a series of diplomatic discussions with the Ammonites. He reviews the history of the disputed territory since Moses. But the efforts fail, and Jepthah declares that "the Lord the Judge be judge this day between the children of Israel and the children of Ammon." On the eve of battle, Jepthah promises God that if he is permitted to defeat the Ammonites, he will deliver as an offering the first person who comes before his doors to greet him. Jepthah defeats the Ammonites, but when he returns to his home he finds his only daughter has come out to welcome him. Jepthah, in anguish, says: "I have opened my mouth unto the Lord and I cannot go back." But the war against the Ammonites has created another conflict. Another tribe, the Ephraimites, have refused to aid Jepthah in the dispute with the Ammonites. Now they argue that Jepthah has slighted them by not seriously seeking an alliance, and they threaten war. Again, Jepthah tells his version of events to no avail, and war again breaks out. During the course of the battle, the Ephraimites become trapped in the fords of Jordan. In order to prevent escapes, the Gileadites require every individual to say the word "shibboleth." An Ephraimite pronounces the word differently from other tribes and, consequently, 42,000 of the enemy are discovered and slain. Jepthah "judges" for six years and is followed by a series of other leaders.

The story of Jepthah is the story of only one of the judges and itself includes a series of micro-stories: the triumphant return of the unjustly exiled, the "rash vow" and its consequences, the exposure of disguise, and the treachery of potential allies. Any of these stories, or a combination, could be the basis for a theoretical point. Locke only casually mentions Jepthah's exile. He ignores Jepthah's tragic loss as well as the episode with the Ephraimites. Instead, he focuses upon the general political conditions in the time of the judges and the events leading up to the armed conflict between the Gileadites and the Ammonites.

Locke's version of the Jepthah story and the broader story of judges is employed to substantiate two theoretical points. First, he wants to show that the origin of political society did not lie in hereditary kingship. That the first leaders were "Captains in War, and Leaders of their Armies . . . appears plainly in the Story of Jepthah."[4]

Jepthah's authority was broadly contractual (he "articled" with the people) and was followed by other judges. All the people wanted to know was, "How can this man save us?" Second, Locke attempts to establish the great difficulties involved in establishing moral right in the absence of political authority. Jepthah had first appealed to historical precedent: "Had there been any such court . . . to determine the right between Jepthah and the Ammonites, they had never come to a state of War . . ." Jepthah was forced to appeal to heaven. In all such cases where there is no judge on earth, "I myself can only be judge in my own Conscience, as I will answer it at the great day, to the Supreme Judge of all Men."[5]

How "good" is the story of the judges and Jepthah in terms of Locke's political theory? The narrative of Jepthah's rise to political power and the circumstances surrounding his war with the Ammonites does effectively establish Locke's theoretical aims. Jepthah's authority, while wide, is contractual and of an emergency nature. His attempts to reason with the leader of a massed army are tragically futile. But the story itself as well as the general political climate at the time of judges creates significant strains in Locke's over-all argument. Locke had boldly employed a scriptural narrative that was part of the patriarchal theory of the origins of government. But however ingenious Locke's effort was, the fact remained that the Book of Judges was designed to tell a different story than the one Locke had carefully reconstructed. The time of judges was hardly a "Golden Age," a "State of Good Will, Mutual Assistance and Preservation." Locke's conception of the state of nature was, on purpose, systematically ambiguous. The state of nature could readily lapse into a state of war, and this was "one great reason of Mens putting themselves into society." But the stories in Judges are truly horrific. There is widespread child sacrifice, treachery (Delilah's betrayal of Samson), gangster rule (Abimelech), gang rape and mutilation (the Benjamites), and, always, mass carnage. The lesson of the time of judges is clear to its authors: "In those days there was no king in Israel; every man did that which was right in his own eyes." The judges may not have been hereditary monarchs, but the moral certainly appears that they should have been. In fact, a kingship was offered to Gideon, and Abimelech attempted to found one.[6]

But the fit between the story of Jepthah and Locke's political theory exhibits other strains. John Dunn has argued that while Locke uses the "exemplary resources as the accredited vocabulary for discussing political issues," there is something wrong with the storytelling and the general theory. It becomes "frictionless, devoid of

external implication, conceptually inert."[7] For Dunn, Locke had created a de-Christianized theory of human society even though the
structure was saturated with Christian assumptions. The state of nature may have been a transposition of Christian theology, but it was
foremost an analytic construct, conceptually independent either of
philosophical anthropology or of conjectural history. Thus, while a
narrative from one society could be more "edifying" than another or
the same at another point in history, "any stage of social development
which was part of the historical story at all, any period within history,
could not in itself be normative for any other period."[8] There is a
sense, then, in which the story of Jepthah is irrelevant to Locke's general theory. At most, it can only serve as a rhetorical thrust against a
theory that is more dependent on storytelling, one such as Filmer's.

Gordon Schochet has discussed this aspect of Locke in his analysis
of the history of patriarchal political thought. Locke's statement that
"an Argument from what has been, to what should of right be, has no
great force" placed historical narrative in an entirely different context
than Filmer had conceived. "The discriminate, self-contained, and personally responsible being that Protestant man was becoming was
surely entitled to affect if not control his own life. Man is real, and his
institutions—to the extent that they are not held to be established by
God—are artificial; they are contrivances designed to meet man's
needs. And if a man's needs differ from those of his ancestors, it
would follow that he is not bound to maintain the institutions of an
earlier age." This movement away from historical narrative as morally
determinative was what defeated patriarchalism, not Locke's arguments, which "could not be ignored" but were not "unanswerable."[9]

The example of Locke's telling of a single story illustrates these
problems. The story of Jepthah as used by Locke is actually a counter-
story from scripture designed to challenge Filmer's contention that
"not only until the Flood but after it . . . patriarchal power did continue." But Locke's story is selectively told and must contend not only
with other events in Judges, but with the explicit theory drawn from
the narrative. Moreover, the story calls into question other aspects of
Locke's theory and reveals in a complex manner the antagonism between Locke's general theory and the whole status of at least one kind
of storytelling. One could conclude that the "fit" between storytelling
and theory is better in Filmer than in Locke, since Filmer's general theory is more epistemologically and morally committed to the stories in
the Old Testament. But if our brief exposition is correct, one could
argue that since Locke had drawn for the reader a model of a looser fit

between the story and the theory, his enterprise is not unsuccessful. There is a sense, then, at least if this single example is generalizable, that what is crucial is the relationship between a *particular* story and a *particular* theory, and we can add this point to our discussion.

JUDITH THOMSON'S STORIES OF KIDNAPPING AND DIALYSIS AND INVASION BY PEOPLE SPORES

Judith Thomson's theoretical initiative is less ambitious than Locke's. She is attempting to clarify the right to life of innocents, particularly the fetus, but her approach is sufficiently broad to require storytelling. "A Defense of Abortion," in fact, includes nearly a dozen stories including variations. I focus on two here. The first involves the Society of Music Lovers who kidnap a person and hook his circulatory system to a violinist so that poisons are extracted from his blood, as well as from that of the kidnapped person. When the victim awakens at the hospital, the doctor explains, "Look, we're sorry the Society of Music Lovers did this to you—we would have never permitted it if we had known. But still they did it, and the violinist now is plugged into you. To unplug you would be to kill him. But never mind, it's only for nine months. By then he will have recovered from his ailment, and can safely be unplugged from you."[10]

One critic has complained that stories such as this are "too clean" to carry the weight assigned to them by the theory.[11] By underspecifying conditions, the storyteller obscures the interaction between moral principles and fails in helping to tell us how to trade one consideration for another. There is a certain excessive cleanliness to Thomson's story. While the victim of an injustice certainly need not know the motivations of oppressors, a story sufficiently removed from our likely experience or those of our acquaintances does require more detail to support the theoretical point. Who are these musicians and why are they driven to such a desperate measure? Why are you, alone, the only person who can save the ailing member? Would the victim be conscious when you pulled the plug? Would he expire in agony? Details can, of course, be supplied by the reader in consciously or unconsciously comparing the kidnapping to a rape (which, of course, is Thomson's intention). But then why not offer an account of a rape itself, either fictional or biographical? Thomson might argue that her story avoids complications that a rape story itself might contain. In her story, the fetus equivalent is a person and, thus, Thomson avoids what she regards as a Gordian knot over the issue of personhood. The aims of the Society are presumably different from those of the rapist, which highlights the question of victims' rights. But the more different the story is in its particulars from the object which her theory is designed to defend, the weaker is the story as a justificatory device. More details would, I think, threaten the analogical connection that is intended.

Nevertheless the story of the Society of Music Lovers is a reasonably good story, although it is not determinative in terms of her theoretical objectives and not for the reasons she intends.[12] For the Society of Music Lovers is a horror story, and like all good horror stories, this one combines elements of the real and the imagined in order to create an empathy for the victim, since for a moment we identify with the victim's condition. In other words, the portion of the story that is specified adequately, the forced dialysis, is sufficiently horrific in itself to bring to the mind of the reader a terror of modern life. Most people know something about the pain involved in this treatment, the lengthy suffering, the terror of possible death. Thus, Thomson need not give any details here. (In fact, further specification would erode her purpose, since pregnancy itself is quite different from the therapy under discussion.) The kidnapping component only provides an added fillip to the horror. We are asked to consider that this whole ordeal is unnecessary!

Like any good horror-storyteller, Thomson carefully manages this sense of terror. The story is told in the second person (". . . imagine this. You wake up in the morning and find yourself . . .") and the conclusion solidifies the appreciated sense of horror between the storyteller and the reader ("I imagine you would regard this as outrageous . . ."). For Thomson to specify the kind of society in which music lovers organize and kidnap people to save ill violinists would remove the whole story farther from our emotional experience, and hence the successful kernel of the story, the horror itself, would disintegrate. What makes this story good, in terms of her theory at least, is not any reasoned argument that alters our intuitions, but the simple paralleling of two horrors that can appear suddenly in the midst of everyday life, rape and debilitating medical treatment. The suddenness of these two horrors, their apparent irrationality, their inexplicability, indeed, their mystery, is captured by the telling of this story.

Partial proof of this point can be ascertained by Thomson's emendations on her own story throughout the essay. A good horror-storyteller knows how to build on the reader's sense of terror, and Thomson, for the most part, does just this. "What if," she asks, the dialysis connection is not for "nine months, but for nine years? Or longer still?"[13] "What if," she asks later, "the treatment is for your whole life? What if," she asks, "the treatment will cause your death within the month?" Note here how the horror is empirically now quite removed from the rape-pregnancy horror story. Pregnancy *can*, of course, be life-threatening, but it cannot last for nine years or for a life-time. Thus, it is the pure emotive force of the horror that makes Thomson's story a good story. In fact, when Thomson returns to the story near the end of her essay to offer a final emendation in order to introduce her concept of the minimally decent samaritan, this tinkering erodes the power of the story by reducing its quotient of horror. She asks, should the kidnap victim be morally required to remain on the machine for "only one hour" and concludes "it seems to me plain you ought to allow him to use your kidney for that hour—it would be indecent to refuse."[14] In this version, the horror has been dissipated, the treatment is not like dialysis or impregnation through rape, because a good portion of the only connecting link between the two stories has been severed. Thomson seems now to be entering a Benthamite world of samaritan calculations, and the reader is led to wonder if it would be okay morally to expect a day on the machine and if a day, how many multiples of weeks or even months? By progressively throwing out longer and more life-threatening burdens in the first version of the story, Thomson could ignore the biological facts of human reproduction because the reader's horror sustains the fiction. When she contracts the burden, the reader is forced to consider the only *real* example available, that is, the nine-month pregnancy, and, consequently, is forced to judge how much time it is minimally decent to expect in assuming the burden. On this question, the kidnapping story is not much help in determining obligations to innocents.

If the story of the Society of Music Lovers is a good story up to a point, the story of the spores is not. Why it is not, is, I think, important to our assessment of storytelling and political theory. After she feels that she has established the argument that "unborn persons whose existence is due to rape have no right to use their mother's bodies, and thus that aborting them is not depriving them of anything they have a right to and, hence, is not unjust killing" on the basis of the music lovers and other stories, Thomson proceeds to consider cases of what might be called diminished responsibility in regard to pregnancy. She says that "there are cases and cases, and the details make a difference." Here is the case that she constructs:

> . . . suppose it were like this: people-seeds drift about in the air like pollen, and if you open your windows, one may drift in and take root

in your carpets or upholstery. You don't want children, so you fix up your windows with fine mesh screens, the very best you can buy. As can happen, however, and on very, very rare occasions does happen, one of the screens is defective; and a seed drifts in and takes root. Does the person-plant who now develops have a right to the use of your house? Surely not—despite the fact that you voluntarily opened your windows, you knowingly kept carpets and upholstered furniture, and you knew that screens were sometimes defective. Someone may argue that you are responsible for its rooting, that it does have a right to your house, because after all you could have lived out your life with bare floors and furniture, or with sealed windows and doors. But this won't do—for by the same token anyone can avoid a pregnancy due to rape by having a hysterectomy, or anyway by never leaving home without a (reliable!) army.[15]

The analogical model at work here is a bit more complicated than that employed in the previous story. The burglary story might be considered as a necessary transitional horror to the people-spore one. That is, the fear of unplanned pregnancy is magnified by the fear of burglary which is then further magnified by the fear of alien intrusion.

But the story doesn't work. Let me show why. While the horror of physical and mental transformation by unknown powers may be a primordial terror, invasion of one's body by people spores is too remote from our experience, except as an unfocused horror, even with the burglary bridge, to provide a clarification of our moral choices regarding unplanned pregnancy. Certainly there is a physical mystery to pregnancy that can terrorize (and/or thrill) a woman (and her spouse). A woman's body undergoes an enormous transformation in ways obvious to the eye and in a thousand unseen chemical alterations. But the people-spore story, rather than focusing directly upon physical fear as in the case of the musician story, introduces a new element. In the first story, the ailing musician, underspecified in the narrative, is a morally neutral character. In the second story, the innocent party becomes a people spore, a being ("person-plant") invisible "like pollen" that can "take root in your carpets." The people spore may be "innocent," but only in the sense that a mosquito is innocent. Indeed, it is even hard for us to attach the concept of innocence at all to a being of which we know so little. While it is certainly not likely for one to attach innocence to the burglar as well, at least we can imagine human attributes and even in the underspecification imagine someone burglarizing because he/she was starving.

Up to this point we can regard the people-spore story as a "flat"

narrative. It is not "good" in the sense of advancing Thomson's theory, but does not challenge it, either. But Gilbert Meilaender's commentary on this story suggests a more damaging assessment.[16]
Meilaender has pondered the significance of the people-spore story
and noted its parallel to a famous image in the history of political
thought. Thomas Hobbes in the *De Cive* announces that he will "consider men as if but even now sprung out of the earth, and suddenly,
like mushrooms, come to full maturity, without all kind of engagement to each other." The Hobbesian invitation to consider humans as
mushrooms leads Meilaender to wonder what "angle of vision"
Thomson is inviting us to adopt when she compares the fetus to a
spore. Thomson, according to Meilaender, has a model of regeneration in this and in other stories that is similar to one employed in nature: parasitism. He considers the analogy through an examination of
Annie Dillard's stories of parasitism. For Dillard, parasitism is a "way
of life" in nature, and she writes of the lives of parasites as a "hellish
hagiography." One which Meilaender cites is the life story of the stylop, a parasite whose hosts are insects such as leaf hoppers, ants, bees,
and wasps. Here is a portion of Dillard's description: "The female
spends her entire life inside the body of her host, with only the tip of
her bean-shaped body protruding. She is a formless lump, having no
wings, legs, eyes, or antennae; her vestigial mouth and anus are tiny,
degenerate and nonfunctional. She absorbs food—her host—through
the skin of her abdomen . . ."[17]

Meilaender compares the vicariousness of the parasite to the fetus:
". . . there is no doubt that the fetus does for nine months live off the
mother and makes use of the mother's circulatory and waste-disposal
system." He then asks, "But shall we acquiesce in this picture of the
fetus as a parasite?" He concludes that the two are "quite different
phenomena," for the vicariousness of the fetus is "strikingly creative—oriented not toward degenerative dependence but toward a
new life that will be able to give as it received."[15]

Let us briefly look at the significance of Meilaender's commentary
in terms of our examination of the relationship of storytelling and political theory. Meilaender is not asserting that the people-spore story is
not fully consistent with Thomson's theory, as we observed could be
done with Locke's story of Jepthah. In fact, he is asserting quite the opposite. We certainly *can* think of individuals in these terms, argues
Meilaender, and in his own essay he does just that. But what Meilaender has done is actually to retell Thomson's story with more specification using Dillard's lifestory of the stylop as his theme to attempt to

show that there is something wrong with Thomson's whole theory. If the spore story includes the premise that human regeneration is like parasitism, then Thomson does not really assume that the fetus is a person, as her theory originally suggests, or "one does not know how she pictures a human being or what she thinks a person is."[19] The second story, then, if Meilaender is correct, and I think he is, illustrates how a narrative can undermine a theory by exposing theoretical assumptions that might have remained unexamined and, hence, hidden from the reader.

THE STORIES OF BRIAN AND MARY IN *HABITS OF THE HEART*

Still another variation can been seen in Bellah, et al., *Habits of the Heart.* The theory which the authors hope to advance is that there are three traditions of discourse in American history (biblical, republican, and individualist), and that while the latter is culturally hegemonic today, at least in the American middle class (which they regard as culturally hegemonic), the other traditions still exist as second languages. The biographic interviews with selected Americans are designed to function as stories to illustrate how individualism (and the other two traditions) informs the lives and social and political commitments of Americans. But the fit between the life histories and the authors' theory is conceived in terms tighter than example. Bellah and his associates see narrative as "a primary and powerful way by which to know about a whole." In fact, their approach can be seen as consisting of two parallel and reinforcing sets of stories constituting a single theory. There are the stories told by the over two hundred Americans, and there are also the exemplary figures of the Anglo-American tradition whose own lives as activists and theorists constitute a set of stories themselves. The task of the authors, then, is not one of illustrating by example the viability of the three traditions, nor even matching the life histories with the historical exemplars. According to the authors, "in talking to our contemporaries, we were listening not only to our predecessors. In our conversations, we were listening not only to voices present but to voices past. In the words of those we talked to, we heard John Calvin, Thomas Hobbes, and John Locke, as well as Winthrop, Franklin, Jefferson, Emerson, and Whitman."[20] The relationship posited here, then, between stories and theory is different from the other examples we have examined. For Bellah, et al., appear to have erased the awkward fit between theory and story. But have they?

The authors, as they hear and then retell the stories of contemporary Americans, openly reject what they call a "scientific version of

Candid Camera," which seeks to capture "beliefs and actions without our subjects being aware of us." Instead they employ an "active, Socratic approach to storytelling, one which does not "seek to impose our ideas" but to create a "public conversation."[21]

Let us examine two of these public conversations. One story is "told" by Brian Palmer, a successful 41-year-old California businessman. Recently divorced and now remarried, Palmer tells the story of his personal crisis. An inveterate planner and "compulsive problem solver," he had neglected his wife and children for career goals. Chastened by the break-up of his marriage, he realized the limitations of the success ethic: "I said bullshit. That ain't the way it should be." In his new life, Palmer talks of the importance of love: "To be able to receive affection freely and give affection and to give of myself and know it is a totally reciprocal type of thing. There's just almost a psychologically buoyant feeling of being able to be so much more involved and sharing. Sharing experiences of goals, sharing of feelings, working together to solve problems, etc. My viewpoint of a true love, husband-and-wife type of relationship is one founded on mutual respect, admiration, affection, the ability to give and receive freely."[22] For the tellers of Brian's story, however, while the life narrative is morally "more coherent than when he was dominated by careerism," it rests upon a "fragile foundation," for "even his deepest impulses of attachment to others are without any more solid foundation than his momentary desires."[23] Palmer "lacks a language to explain what seem to be the real commitments that define his life, and to that extent the commitments themselves are precarious."[24]

A major reason for the assessment of Palmer above is based upon a "public conversation" initiated by the interviewer, Ann Swidler, on the subject of lying. The authors reprint a small portion of the conversation in the appendix of *Habits of the Heart*:

> . . . Swidler, trying to get Brian Palmer to clarify the basis of his moral judgments, responded to his statement that "lying is one of the things I want to regulate" by asking, "Why?"

A: Well, it's a kind of thing that is a habit you get into. Kind of self-perpetuating. It's like digging a hole. You just keep digging and digging.

Q: So why is it wrong?

A: Why is integrity important and lying bad? I don't know. It just is. It's just so basic. I don't want to be bothered with challenging that. It's part of me. I don't know where it came from, but it's very important.

Q: When you think about what's right and what's wrong, are things bad because they are bad for people, or are they right and wrong in themselves, and if so how do you know?

A: Well, some things are bad because . . . I guess I feel like everybody on this planet is entitled to have a little bit of space, and things that detract from other people's space are kind of bad . . .[25]

This brief telling of how Palmer's story was re-told reveals a good deal about the status of storytelling, generally, in *Habits of the Heart*. In the story itself, which begins the entire book, Palmer is characterized as holding values as "matters of personal preference . . . detached from any social or cultural base that could give them broader meaning." His second answer reproduced above is offered as evidence of this assessment. But does the public conversation initiated by the interviewer, including the last question above which would be a difficult query in a Ph.D. examination, tell the story of a man whose "deepest impulses" are no more than "momentary desires?" Palmer cannot explain the first principles of his moral beliefs, and when forced to do so reaches for the language of individualism. But as one critic of this story has observed, "like C. S. Pierce, Brian doesn't know how to answer questions that aren't connected to real doubts," and that like Wittgenstein, "he can't think of anything more certain than the wrongness of lying that might be introduced to support the idea that lying is wrong."[26]

Palmer might not be a particularly philosophically inclined citizen (except in his moment of life crisis); he may hold to a philosophical theory not accepted by the storytellers (though it still may not be an individualistic one). But do any of these conclusions justify the categorization of his life story as one of "comic tragedy" based upon "precarious" commitments and "momentary desires?" This I would contend is the story of the authors of *Habits of the Heart*. It is not Brian's story, and one wonders if the public conversations involve the telling of the stories of the authors rather than those of Brian Palmer.

Partial proof that the stories in *Habits of the Heart* are less the stories of Americans than the theories of the authors recast in narrative form can be gained by a brief examination of another life story, that of Mary Taylor. Taylor, a member of the California Coastal Commission, is described by the authors as "a civic-minded professional who was able to move from the cosmopolitan value of relative tolerance toward the kind of commitment to the common good that is necessary to assure the integrity of the community."[27] Unfortunately, say the authors, they "did not meet many Mary Taylors," but they were impressed with her "remarkable strengths—her courage, vision, and commit-ment." Her life story "show(s) us a conception of citizenship that is still alive in America."[28] By talking to Taylor, the authors were talking to Jefferson and Winthrop and a civil self just as when they were talk-ing to Palmer, they were talking to Franklin and a utilitarian self.

Yet the authors do seem to neglect the parallels between both sto-ries. Taylor speaks of the importance of realizing "that other people have other values, but they must be respected." "That," she says, "is what freedom is all about." When Palmer speaks of his belief that "everybody on this planet is entitled to a little bit of space," he is criti-cized for justifying his deepest ethical virtues in terms of personal preference. For Mary Taylor, tolerance shows her concern for "mutual respect among members of society." When Taylor states that one should not engage in political work "unless you get satisfaction out of it," this shows she is not a "martyr." When Palmer describes his job in terms of self-satisfaction, this is evidence of the "voice of a utilitarian self seeking its separate identity in the exercise of its growing pow-ers." When Palmer describes his departure from church going because of hypocrisy among Christians, this is evidence of the unwillingness of Americans to invest in community when that entails divesting at least part of an autonomous self. When Taylor announces that she does not go to church any longer despite her Catholic upbringing because she has concluded that religion is "too sentimental," this is because "the main source of her sense of social responsibility seems to be the expe-rience of caring and being cared for in the course of her volunteer work." Palmer's confessed loneliness is evidence of the shallowness of his life; Taylor's is the loneliness of the steward. When Taylor is reluc-tant to define the public good, the authors, presumably from their public conversations, contend that "such professions of agnosticism do not mean that Mary is totally without any substantive conception of the public good." Palmer's inability to determine if lying is wrong in itself or because of its consequence is evidence of the fragility of his autobiographical vision.

On the basis of this brief comparison, one can hypothesize that the stories the authors of Habits of the Heart tell involve less a conversation with three traditions than a conversation with one tradition, admit-tedly with some variation. That is, the stories of Palmer and Taylor converge once the theory is lifted. Palmer's life story is hardly bereft of communitarian elements, although the authors may not approve of the "symbolic cosmos" in which they are framed. Taylor's story high-lights her effort to convey her life in communitarian language, but the justification of her beliefs is studded with individualistic premises. The public conversation permits the authors as retellers of both stories to expose the individualistic framework of Palmer's communitarian language and largely to ignore the possibilities for exposing Taylor's communitarian framework while searching for communitarian elements in individualistic responses.

The public conversation, then, is the device that disguises the awkwardness between the stories and the theory. Are the stories in *Habits of the Heart* good stories? To the extent that the authors believe that they have established the existence of second languages separately identifiable in the stories of American citizens, they are not. Although we have only examined two stories in any detail, we can argue that without the method of public conversation, the habits of the heart that are described in the narrative would be more incoherent and unstable than they appear. When the authors speak to Palmer, they contend that they hear Franklin. But if they listened more carefully, they would have heard Jefferson, too, especially the latter's concern with organized religion and yearning for a stable private life. When Taylor speaks, we certainly hear Jefferson, as the authors suggest, but despite their best efforts, we also hear Franklin and Whitman. This is not to say that the authors are deceptive, but that they are often telling different stories than simply those of Palmer and Taylor. Sometimes they are telling their own stories in narrative form, and sometimes they are arguing with the storytellers and their theoretical predecessors. That these three stories are mixed up ironically leads to the cohesion of the theory. When untangled, as we have tried to accomplish here, all of these stories produce an incoherence in the theory.

But viewed from another angle, the stories of *Habits of the Heart* are, or could be, good stories. Clearly, in the case of Palmer, the authors chose to argue with the storyteller. In the case of Taylor, they did not; they chose to agree. In the former case, the authors present the result of the argument; in the latter, the result of their agreement. Only in the appendix do we learn of the process of argumentation and that in only two instances with two storytellers. The stories being told, then, are stories of arguments/agreements, not simply "conversations" with "particular individuals" to uncover the possibility of our cultural traditions. When the authors chose to agree, we hear primarily the story of the storyteller (or at least that portion with which the authors agree). If we look, then, at the stories themselves in *Habits of the Heart* as stories hovering somewhere between the narrative without "public conversation" and the general theory, we have a set of "good" stories.

WALZER'S STORIES OF CIVIL WAR DRAFT LAWS, THE MACY AND STRAUSS BROTHERS, AND WASHING MACHINES

Spheres of Justice attempts to facilitate a *via media* between the demands of liberal and socialist thought. To socialists, Walzer insists that "complex equality" is the only viable conception of justice in most spheres. To liberals, Walzer argues that the domination of money requires a broader pluralism. *Spheres of Justice* also offers a praxis for social democratic thought. Walzer sets out to show that a "decentralized democratic socialism" and "a strong welfare state, at least in part, run by local and amateur officials" is partially discernible from the social meanings people have already assigned to goods.[29] To achieve these goals, Walzer tells stories. "I have tried," he writes in his preface, "to work my argument through contemporary and historical examples . . . My examples are rough sketches, sometimes focused on the agents of distribution, sometimes on the procedures, sometimes on the criteria, sometimes on the use and meaning of the things we share, divide, and exchange."[30]

In the arena of money and commodities, Walzer attempts to mark off a sphere that makes considerable concessions to the liberal idea. He readily accepts Locke's observation about the tacit agreement of men to put a value on "a little piece of yellow metal." There will always be money (Walzer cannot imagine a society without it), and there will always be some market in commodities (commodities are our anchors in the world). But he does want to keep money and the purchase of commodities in their place. He asks: "What is the proper sphere of money? What social goods are rightly marketable?"[31]

His paradigmatic story here is the practice of simony and the objections to it. The Christian understanding of a social good, ecclesiastical office and God's grace were not things that could be for sale. Walzer's stories about American society are used to establish an analogical connection to the sin of simony and so establish the principle that there are things that money can't buy. One concerns the Conscription Act of 1863, which permitted the exemption of any man from service if he were willing and able to pay $300 to pay a substitute. For Walzer, this law was "bad business in a republic, for it seemed to abolish the *public thing* and turn military service (even when the republic was at stake!) into a private transaction."[32] Another concerns the invention of the department store by Rowland Macy and the Strauss brothers. Walzer expresses only the barest sympathy for the small-scale merchants who were ruined by this new retailing structure.

Only simple equality through an elimination of buying and selling could eliminate this kind of development. He is also relatively unconcerned about the accumulation of wealth by these entrepreneurs: "the rest of us can only watch it with admiration (or envy)." But Walzer is concerned about the political ascendancy of these entrepreneurs and their heirs. The question is not that they were not "decent and capable public servants," but that "they owed their political influence to their wealth and continuing business success."[33] The third story is a gloss on André Gorz's account of the insidious economic and social consequences of private consumption of commodities. Appliances designed for individuals, Gorz argues, erode those which could be used or designed for public use. The privately owned washing machine, for example, operates against the installation of public laundries. The same can be said for the automobile and public transportation, the television and, more recently, the VCR and the movie house. Walzer has a great deal of sympathy for this argument. There should be some forum in which the consequences of commodity acquisition are discussed, although contrary to Gorz, he contends that such collective decisions should be made at the level of the apartment house or the city block.

Walzer's case against the Civil War legislation becomes his case for blocked exchanges. But had the legislators "failed to understand the logic of their own institutions," or worse, enacted class legislation? Only if one assumes as Walzer does that a national draft is a morally justifiable institution in a republic. Most Americans did not. Blaine's remarks in 1864 illustrate the nature of a belief system unexplored in Walzer's story: "Do not, I pray you by any action here proclaim to the world that you have no faith in the loyal people of the United States. Do not allow it to appear, even by implication, that the *people* need to be goaded and driven into support for a people's war . . . Just let it be understood that whoever·the lot falls on *must go*, regardless of all business considerations, all private interests, all personal engagements, all family obligations; that the draft is to be sharp, decisive, final, and inexorable, without commutation and without substitution, and my word for it you will create consternation in all the loyal States."[34] Blaine went on to suggest that only Napoleon had resorted to such measures. To attempt to introduce a system in the United States would be "to ignore the first principles of republican government."

The *levée en masse* was regarded with horror by nearly all politicians. Only anti-war democrats referred to the 1863 act as a "conscription" bill. In this climate the commutation clause was justified as a "democratic" measure. Should only substitutions be permitted (and few were willing to remove this exemption), the poor would be in an even worse position. The $300 commutation would, so it was argued, actually keep down the price of securing substitutes. Fred Shannon, in his classic study of the Union Army, summarizes the majority position:[35]

> One brother might serve for another, a son for a father or vice versa. A friend might serve for another who would look out for his interests. Or if a rich man found it less inconvenient to hire a substitute than to procure one in any other fashion, that was his privilege. There would surely be enough to go around without working any hardship on anybody. By this method the draft would merely be a method of placing upon a given number of individuals the personal responsibility of procuring one soldier each, either themselves or substitutes. By this means sources of recruiting would be utilized which had hitherto been unexplored and, at the same time, each citizen could exercise his choice as to whether or not he would render personal service. What could be more democratic?[36]

Indeed, what could be more democratic from the perspective of a commitment to avoid a *levée en masse*? In fact, between 1863 and 1864 there were scores of attempts to tinker with the commutation system. One amendment in the 1863 act proposed to fine an individual who refused the draft and could not afford the commutation fee. The "fine" was to range from $20 to $200, presumably to be based upon the individual's economic circumstances. New York City aldermen appropriated $42.5 million dollars to pay the commutation fees of individuals who could not afford the $300. No less than twelve amendments to section 13 (the commutation and substitution provision) were proposed in the 1864 extension of the enrollment act. One proposed a plan of graduated commutation with taxes of 10, 20, and 30 percent on incomes above $600, $2,000, and $5,000, respectively.

Walzer does not discuss these efforts, but his general attitude toward them could be summarized by his comment that "when people sneak across the boundary of the sphere of money, they advertise the existence of the boundary. It's there, roughly at the point where they begin to hide and dissemble."[37] But Americans did learn about the draft, exemptions, and blocked exchanges. The "logic of our institutions" taught us to "acknowledge now the principle of equal treatment," and now "because of the political struggles of 1863 . . . we know roughly where the boundary is that it marks out."[38] The draft is precisely where it ought to be, and the sale of exemptions is a blocked exchange.

But is this the story of the Conscription Act of 1863 and its amendments? There certainly was an attempt, in the words of legislators, to protect the "great middle interest" of the population. But was the legislation and the subsequent tinkering totally an example of dissembling? Might not the thrust of the debates and the amendments have been a groping effort to avoid both a national draft *and* create the conditions for blocked exchanges? Had communities widely subsidized commutation fees for the poor and had the national government developed a system of graduated fees, exchanges would not have been as blocked as in the levee en masse. On the other hand, if conscription is wrong even when the republic is at stake (as Blaine, who was no Copperhead, argued), commutation in some form is preferable to the institution of a Napoleonic republic. If the volunteer is the only republican hero, and if there are not enough people to fight a "people's" war, then maybe it ought not be fought at all.

Walzer's other stories function even more problematically as routes to his theory. Section 13 of the Enrollment and Conscription Act permits Walzer to conclude that the *levée en masse* is the only institution that effectively avoids the problem of blocked exchanges and military service. For Macy and the Strauss brothers, he simply has no recommendations save that citizens must be careful not to conflate the economic skills of the entrepreneur with political talent. To permit oneself to be governed by talented men and women as a consumer and as a citizen "must be two entirely separate decisions." As to the washing machine question, it is difficult to imagine, even should the market respond, the forsaking of the "private" television or Maytag. There will always be groups like the Amish in a liberal society. They evoke our admiration and even occasionally our envy, but no number of stories about communes in America can establish even a modified version of Gorz's utopian vision. Why? The answer involves an acceptance of the essence of life in a bourgeois society, an acceptance that Walzer cannot entertain. It is possible to devise election laws that permit citizens to run for office without the personal power of money (although, even these sorts of measures are more difficult than first appearances suggest). It is much more difficult to separate admiration of entrepreneurial success from confidence in governing in a society in which the former is a paramount value. Shrewdness, perseverance, the ability to "meet a payroll," "realism": these are what Americans more often than not see as political attributes as well as economic ones. There are periods of protest, of course, but even the American reform mentality historically has taken a business cast. The line from Franklin to Iaccocca has few interruptions. The Macy-Strauss

economic-political success story is not, in terms of our social needs, a
basis for limiting the power of money; in fact, it could be seen as a
story that establishes the argument for the responsibility and legitimacy of bourgeois rule in America. Walzer admits this crucial aspect
of American culture in terms of commodities when, after reviewing
Gorz's critique of the automobile and its supporting infrastructure, he
says, "He is probably right, but the car is also a symbol of individual
freedom; and I doubt that any democratic public within living memory would have voted against it, even if the long term consequences of
its mass production were known in advance."[39]

The story of the Civil War draft, then, rather than taken as a story
that illustrates the proposition that exemption is to military service as
simony is to ecclesiastical office, could be read as a story that illustrates something quite different, such as that conscription is to republicanism as freedom is to slavery. If it is the latter story that is being told,
then Americans did not finally get the logic of their institutions right
after 1863, but began the first step on a long road toward a Napoleonic
empire. More generally, a reinterpretation of the story raises questions
about the logic implied by Walzer's other stories designed to establish
that a system of blocked exchanges is required by the logic of our own
social meanings. The Macy and Strauss and Maytag stories are stories
that are certainly about what money can buy. But in the context in
which Walzer has chosen to tell his stories, it is not money that buys
political office, but shrewdness and realism which legitimizes both,
and it is not commodities that enslave us or even give us solace, but it
is commodities that give us freedom individually.

Walzer's stories are designed to achieve an objective as bold and
ingenious as Locke's. As Locke had tried to use the patriarchal story of
Jepthah to establish the legitimacy of liberalism, Walzer uses his stories from American history in order to show that there exists a praxis
for a social-democratic America. But Walzer's theoretical project necessarily requires a closer fit than Locke's did. Walzer's stories are
"good" stories as illustrations of his theory of complex justice, but are
they "good stories" for describing American practices?

CONCLUSION

We began this essay with the contention that despite the penchant for
storytelling among political theorists, the fit between a story and a theory can best be described as awkward. Figure 13.1 illustrates in very
simplified form how a deconstructive structure parallels each effort at
theory construction through storytelling. Each story seems to require a

Figure 13.1. Theory Construction (Deconstruction) and Story-Telling

	Locke	Thomson	Bellah et. al.	Walzer
Theoretical Objective	Origin of political authority in consent	Justification of killing of innocents	Existence of second languages in American culture	Complex equality; social democratic praxis in America
Bridges	Authority temporary, limited, not hereditary	Kidnapping-dialysis/ rape; burglary/spore invasion/pregnancy	American exemplars in three languages	Logic of our institutions
(Counter-Bridges)	(Anarchy; state of war)	(Specification)	(Stories as authors' narratives)	(Exemptions attempt to avoid *levée en masse*; Macy and Strauss as bourgeois heroes; Maytags = freedom)
(Counter-Stories)	(Moral of Judges: "In those days there was no king")	(Meilaender's stylops; Thomson's own emendations)	(Brian's communitarianism; Mary's individualism)	(Draft as anti-republican institution; Macy's and Strauss' transferability of economic skills; washing machines and cultural consensus)
Stories	Jepthah in Book of Judges	Kidnapping and dialysis; invasion of people spores	Brian's and Mary's oral histories	Civil War draft; Macy's and Strauss' "buying" political office retail; new consumer durables and democratic ratification

bridge to the theory which can be substituted with a counterbridge based upon a reinterpretation of the proposed story or the introduction of another story. These "counter-stories" connect to the different bridge that prevents completion of the theory or serves to undermine the theory itself.

In our examination of selected stories, we have seen how this process works in particular ways. Locke's story of Jepthah, while a bold story to tell in terms of his theory, contains powerful counter-concepts to his own theoretical project and, perhaps more importantly, highlights the analytic nature of his theory. Thomson's stories seem to force the hearer to produce counter-stories as much as they provide a connection to her theoretical point. One story pursued on its own terms seems actually to invite a re-examination of her entire theory. We offered a reinterpretation of Walzer's stories that challenges his assertion that a praxis exists for a social democratic America, and suggested that the stories in *Habits of the Heart* are different from the ones the authors say they are telling, at least if the steps from storytelling to theory construction are to be coherent.

Despite these problems, we can identify aspects of these narratives that make them "good" stories. Locke's story of Jepthah carries his case to the "home base" of a competing theory, although at a cost. Thomson's kidnapping story captures in vivid terms the horror of rape and attendant pregnancy through the hearer's identification with the victim of life-threatening disease. Walzer's narrative of the Conscription Act forces us to think about the basis of distributive justice even if his effort to relate it to an American praxis is overdrawn. Bellah's stories of American autobiographies, if seen as arguments, reinforce the authors' jeremiadic critiques of modern American culture. Even when stories don't fit, or don't quite fit, they engage us in the theorist's project. This, I think, may be the standard for assessing stories that political theorists tell, despite their vulnerability to deconstruction. Thus, while the theorists' stories might not "clinch" their theory and always "break down," as Guttman suggests, or might not prevent recourse to impersonal rational arguments, as MacIntyre argues, good stories succeed in doing something else, something that is as important. They convey to us something both about the tenacity of the theorist's endeavor and the nature of his/her enterprise.

Let me illustrate by briefly discussing C. S. Lewis' essay, "On Stories."[40] Lewis' focus is not precisely the same as mine here.[41] He is concerned about the relationship between theme and plot in stories. For Lewis, stories with the most breathtaking plots, but without theme, are bad stories and, conversely, stories that attempt to combine theme and plot, while Lewis' favorites, ultimately fail to sustain the atmosphere they attempt to create. For example, in Wells' *War of the Worlds*, the horror of extra-territoriality is captured when the projectile first lands on Horsell Common. "In the later horrors," says Lewis, "excellently as they are done, we lose the feeling of it." Similarly, in Homer (Lewis' selection of stories is disarmingly eclectic), the anticipation created when Odysseus' ship lands on Circe's island ("the sight of smoke going up from amidst those unexplored woods, the god meeting us") is somehow unfulfilled. Other stories do a bit better (the celebration of everyday life in *The Hobbit*; the exploration of a "central region of reality" in the story of Oedipus), but they, too, seem eventually to falter.

Stories, then, need plot; but when only plot is delineated, the stories have limited interest. So stories need theme as well, but somehow theme cannot be sustained simply in a story. Why? For Lewis, the answer lies in the resemblance of the story to life. "In real life, as in a story, something must happen. That is just the trouble. We grasp at a state and find only a succession of events in which the state is never quite embodied." Our "grand ideas contained in stories—excitement, awe, homecoming, leaving" are "delightful," but then "something must happen, and after that something else."[42] Lewis sees the story in terms of a net (plot) designed to catch a bird (theme). But the bird always escapes. Yet, if it is not caught, then we never get to see it at all.

Lewis' discussion of the relation between theme and plot in stories is relevant to our discussion of story and theory. The theorist attempts to capture his vision in narrative form, not simply as a rhetorical device, but as part of an attempt to refresh our perception of the theory. The story here is the net. The theory, trapped for a moment in the net, allows us to see it, perhaps, for the time or, perhaps, from an angle of vision not heretofore available. In a sense, the story is the enemy of the theory. We have seen how often the theory escapes from the net even in good stories, and in bad ones how the theory becomes hopelessly entangled in it and is sometimes mangled or destroyed. But without the story we often cannot see the theory at all, at least not as the theorist hopes we will. By submitting the theory to the story, to the demand that "something must happen, and after that, something else," the writer submits his theory to the narrativeness of political life. The theorist's enterprise is then destined to failure, but it is nonetheless an effort that the reader should demand and the theorist accept. In Lewis' words, "the bird always escapes us, but we saw it close and enjoyed the plumage." When we are able to see in this way, we have found a good story and a good theorist.

NOTES

1. I make no attempt here to present a topology of stories, nor to offer a general definition, except to note that the stories discussed are "short stories," as distinct from long ones such as Tocqueville's *The Ancien Regime and the French Revolution*, Montesquieu's *Persian Letters*, or Engels' *The Condition of the Working Class in England*.

2. Amy Guttman, "Moral Philosophy and Political Problems," *Political Theory*, vol. 10 (1982), pp. 33–47, at p. 38.

3. John Locke, *Two Treatises of Government* (New York: New American Library, 1965), I: pp. 158, 163, 167; II: pp. 109, 241.

4. Ibid., II: p. 109.

5. Ibid., II: p. 21.

6. One hundred years later, Paine openly rejected the "lessons of Judges," complaining about the "hankering" for kings and citing Gideon's refusal to accept the crown as the real paradigmatic lesson. See Thomas Paine, *The Essential Thomas Paine* (New York: New American Library, 1969), pp. 30–31. For a more complex assessment which sees "Judges" as a story of deliverers and "anti-deliverers," see Abraham Malamat, "Charismatic Leadership in the Book of Judges," *The Mighty Acts of God*, ed. Frank Moore et al. (New York: Doubleday, 1980), pp. 152–68.

7. John Dunn, *The Political Thought of John Locke* (Cambridge: Cambridge University Press, 1969), p. 99.

8. Ibid., p. 102.

9. Gordon Schochet, *Patriarchalism in Political Thought* (New York: Basic Books, 1975), pp. 274–75.

10. Judith Thomson, "A Defense of Abortion," *Philosophy and Human Affairs*, vol. 1 (Fall, 1971), pp. 47–66, at p. 49.

11. Robert Goodin, *Political Theory and Public Policy* (Chicago: University of Chicago Press, 1982), pp. 8–9.

12. I should note that I use "good" here only in terms of internal theoretical commensurability and not in a moral sense. For an evaluation of the latter, see Philip Abbott, "Philosophers and the Abortion Question," *Political Theory*, vol. 6 (1978), pp. 313–35.

13. Thomson, "A Defense of Abortion," p. 49.

14. Ibid., p. 60.

15. Ibid., p. 59.

16. Gilbert Meilaender, *The Limits of Love* (University Park: Pennsylvania State University Press, 1987), pp. 48–59.

17. Ibid., p. 53.

18. Ibid., p. 55.

19. Ibid., p. 59.

20. Robert Bellah et al., *Habits of the Heart* (Berkeley: University of California Press, 1985), p. 306.

21. Ibid., p. 304.

22. Ibid., p. 5.

23. Ibid., p. 8.

24. Ibid.

25. Ibid., pp. 304–5.

26. Jeffrey Stout, "Liberal Society and the Languages of Morals," *Community in America: The Challenge of Habits of the Heart* (Berkeley: University of California Press, 1988), p. 129.

27. Bellah et al., *Habits of the Heart*, p. 192.

28. Ibid., p. 195.

29. Michael Walzer, *Spheres of Justice: A Defense of Pluralism and Equality* (New York: Basic Books, 1983), p. xiv.

30. Ibid.

31. Ibid., p. 103.

32. Ibid., p. 99.

33. Ibid., pp. 111–12.

34. Fred A. Shannon, *The Organization of the Union Army, 1861–1865*, vol. II (Cleveland: Arthur Clark, 1928), pp. 39–40.

35. It should be noted that Shannon himself was hardly a defender of Section 13, which he regarded as a "concession to the bourgeoisie."

36. Shannon, *Union Army*, p. 12.

37. Walzer, *Spheres of Justice*, p. 98.

38. Ibid., p. 99.

39. Ibid., p. 115.

40. C. S. Lewis, *Of Other Worlds* (New York: Harcourt, Brace and World, 1966), pp. 3–21.

41. Lewis' comments on story-telling were brought to my attention by Meilaender, *The Limits of Love*, pp. 19–31, who notes the importance of Lewis' own stories for conveying Christian belief.

42. Lewis, *Of Other Worlds*, p. 20.

14

Narration, Reason, and Community

Walter R. Fisher

"What matters at this stage" of the late twentieth century, Alasdair MacIntyre contends, "is the construction of local forms of community within which civility and the intellectual and moral life can be sustained through the dark ages which are already upon us."[1] As I shall argue, the constitution of communities requires the existence of certain modes of communication. To begin, however, a context is necessary. Every story must have its exposition. This one will be synopses of the stories about community and communication told by John Dewey, Martin Buber, Jürgen Habermas, and Hans-Georg Gadamer. Notice will also be given to the notions of certain postmodern storytellers. The argument of this survey is that conceptions of communication imply forms of community, that community depends on particular forms of communication, and that a dialectical tension exists between ideal conceptions of communication and the realization of ideal community beyond the local and ephemeral. When ideal conceptions are applied to ongoing associations, such as society, communication is seen as distorted and community is seen as a distant dream. The burden of the story itself is the argument that a narrational view of communication clarifies the constitution of community and adds an essential consideration, the role of reason in the process. The epilogue is more by way of suggestion than argument; it raises questions, proposes possible answers, and comments on the relationship between local and metanarratives and their communities.

Dewey maintained that there could be "no such thing as community" if people were not interested in others, "in entering into the

activities of others and taking part in conjoint and cooperative doings."[2] Because people do have this inclination, along with their private proclivities, community is not only possible, it happens. It comes
into being through communication, by which Dewey meant "a process
of sharing experience till it becomes a common possession. It modifies
the disposition of both parties who partake in it."[3] The impetus for
and realization of communication is understanding. "Society," for
Dewey, "not only continues to exist *by* transmission, *by* communication, but it may fairly be said to exist *in* transmission, *in* communication."[4] He did not limit the forms of communication that contribute to
community. Everyday discourse counted, as did artistic and scientific
expressions. He was, however, concerned about the negative character
of public debate, comparing it to a "watered-down version of the
Hegelian dialectic."[5] Persuasion, in his view, was an inevitable consequence of genuine communication, but such discourse had to be a
nonmanipulative form, a mutual educative experience.

In regard to community, Dewey held two views: (1) that a real
community already exists by virtue of "the infinite relationships of
man with his fellows and with nature;"[6] and (2) that an ideal community only exists in democratic experience. His conception of communication was tied to this ideal. The connection between ideal community
and ideal communication is established clearly in this passage from
Problems of Men:

> What is the faith in democracy in the role of consultation, of confer-
> ence, of persuasion, of discussion, in the formulation of public opin-
> ion . . . except faith in the capacity of the intelligence of the common
> man to respond with common sense to the free play of acts and ideas
> which are secured by effective guarantees of free inquiry, free assem-
> bly and free communication.[7]

Given this faith, along with common agreement about common
ends sought by conjoint action, understanding would follow and democratic community would thrive. "Consensus," he wrote, "demands
communication."[8] And, he maintained, "Democracy is not an alternative to other principles of associated life. It is the idea of community
life itself."[9]

Foreshadowing the position of Buber, Dewey held that democracy
was not a mode of nation-state governance but a "mode of associated
living, of conjoint communicated experience."[10] He anticipated Habermas's views of communicative action, not only in his stress upon

understanding and consensus, but also in his conception of genuine communication as an ideal transaction, one of uncoerced, mutual, educative exchange. And like MacIntyre, Dewey despaired the possibility of community beyond local associations. I share the despair, at least in regard to Dewey's observation that "no government of experts in which the masses do not have a chance to inform experts as to their needs can be anything but an oligarchy managed in the interests of the few."[11] I also believe him when he writes: "no matter how ignorant any person is, there is one thing he knows better than anybody else and that is where the shoe pinches on his own feet."[12] I shall have more to say about experts later.

As I move to the views of Buber on community and communication, I have the feeling of introducing someone to his or her own best friend or loved one. It can hardly be the case that everyone interested in the subject does not know as much or more than I about Buber's thought. This is especially true of Ronald C. Arnett, who has written an excellent book, *Communication and Community: Implication of Buber's Dialogue.*[13] So, my purpose here is to touch on essential ideas for this contextualization of my views. The passage that captures Buber's vision of community as well as any, is this one:

> On the far side of the subjective, on this side of the objective, on the narrow ridge, where I and Thou meet, there is the realm of "between." This reality, whose disclosure has begun in our time, shows the way, leading individualism and collectivism, for the life decision of future generation. Here the genuine third alternative is indicated, the knowledge of which will help to bring about the genuine person again and to establish genuine community.[14]

If another passage is needed to clarify his position, I offer this one: "The real living together of man with man can only thrive where people have the real things of their common life in common; where they can experience, discuss and administer them together, where real fellowship and real work guilds exist."[15] In short, for Buber, genuine community, as an ongoing association, is a commune inspirited by Hasidic and socialist ideals.

It immediately follows from this conception of genuine community that genuine communication cannot be the usual forms of monologic discourse. Whenever communication is strictly monologic, whether in debate, in conversations, in friendly chats, or in lovers' talk, real relationship is nonexistent. The same applies to technical communication, which Buber ironically says is "the inalienable sterling quality of 'modern' existence." On rare occasions, at times even in the sorts of communication just enumerated, dialogic communication may emerge. Genuine dialogue appears in those encounters "no matter whether spoken or silent—where each of the participants really has in mind the other or others in their present and particular being and turns to them with the intention of establishing a living mutual relation between himself and them."[16] As with Dewey's notions, Buber's can also lead to despair: waiting for dialogue to occur can be like waiting for Godot.

Consider again the themes that arise from Dewey's and Buber's views. The realization of community in Dewey's thought depends on human intelligence and mutual, educative exchange.[17] The actualization of community in Buber's thinking relies on the human capacity to enter the "in-between," to be genuinely in relation to others through dialogic communication. Since the potential for intelligence and authenticity is rarely achieved, mutual, educative exchange and dialogue are rare. Since these forms of communication are seldom in existence, democratic and socialist communities are seldom in existence. When they do exist, they appear in local and short-lived encounters. As ideal achievements, they serve as standards by which ordinary experience and public discourse must be seen as distorted and counterproductive to life as we would want it to be. Reverberations of these themes recur in the writings of Habermas and Gadamer.

Habermas's notion of an emancipated, rational society has strong conceptual affinities with Dewey's construction of democracy. Like Dewey, Habermas stresses human intelligence, the capacity of people to reason and to be rational. This potential is evident in argumentation, which he defines as "that type of speech in which participants thematize contested validity claims and attempt to vindicate them through arguments."[18] "An argument," he writes, "contains reasons or grounds that are connected in a systematic way with the validity claim of a problematic expression."[19] The aim of such discourse, in line with Dewey's ideas again, is understanding, or "valid agreement," and consensus. The model underlying Habermas's view of argumentation resembles Buber's notion of encounter. Habermas envisions an "ideal speech situation," a symmetrical and noncoercive transaction. There would be equal opportunity to participate, to criticize, to express personal aims and attitudes, and to perform these acts without regard to power or ideology. The paucity of argumentation based on this model accounts for the lack of an emancipated, rational society, and when the model is used to assess ordinary and public discourse, such discourse must be viewed as distorted.

Gadamer's concept of conversation, also like Buber's view of encounter, leads to the same conclusion when applied to everyday discourse. "It is characteristic of every true conversation," he maintains, "that each opens himself to the other person, truly accepts his point of view as worthy of consideration and gets inside the other to such an extent that he understands not a particular individual, but what he says."[20] True conversation for Gadamer is dialogue, question and answer, in which there is a "fusion of horizons," an encounter of "transformation into a communion, in which we do not remain what we were."[21] The result is understanding, not just valid agreement. Gadamer privileges linguisticality rather than intelligence, the capacity for authenticity, or argumentative ability. "Language," he insists, "is not just one of man's possessions in the world, but on it depends the fact that man has a world at all."[22] From this view, communication is "a living process in which a community is lived. . . . All forms of human community of life are forms of linguistic community: even more, they constitute language."[23] Gadamer is talking here about communication and community with their initial "cees" lowercase. When the "cees" are capitalized, when the stress is on true conversation, ordinary, usual communication and community fall short of the ideal, and again, we are left with the local and isolated realizations of what communication and community can be.

A glimmer of hope exists in each of these writer's views: people do have intelligence, the capacity for authenticity, the ability to argue, and a desire for understanding. This is not the case with the leading theorists of postmodernism. Most vocal among them are Foucault, Derrida, and Lyotard. For Foucault, all public discourse is infected with power;[24] for Derrida, all discourse is condemned to totalization through logocentric distinctions that marginalize people, ideas, institutions, and so on.[25] Lyotard, for his part, declares the end of all metanarratives—the stories that have aspired to universal application and on which dreams of transcendental community have depended.[26] Consensus, as conceived by Dewey and Habermas, he says, is "outmoded and suspect."[27] Community on any large scale is foreclosed by the fact that communication in society has been reduced, fragmented into language games."[28] Because this is the case, he thinks that "the idea . . . we need today in order to make decisions in political matters cannot be the idea of the totality, or of the unity, of a body. It can only be the idea of multiplicity or of a diversity."[29]

Interestingly, our most adamant antimodernist, MacIntyre, agrees with the underlying observation of Lyotard: ours is a time marked by incommensurate notions of rationality, justice, and ethics. Lyotard accepts the fact; MacIntyre deplores it. Insofar as incommensurability does reign, the dream of community beyond the local must remain a distant, if not impossible, dream. Yet, as I wrote in a review of MacIntyre's book, *Whose Justice? Which Rationality?*, there will always be conceptual and/or logical incommensurability between or among people who are certain of their own version of truth and their own particular vocabulary and grammar.[30] Fortunately, for the world to go on, they do not need to convince or to persuade one another. They must only gain the adherence of a relevant audience, others who are affected by the matter at hand and whose values are fundamental but not beyond discussion and debate. Protesters, as MacIntyre notes in *After Virtue*, talk past one another, as one side grounds arguments in "rights" and the other in "law."[31] He is correct; they do talk past one another. But, they do not talk past those who will decide the outcome of the controversy. The coherence and fidelity of the rival stories told by these factions are assessed and decisions are made and, insofar as these principles are enacted, the assessments and decisions are rational. This sort of rationality will not satisfy those who demand "rational persuasion" or consensus, but then it does comply with another notion of rationality, the idea that rationality is displayed when people are open to argument and have an ability and willingness to participate in it.

To all this—the thinking of pre- and postmodernists alike—our leading neopragmatist, Richard Rorty, says: "We need a redescription of liberalism as the hope that culture as a whole can be 'poeticized' rather than as the Enlightenment hope that it can be 'rationalized' or 'scientized.' That is, we need to substitute the hope that chances for fulfillment of idiosyncratic fantasies will be equalized for the hope that everyone will replace 'passion' or fantasy with 'reason'."[32] This new hope, he hopes, will be kept alive by keeping the conversation of humankind going.[33] Perhaps needless to say, it is not Gadamer's concept of conversation that he has in mind. It is simply talk that recognizes contingency, irony, and solidarity.

In response to these various notions of communication and community, I offer an alternative way of thinking, one that does not deny people's intelligence, the capacity for authenticity, the ability to argue, or the desire for understanding. It is a view that provides a construct that subsumes these human attributes: put succinctly, I argue that human beings are most aptly designated *homo narrans*. This view speaks not only to the idealistic conceptions of communication and community; it also addresses the implications inherent in postmodern theories that privilege ideology, power, desire, and deconstruction in human decision-making and action. To these theories, it says: Decision and action are inevitable; if ideology, power, desire, and indeterminacy are the only features of human decision and action, then the only choice is that of whose domination will prevail, whose oppression shall one submit to and live by. The feature of human decision-making and action left out here is reason. The narrative perspective on human beings restores this feature by reconstructing it in terms of narrative rationality, which I will explain shortly. Narrative reason incorporates traditional logics as they pertain to communicative practices, but reinstates significant questions of values so that intelligence, authenticity, argumentative ability, and understanding are enhanced.

TEXT

The foundation of my proposal, which is definitely a proposal and not a panacea, is, as I have indicated, the assumption that human beings are essentially storytellers. The assumption derives authority from thinkers as different as MacIntyre and Gregory Bateson. MacIntyre maintains that "man is in his actions and practice, as well as in his fictions essentially a storytelling animal";[34] that "enacted dramatic narrative is the basic and essential characterization of human actions."[35] Bateson opined, "If I am at all fundamentally right in what I am saying, the thinking in terms of stories must be shared by all mind or minds, whether ours or those of redwood forests and sea anemones."[36] The ultimate authority for the belief in the narrative nature of human beings, however, is experiential. Whatever form of communication a person may use, the result will always be an interpretation of some aspect of the world that is historically and culturally grounded and shaped by a fallible human being. There is, in other words, no form of human communication that presents uncontested truths, including this one. Thus, when I use the term narration, I have in mind not the specific individuated forms or genre that we call narrative, but a conceptual frame that would account for the "stories" we tell each other—whether such "stories" are in the form of argumentation, narration, exposition, or esthetic writings and performance. This view is at one with the perspective of Hauerwas and Jones: "Narrative is neither just an account of genre criticism nor a faddish appeal to the importance of telling stories; rather it is a crucial conceptual category for such matters as understanding issues of epistemology and methods of argument, depicting personal identity, and displaying the content of Christian [and, I would add, secular] convictions."[37]

Stories, in my view, are not isolated utterances or gestures but symbolic actions—words and/or deeds—that have sequence and meaning for those who live, create, or interpret them. So understood, they have relevance to real as well as to fictive experiences. Regardless of form, discursive or nondiscursive texts are meant to give order to life by inducing others to dwell in them to establish ways of living in common, in intellectual and spiritual communities in which there is confirmation for the story that constitutes one's life. This presentation is meant to be such a story.

The second component of my proposal is that the material or stuff of stories is "good reasons." By this term, I mean *elements that provide warrants for accepting or adhering to the advice fostered by any form of human communication that can be considered rhetorical.* And it is my view that there is no form of discourse that cannot be so construed. All forms of human communication function to influence the hearts and minds of others—their beliefs, values, attitudes, and/or actions. The concept of good reasons coincides with the assumption that human beings are as much valuing as they are reasoning beings. The fact is that values may serve as reasons, and what we usually call reasons are value-laden.

I call my proposal the narrative paradigm, meaning by paradigm a philosophical representation designed to formalize the structure of a component of experience and to direct understanding and inquiry into the nature and functions of the experience—in this instance, the experience of human communication. In line with the assumptions and definitions just delineated, the paradigm has five presuppositions:

1. Humans are essentially storytellers.

2. The definitive modes of human decision and action are good reasons, which vary in form among situations, genre, and media of communication.

3. The production and use of good reasons are ruled by matters of history, culture, and character along with the specific constraints of time and place of presentation.

4. Rationality is grounded in the nature of persons as narrative beings, in their inherent awareness of narrative coherence—whether or not a story hangs together and narrative fidelity—whether or not the stories they experience ring true to the stories they know or believe to be true.

5. The world as we live it is a series of stories that must be chosen among in order for us to live life in a process of continual re-creation.

Two features of the paradigm are particularly relevant to the theme of narrativity and community. First is its construction of rationality, narrative rationality, which concerns the quality of stories that entice one to belong to one community or another. As already indicated, narrative rationality has two basic principles: coherence and fidelity.

Before I outline the specific tests used to employ these principles, l would like to note the standards proposed by Hauerwas and David Burrell, from an ethical standpoint, and by Chaim Perelman, from an informal logic perspective. Hauerwas and Burrell hold, "The test of each story is the sort of person it shapes."[38] (I should mention in passing that this is the hallmark of Wayne Booth's book, *The Company We Keep: An Ethics of Reading.*[39]) Perelman took the position that an argument is as good as the audience that would adhere to it, strongly suggesting that the best such audience would be a universal one.[40] I endorse both of these standards, but I believe that people need more specific guidance than these rules, which are reminiscent of Kant's moral imperative.

In fairness to Hauerwas and Burrell, I want to acknowledge that they do provide criteria by which their standard may be employed. They write:

> Any story which we adopt, or allow to adopt us, will have to display:
> 1. power to release us from destructive alternatives;
> 2. ways of seeing through current distortions;
> 3. room to keep us from having to resort to violence;
> 4. a sense for the tragic: how meaning transcends power.

But, as they go on to say, "It is inaccurate . . . to list these criteria as features a story must display."[41] They concern the effects a story may have, not how it induces us to believe or to act. The position I have taken is that good reasons are the features of stories that persuade us and that by testing their coherence and fidelity, we can discern whether or not they are deserving of our adherence.

Testing for coherence requires attention to three aspects of a story. First, *structural* or *argumentative coherence.* Here the interest is the traditional one of determining whether or not a message is consistent, whether or not it involves a contradiction in form or reasoning. Second, *material coherence.* Here one is concerned about how an immediate story compares with other stories that deal with the same subject. A story may be internally consistent, but important facts may be omitted, counterarguments ignored, and relevant issues overlooked. *There is no story that is not embedded in other stories.* The meaning and merit of a story are always a matter of how it stands with or against other stories. Third, *characterological coherence.* Concern for this third type of coherence is one of the key differences between the concept of narrative rationality and traditional formal and informal logics, and needs some explanation.

Central to all stories is character. Whether or not a story is believable depends on the reliability of characters, both as narrators and actors. Determinations of one's character are made by interpretations of a person's decisions and actions that reflect values. In other words, character may be considered an organized set of actional tendencies. If these tendencies contradict one another, change significantly, or alter in "strange ways," the result is a questioning of character. Coherence in life and literature requires that characters behave characteristically. Without this kind of predictability, there is no trust, no rational order, no community.

To illustrate the importance of characterological coherence, one may consider the rhetoric of former President Reagan. The question is this: how is it that President Reagan enjoyed a nearly unanimous evaluation as a "Great Communicator" despite the fact that he was also noted for making factual errors, making inconsistent statements, reasoning in only limited fashion, and frequently diverting attention from relevant issues and inquiries? Part of the answer to this question has to do with esthetics, his skill as a performer. Part of the answer has to do with the consistency of his story with the story of America. Part of the answer has to do with his implied audience—the idea that we are all heroes. But, a very important part of the answer has to do with character.

When one has determined that a person—ordinary or presidential—has a trustworthy and reliable character, that his or her heart is in the right place, one is willing to overlook or forgive many things: factual errors if not too dramatic, lapses in reasoning, and occasional discrepancies. These come to be seen as aberrations, probably induced by circumstances but not incompetence. One can see this kind of judgment rendered in obvious forms where friends, loved ones, heroes, and saints are concerned. Those who would criticize such figures become the ones who are criticized. Because President Reagan was considered such a figure, commentators said he had a "Teflon personality." How one achieves this kind of character perception is an interesting question, but now is not the time to pursue it. The point is that character can be a decisive feature of any story and must be assessed carefully.

Testing for fidelity, for the truth qualities of a story, entails two major considerations: weighing the elements of a message usually regarded as its reasons and weighing the values it explicitly or implicitly conveys. In the first instance, one does what one has always been taught to do: determine whether the statements in a message that purport to be fact are indeed facts, that is, confirmed by consensus or reliable, competent witnesses; determine whether relevant facts or arguments have been omitted or misrepresented; determine whether the individuated forms of reasoning in it are sound, that is, assess the sign, cause, definition, analogy, example, and authority arguments—using standards from formal or informal logics; and determine whether the key issues have been addressed, the questions on which decision and action should turn.

In the second instance, one tries to answer the following questions related to values: What are the explicit and implicit values in the story? Are the values appropriate to the nature of the decision or beliefs that the story concerns? What would be the effects of adhering to the values in regard to one's concept of self, to one's behavior, to one's relationship with others and society? Are the values confirmed or validated in one's experience, in the lives and statements of others whom one admires and respects? And even if a *prima facie* case has been made or a burden of proof has been established, are the values fostered by the story those that would constitute an ideal basis for human conduct? This final question is clearly the paramount issue that confronts those responsible for decisions that impinge on the nature, quality, and continued existence of human life, especially in the fields of medicine and weapons technology and employment.

My intention in developing these questions about values was to offer a scheme to generate a sense of what is good as well as what is strictly logical in the stories that people might adopt. It is a scheme that does not dictate what one should believe, but it does necessarily involve one in considering one's relations with others and the pragmatic consequences of one's choices in regard to self and society.

One answer, then, to the question posed by the title of Stanley Hauerwas and Gregory Jones's book, *Why Narrative?*, is that narration, considered as a paradigm, provides a logic consonant with the nature of persons as narrative beings by which the features of stories—good reasons—can be assessed systematically. It is important to note that this logic does not deny the utility of traditional tests of facts and arguments. It differs from formal logic in that it does not presume a world constituted by analytic structures. And it differs from the leading conceptions of informal logic advanced by Stephen Toulmin and Chaim Perelman in that it does not presume that the everyday world is analogous to the world of the courtroom, at least as the world of the courtroom is conceived in terms of argument rather than stories. The narrative paradigm presupposes a world constituted by stories and the view that no form of discourse is to be privileged over others because its form is predominantly argumentative. No matter how strictly a case is argued—theologically, scientifically, philosophically, or legally—it will always be a story.

The second feature of the paradigm particularly relevant to the theme of narrative and community is its intrinsic egalitarian bias. This feature answers, again, to the question posed by Hauerwas and Jones's *Why Narrative?* By insisting on the rationality of all normal persons, the paradigm legitimates their membership in the public, that is, the kind of society envisioned by Dewey. That many people forsake or only nominally exercise the privileges of this membership is due, at least in part, to the elitism of traditional conceptions and practices that purport to represent true reason and rationality. These conceptions and the practices that follow from them imply a hierarchical system, a community in which some persons are qualified to judge and to lead and other persons are to follow. Those who are at the top of the hierarchy are experts, persons who know specialized subject matters, and the nature of argumentative issues, forms of reasoning, and rules of advocacy in particular fields of knowledge. Their discourse dominates public decision-making and renders nonexperts spectators of their performances. As Robert N. Goodman has observed: "We have abdicated power over our future to the experts."[42] One way to overcome or to move against this reality is to reconceptualize reason and rationality—along the lines I have outlined. Just as literacy—whether conceived in terms of communication competence or cultural knowledge—is prerequisite to participation in the political, economic, and social life of the society, so is awareness of and sophistication in one's own reason and rationality. Both are essential grounds of social and political empowerment.

I would like to make it clear before I move on to further observations about communication and community that I do not deny the legitimacy (the inevitability) of hierarchy. History records no community, uncivilized or civilized, without key storymakers and storytellers, whether sanctioned by God, a "gift," heritage, power, intelligence, or election. Narration implies, however, that the people do judge the stories that are told for and about them and that they have a rational capacity to make such judgments. To apply a narrative paradigm to communication is to hold, along with Aristotle, that people have a natural tendency to prefer what they perceive as the truth and the just.[43] It is also to concur with Gadamer, who holds that "there are no people who do not 'think' sometime and somewhere. That means that there is no one who does not form general views about life and death, about freedom and living together, about the good and about happiness."[44] Furthermore, the narrative paradigm does not deny that the people can be wrong. But, then, so can elites, especially when a decision is social or political. There is no evidence that I know of to support the claim that experts know better than anyone else when it comes to such decisions. Nor does the theory behind the narrative paradigm deny the existence and desirability of genius in individuals or the capacity of the people to formulate and adopt new stories that better account for their lives or the mystery of life itself. The sort of hierarchy to which the paradigm is inimical is hierarchy based on the assumption that some people are qualified to be rational and others not.

I have suggested that there are two considerations in regard to community: the grounds of its constitution and the nature of the communication that provides the forms and fabric of its existence. Since I feel more confident in my views of communication, believing them less controversial than my notions about community, I shall start with them, that is, with my perspectives on communication and community.

While the principles of coherence and fidelity—narrative rationality—are relevant to all forms of human communication, there are different forms of human communication with different relationships to community. The sort of communication that gives rise to community is what I call *affirmative rhetoric*. It is the kind of discourse that is designed to overcome doubt, to gain unity of belief, attitude, value, and action in accord with a "new" idea, ideology, or practice. Adherence by two or more people to such discourse is tantamount to the creation of a community. When the community's ideas or adherents are attacked for violating the norms of the association, from within or without, there will be what I call *purification rhetoric*, an attempt to rid them of the specter of sin, error, or aberration. And when the community's fundamental tenets are challenged by rival tenets proposing a radically different or new association, what I call *subversion rhetoric* will emerge, discourse meant to undermine the coherence and fidelity of the opposing story.

The clearest evidence of the existence of a community is the presence of what I call *reaffirmative rhetoric*. Its characteristic forms are arguments reasserting the validity of the community's creed or modes of ceremonial, communal transactions. The argumentative form of reaffirmative rhetoric is like the modes of affirmative, purification, and subversion rhetorics. It is meant to remove doubt and uncertainty. The ceremonial, communal modes of reaffirmative rhetoric, on the other hand, presume an identity of heart and mind, a commitment beyond doubt or dispute. Such communication may be verbal or nonverbal, as in such expressions as "I love you" and "I pledge allegiance" and in such acts as participating in communion and in gestures of caring, compassion, wonder, and awe. Where the other forms of rhetoric promote ways of becoming, ceremonial, communal modes of communication signify a way of being, a living presence in relation to an other. In their uncontaminated experiences, they are what others have called dialogic communication. In my view, the other forms of rhetoric only achieve a dialogic dimension when they imply an honored perception of the intended audience: its humanity, divinity, inherent dignity, intelligence, and so on. The one sort of communication that is inimical to community is what I call *evisceration rhetoric*. This is the discourse that asserts nihilism, the absurdity of life itself.

The question at this point is, What informs the forms and modes of rhetoric I have outlined? Here is where I venture my ideas about community. It seems to me that there are two essential sites of community: interpersonal relationships, such as families, friendships, social groupings, and some professional associations. The other site is what MacIntyre calls practices, including medicine and law, sport and scholarship. Each of these sites is the home of a set of values that constitute a community, specifying norms of character, role performance, interaction, and ideal aspiration. Put another way, a community is at bottom an ethical construction.

Although the ethical ground of communities is their most important feature, there are others that are also important. First, communities are not constrained by time or place. No doubt communities are enhanced by "physical space which encourages the encounter of strangers," as Parker Palmer has observed.[45] And so are they enhanced by face-to-face interactions, whether public or private. But if such contact were a necessary condition of their existence, they would not only always be local, they would also always be ephemeral. That communities are not always local or ephemeral is demonstrated by the existence of tradition and by professional and other gatherings in which we enact the values I cited from MacIntyre at the outset: civility, intellect, and morality. Adherence to these values did not begin, nor will it end, at any given gathering. Moreover, these values coincide with the values celebrated long ago, in the representation of Socrates, who spoke for the good, beauty, health, wisdom, courage, temperance, justice, harmony, order, friendship, and a oneness with the meaning of life here and hereafter. At the same time that these values affect our lives, there is another set of values that persists as well. There is a community that adheres to the values of Callicles: pleasure, expediency, self-aggrandizement, strength, political acumen, material success, and power. And yet, these values are not unknown to us, or at least to me, and this raises a second observation.

We belong not to one community but several, and the values that constitute them can well be in conflict. A case in point is the "American dream," which is the embodiment of values that define what it means to be a citizen in the American community. In writing about the 1972 presidential election, I proposed the idea that the American dream is actually two dreams, or better yet, two myths, a materialistic one and a moralistic one. The materialistic myth is expressed in the "rags to riches" story; it espouses a work ethic and endorses such values as effort, persistence, "playing the game," initiative, self-reliance, achievement, and success. Competition is its presumed way of pursuing the dream. Unlike the moralistic myth, the materialistic myth does not require a regeneration or sacrifice of self; rather, it promises that if one employs one's energies and talents to the fullest, one will reap the rewards of status, wealth, and power. In naked form, the materialistic myth is compassionless and self-centered; it encourages manipulation and exploitation.

The moralistic myth gains authority from the Declaration of Independence, which states that "all men are created equal"; they are "endowed by their Creator with certain inalienable rights"; "among these are life, liberty and the pursuit of happiness." Cooperation is its favored way of being and its principal values are tolerance, charity, compassion, and true regard for the dignity and worth of each individual. One who stresses these values too much runs the risk of being considered self-righteous and unrealistic.

My point here is that adherence to both myths is what defines one as being American. No American can escape the whole dream. When one of the myths dominates, whether in the polity at large or in a particular individual, the other myth is hauntingly there in the background. Robert Bellah and his coauthors may be correct, in their book *Habits of the Heart*, when they maintain that it is "individualism, and not equality, that has marched inexorably through our history,"[46] but I would maintain it has not done so without equality taunting its every step. As Kenneth L. Karst observed: "At some deep level Americans have always understood: equality among citizens is essential to the community of meaning that defines the American nation."[47]

This brings me to a third observation. Not only do people belong to multiple, competing communities, it has always been so. I agree with MacIntyre that there are distinct traditions that transcend time and place (I have said as much already), but I disagree with the notion that there was a time or place when communities were not local, that is, circumscribed by limited groups of adherents of certain values or arguments within any given polity.[48] I also agree with Jeffrey Stout's analysis of how communities related to practices, such as medicine and law, become corrupt when their practitioners pursue values external to them.[49] When doctors and lawyers pursue money, power, and prestige to the detriment of health and justice, their professions suffer and so do their characters, at least within those professions by those who still adhere to the ideals that constitute the practice. In other communities, however, their behavior may be hailed as a model. One's membership in multiple, competing communities means that one can be an upstanding character and a rogue at the same time.

EPILOGUE

The most obvious question to be raised now is, How do people come to be members of a community, or, put another way, how are they induced to recognize that they are, in fact, members of a community? Given urbanization and the breakdown of neighborhoods, given the fragmentation of society and the problems of legitimation, given the renascence of nationalism and the struggle among people within and among nations over economic, ecological, and military enterprises, and given the control of media by commercial interests and power elites, the question might even be better put this way: How can dissociated, or unhappily associated, or unreflectively entangled people be brought to a sense of interdependence and common fate that leads to joint actions, to a sense of community, without individuals being homogenized into conformist or repressive collectivities?[50] One answer, perhaps the dominant one today, is to give up on the idea of community beyond the local and ephemeral, to celebrate diversity, difference, and democracy in its limited moments of realization. For my part, I have no answer beyond the one I have offered: Communities are co-constituted through communication transactions in which participants coauthor a story that has coherence and fidelity for the life that one would lead. One may adhere to a story because it sanctions a life one must live in order to survive or to succeed. This sort of adherence creates communities by concession or conformity. One may also adhere to a story because one senses in it an honored perception of oneself. Such adherence creates communities by election or conversion. From this view, truly transcendental stories are those that show or reveal us to ourselves ontologically, they account for our Being—what we are and what we can be.[51] As I have maintained elsewhere: "Any story, any form of rhetorical communication, not only says something about the world, it also implies an audience, persons who conceive of themselves in very specific ways."[52] The task, as Perelman clearly saw, "is not, as often assumed, to address *either* a particular audience *or* a universal audience, but in the process of persuasion to adjust to and then to transform the particularities of an audience into universal dimensions."[53]

The point I would stress is that embedded in some local narratives are narratives with potential universal application. For instance, in the example MacIntyre cites of protesters arguing past one another: At the same time that they tell rival stories about a given issue, they also participate in a story about how dispute in a democratic society should be conducted. The basic plot line of this story is respect for the dignity and worth of all people. Acting in accord with this story would transform the dispute into dialogue. And, it should be noted, this story, regarding the dignity and worth of all people, like other metanarratives, began as a local narrative.

Finally, it seems to me that the calls for community today are like the parallel calls for a return to values. The fact of the matter is that there has never been a time without communities and never a human decision or action that did not reflect values. So, in a sense, these calls bounce against reality. They are, in effect, calls for a particular but transcendental community and a specific but unifying set of values. What is desired, in short, is an ideal—a true democracy, a socialist commune, an emancipated society, or a civil, intellectual, moral enclave. The realization of these ideals, or their closer approximation, depends, I think, on having realistic conceptions of communication and the material conditions that mitigate them. The narrative paradigm is one such conception: it sees people as they are and as what they can be—with reason.

ACKNOWLEDGMENTS

Portions of this essay are taken from my book, *Human Communication as Narration: Toward a Philosophy of Reason, Value, and Action* (Columbia: University of South Carolina Press, 1987). I am grateful to Thomas A. Hollihan, Stephen D. O'Leary, Peter J. Marston, Allen Scult, and John R. Stewart for constructive readings of this essay.

NOTES

1. Alasdair MacIntyre, *After Virtue* (Notre Dame, Ind.: Notre Dame University Press, 1981), p. 245.

2. John Dewey, *Democracy and Education* (New York: Macmillan, 1916), p. 24.

3. Ibid., p. 9.

4. Ibid., p. 4.

5. John Dewey, *Liberalism and Social Action* (New York: Capricorn, 1935), p. 71.

6. John Dewey, *Human Nature and Conduct* (New York: Modern Library, 1930), p. 330.

7. John Dewey, *Problems of Men* (Totowa, N.J.: Littlefield, Adams, 1958), p. 5.

8. Dewey, *Democracy and Education*, p. 5.

9. John Dewey, *The Public and Its Problems* (Chicago: Swallow Press, 1927), p. 148.

10. Dewey, *Democracy and Education*, p. 87.

11. Dewey, *The Public and Its Problems*, p. 208.

12. Ibid., p. 207.

13. Ronald Arnett, *Communication and Community: Implications of Buber's Dialogue* (Carbondale, Ill.: Southern Illinois University Press, 1986). See also Tullio Maranhao, ed., *The Interpretation of Dialogue* (Chicago: University of Chicago Press, 1990); Floyd Matson and Ashley Montague, eds., *The Human Dialogue: Perspectives on Communication* (New York: Free Press, 1967); John R. Stewart, "Foundations of Dialogic Communication," *Quarterly Journal of Speech*, vol. 64 (1978), pp. 183–201.

14. Martin Buber, *Between Man and Man*, trans. Roger G. Smith (New York: Macmillan, 1967), pp. 204–5; see also Parker Palmer, *To Know as We Are Known: A Spirituality of Education* (San Francisco: Harper and Row, 1983), pp. 99–103.

15. Martin Buber, *Paths to Utopia*, trans. R. F. C. Hull (Boston: Beacon Press, 1958), p. 19.

16. Buber, *Between Man and Man*, p. 19.

17. Lloyd Bitzer, "Rhetoric and Public Knowledge," *Rhetoric, Philosophy, and Literature: An Exploration*, ed. Don Burks (West Lafayette, Ind.: Purdue University Press, 1978), pp. 67–93; Thomas Farrell, "Knowledge, Consensus, and Rhetorical Theory," *Quarterly Journal of Speech*, vol. 62 (1976), pp. 1–14; Parker Palmer, *The Company of Strangers: Christians and the Renewal of America's Public Life* (New York: Crossroad, 1981), pp. 71ff.

18. Jürgen Habermas, *The Theory of Communicative Action*, vol. I: *Reason and the Rationalization of Society*, trans. Thomas McCarthy (Boston: Beacon Press, 1981), p. 18.

19. Ibid., p. 249.

20. Hans-Georg Gadamer, *Truth and Method* (New York: Crossroad, 1982), p. 347; see Thomas Frentz, "Knowledge, Consensus, and Rhetorical Theory," *Quarterly Journal of Speech*, vol. 71 (1985), pp. 1–18.

21. Gadamer, *Truth and Method*, p. 340.

22. Ibid., p. 401.

23. Ibid., p. 404.

24. Michel Foucault, *Power/Knowledge: Selected Interviews and Other Writings*, ed. Colin Gordon, trans. Colin Gordon, Lee Marshall, John Mepham, and Kate Soper (New York: Pantheon, 1980), pp. 109–33.

25. Jacques Derrida, *Of Grammatology*, trans. Gayatri Spivak (Baltimore: Johns Hopkins University Press, 1976), pp. 6–93; Jacques Derrida, *Dissemination*, trans. Barbara Johnson (Chicago: University of Chicago Press, 1981), pp. 61–171.

26. Jean-François Lyotard, *The Postmodern Condition*, trans. Geoff Bennington and Brian Massumi (Minneapolis: University of Minnesota Press, 1984), p. 37.

27. Ibid., p. 66.

28. Ibid., p. 41.

29. Jean-François Lyotard and Jean-Luc Thebaud, *Just Gaming*, trans.

Wlad Godzich (Minneapolis: University of Minnesota Press, 1985), p. 94; Lyotard, *Postmodern Condition*, p. 23.

30. MacIntyre, *After Virtue*, pp. 69ff.; Alasdair MacIntyre, *Whose Justice? Which Rationality?* (Notre Dame, Ind.: Notre Dame University Press, 1988), pp. 326–48.

31. MacIntyre, *After Virtue*, p. 66.

32. Richard Rorty, *Contingency, Irony, Solidarity* (Cambridge: Cambridge University Press, 1989), p. 53.

33. Richard Rorty, *Philosophy and the Mirror of Nature* (Princeton, N.J.: Princeton University Press, 1979), p. 394; Rorty, *Contingency*, p. 52.

34. MacIntyre, *After Virtue*, p. 201.

35. Ibid., p. 194.

36. Gregory Bateson, *Mind and Nature: A Necessary Unity* (New York: Bantam, 1980), p. 14.

37. Stanley Hauerwas and L. Gregory Jones, eds., *Why Narrative? Readings in Narrative Theology* (Notre Dame, Ind.: Notre Dame University Press, 1989), p. 5.

38. Stanley Hauerwas and David Burrell, "From System to Story: An Alternative Rationality," *Why Narrative?*, ed. Hauerwas and Jones, pp. 158–90, at p. 185.

39. Wayne Booth, *The Company We Keep: An Ethics of Reading* (Berkeley: University of California Press, 1988). See also Ronald Beiner, *Political Judgment* (Chicago: University of Chicago Press, 1983), pp. 127–28.

40. Chaim Perelman and L. Olbrechts-Tyteca, *The New Rhetoric: A Treatise on Argumentation*, trans. John Wilkinson and Purcell Weaver (Notre Dame, Ind.: Notre Dame University Press, 1969), p. 31; Chaim Perelman, "The New Rhetoric: A Theory of Practical Reasoning," *The New Rhetoric and the Humanities: Essays in Rhetoric and Its Applications* (Dordrecht, Holland: D. Reidel, 1979), p. 14; Chaim Perelman, "The New Rhetoric and the Rhetoricians," *Quarterly Journal of Speech*, vol. 70 (1984), pp. 188–96, at p. 191.

41. Hauerwas and Burrell, "From System to Story," p. 185.

42. Robert Goodman, "Technological Arrogance, Plus Ignorance, Spells Disaster," *Los Angeles Times*, Part II, 1986, p. 5. See also Frank Fischer, *Technocracy and the Politics of Expertise* (Newbury Park, Calif.: Sage, 1990), pp. 40–55.

43. Aristotle, *Rhetoric*, trans. W. Rhys Roberts (New York: Modern American Library, 1954), section 1.1.1355.

44. Hans-Georg Gadamer, *Reason in the Age of Science*, trans. Frederick Lawrence (Cambridge, Mass.: MIT Press, 1981), p. 58.

45. Palmer, *Company of Strangers*, pp. 46ff.

46. Robert Bellah, Richard Madsen, William Sullivan, Ann Swidler, and Stephen Tipton, *Habits of the Heart* (Berkeley: University of California Press, 1985), p. viii.

47. Kenneth Karst, *Belonging to America: Equal Citizenship and the Constitution* (New Haven, Conn.: Yale University Press, 1989), p. 196.

48. MacIntyre, *Whose Justice?*, pp. 349ff.

49. Jeffrey Stout, *Ethics After Babel: The Languages of Morals and Their Discontents* (Boston: Beacon Press, 1988), pp. 267ff.

50. Raymond Williams, *Resources of Hope: Culture, Democracy, and Socialism*, ed. Robin Gable (London: Verso, 1989), pp. 19–38, 111–19; Raymond Williams, *The Politics of Modernism: Against the New Conformists*, ed. Tony Pinckney (London: Verso, 1989), pp. 177–97.

51. Allen Scult, "Deconstructed Discourse and Rhetorical Truth: The Journey of a Narrative in Time" (paper presented at the International Society for the Study of Rhetoric, Biennial Congress, Ottingen, Germany, 1989).

52. Walter Fisher, *Human Communication as Narration: Toward a Philosophy of Reason, Value, and Action* (Columbia: University of South Carolina Press, 1987), pp. 75, 187.

53. Perelman, "The New Rhetoric and the Rhetoricians," p. 192.

15

Postmodern Environmental Ethics: Ethics as Bioregional Narrative

Jim Cheney

POSTMODERNISM AND PRIVILEGED DISCOURSE

"But you know, grandson, this world is fragile."
The word he chose to express "fragile" was filled with the intricacies of
a continuing process, and with a strength inherent in spider webs. . . . It
took a long time to explain the fragility and intricacy because no word
exists alone, and the reason for choosing each word had to be explained with
a story about why it must be said this certain way. That was the
responsibility that went with being human . . . and this demanded great
patience and love. —Leslie Marmon Silko, Laguna Pueblo[1]

The question which this section addresses might be put as follows: in the light of postmodernist deconstruction of modernist totalizing and foundationalist discourse, can we any longer make sense of the idea of privileged discourse, discourse which can lay claim to having access to the way things are? The dominant postmodernist view is that this is not possible, that language can be understood only as either a set of tools created for various human purposes or as the free creation of conscious persons or communities. This being so, it is argued, we should practice ontological abstinence in our beliefs about the relation between language and world. To the extent that the notion of objectivity enters into postmodernist discourse at all it tends to take the form that "truth" is simply the result of social *negotiation*, agreement achieved by the participants in particular conversations.

A more useful conception of objectivity has been suggested by some feminist postmodernists in an attempt to privilege discourses

328

constructed in opposition to the totalizing and colonizing discourses constructed by the dominant culture. It is within this basic framework that Sandra Harding, for example, tries to weave a place for a feminist standpoint epistemology within postmodernism:

> . . . if there can be "a" feminist standpoint, it can only be whatever emerges from the political struggles of "oppositional consciousness"— oppositional precisely to the longing for "one true story" that has been the psychic motor for Western science. . . . The greatest resource for would-be "knowers" is our nonessential, non-naturalizable, fragmented identities and the refusal of the delusion of a return to an "original unity."[2]

Objectivity is defined negatively in relation to those views which oppositional consciousness deconstructs. A voice is privileged to the extent that it is constructed from a position that enables it to spot distortions, mystifications, and colonizing and totalizing tendencies within other discourses.

More can be said on behalf of privileged discourses. John Caputo, for example, has pointed to significant differences in the views of Heidegger and Rorty, both writers in the deconstructionist tradition.[3] One way of stating Heidegger's position would be to say that he thinks that postmodernist deconstructionism of the sort exemplified by Rorty must itself be deconstructed; Rorty is still working within the metaphysical framework he sought to dismantle by deconstructing that framework's foundationalist epistemology. Rorty has, in effect, accepted the view of language embedded in the correspondence theory of truth, rejecting merely its pretensions to be a "mirror of nature." We are left with the same old dualistic view of language and its relationship to the world, minus only the idea that language mirrors nature. Since this mirroring was supposed to provide the link between language and world, language now floats free of the world— it's language all the way down. What we are left with are conversations sustained only by the criteria of internal self-coherence and adequacy to the purposes for which they are constructed—which, of course, are freely constructed purposes of conscious human beings, not purposes given to us, as it were, by the world. Because it is language all the way down, Heidegger would deconstruct these language games as well.

Exposing the errors in the correspondence theory of truth and its foundationalist epistemology exposes the bankruptcy of the view that language is rooted solely in conscious human projects and validated solely by reference to canons of internal consistency and adequacy to those projects. Rorty dismantles the correspondence theory of truth, with its hope of finding a way for the transcendental subject to touch the world with its words, only to leave the transcendental subject in place, freely creating world upon world of words—finally not taking responsibility for its words, but merely pouring them forth in conversation after conversation. Surely a thorough-going postmodernism would deconstruct the modernist transcendental subject along with the foundationalist epistemologies modernism has constructed in its attempt to regain the world.

When this transcendental subject is also deconstructed, we are left with the world and words in it, emergent from it. Heidegger, for example, opts for a new relation to language altogether, one which results from a "meditative openness" to the world. The world speaks through us when we let go of the metaphysical voice. Language of this sort is a "listening," a "gift in which things come to presence." Language doesn't trap us in a world of words, but is the way in which the world is present to us. The difference in the languages Heidegger describes is said to be a difference between "primordial" language, as a way in which the world discloses itself by our being rooted in the world, and "fallen" language, which constructs itself as a mirror of nature and uproots itself from the world by employing the criteria of adequacy to human purposes and internal coherence (not problematic in themselves) at the expense of faithfulness to experiential embedment in the world—a loss of hearing in the hegemony of constructed vision, a hegemony which did not abate, as it should have, with the rise of postmodernism.

Language as so conceived does not pretend to be giving the "one true story" any more than language does in Rorty's view. Just as a particular wolf is only one of the ways in which the world has expressed itself, so the stones and narratives which emerge in various physical, cultural, and linguistic settings give expression to human "being-in-the-world" in various ways. In the end even instrumental rationality gives expression to the world in this way, though it is a distorted expression, distorted precisely through denying its own origins as a particularized expression of the world and setting up shop as a "mirror of nature" certified by a foundationalist epistemology or by cutting itself free from the world altogether. Like the conscious ego which has turned its back on the id out of which it grew, such language becomes subject to bad dreams, neurosis, and psychosis—the return of the repressed. The truth of "It's language all the way down" must be understood in light of the equal truth of "It's world all the way up"—though it gets perverse in its upper reaches as the world as language closes in on itself, becoming inbred and pretending to totalization and foundationalist philosophy.

The possibility of totalizing, colonizing discourse arises from the fact that concepts and theories can be abstracted from their paradigm settings and applied elsewhere. Although these abstractions are fully intelligible only within the paradigm settings which gave birth to them, such abstractions can achieve a life of their own; they can be articulated in accordance with canons of coherence and made into apparently self-contained wholes ready for export and application to a variety of situations. The situations to which a theory is deemed applicable, however, are specified within the theory, by the theory as articulated in abstraction from its paradigm setting. The danger is that the theory when applied to a situation specified *by* the theory will serve not to *articulate* that new situation, that is, bring it to experiential and moral coherence, but rather will serve as a mechanism of *de facto* repression of at least some of the experiential dimensions of the situation and lead to confusion and bafflement at the level of action and conscious attempts to understand one's situation and what one is about.[4] Vine Deloria, Jr. and other Native American writers make this point about Christianity, for example, and contrast it with Native American spirituality, which is closely tied to place and, for that reason, is not thought of as exportable.[5] To prepare a theory, religion, or culture for export is to turn it into a potential tool for the colonization of the minds of other people.

The effect of totalizing language is to assimilate the world to it. Totalizing language provides an abstract understanding that cuts through individual differences when these are irrelevant to its purposes. Nested, logically related concepts are employed to draw the (to it) idiosyncratic up into language and give it a place in its schema of the real. Contextual discourse reverses this; it assimilates language to the situation, bends it, shapes it to fit. Contextual discourse is not fundamentally concerned with issues of overall coherence. Or, rather, the kind of overall coherence for which it strives is different: a mosaic of language which serves as a tool of many purposes at once. In the life of a tribal community, for example, it must articulate a sense of those processes which bind the community together and to the land; and it must do this in a language which functions effectively to call forth appropriate responses. It must provide a means whereby individuals can come into their own in nonrepressive ways; yet, individual identities must be articulated in a language that makes these individuals intelligible to the community. Culturally understood conceptions of self, that is to say, must come to articulate individual experience without being imposed on individuals in a way that sets up psychic splits. The language must also articulate a process of human interaction with the land which ensures the health[6] both of the land and the community. Contextualized language is tuned to quite specific situations and forgoes the kind of totalizing coherence with which we have been so preoccupied in the modern world.

Tom Jay in his lyrical essay, "The Salmon of the Heart," is concerned with just such contextualized language. He reports that

> . . . the "flash" in our phrase "flash of inspiration" is etymologically grounded not in lightning but in the flash-splash of a fish. Ideas do not flash like lightning but rise like trout to caddis flies.[7]

Here we have a lovely image of the difference between the totalizing overlays of which I have been speaking and contextualized languages which percolate upward through the contexts they are bringing to voice in language shaped by this percolating process.[8] A striking feature of contextualized language, particularly in traditional cultures such as those of Native Americans, is that it

> . . . bridges subject and object worlds, inner and outer. Language is the path, the game trail, the river, the reverie between them. It shimmers there, revealing and nourishing their interdependence. Each word *bears* and *locates* our meetings with the world. A word is a dipped breath, a bit of spirit *(inspire, expire)* wherein we hear the weather. Our "tongues" taste the world we eat. At root [this] language is sacramental.[9]

This observation is commonplace concerning discourse in traditional cultures. The construction of the modernist subject has been a long time in the making. It took much time and cultural effort to generate the intuitive "obviousness" of the Cartesian privatized self. The modernist period in philosophy, with its creation of absolute subjectivity and the need for a foundationalist epistemology to regain connection with the world, is only the latest installment in the story of the cultural construction of the subjective self. We can now tell coherent stories of this cultural construction which take us back to the agrarian revolution, some nine or so millennia ago. As we read these accounts, contextualized discourse seems to emerge as our mother tongue; totalizing, essentializing language emerges as the voice of the constructed subjective self, the voice of dissociated, gnostic alienation.[10]

As an example of language which "bridges subject and object worlds," Tom Jay refers to the place of the salmon in the lives of Northwest Coast Indians, the way in which what is said and done in relationship to salmon incorporates an understanding, including a *moral* understanding, of health—health in self, community, earth, and the relationships between these:

> ... [S]almon ... are literal *embodiments* of the wisdom of the *locale,* the resource. The salmon are the wisdom of the northwest biome. They are the old souls, worshipful children of the land. *Psychology without ecology is lonely* and vice versa. The salmon is not merely a projection, a symbol of some inner process, it is rather the embodiment of the soul that nourishes us all. ... [T]o the original peoples of the Pacific Northwest, salmon were not merely food. To them, salmon were people who lived in houses far away under the sea. Each year they undertook to visit the human people because the Indian peoples always treated them as honored guests. When the salmon people traveled, they donned their salmon disguises and these they left behind perhaps in the way we leave flowers or food when visiting friends. To the Indians the salmon were a resource in the deep sense, great generous beings whose gifts gave life. The salmon were energy: not "raw" energy, but intelligent perceptive energy. The Indians understood the salmon's gift involved them in an ethical system that resounded in every corner of their locale. The aboriginal landscape was a democracy of spirits where everyone listened, careful not to offend the *resource* they were a working part of. [11]

This understanding of the salmon performs a major integrative function in Northwest Coast Indian society. It is this integrative function which is the criterion which guides development of the image. In the interest of fulfilling this function the account does forgo another sort of "truth," but this should not blind us to the fact that there is truth here, too, a truth which, perhaps, *must* be embodied in some such way as this.

The epistemological function of contextualist discourse is underscored in Robin Ridington's account of the place of myth in the life of the Beaver Indians, a northern hunting people. Ridington points out that for nomadic people such as these, survival "depends upon artifice rather than artifact. They live by knowing how to integrate their own activities with those of the sentient beings around them." It is what we call *mythic* thinking which carries this knowledge. "Their dreaming provides them access to a wealth of information. Their vision quests and their myths integrate the qualities of autonomy and community that are necessary for successful adaptation to the northern forest environment." As Ridington points out, "the true history of these people will have to be written in a mythic language."[12]

Paula Gunn Allen (Laguna Pueblo/Lakota) refers to the Western "meta-myth" that "there is such a thing as determinable fact, natural—that is, right— explanations, and reality that can be determined outside the human agency of discovery and fact finding." The account she gives of myth, ritual, and vision in her tribal culture is distinctively postmodern. She notes that "myth" is synonymous with "fable," not "belief," and that it has the connotation of "moral story." Myth, she says, "is an expression of the tendency to make stories of power out of the life we live in imagination." Here she is noting the intimate connection between myth and ritual—myth as "a language construct that contains the power to transform. . . . Of course it reflects belief . . . but it is at base a vehicle. . . ." Myth, then, is knowledge shaped by transformative intent: "Myth may be seen as a teleological statement, a shaped system of reference that allows us to order and thus comprehend perception and knowledge. . . ."[13] We in the postmodernist West are only beginning to see such possibilities in language. Postmodernism makes possible for us the conception of language conveying an understanding of self, world, and community which is consciously tuned to, and shaped by, considerations of the health and well-being of individual, community, and land and our ethical responsibilities to each. This postmodernist possibility is an actuality in the world of tribal myth and ritual.[14]

The current emphasis in contemporary feminist thought on contextualism, narrative discourse, standpoint epistemologies, and "cultural and discursive birthplaces"[15] helps give us access to the discourse of tribal peoples, with which it has significant affinities. In addition, the role of the land in tribal discourse as well as the details of its narrative and mythic style can significantly inform postmodernist thought on discourse. The postmodernist account of ethics as bioregional narrative which I explore in the next section owes much to meditation on the role of land in tribal discourse.

ENVIRONMENTAL ETHICS AS BIOREGIONAL NARRATIVE

The landscape and the language are the same,
And we ourselves are language and are land.   —Conrad Aiken[16]

I can only answer the question "What am I to do?" if I can answer the prior
question "Of what story or stories do I find myself a part?" . . . Mythology,
in its original sense, is at the heart of things.   —Alasdair MacIntyre[17]

An environmental ethic does not want to abstract out universals, if such
there be, from all this drama of life, formulating some set of duties
applicable across the whole. . . . The logic of the home, the ecology, is finally
narrative. . . . If a holistic ethic is really to incorporate the whole story, it
must systematically embed itself in historical eventfulness. Else it will not
really be objective. It will not be appropriate, well adapted, for the way
humans actually fit into their niches.   —Holmes Rolston, III[18]

In *A Sand County Almanac* Aldo Leopold offers the following general principle: "A thing is right when it tends to preserve the integrity, stability, and beauty of the biotic community. It is wrong when it tends otherwise."[19] Holmes Rolston, III suggests that we understand this principle as "deeply embedded in [Leopold's] love for the Wisconsin sand counties,"[20] that we understand it as belonging to Leopold's "storied residence" in those counties. Rather than view it simply as a universal norm perhaps *suggested* to Leopold by his life and work, we are urged to understand it as inflected by historicity, as *essentially* tied to place and Leopold's narrative embedment in, and understanding of, the sand counties of Wisconsin.

Rolston's notion of "storied residence" can be understood as urging environmental ethicists to make the postmodern turn. It can also be understood in the spirit of Alasdair MacIntyre's insistence upon the central importance of narrative to ethical thought, an insistence which is, likewise, a rejection of modernist ethical thought. In this section I pick up on Rolston's suggestion in an indirect way by sketching a path for a postmodernism which makes use of certain notions current in contemporary environmentalism. In so doing, I hope to show that this transformed postmodernism will, in turn, have a transformative effect on environmental ethics which, protestations to the contrary notwithstanding, has almost always been conceived of in modernist ethical terms. In reconstructing postmodernism I am at the same time setting an agenda for reconceiving environmental ethics in contextual and postmodern terms.

In a recent article, Biddy Martin and Chandra Talpade Mohanty
state with admirable clarity both the limitations and potential of postmodernism for feminist discourse in particular (and, by implication,
for any discourse aimed at the deconstruction of totalizing and colonizing discourse). In discussing the work of Minnie Bruce Pratt, Martin and Mohanty contrast her insistence upon "our responsibility for
remapping boundaries and renegotiating connections" with

> . . . the more abstract critiques of "feminism" and the charges of total-
> ization that come from the ranks of antihumanist intellectuals. For
> without denying the importance of their vigilante attacks on human-
> ist beliefs in "man" and Absolute Knowledge wherever they appear,
> it is equally important to point out the political limitations of an in-
> sistence on "indeterminacy" which implicitly, when not explicitly,
> denies the critic's own situatedness in the social, and in effect refuses
> to acknowledge the critic's own institutional home.

The project that emerges from the acknowledgment of situatedness
while refusing modernist essentialism and totalization is that of initiating a "complicated working out of the relationship between home,
identity, and community that calls into question the notion of a coherent, historically continuous, stable identity and works to expose the
political stakes concealed in such equations." This is accomplished by
grounding the narrative account not in a "coherent, historically continuous, stable identity," but rather

> . . . in the geography, demography, and architecture of the communi-
> ties that are [Pratt's] "homes"; these factors function as an organizing
> mode in the text, providing a specific concreteness and movement for
> the narrative.

Further,

> Geography, demography, and architecture, as well as the configura-
> tion of her relationships to particular people . . . serve to indicate the
> fundamentally relational nature of identity and the negations on
> which the assumption of a singular, fixed, and essential self is based.

Relations to people are elaborated "through spatial relations and historical knowledges," the importance of which "lies in the contextualization of [those relations], and the consequent avoidance of any
purely psychological explanation."[21]

Narrative is the key then, but it is narrative grounded in geography rather than in a linear, essentialized narrative self. The narrative style required for situating ourselves without making essentializing or totalizing moves is an elaboration of relations which forgoes the coherence, continuity, and consistency insisted on by totalizing discourse. Our position, our *location*, is understood in the elaboration of relations in a nonessentializing narrative achieved through a grounding in the geography of our lives. Self and geography are bound together in a narrative which locates us in the moral space of defining relations. *"Psychology without ecology is lonely and vice versa."*[22] Mindscapes are as multiple as the landscapes which ground them. Totalizing masculine discourse (and essentializing feminist discourse) give way to a contextualized discourse of place.

Why a discourse or narrative of relation to place? And what is meant by "place" here? We can work toward an answer to these questions by considering some of the possible alternatives for a contextualizing narrative as the means for locating oneself in a moral space out of which a whole and healthy self, community, and earth can emerge.

The fragility of the inturning process, the internal narrative in isolation from community and world, is obvious. A particularly poignant example of this fragility is related by Edith Cobb in her book *The Ecology of Imagination in Childhood*. She relates the story of Alice, a child she describes as "surrounded by empty psychological space"; her narrative construction of self had to operate entirely within the confines of her own interior space. The result (or actuality) of this is schizophrenia. In extreme cases such as this it is brought home to us that what we take to be the interior space of the self, our individual essence, is really an internalized landscape or, better, one term of a constructed narrative of self-in-place. Cobb's account of Alice's life brings this out clearly. In one situation only is Alice embedded in a geography larger than her own closed-in self. This occurs in yearly visits to the family summer home, when a "sea change" comes over her in the context of an immersion in the natural world. Alice's lyrical portrait of these summers poignantly illustrates the necessity of landscape for the coherent construction of a self.

What happens when the landscape includes only the human community and its institutions? Here Martin and Mohanty's analysis of Pratt's autobiographical narrative is illuminating. We have looked at the positive side of narrative contextualized by reference to geography. There is a negative aspect, however, when that geography is one of human making:

... the very stability, familiarity, and security of these physical structures are undermined by the discovery that these buildings and
streets witnessed and obscured particular race, class, and gender
struggles. The realization . . . politicizes and undercuts any physical
anchors she might use to construct a coherent notion of home or her
identity in relation to it.

This cultural geography serves as well to indicate

... the negations on which the assumption of a singular, fixed, and
essential self is based. For the narrator, such negativity is represented
by a rigid identity such as that of her father, which sustains its appearance of stability by defining itself in terms of what it is not. . . .
The "self" in this narrative is not an essence or truth concealed by patriarchal layers of deceit and lying in wait of discovery, revelation or
birth.
        It is this very conception of self that Pratt likens to entrap-
ment. . . .[23]

When "unity is exposed to be a potentially repressive fiction"[24] in this
way, one of the critical functions of narrative is to undercut such identities, such "homes":

"The system" is revealed to be not one but multiple, overlapping in-
tersecting systems or relations that are historically constructed and
recreated through everyday practices and interactions and that im-
plicate the individual in contradictory ways. . . .
        Community, then, is the product of work, of struggle, it is inher-
ently unstable, contextual, it has to be constantly reevaluated in relation to critical political priorities. . . . There is also, however, a strong
suggestion that community is related to experience, to history. For if
identity and community are not the product of essential connections,
neither are they merely the product of political urgency or necessity.
For Pratt, they are a constant recontextualizing of the relationship between personal/group history and political priorities.[25]

Within the geography of human landscape the contextual voice can
emerge in clarity and health only through a "constant recontextualizing" which prevents the oppressive and distorting overlays of cultural
institutions (representing a return of the repressed) from gathering
false, distorting, and unhealthy identities out of "the positive desire
for unity, for Oneness."[26]
        Is there any setting, any landscape, in which contextualizing
discourse is not constantly in danger of falling prey to the distortions

of essentializing, totalizing discourse? Perhaps not. A partial way out might be envisioned, however, if we expand the notion of a contextualizing narrative of place so as to include nature—nature as one more player in the construction of community. My suggestion is that a postmodernist emphasis on contextualism and narrative as a means of locating oneself offers us an alternative mode of understanding bioregionalism and, conversely, that bioregionalism is a natural extension of the line of thought being developed by those advocating a view of ethics as contextualist and narrative. What I propose is that we extend these notions of context and narrative outward so as to include not just the human community, but also the land, one's community in a larger sense. Bioregions provide a way of grounding narrative without essentializing the idea of self, a way of mitigating the need for "constant recontextualization" to undercut the oppressive and distorting overlays of cultural institutions.

Listen to the following passage concerning the Ainu, the indigenous people of Japan (the Kamui referred to are spirits of natural phenomena—everything is a Kamui for the Ainu):

> The Ainu believed that the housefire was an eye of the Kamui that watched and welcomed all game that entered through the hunting window. As game entered through the hunting window . . . the fire reported its treatment back to the appropriate Kamui community. Fire is the appropriate witness for the *resource*, flickering warm light rising from the broken limbs of trees. . . . The mythic images circle and knot together into a reality that is a story, a parable, where facts are legendary incidents, not data.[27]

One significant feature of this passage is that it locates moral imperatives in the watchful eye of the housefire. The reality that is knit together as story and parable carries not the "intrinsic value" so much discussed in the literature in environmental ethics, but rather actual moral *instruction*. An important aspect of the construction or evolution of mythic images is their ability to articulate such moral imperatives and to carry them in such a way that they actually *do* instruct; that they *locate* us in a *moral* space which is at the same time the space we live in physically; that they locate us in such a way that these moral imperatives have the lived reality of fact. In the case of the Ainu this is achieved, in part, by including all of nature within the moral community. For a genuinely contextualist ethic to include the land, the land must *speak* to us; we must stand in *relation* to it; it must *define* us, and we it.

It has often been noticed that mythical cosmologies carry thought, that they are the vehicles of richly textured understandings of human nature and community cohesion. John Wisdom and Paul Ricoeur, for example, have noted the quite sophisticated and complex understandings of human psychology embedded in Christian cosmology.[28] The difficulty with that cosmology in particular is in its relationship to the land. It has been argued by Shepard[29] and others that although the religion of the Desert Fathers *was* a response to the desert landscape, it was one of denial, one which set culture over and against nature, history over and against cyclical mythologies firmly embedded in place. James Hillman has noted that monotheism functions as a mechanism to deny the voices of polytheism, those voices which speak from all dimensions and aspects of one's experience of, and relation to, the world, voices which, if allowed to speak, would tell not only of distortions, but of the health that is there, or might be there.[30] These voices can also be found in a monotheistic cosmology, but they come through indirection or as background, subliminal, buried, as in dreams. The monotheistic overlay, the narrative of a totalizing history, a salvation history rooted in the beyond of a father god distinct from his creation, is a rejection of precisely those elements which make mythical images bearers of health, images which gather to themselves knowledge of place and its health, community and the dynamics of community health—all woven together in a narrative that *instructs* by locating us in a moral space in which moral imperatives are present to the community with the force and presence of reality, of fact. The mythic images and narratives which gather to themselves knowledge of place and community and the health of each must be free of the influence of such world-denying and self-truncating projects so that they can be responsive to world and self. In addition, they must be rich and complex enough to articulate an understanding of both self and world and to weave them together into a unity in which an understanding of self and community is an understanding of the place in which life is lived out and in which an understanding of place is an understanding of self and community.

Where are *we* to find those "mythic images" which "circle and knot together into a reality" that is life-giving, healthy, liberating? Where we must look is to the *mind*scape/*land*scape which emerges from our narrative and mythical embedment in some particular place. This begins with the inscribing of the nervous system *in* the landscape; the body is the instrument of our knowledge of the world.[31]

With language comes a taxonomy of the world, an ordering of our cosmos, and a positioning of ourselves within this matrix. Eventually the cosmos comes to express a moral order—it instructs us in virtue of its very manner of containing us. Shepard argues for the critical importance of the early taxonomic stage, the first ordering of one's cosmos. It is critical that just as the infant passes from the nurturing womb into a nurturing relationship with the first caretaker(s), so the child must pass from this to a sense of embedment in a nurturing cosmos. The claim is that without this there is fixation at the earlier developmental level, a fixation on ambivalences engendered in relation to one's first nurturer(s) which would have been resolved by passing into what Shepard calls the "earth matrix." This second "grounding" or "bonding" to the earth matrix nourishes the growing child in ways that the earlier bonding cannot achieve by itself. By satisfying emerging urges, the earlier bonding is incorporated in the later bonding; the ambivalences which begin to emerge do not become objects of fixation. The result is not an *identification* with nature; identification is an essentializing move motivated by attempts to deal with ambivalence. As Shepard notes, the lovers of the earth and the destroyers of the earth often have one thing in common: the attempt to handle ambivalence without resolving it, using the defective tools of identification or dichotomization, respectively.[32] What one should do is *relate* to nature as "satisfying other."

Shepard's account of the ways in which we have lost this bioregional connectedness is instructive, for it points to the difficulties that must be faced in the "constant recontextualization" discussed by Martin and Mohanty as well as to some features of "storied residence" that might temper these difficulties. The central claim is that when social structures emerged in an agrarian society which no longer allowed for the broadening of the child's relationship from the human nurturer to nature as the nurturing other in a wider sense, rather than establishing relationships to nature as nurturing other, the image of the mother, with all its ambivalence, was *projected* onto nature. The result was a representation of the mother rather than a clear vision of nature as nurturer but *not* mother. The whole complex of Mother Earth imagery is the result of this projection, making Mother Earth the object of highly ambivalent attitudes and behavior. The love-hate relationship to nature and the need to dominate nature seems to begin precisely with the rise into prominence of Mother Earth imagery. To resolve this particular problem it should not be necessary to return to a preagrarian, gatherer-hunter life. It is necessary, however, that we not take existing, humanly constructed models such as machines, words, and human society as our models and metaphors of order, for these already embed our projections and carry with them the return of the repressed. One consequence of this tendency is a literalization of nature at the conscious level and its use as a projection screen by unconscious processes. Bioregionalism could help turn this around if it were understood in light of the kind of contextualist approach I have been advocating.

The cosmos constructed as a result of a sense of embedment in the "earth matrix" first nourishes and then later instructs. "Through myth and its ritual enactments," Shepard says, "natural things are not only themselves but a speaking." Passage into adolescence *not* marked by ambivalence and fixation at earlier levels precludes perception of the world as an illusion to be transcended. Rather than graduating *"from the world,"* Shepard says, the child graduates "into its significance."[33]

That this second grounding is in the natural world is important. As the ground out of which we have evolved, it can be satisfying in a way that no substitute for this matrix could be. What is desired is a complex system of images or myths of the human-land community which *instructs* and does so in a way that is felt to be both obligatory and fostering of individual and community health. These purposes can be accomplished best when the community has before it a coherent model of health to draw on. When this model is the one within which, and in interaction with which, both the individual and the community must live, we get precisely the images we need to mediate our relationships to one another and to the land. But nature must be transformed in image to perform this function. A Western scientific description of the specifics of the ecosystem within which one lives is not adequate. It provides the wrong kind of myth. It can and ought to *inform* our construction of appropriate mythical images, but it cannot function as the centerpiece of a viable environmental ethic, much less a *mythos* for our times. Elizabeth Bird asks whether we would want "the world [that] ecology would construct for us if it were to win political hegemony in the sciences?"[34] The *mythos* into which modem ecology is drawn in the minds of many radical environmentalists is that of organicism, the "dream of natural (unforced) community":

> For many radical and antiliberal thinkers, including many feminists considering sciences and technologies, [organicism] has . . . appeared to be an alternative to both antagonistic opposition and to regulatory functionalism. It is easy to forget that organicism is a form of longing for a spontaneous and always healthy body, a perfect opposite to the

technicist and reductionist boogey man. . . . Organicism is the analytical longing . . . for purity outside the disruptions of the "artificial." It is the reversed, mirror image of other forms of longing for transcendence.[35]

The integrity of the objective scientific model must, for the purposes I have been sketching (but not for all purposes), give way to the requirement of the health and well-being of individual, community, and land in the construction of an image of nature (with us in it) which effectively instructs. If value is implicit in our descriptions of the world and our place in it, then the narratives we construct will embody value and orient us.

What we want then is language that grows out of experience and articulates it, language intermediate between self and world, their *intersection*, carrying knowledge of both, knowledge charged with valuation and instruction. This is language in which "the clues to the meaning of life [are] embodied in natural things, where everyday life [is] inextricable from spiritual significance and encounter."[36] The vision received in the Native American vision quest, for example, is a culturally mediated intersection of self and world. It is a gift and must be located in the world. It is important not to conceive of these images as projections; they are intersections, encounters. This way of putting it acknowledges both our active construction of reality and nature's role in these negotiations. We should say with Aiken that "The landscape and the language are the same,/And we ourselves are language and are land."[37] Such language mediates experience and the world with language alive and responsive to our interaction with the world, language which articulates not the *logos* of the system as we in the West have come to understand this, but our *telos* within it. It is a language of instruction; and in order to instruct it must embed an understanding of self and world and the relation between the two. The task then is to tell the best stories we can. The tales we tell of our, and our communities', "storied residence" in place are tales not of universal truth, but of local truth, bioregional truth.

The notion of a mythic, narrative, and bioregional construction of self and community, and the "storied residence" out of which action proceeds, has a close affinity with, and relevance to, feminist postmodernist attempts to deal with the "fractured identities" of multiple female voices in the wake of the deconstruction of patriarchal totalizing and essentializing discourse. Listen to the following comparison of Australian aboriginal people with the villager/farmer:

[For the aboriginal peoples the] topographic features and creatures were diffused throughout a vast region. They were not all visible at once and human products were always mixed with the nonhuman. The villager[s] [by contrast] did not rove through these physical extensions of the self; [they] occupied them. [The aborigine] seemed to inhabit the land like a blood corpuscle, while the farmer was centered in it and could scan it as a whole.[38]

The gatherer-hunter who wanders through "physical extensions of the self" "like a blood corpuscle" is certainly not subject to many of the essentializing pressures brought to bear on "civilized" people since the agrarian revolution. The "centered" point of view of the farmer and the diminished natural landscape available for articulating both self and community (as well as its virtual replacement by a humanly contrived world) are simply the first of many such pressures. The totalizing, essentializing discourse of patriarchal consciousness is the latest of such pressures. Dismantling patriarchal discourse is not likely by itself to eliminate the forces of essentialization and totalization. If the above description is right, the price that was paid by the human move away from the gatherer-hunter condition was precisely the setting in motion of those forces of essentialization and totalization. In the modern world the constant "recontextualization" that Martin and Mohanty speak of is likely to be an ever necessary feature of attempts to produce health and well-being. The concept of "storied residence" or "bioregional narrative" that I have been articulating seems increasingly important once we see the omnipresent nature of the forces of essentialization and totalization. In fact, "storied residence" seems to be a necessary part of the deconstructive process, the dismantling of the manifestations of these forces.

But beyond the project of deconstruction is the goal of health and well-being, which is the primary reason for introducing the idea of bioregional narrative. Authentic existence is not a matter of discovering a "real" self (it is still a social self, a construct); there is just the project of bringing into being healthy communities, healthy selves— an *achievement*, not a discovery of something that is hidden, covered over. But landscapes can be hard, or diminished and distorted, and the health in them and, consequently, in us comes at a price and only with much labor.

What has emerged is a conception of bioregional truth, local truth, or ethical vernacular.[39] The fractured identities of postmodernism, I suggest, can build health and well-being by means of a bioregional contextualization of self and community. The voices of health will be as various and multiple as the landscapes which give rise to them—landscapes which function as metaphors of self and community and figure into those mythical narratives which give voice to the emergence of self and community. The notion of socially constructed selves gives way to the idea of bioregionally constructed selves and communities. In this way, bioregionalism can "ground" the construction of self and community without the essentialization and totalization typical of the various "groundings" of patriarchal culture.

CONCLUSION

My objective in this paper has been to suggest a direction for postmodernism which at the same time sets an agenda for any environmental ethic that opts for the postmodern turn. The central notion of such an ethic, I have suggested, is that of bioregional narrative. In setting this agenda I have for the most part bypassed the difficulties attendant upon the satisfactory articulation of this notion and its embedment in an environmental ethic. Bioregional narratives are normative; and they are the subject of social negotiation. What I *have* been at pains to do is to avoid the foundationalist suggestion that these narratives are *givens* from which ethical injunctions *follow*, to resist, that is, a form of naturalism which would preclude the social negotiation of the stories we tell and the concepts of health and well-being embedded in them. I have not, in this paper, begun the work of such negotiation for the culture in which I find myself.

ACKNOWLEDGMENTS

An earlier version of this paper was presented at the "EcoFeminist Perspectives: Culture, Nature, Theory" conference at the University of Southern California, March 1987. The author wishes to thank the following people for comments and criticism: Sally Abbott, David Abram, Tom Birch, Elizabeth Bird, Alison Jaggar, Carolyn Merchant, Patrick Murphy, Linda Nicholson, Karen Warren, Michael Zimmerman, and two anonymous referees.

NOTES

1. Leslie Marmon Silko, *Ceremony* (New York: New American Library, 1977), pp. 36–37

2. Sandra Harding, *The Science Question in Feminism* (Ithaca, N.Y.: Cornell University Press, 1986), p. 193. See also Linda Alcoff, "Cultural Feminism

versus Post-Structuralism: The Identity Crisis in Feminist Theory," *Signs* 13 (1988): pp. 405–36.

3. John D. Caputo, "The Thought of Being and the Conversation of Mankind: The Case of Heidegger and Rorty," *Review of Metaphysics* 36 (1983): pp. 661–85.

4. See Jim Cheney, "The Intentionality of Desire and the Intentions of People," *Mind* 87 (1978): pp. 517–32.

5. See Vine Deloria, Jr. (Standing Rock Sioux), *God Is Red* (New York: Dell Publishing Company, 1973); various Native American contributors to Calvin Martin, *The American Indian and the Problem of History* (Oxford: Oxford University Press, 1987): Paula Gunn Allen (Laguna Pueblo/Lakota), *The Sacred Hoop: Recovering the Feminine in American Indian Traditions* (Boston: Beacon Press, 1986). Margaret Atwood's depiction of the overthrow of a colonizing consciousness by immersion in the mythos of indigenous people in her novel *Surfacing* (New York: Popular Library 1972) is instructive. See also Paul Shepard, *Nature and Madness* (San Francisco: Sierra Club Books 1982) on the issue of ideas and their habitats.

6. Elizabeth Bird (correspondence) points out that health is a *political* concept. It is not only reality which must be negotiated but also such notions as health and well-being.

7. Tom Jay, "The Salmon of the Heart," in Finn Wilcox and Jeremiah Gorsline, eds., *Working the Woods, Working the Sea* (Port Townsend, Wash.: Empty Bowl, 1986), p. 116.

8. This last statement should not be taken to imply, however, that there is some one true account of each situation. I am not offering an *anti*postmodernist account. Elizabeth Bird, who urged clarification on this point, asks: "Couldn't a single contact percolate multiple accounts?" Yes. Discourse is privileged on this account not in virtue of being the one true story certified by a foundationalist epistemology, but because it arises in such a way as to enhance the possibility that it will be free of the distorting influence of totalizing overlays.

9. Jay, "Salmon," pp. 101–2.

10. It is an old, old story. One such account is offered by Hans Jonas (*The Gnostic Religion: The Message of the Alien God and the Beginnings of Christianity* [Boston: Beacon Press, 1963]) of the rise of Gnosticism in the early Christian era. As Jonas shows, the parallels between ancient Gnosticism and the spirit of modernism are, in fact, deep and striking. Another story is told by Julian Jaynes (*The Origin of Consciousness in the Breakdown of the Bicameral Mind* [Boston: Houghton Mifflin Company, 1976]), who locates the creation of a

distinctively psychological vocabulary and unified concept of the self as having taken place, for the Greeks, somewhere between the composition of *The Iliad* and the composition of *The Odyssey*. Shepard traces "culturally-ratified distortions of childhood," "massive disablement of ontogeny" *(Nature and Madness,* p. ix) leading eventually to the creation of the modern subject back to the agrarian revolution. A reasonable story can also be told which locates these distortions as far back as the Upper Paleolithic, the time of the cave paintings at Lascaux and elsewhere (see John E. Pfeiffer, *The Creative Explosion* [New York: Harper and Row, 1982]). On the construction of the modernist self, see Susan R. Bordo, *The Flight to Objectivity* (Albany: State University of New York Press, 1987). A fascinating account for the Orient can be found in Herbert Fingarette's reading of the Confucian texts *(Confucius—The Secular as Sacred* [New York: Harper and Row, 1972]).

11. Jay, "Salmon," p. 112.

12. Robin Ridington, "Fox and Chickadee," in Martin, ed., *The American Indian,* pp. 134–35.

13. Allen, *The Sacred Hoop,* pp. 103–5.

14. This is not to say, however, that such potential is, in fact, realized by all tribal cultures. There are, even in tribal cultures, various pressures at work which all too often result in, for example, male dominance, erosion of female power, and dramatic increases in the level of inter- and intratribal violence. The anthropologist Peggy Reeves Sanday, in her wide-ranging, cross-cultural study of tribal cultures *(Female Power and Male Dominance: On the origins of sexual inequality* [Cambridge: Cambridge University Press, 1981]), provides a perceptive account of the conditions under which such deterioration either takes place or is held at bay. Such factors include recentness of migration to a new home, environmental stress, reproductive difference, and the type of story of origin told by the culture. The interaction between these and other factors in producing or precluding domination and violence is complex. Even under the best of conditions some form of culturally constructed vigilance seems necessary. In many Native American tribes this takes the form of the trickster or clown. For excellent examples see Anne Cameron, *Daughters of Copper Woman* (Vancouver: Press Gang Publishers, 1981), pp. 107–14, and Hyemeyohsts Storm, *Song of Heyoehkah* (New York: Ballantine Books, 1981).

15. See Harding, *The Science Question;* Carol Gilligan, *In a Different Voice: Psychological Theory and Women's Development* (Cambridge: Harvard University Press, 1982); Terry Winant, "The Feminist Standpoint: A Matter of Language," *Hypatia* 2 (1987): 123–48.

16. Conrad Aiken, quoted in Edith Cobb, *The Ecology of Imagination in Childhood* (New York: Columbia University Press, 1977), p. 67.

17. Alasdair MacIntyre, *After Virtue* (Notre Dame, Ind.: University of Notre Dame Press, 1981), p. 216.

18. Holmes Rolston, III, "The Human Standing in Nature: Storied Fitness in the Moral Observer," presented at the Values and Moral Standing Conference at Bowling Green State University, April 1986.

19. Aldo Leopold, *A Sand County Almanac* (New York: Ballantine Books, 1970) p. 262.

20. Rolston, "Storied Fitness."

21. Biddy Martin and Chandra Talpade Mohanty, "Feminist Politics: What's Home Got to Do with It?" in Teresa de Lauretis, ed., *Feminist Studies/ Critical Studies* (Bloomington: Indiana University Press, 1986), pp. 193–200. See also Alcoff, "Cultural Feminism."

22. Jay, "Salmon," p. 112.

23. Martin and Mohanty, "Home," pp. 196–97.

24. Ibid., p. 204.

25. Ibid., pp. 209–10.

26. Ibid., p. 208.

27. Jay "Salmon," p. 117.

28. John Wisdom, "Gods," *Proceedings of the Aristotelian Society* 45 (1944–45): 185–206; Paul Ricoeur, *The Symbolism of Evil* (Boston: Beacon Press, 1967).

29. Shepard, *Nature and Madness*, chapter 3.

30. James Hillman, *Re-Visioning Psychology* (New York Harper and Row, 1975).

31. I use the paradoxical-sounding phrase "inscribing of the nervous system *in* the landscape" to avoid the modernist empiricism which would be suggested were I to interchange "nervous system" and "landscape." See David Abram, "The Perceptual Implications of Gaia," *The Ecologist 15* (1985): pp. 96–103, for an overview of some of the literature concerning the views (1) that perception must be studied as an attribute of an organism and its environment taken together, (2) that psyche is a property of the ecosystem as a whole, and (3) that the intellect is an elaboration of creativity at the level of bodily experience.

32. Shepard, *Nature and Madness*, p. 123.

33. Ibid., p. 9.

34. Elizabeth Ann R. Bird, "The Social Construction of Nature: Theoretical Approaches to the History of Environmental Problems," *Environmental Review* 11 (1987): p. 262.

35. Donna Haraway, "Primatology Is Politics by Other Means," in Ruth Bleier, ed., *Feminist Approaches to Science* (New York: Pergamon Press, 1984), p. 86.

36 Shepard, *Nature and Madness*, p. 6.

37. See note 13.

38. Shepard, *Nature and Madness*, pp. 23–24.

39. My thanks to Carolyn Merchant for suggesting the wonderful term *ethical vernacular*.

Bibliography

Abell, Peter. *The Syntax of Social Life: The Theory and Method of Comparative Narratives*. New York: Oxford University Press, 1987.

Abbott, Andrew. "From Causes to Events: Notes on Narrative Positivism." *Sociological Methods and Research*, vol. 20 (1992), pp. 428–55.

Abbott, Philip. "Story-Telling and Political Theory." *Soundings*, vol. 74, no. 3–4 (Winter, 1991), pp. 369–97.

Abrams, Kathryn. "Hearing the Call of Stories." *California Law Review*: vol. 79, no. 4 (July, 1991), pp. 971–1052.

Abu-Lughod, Lila. *Writing Women's Worlds: Bedouin Stories*. Berkeley: University of California Press, 1993.

Adams, Jeff. *The Conspiracy of the Text: The Place of Narrative in the Development of Thought*. New York: Routledge and Kegan Paul, 1986.

Aftel, Mandy. *The Story of Your Life: Becoming the Author of Your Own Experience*. New York: Simon and Schuster, 1995.

Agar, Michael. "Stories, Knowledge, and Themes." *American Ethnologist*, vol. 7 (1980), pp. 223–39.

Ankersmit, Franklin R. *Narrative Logic: A Semantic Analysis of the Historian's Language*. Norwell, Mass.: Kluwer Academic, 1993.

Antonio, Robert. "Postmodern Storytelling versus Pragmatic Truth-Seeking." *Sociological Theory*, vol. 9 (1991), pp. 154–63.

Appignanesi, Lisa, ed. *Identity: The Real Me*. London: Institute of Contemporary Art, 1987.

Arendt, Hannah. *The Human Condition*. Chicago: University of Chicago Press, 1958, pp. 175–99, 207–12.

Ariel, Mira, and Rachel Giora. "The Role of Women in Linguistic and Narrative Change: A Study of Hebrew Pre-State Literature." *Journal of Narrative and Life History*, vol. 2, no. 4 (1992), pp. 309–32.

Armstrong, Nancy, and Leonard Tennenhouse. "History, Poststructuralism, and the Question of Narrative." *Narrative*, vol. 1, no. 1 (January, 1993), pp. 45–58.

Attwod, Bain, ed. *In the Age of Mabo: History, Aborigines and Australia*. St. Leonards, NSW: Allen and Unwin, 1996.

Bal, Mieke. "First Person, Second Person, Same Person: Narrative as Episte-mology." *New Literary History*, vol. 24 (1993), pp. 293–320.

———. *Narratology: Introduction to the Theory of Narrative*, trans. Christine Van Boheemen. Toronto: University of Toronto Press, 1985.

Baltes, Paul, and Orville Brim, eds. *Life-Span Development and Behavior*. New York: Academic Press, 1982.

Bannet, Eve. "Pluralist Theory: Fictions and Fictional Politics." *Philosophy and Literature*, vol. 13 (April, 1989), pp. 28–41.

Barber, Benjamin. *The Conquest of Politics*. Princeton: Princeton University Press, 1983.

Barry, Anita. "Narrative Style and Witness Testimony." *Journal of Narrative and Life History*, vol. 1, no. 4 (1991), pp. 281–93.

Barthes, Roland. *S/Z*. New York: Hill and Wang, 1974.

Baxter, Charles. "No-Fault Fiction: Blame the Presidents." *Harper's*, no. 289 (November, 1994), pp. 13–15.

Bell, Michael. "How Primordial Is Narrative?" *Narrative in Culture*, ed. Christopher Nash. New York: Routledge, 1990, pp. 172–98.

Bellah, Robert, Richard Madsen, William Sullivan, Ann Swidler, and Steven Tipton. *Habits of the Heart: Individualism and Commitment in American Life*. New York: Harper and Row, 1985.

Benhabib, Seyla. "Hannah Arendt and the Redemptive Power of Narrative." *Social Research*, vol. 57, no. 1 (1990), pp. 167–96.

Benjamin, Walter. "The Storyteller." *Illuminations*, ed. Hannah Arendt. New York: Harcourt Brace and World (1955), pp. 83–109.

Bennett, W. Lance. "Political Campaign Literature." *Quarterly Journal of Speech*, vol. 63, no. 3 (October, 1977), pp. 219–38.

———. "Storytelling in Criminal Trials: A Model of Social Judgment." *Quarterly Journal of Speech*, vol. 64 (1978), pp. 1–22.

Bennett, W. Lance, and Martha S. Feldman. *Reconstructing Reality in the Court-room*. New Brunswick, N.J.: Rutgers University Press, 1981.

Benstock, Shari. *The Private Self*. London: Routledge, 1988.

Benveniste, Emile. *Problems in General Linguistics*, trans. Mary Meek. Coral Gables: University of Miami Press, 1971.

Berger, Peter, and Hansfried Kellner. "Marriage and the Construction of Real-ity." *Diogenes*, vol. 46, no. 1 (1964), pp. 1–24.

Berkowitz, Leonard, ed. *Advances in Experimental Social Psychology*, vol. 21. San Diego: Academic Press, 1988.

Bernstein, J. M. "Self-Knowledge as Praxis: Narrative and Narration in Psychoanalysis." *Narrative in Culture*, ed. Christopher Nash. New York: Routledge, 1990, pp. 51–77.

Bernstein, Richard J. *Beyond Objectivism and Relativism*. Lanham, Md.: University Press of America, 1983.

Berry, Thomas. *The Dream of the Earth*. San Francisco: Sierra Club Books, 1988, pp. xi–xii, 123–79.

Bertaux, Daniel, ed. *Biography and Society: The Life History Approach in the Social Sciences*. Beverly Hills, Calif.: Sage Publications, 1981.

Berthoff, Warner. "Fiction, History, Myth: Notes Toward the Discrimination of Narrative Forms." *The Interpretation of Narrative: Theory and Practice*. Cambridge: Harvard University Press, 1970, pp. 263–87.

Bettelheim, Bruno. *The Uses of Enchantment*. New York: Alfred A. Knopf, 1976.

Bhabba, Homi K., ed. *Nation and Narration*. New York: Routledge, 1990.

Bleicher, Joseph. *Contemporary Hermeneutics*. London: Routledge, 1980.

Bochner, Arthur, and Carolyn Ellis. "Personal Narrative as a Social Approach to Interpersonal Communication." *Communication Theory*, vol. 2 (1992), pp. 165–72.

Boje, David. "The Storytelling Organization: A Study of Story Performance in an Office-Supply Firm." *Administrative Science Quarterly*, vol. 36 (1991), pp. 106–26.

Brady, Margaret. "Narrative Competence: A Navajo Example of Peer Group Evaluation." *Journal of American Folklore*, vol. 93 (1980), pp. 158–81.

Braudel, Fernand. *The Mediterranean and the Mediterranean World in the Age of Philip II* (2 Vols.), trans. Sian Reynolds. New York: Harper and Row, 1972–74.

Braudy, Leo. *Narrative Form in History and Fiction*. Princeton: Princeton University Press, 1970.

Bremond, Claude. "The Logic of Narrative Possibilities." *New Literary History*, vol. 11, no. 3 (1980), pp. 387–412.

Brewer, Maria. "A Loosening of Tongues: From Narrative Economy to Women Writing." *MLN*, vol. 99 (December, 1984), pp. 1141–61.

Brockelman, Paul. *The Inside Story: A Narrative Approach to Religious Understanding*. Albany: State University of New York Press, 1992.

Brody, Howard. *Stories of Sickness*. New Haven: Yale University Press, 1987.

Brooks, Peter. *Reading for the Plot: Design and Intention in Narrative*. New York: Alfred A. Knopf, 1984.

Brooks, Peter, and Paul Gewirtz, eds. *Law's Stories: Narrative and Rhetoric in the Law*. New Haven, Con.: Yale University Press, 1996.

Brown, Richard Harvey. "Narrative in Scientific Knowledge and Civic Discourse." *Current Perspectives in Social Theory*, ed. John Wilson. Greenwich, Conn.: JAI Press, 1991, pp. 313–29.

———. "The Position of the Narrative in Contemporary Society." *New Literary History*, vol. 11, no. 3 (1980), pp. 545–50.

———. *Society as Text*. Chicago: University of Chicago Press, 1987.

———, ed. *Writing the Social Text: Poetics and Politics in Social Science Discourse*. New York: Aldine De Gruyter, 1992.

Bruner, Edward. "Ethnography as Narrative." *The Anthropology of Experience*, ed. Victor Turner and Edward Bruner. Chicago: University of Chicago Press, 1986, pp. 139–55.

Bruner, Jerome. *Actual Minds, Possible Worlds*. Cambridge: Harvard University Press, 1986.

———. "Life as Narrative." *Social Research*, vol. 54, no. 1 (Spring, 1987), pp. 11–32.

———. "The Narrative Construction of Reality." *Critical Inquiry*, vol. 18, no. 1 (Autumn, 1991), pp. 1–21.

Brunner, Diane. *Inquiry and Reflection: Framing Narrative Practice on Education*. Albany: State University of New York Press, 1994.

Buker, Eloise. *Politics Through a Looking-Glass: Understanding Political Cultures Through a Structuralist Interpretation of Narratives*. New York: Greenwood Press, 1987.

Burrell, David. "Stories of God: Why We Use Them and How We Judge Them." *Is God* God? ed. James Mcclendon and Axel Steuer. Nashville: Abingdon Press, 1981, pp. 206–29.

Campbell, Joseph. *The Hero with a Thousand Faces*. New York: Pantheon, 1949.

Canary, Robert, and Henry Kozicki, eds. *The Writing of History*. Madison: University of Wisconsin Press, 1978.

Carr, David. "Narrative and the Real World: An Argument for Continuity." *History and Theory*, vol. 25, no. 2 (1986a), pp. 117–31.

———. *Time, Narrative, and History*. Bloomington: Indiana University Press, 1986b.

Cartwright, Rosalind. *Crisis Dreaming*. New York: HarperCollins, 1992.

Cazden, Courtney and Dell Hymes. "Narrative Thinking and Story-Telling Rights." *Keystone Folklore*, vol. 22, no. 1–2 (1978), pp. 21–36.

Chafe, Wallace. *Discourse, Consciousness, and Time*. Chicago: University of Chicago Press, 1994.

———, ed. *The Pear Stories*. Norwood, N.J.: Ablex, 1980.

Chatman, Seymour. *Coming to Terms: The Rhetoric of Narrative in Fiction and Film*. Ithaca: Cornell University Press, 1990.

———. "Towards a Theory of Narrative." *New Literary History*, vol. 6 (1975), pp. 295–318.

Cheney, Jim. "Postmodern Environmental Ethics: Ethics as Bioregional Narrative." *Environmental Ethics*, vol. 11 (1987), pp. 115–46.

Clayton, Jay. "Narrative and Theories of Desire." *Critical Inquiry*, vol. 16 (Autumn, 1989), pp. 33–53.

Cohler, Bertram. "The Life Story and the Study of Resilience and Response to Adversity." *Journal of Narrative and Life History*, vol. 1, no. 2–3 (1991), pp. 169–200.

———. "Personal Narrative and Life Course." *Life-Span Development and Behavior*, vol. 4, ed. Paul Baltes and Orville Brim. New York: Academic Press, 1982, pp. 205–41.

Coles, Robert. *The Call of Stories: Stories and the Moral Imagination*. New York: Houghton Mifflin, 1989.

Collingwood, R. G. *The Idea of History*. Oxford: Clarendon Press, 1946.

Coste, Didier. *Narrative as Communication*. Minneapolis: University of Minnesota Press, 1989.

Couto, Richard. "Narrative, Free Space, and Political Leadership in Social Movements." *Journal of Politics*, vol. 55 (February, 1993), pp. 57–79.

Cowley, Geoffrey, and Karen Springen. "Rewriting Life Stories." *Newsweek* (April 17, 1995), pp. 70–74.

Cox, Harvey. *The Seduction of the Spirit*. New York: Simon and Schuster, 1973.

Crites, Stephen. "The Narrative Quality of Experience." *Journal of the American Academy of Religion*, vol. lix, no. 3 (September, 1971), pp. 291–311.

———. "Storytime: Recollecting the Past and Projecting the Future." *Narrative Psychology*, ed. Theodore Sarbin. New York: Praeger, 1986, pp. 152–73.

Cronon, William. "A Place for Stories: Nature, History, and Narrative." *Journal of American History*, vol. 78, no. 4 (1992), pp. 1347–76.

Crowley, Daniel. "Bahamian Narrative as Art and as Communication." *Western Folklore*, vol. 49 (October, 1990), pp. 349–69.

Danto, Arthur. *Analytic Philosophy of History*. Cambridge: Cambridge University Press, 1965.

———. *Narration and Knowledge*. New York: Columbia University Press, 1985.

Davis, F. James. "Stories and Sociology." *Urban Life and Culture*, vol. 3 (1974), pp. 310–16.

Davis, Madeline, and Elizabeth Lapovsky Kennedy. "Oral History and the Study of Sexuality in the Lesbian Community." *Feminist Studies*, vol. 12, no. 1 (Spring, 1986), pp. 7–26.

Dennett, Daniel. *Consciousness Explained*. Boston: Little, Brown, 1991.

Delgado, Richard. "Storytelling for Oppositionists and Others: A Plea for Narrative." *Michigan Law Review*, vol. 87 (August, 1989), pp. 2411–41.

———. "When a Story Is Just a Story: Does Voice Really Matter?" *Virginia Law Review*, vol. 76 (1990), pp. 95–111.

Demallie, Raymond. "'These Have No Ears': Narrative and the Ethnohistorical Method." *Ethnohistory*, vol. 40, no. 4 (Fall, 1993), pp. 515–38.

Denzin, Norman. "The Alcoholic Self: Communication, Ritual, and Identity Transformation." *Communication and Social Structure*, ed. David Maines and Carl Couch. Springfield, Ill.: Charles C. Thomas, 1988, pp. 59–74.

Didion, Joan. *After Henry*. New York: Simon and Schuster, 1992, pp. 47–91, 198–209, 220–319.

———. *Miami*. New York: Simon and Schuster, 1987.

———. *The White Album*. New York: Simon and Schuster, 1979, pp. 11–47.

Diengott, Nilli. "Narratology and Feminism." *Style*, vol. 22 (1988), pp. 42–51.

Disch, Lisa. *Hannah Arendt and the Limits of Philosophy*. Ithaca: Cornell University Press, 1994.

———. "More Truth Than Fact: Storytelling as Critical Understanding in the Writings of Hannah Arendt." *Political Theory*, vol. 21, no. 4 (1993), pp. 665–94.

Dolan, Frederick M. *Allegories of America: Narratives, Metaphysics, Politics*. Ithaca: Cornell University Press, 1994.

Downing, David, and James Sosnoski. "Working with Narrative Zones in a Postdisciplinary Pedagogy." *Narrative*, vol. 3, no. 3 (October, 1995), pp. 271–86.

Doyle, Laura. "The Folk, the Nobles, and the Novel: The Racial Subtext of Sentimentality." *Narrative*, vol. 3, no. 2 (May, 1995), pp. 161–87.

Dray, W. H. "Narrative versus Analysis in History." *Rationality, Relativism and the Human Sciences*, ed. J. Margolis, M. Krausz, and R. M. Burian. Boston: Martinus Nijhoff, 1986, pp. 23–42.

———. "On the Nature and Role of Narrative in Historiography." *History and Theory*, vol. 10 (1971), pp. 153–71.

Dryzek, John. "Policy Analysis as a Hermeneutic Activity." *Policy Sciences*, vol. 14 (1982), pp. 309–29.

Dunne, John. *Time and Myth*. New York: Macmillan, 1973.

Dunn, Judy. *The Beginnings of Social Understanding*. Cambridge: Harvard University Press, 1988.

Eagle, Morris. "Psychoanalysis and 'Narrative Truth': A Reply to Spence." *Psychoanalysis and Contemporary Thought*, vol. 7 (1984), pp. 629–40.

Eagleton, Terry. "History, Narrative, and Marxism." *Reading Narrative*, ed. James Phelan. Columbus: Ohio State University Press, 1989, pp. 272–81.

———. *Literary Theory*. Minneapolis: University of Minnesota Press, 1983.

Eakin, P. J. *Fictions in Autobiography*. Princeton: Princeton University Press, 1985.

Eder, Donna. "Building Cohesion Through Collaborative Narration." *Social Psychology Quarterly*, vol. 51, no. 3 (September, 1988), pp. 225–35.

Eichorn, D. H. et al. *Present and Past in Midlife*. New York: Academic Press, 1981.

Estrich, Susan. "Rape." *Yale Law Journal*, vol. 95, no. 6 (1986), pp. 1087–1184.

Ettema, James, and Theodore Glasser. "Narrative Form and Moral Force: The Realization of Innocence and Guilt Through Investigative Journalism." *Journal of Communication*, vol. 38 (Summer, 1988), pp. 8–26.

Falck, Colin. *Myth, Truth, and Literature*. Cambridge: Cambridge University Press, 1989.

Feinstein, A. David. "Personal Mythology as a Paradigm for Holistic Public Psychology." *American Journal of Orthopsychiatry*, vol. 49, no. 2 (1979), pp. 198–217.

Fercerro, John. "Autobiography and Narrative." *Reconstructing Individualism*, ed. Thomas Heller, Morton Sosna, and David Wellbery. Stanford: Stanford University Press, 1986, pp. 16–29.

Fisher, Walter. *Human Communication as Narration*. Columbia: University of South Carolina Press, 1987.

———. "Narration, Reason and Community." *Writing the Social Text*, ed. Richard Harvey Brown. New York: Aldine De Gruyter, 1992, pp. 199–217.

———. "Narrative as a Human Communications Paradigm," *Communication Monographs*, no. 511 (1984), pp. 1–22.

———. "Narration, Knowledge, and the Possibility of Wisdom." *Rethinking Knowledge: Reflections Across the Disciplines*, ed. Walter Fisher and Robert F. Goodman. Albany: State University of New York Press, 1995, pp. 169–92.

Fivush, Robyn, "Gender and Emotion in Mother-Child Conversations about the Past." *Journal of Narrative and Life History*, vol. 1, no. 4 (1991), pp. 325–41.

Ford, David. "System, Story, Performance: A Proposal about the Role of Narrative in Christian Systematic Theology." *Why Narrative?*, ed. Stanley

Hauerwas and L. Gregory Jones. Grand Rapids, Mich.: William B. Eerd-mans, 1989, pp. 191–215.

Flynn, Thomas, and Dalia Judovitz, eds. *Dialectic and Narrative*. Albany: State University of New York Press, 1993.

Freed, Richard, and Glenn Broadhead. "Discourse Communities, Sacred Texts, and Institutional Norms." *College Composition and Communication*, vol. 38 (1987), pp. 154–65.

Freeman, Mark. "History, Narrative, and Life-Span Developmental Knowledge." *Human Development*, vol. 27 (1984), pp. 1–19.

Frei, Hans. "Apologetics, Criticism, and the Loss of Narrative Interpretation." *Why Narrative?*, ed. Stanley Hauerwas and L. Gregory Jones. Grand Rapids, Mich.: William B. Eerdmans, 1989, pp. 45–64.

Friedman, Susan Stanford. "Spatialization: A Strategy for Reading Narrative." *Narrative*, vol. 1, no. 1 (January, 1993), pp. 12–23.

Friedman, Thomas. "A Nixon Legacy Devalued by a Cold War Standard." *New York Times* (May 1, 1994), p. 4-E.

Furet, François. "From Narrative History to History as Problem." *Diogenes*, no. 89 (Spring, 1975), pp. 106–23.

Gadamer, Hans-Georg. *Truth and Method*, trans. Joel Weinshemer and Donald Marshall. New York: Continuum Publishing Co., 1993.

Galda, Lee, and Anthony Pellegrini, eds. *Play, Language, and Stories: The Development of Children's Literate Behavior*. Norwood, N.J.: Ablex Publishing Corp., 1985.

Gallie, W. B. *Philosophy and the Historical Understanding*. New York: Schocken Books, 1968.

Garro, Lisa. "Narrative Representations of Chronic Illness Experience." *Social Science and Medicine*, vol. 38, no. 6 (1994), pp. 775–88.

Gee, James. "A Linguistic Approach to Narrative." *Journal of Narrative and Life History*, vol. 1, no. 1 (1991), pp. 15–39.

———. "The Narrativization of Experience." *Journal of Education*, vol. 167 (1985), pp. 9–35.

Geertz, Clifford. "Blurred Genres." *The American Scholar*, vol. 80 (1980), pp. 165–79.

———. "Deep Play." *Interpretive Social Sciences: A Second Look*, eds. Paul Rabinow and William Sullivan. Berkeley: University of California Press, 1987, pp. 195–240.

———. *The Interpretation of Cultures*. New York: Basic Books, 1973.

———. *Works and Lives: The Anthropologist as Author*. Stanford: Stanford University Press, 1988.

Gellner, Ernest. "The Stakes in Anthropology." *American Scholar*, vol. 57 (Winter, 1988), pp. 17–30.

Genette, Gerard. "Boundaries of Narrative." *New Literary History*, vol. 8 (1976), pp. 1–13.

———. *Narrative Discourse: An Essay in Method*, trans. Jane Lewin. Ithaca: Cornell University Press, 1980, pp. 25–32.

———. *Narrative Discourse Revisited*, trans. Jane Lewin. Ithaca: Cornell University Press, 1988.

Georges, Robert. "Toward an Understanding of Storytelling Events." *Journal of American Folklore*, vol. 28 (1969), pp. 313–28.

Gergen, Kenneth. "Social Psychology as History." *Journal of Personality and Social Psychology*, vol. 26 (1973), pp. 309–20.

Gergen, Kenneth, and Mary Gergen. "Narrative and the Self as Relationship." *Advances in Experimental Social Psychology*, ed. Leonard Berkowitz. San Diego: Academic Press, 1988, pp. 17–56.

———. "Narrative Form and the Construction of Psychological Science." *Narrative Psychology*, ed. Theodore Sarbin. New York: Praeger, 1986, pp. 22–44.

———. "Narratives of the Self." *Studies in Social Identity*, ed. Theodore Sarbin and Karl Scheibe. New York: Praeger, 1983, pp. 254–73.

———. "The Social Construction of Narrative Accounts." *Historical Social Psychology*, ed. Kenneth Gergen and Mary Gergen. Hillsdale, N.J.: Lawrence Erlbaum Associates, 1984, pp. 173–89.

Gergen, Mary. "Finished at Forty: Women's Development Within the Patriarchy." *Psychology of Women Quarterly*, vol. 14 (1990), pp. 471–93.

———. "Life Stories: Pieces of a Dream." *Storied Lives*, ed. George Rosenwald and Richard Ochberg. New Haven: Yale University Press, 1992, pp. 127–44.

Gerhardt, Julia. "The Nature of Therapeutic Discourse." *Journal of Narrative and Life History*, vol. 4, no. 3 (1994), pp. 151–92.

Gidenose, Hendrik, ed. *Teacher Education Policy: Narratives, Stories, and Cases*. Albany: State University of New York Press, 1992.

Gilligan, Carol. in *A Different Voice: Psychological Theory and Women's Development*. Cambridge: Harvard University Press, 1982.

Gitlin, Todd. "Glib, Glib, Glib." *Utne Reader* (March/April 1994), pp. 115–16.

Goffman, Erving. *Frame Analysis*. New York: Harper and Row, 1974.

Goldberg, Michael. "God, Action, and Narrative." *Why Narrative?*, ed. Stanley Hauerwas and L. Gregory Jones. Grand Rapids, Mich.: William B. Eerdmans, 1989, pp. 348–65.

Goldman, Susan, and Connie Varnhagen. "Memory for Embedded and Sequential Story Structures." *Journal of Memory and Language*, vol. 25 (August, 1986), pp. 401–18.

Goodwin, Marjorie. "'Instigating': Storytelling as Social Process." *American Ethnologist*, vol. 9 (1982), pp. 799–819.

Gottdiener, Mark, and Alexander Lagopoulos, eds. *The City and the Sign*. New York: Columbia University Press, 1986.

Greeley, Andrew. "Why Do Catholics Stay in the Church? Because of the Stories." *New York Times Magazine* (July 10, 1994), pp. 38–41.

Greenberg, Gary. "If a Self Is a Narrative: Social Constructionism in the Clinic." *Journal of Narrative and Life History*, vol. 5, no. 3 (1995), pp. 269–83.

Greenspan, Henry. "Lives as Texts: Symptoms as Modes of Recounting in the Life Histories of Holocaust Survivors." *Storied Lives*, ed. George Rosenwald and Richard Ochberg. New Haven: Yale University Press, 1992, pp. 145–64.

Gregory, Marshall. "The Sound of Story: Narrative, Memory, and Selfhood." *Narrative*, vol. 3, no. 1 (January, 1995), pp. 33–56.

Griffin, Larry. "Narrative, Event-Structure Analysis, and Causal Interpretation in Historical Sociology." *American Journal of Sociology*, vol. 98 (March, 1993), pp. 1094–1133.

Gutting, Gary. *Paradigms and Revolutions*. Notre Dame: University of Notre Dame Press, 1980.

Hall, Pamela. *Narrative and the Natural Law: An Interpretation of Thomistic Ethics*. Notre Dame: University of Notre Dame Press, 1994.

Hall, Stephen. "The Language of Dreams." *Vogue* (August, 1992), pp. 166, 168, 170.

Hamerow, Theodore. "The Bureaucratization of History." *American Historical Review*, vol. 94, no. 3 (1989), pp. 654–60.

Haraway, Donna. "Manifesto for Cyborgs." *Socialist Review*, vol. 14, no. 2 (1985), pp. 65–107.

———. "Situated Knowledges." *Feminist Studies*, vol. 14 (1988), pp. 575–99.

Hardy, Barbara. "Towards a Poetics of Fiction: An Approach Through Narrative." *Novel: A Forum on Fiction*, vol. 2, no. 1 (1968), pp. 5–14.

Harkin, Michael. "History, Narrative, and Temporality: Examples from the Northwest Coast." *Ethnohistory*, vol. 35 (Spring, 1988), pp. 99–130.

Harré, Rom. "Some Narrative Conventions of Scientific Discourse." *Narrative in Culture*, ed. Christopher Nash. New York: Routledge, 1990, pp. 81–101.

Hart, Janet. "Cracking the Code: Narrative and Political Mobilization in the Greek Resistance." *Social Science History*, vol. 16, no. 4 (1992), pp. 631–68.

Hartt, Julian. "Theological Investments in Story." *Why Narrative?*, ed. Stanley Hauerwas and L. Gregory Jones. Grand Rapids, Mich.: William B. Eerdmans, 1989, pp. 279–92.

Hauerwas, Stanley, and David Burrell. "From System to Story: An Alternative Pattern for Rationality in Ethics." *Why Narrative?*, ed. Stanley Hauerwas and L. Gregory Jones. Grand Rapids, Mich.: William B. Eerdmans, 1989, pp. 158–90.

———. *Truthfulness and Tragedy*. Notre Dame: University of Notre Dame Press, 1977.

Hauerwas, Stanley, and L. Gregory Jones. *Why Narrative? Readings in Narrative Theology*. Grand Rapids, Mich.: William B. Eerdmans, 1989.

Heath, Shirley. *Way with Words: Life and Work in Communities and Classrooms.* New York; Cambridge University Press, 1983.

Hillman, James. *Healing Fiction*. Barrytown, N.Y.: Station Hill, 1983.

———. "A Note on Story." *Parabola*, vol. 4, no. 4 (1979), pp. 43–45.

———. *Re-Visioning Psychology*. New York: Harper and Row, 1975.

Himmelfarb, Gertrude. "Denigrating the Rule of Reason." *Harper's,* no. 268 (April, 1984), pp. 84–90.

———. "Is It a Plot?" *New York Times Book Review* (October 30, 1994), pp. 40–41.

———. *The New History and the Old*. Cambridge: Harvard University Press, 1987.

———. "Some Reflections on the New History." *American Historical Review,* vol. 94, no. 3 (1989), pp. 661–70.

Hohler, Thomas. "Storytelling and Human Experience." *Research in Phenomenology,* vol. 17 (1987), pp. 291–303.

Holland, Norman. "Unity, Identity, Text, Self." *Reader-Response Criticism: From Formalism to Post Structuralism*, ed. Jane Tompkins. Baltimore: Johns Hopkins University Press, 1980, pp. 118–33.

Howard, George. "Culture Tales." *American Psychologist*, vol. 46, no. 3 (March, 1991), pp. 187–97.

———. *A Tale of Two Stories: Excursions into a Narrative Approach to Psychology.* Notre Dame, Ind.: Academic Publications, 1989.

Hudson, Judith. "Learning to Reminisce: A Case Study." *Journal of Narrative and Life History*, vol. 1, no. 4 (1991), pp. 295–324.

———. "Reminiscing with Mother and Others." *Journal of Narrative and Life History*, vol. 3, no. 1 (1993), pp. 1–32.

Hutcheon, Linda, and Michael Hutcheon. "Otherhood Issues: Post-National Operatic Narratives." *Narrative*, vol. 3, no. 1 (January, 1995), pp. 1–17.

Invernizzi, Marcia, and Mary Abouzeid. "One Story Map Does Not Fit All: A Cross-cultural Analysis of Children's Written Story Retelling." *Journal of Narrative and Life History*, vol. 5, no. 1 (1995), pp. 1–19.

Irele, Abiola. "Narrative, History, and the African Imagination." *Narrative*, vol. 1, no. 2 (May, 1993), pp. 156–72.

Iser, Wolfgang. *The Fictive and the Imaginary: Charting Literary Anthropology.* Baltimore: Johns Hopkins University Press, 1993.

———. *The Implied Reader.* Baltimore: Johns Hopkins University Press (1974), pp. xii–xiii.

Jackson, Bernard. "Narrative Theories and Legal Discourse." *Narrative in Culture*, ed. Christopher Nash. New York: Routledge, 1990, pp. 23–50.

Jameson, Frederic. *The Political Unconscious: Narrative as a Socially Symbolic Act.* Ithaca: Cornell University Press, 1981.

Jauss, Hans. *Toward an Ethic of Perception*, trans. Timothy Bahti. Minneapolis: University of Minnesota Press, 1982.

Jefferson, Gail. "Sequential Aspects of Storytelling in Conversation." *Studies in the Organization of Conversational Interaction*, ed. Jim Schenkein. New York: Academic Press, 1978.

John-Steiner, Vera, and Carolyn Panofsky. "Narrative Competence: Cross-Cultural Comparisons." *Journal of Narrative and Life History*, vol. 2, no. 3 (1992), pp. 219–33.

Johnstone, Barbara. *Stories, Community, and Place.* Bloomington: Indiana University Press, 1990.

Josselyn, Ruthellen, and Amia Lieblich, eds. *The Narrative Study of Lives.* Newbury Park, Calif.: Sage Publications, 1993.

Kaplan, Thomas. "The Narrative Structure of Policy Analysis." *Journal of Policy Analysis and Management*, vol. 5, no. 4 (1986), pp. 761–78.

Katriel, Tamar, and Aliza Shenhar. "Tower and Stockade: Dialogic Narration in Israeli Settlement Ethos." *Quarterly Journal of Speech*, vol. 76 (1990), pp. 359–80.

Keen, Ernest. "Narrative Construction in Treating Multiple Personality Disorder." *Journal of Narrative and Life History*, vol. 5, no. 3 (1995), pp. 247–53.

———. "Paranoia and Cataclysmic Narratives." *Narrative Psychology*, ed. Theodore Sarbin. New York: Praeger, 1986, pp. 174–90.

Keen, Sam. *To a Dancing God.* New York: Harper and Row, 1970.

Keen, Sam, and Anne Valley Fox. *Telling Your Story.* Garden City, N.Y.: Doubleday, 1973.

Keeshig-Tobias, Lenore. "Poaching: Is It Irresponsible to Appropriate Native American Stories?" *Utne Reader* (March/April 1994), pp. 118–19.

Kellner, Hans. "Narrativity in History: Poststructuralism and Since." *History and Theory*, vol. 26, no. 4 (September, 1987), pp. 1–29.

Kemp, Peter. "History as Narrative and Practice" (interview with Paul Ricoeur). *Philosophy Today*, vol. 29 (Fall, 1985), pp. 213–22.

Kerby, Anthony Paul. "The Adequacy of Self-Narration: A Hermeneutical Approach." *Philosophy and Literature*, vol. 12 (1988), pp. 232–44.

———. "The Language of the Self." *Philosophy Today* (Fall, 1986), pp. 210–23.

———. *On Narrative and the Self*. Bloomington: Indiana University Press, 1991.

Klass, Perri. "The Narrated Life." *Victoria* (Sept. 1994), pp. 122, 116.

Kleinman, Arthur. *The Illness Narratives: Suffering, Healing, and the Human Condition*. New York: Basic Books, 1988.

Kling, Joseph. "Complex Society/Complex Cities: New Social Movements and the Restructuring of Urban Space." *Mobilizing the Community*, ed. Robert Fisher and Joseph Kling. Newbury Park, Calif.: Sage Publishing, 1993, pp. 28–51.

Knight, Deborah. "Selves, Interpreters, Narrators." *Philosophy and Literature*, vol. 18, no. 2 (1994), pp. 274–86.

Kris, Ernst. "The Personal Myth." *Journal of the American Psychoanalytic Association*, vol. 4 (1956), pp. 653–81.

Labov, William and Joshua Waletzky. "Narrative Analysis: Oral Versions of Personal Experience." *Essays on the Verbal and Visual Arts*, ed. June Helm. Seattle: University of Washington Press, 1987, pp. 12–44.

Labov, William. "Speech Acts and Reactions in Personal Narrative." *Analyzing Discourse: Text and Talk*, ed. Deborah Tannen. Washington, D.C.: Georgetown University Press, 1982, pp. 219–47.

Lacan, Jacques. "The Neurotic's Individual Myth." *Psychoanalytic Quarterly*, vol. 48 (1979), pp. 405–25.

Lamarque, Peter. "Narrative and Invention: The Limits of Fictionality." *Narrative in Culture*, ed. Christopher Nash. New York: Routledge, 1990, pp. 131–53.

Landau, Misia. "Human Evolution as Narrative." *American Scientist*, vol. 72 (1984), pp. 262–68.

———. "Trespassing in Scientific Narrative: Grafton Elliot Smith and The Temple of Doom." *Narrative Psychology*, ed. Theodore Sarbin. New York: Praeger, 1986, pp. 45–64.

Langer, Lawrence. *Holocaust Testimonies*. New Haven: Yale University Press, 1991.

Lanser, Susan S. "Toward a Feminist Narratology." *Style*, vol. 20 (1986), pp. 341–63.

La Rue, Lewis Henry. *Constitutional Law as Fiction: Narrative in the Rhetoric of Authority*. University Park: Pennsylvania State University Press, 1995.

Leitch, Thomas. *What Stories Are: Narrative Theory and Interpretation*. University Park: Pennsylvania State University Press, 1986.

Lempert, Lora Bex. "A Narrative Analysis of Abuse: Connecting the Personal, the Rhetorical, and the Structural." *Journal of Contemporary Ethnography*, vol. 22, no. 4 (January, 1994), pp. 411–41.

Lentricchia, Frank, and Thomas Mclaughlin, eds. *Critical Terms for Literary Study*. Chicago: University of Chicago Press, 1990.

Levine, Lawrence. "The Unpredictable Past: Reflections on Recent American Historiography." *American Historical Review*, vol. 94, no. 3 (1989), pp. 671–79.

Lewis, Justin. "The Absence of Narrative: Boredom and the Residual Power of Television News." *Journal of Narrative and Life History*, vol. 4, no. 1 (1994), pp. 25–40.

Lewis, William. "Telling America's Story: Narrative Form and the Reagan Presidency." *Quarterly Journal of Speech*, vol. 73 (August, 1987), pp. 280–302.

Liebos, Tamar. "Narrativization of the News." *Journal of Narrative and Life History*, vol. 4, no. 1 (1994), pp. 1–8.

Linde, Charlotte. *Life Stories: The Creation of Coherence*. New York: Oxford University Press, 1993.

———. "Private Stories in Public Discourse: Narrative Analysis in the Social Sciences." *Poetics*, vol. 15 (1986), pp. 183–202.

Lloyd, Genevieve. "The Self as Fiction: Philosophy and Autobiography." *Philosophy and Literature*, vol. 10, no. 2 (1986), pp. 168–85.

Luban, David. "Explaining Dark Times: Hannah Arendt's Theory of Theory." *Social Research*, vol. 57, no. 1 (1983), pp. 213–48.

———. "Difference Made Legal: The Court and Dr. King." *Michigan Law Review*, vol. 87 (August, 1989), pp. 2152–2224.

Lyotard, Jean-François. *The Postmodern Condition: A Report on Knowledge*, trans. Geoff Bennington and Brian Massumi. Minneapolis: University of Minnesota Press, 1984.

MacIntyre, Alasdair. *After Virtue*. Notre Dame: University of Notre Dame Press, 1981, pp. 190–209.

———. "The Intelligibility of Action." *Rationality, Relativism and the Human Sciences*, ed. J. Margolis, M. Krausz, and R. M. Burian. Boston: Martinus Nijhoff Publishers, 1986, pp. 63–80.

McAdams, Don. *Power, Intimacy, and the Life Story*. Homewood, Ill.: Dorsey Press, 1985.

————. *The Stories We Live By: Personal Myths and the Making of the Self.* New York: William Morrow, 1993.

McClendon, James. *Biography as Theology.* Nashville: Abingdon Press, 1974.

McCloskey, David. "Storytelling in Economics." *Narrative in Culture,* ed. Christopher Nash. New York: Routledge, 1990, pp. 5–22.

McCullagh, C. Behan. "Narrative and Explanation in History." *Mind,* vol. 78 (1969), pp. 256–61.

McFague, Sallie. *Metaphorical Theology.* Philadelphia: Fortress Press, 1982.

McGoldrick, Monica, Froma Walsh, and Carol Anderson, eds. *Women in Families.* New York: W. W. Norton, 1982.

Mahoney, Martha. "Legal Images of Battered Women: Redefining the Issue of Separation." *Michigan Law Review,* vol. 90, no. 1 (1991), pp. 1–94.

Maines, David. "Narrative's Moment and Sociology's Phenomena: Toward a Narrative Sociology." *Sociological Quarterly,* vol. 34, no. 1 (1993), pp. 17–38.

————. "The Storied Nature of Health and Diabetic Self Help Groups." *Advances in Medical Sociology,* ed. Gary Albrecht and Jay Levy. Greenwich, Conn.: JAI Press, 1991, pp. 185–202.

Maines, David, and Jeffrey Bridger. "Narratives, Community and Land Use Decisions." *Social Science Journal,* vol. 29, no. 4 (1992), pp. 363–80.

Mair, Miller. *Between Psychology and Psychotherapy: A Poetics of Experience.* London: Routledge, 1988.

————. "Psychology as Storytelling." *International Journal of Personal Construct Psychology,* vol. 1 (1988), pp. 125–37.

————. "Telling Psychological Tales." *International Journal of Personal Construct Psychology,* vol. 3 (1990), pp. 121–35.

Mancuso, James. "The Acquisition and Use of Narrative Grammar Structure." *Narrative Psychology,* ed. Theodore Sarbin. New York: Praeger, 1986, pp. 91–110.

Mancuso, James, and Theodore Sarbin. "The Self-Narrative in the Enactment of Roles." *Studies in Social Identity,* ed. Theodore Sarbin and Karl Scheibe. New York: Praeger, 1986, pp. 233–53.

Mandelbaum, Maurice. "A Note on History as Narrative." *History and Theory,* vol. 6 (1967), pp. 414–19.

————. *The Anatomy of Historical Knowledge.* Baltimore: Johns Hopkins University Press, 1977.

Mandler, Jean. *Stories, Scripts, and Scenes: Aspects of Schemata Theory.* Hillsdale, N.J.: Lawrence Erlbaum, 1984.

Mandler, Jean, and Nancy Johnson. "Remembrance of Things Parsed: Story Structure and Recall." *Cognitive Psychology,* vol. 9 (1977), pp. 111–51.

Martin, Wallace. *Recent Theories of Narrative*. Ithaca, N.Y.: Cornell University Press, 1986.

Massaro, Toni. "Empathy, Legal Storytelling, and the Rule of Law: New Words, Old Wounds?" *Michigan Law Review*, vol. 87 (August 1989), pp. 2099–2127.

Maynard, Douglas. "Narratives and Narrative Structure in Plea Bargaining." *Law and Society Review*, vol. 22, no. 3 (1988), pp. 449–81.

Maynes, Mary Jo. "Autobiography and Class Formation in Nineteenth-Century Europe: Methodological Considerations." *Social Science History*, vol. 16, no. 3 (Fall, 1992), pp. 517–37.

Megill, Allan. "Recounting the Past: 'Description,' Explanation, and Narrative in Historiography." *American Historical Review*, vol. 94, no. 3 (June, 1989), pp. 627–53.

Mehan, Hugh, and Houston Wood. *The Reality of Ethno-Methodology*. New York: John Wiley, 1975.

Meilaender, Gilbert. *The Limits of Love: Some Theological Explorations*. University Park: Pennsylvania State University Press, 1987, pp. 19–31.

Metz, Johann Baptist. "A Short Apology of Narrative." *Why Narrative?*, ed. Stanley Hauerwas and L. Gregory Jones. Grand Rapids, Mich.: William B. Eerdmans, 1989, pp. 251–62.

Michaels, Sarah Ann. "Sharing Time: Children's Narrative Styles and Differential Access to Literacy." *Language and Society*, vol. 10 (1981), pp. 423–42.

Miller, David L. *The New Polytheism*. Dallas: Spring Publications, 1981.

Miller, Peggy, and Barbara Moore. "Narrative Conjunctions of Caregiver and Child: A Comparative Perspective on Socialization Through Stories." *Ethos*, vol. 17 (1989), pp. 43–64.

Miller, Peggy, Randolph Potts, Heidi Fung, Lisa Hoogstra, and Judy Mintz. "Narrative Practices and the Social Construction of Self in Childhood." *American Ethnologist*, vol. 17 (1990), pp. 292–311.

Mink, Louis. "History and Fiction as Modes of Comprehension." *New Literary History*, vol. 1 (1970), pp. 541–58.

———. "Narrative Form as a Cognitive Instrument." *The Writing of History: Literary Form and Historical Understanding*, ed. Robert Canary and Henry Kozicki. Madison: University of Wisconsin Press, 1978, pp. 129–49.

———. "Philosophical Analysis and Historical Understanding." *Review of Metaphysics*, vol. 21 (1968), pp. 667–98.

Minnow, Martha, and Gary Bellow, eds. *Law Stories*. Ann Arbor: University of Michigan Press, 1996.

Mishler, Elliot. "The Analysis of Interview-Narratives." *Narrative Psychology*, ed. Theodore Sarbin. New York: Praeger, 1986, pp. 233–55.

———. "Models of Narrative Analysis: A Typology." *Journal of Narrative and Life History*, vol. 5, no. 2 (1995), pp. 87–123.

Mitchell, W. J. T., ed. *On Narrative*. Chicago: University of Chicago Press, 1981.

Moi, Toril. *Sexual/Textual Politics*. London: Routledge, 1985, pp. 7–11.

Morson, Gary Saul. *Narrative and Freedom: The Shadows of Time*. New Haven: Yale University Press, 1994.

Munz, Peter. "History and Myth." *Philosophical Quarterly*, vol. 6 (1956), pp. 1–17.

———. "The Skeleton and the Mollusc: Reflections on the Nature of Historical Narratives." *New Zealand Journal of History*, vol. 1 (1967), pp. 107–23.

Murray, Keith. "Literary Pathfinding: The Work of Popular Life Constructors." *Narrative Psychology*, ed. Theodore Sarbin. New York: Praeger, 1986, pp. 276–92.

Muske, Carol. "Oppressed by Narrative." *New York Times Book Review* (November 6, 1994), p. 18.

Myers, Greg. "Making a Discovery: Narratives of Split Genes." *Narrative in Culture*, ed. Christopher Nash. New York: Routledge, 1990, pp.102–26.

Nash, Christopher, ed. *Narrative in Culture: The Uses of Storytelling in the Sciences, Philosophy, and Literature*. New York: Routledge, 1990.

Natanson, Maurice. *The Journeying Self: A Study in Philosophy and Social Role*. Reading, Mass.: Addison-Wesley, 1970.

Nelson, Katherine, ed. *Narratives from the Crib*. Cambridge: Harvard University Press, 1989.

———. "Perspectives on Embodiment: The Uses of Narrativity in Ethnographic Writing." *Journal of Narrative and Life History*, vol. 1, no. 2–3 (1991), pp. 213–43.

———. "Remembering and Telling: A Developmental Story." *Journal of Narrative and Life History*, vol. 1, no. 2–3 (1991), pp. 109–27.

Newton, Adam Z. *Narrative Ethics*. Cambridge: Harvard University Press, 1995.

Niebuhr, H. Richard. "The Story of Our Life." *Why Narrative?*, ed. Stanley Hauerwas and L. Gregory Jones. Grand Rapids, Mich.: William B. Eerdmans, 1989, pp. 21–64.

Novak, Michael. "'Story' and Experience." *Religion as Story*, ed. James Wiggins. New York: Harper and Row, 1975, pp. 175–200.

Novick, Peter. *That Noble Dream*. Cambridge: Cambridge University Press, 1988.

Novitz, David. "Art, Narrative, and Human Nature." *Philosophy and Literature*, vol. 13, no. 1 (1989), pp. 57–74.

————. *Knowledge, Fiction and Imagination*. Philadelphia: Temple University Press, 1987.

Nussbaum, Martha. *The Fragility of Goodness*. New York: Cambridge University Press, 1986.

————. *Love's Knowledge: Essays on Philosophy and Literature*. New York: Oxford University Press, 1990.

————. *Poetic Justice: The Literary Imagination and Public Life*. Boston: Beacon Press, 1996.

Olafson, Frederick, "Narrative History and the Concept of Action." *History and Theory*, vol. 9 (1970), pp. 265–89.

O'Neill, Patrick. *Fictions of Discourse: Reading Narrative Theory*. Toronto: University of Toronto Press, 1994.

Ong, Walter. "Oral Remembering and Narrative Structures." *Analyzing Discourse: Text and Talk*, ed. Deborah Tannen. Washington, D.C.: Georgetown University Press, 1982, pp. 12–24.

Outka, Gene. "Character, Vision, and Narrative." *Religious Studies Review*, vol. 6, no. 2 (1980), pp. 110–18.

Passerini, Luisa. "A Memory for Women's History: Problems of Method and Interpretation." *Social Science History*, vol. 16, no. 4 (1992), pp. 669–94.

Pellauer, David. "Time and Narrative and Theological Reflection." *Philosophy Today*, vol. 31 (Fall, 1987), pp. 262–86.

Personal Narratives Group. *Interpreting Women's Lives*. Bloomington: Indiana University Press, 1989.

Peterson, Carole, and Alyssa McCabe. *Developmental Psycholinguistics: Three Ways of Looking at a Child's Narrative*. New York: Plenum Press, 1983.

Phelan, James, ed. *Reading Narrative: Form, Ethic, Ideology*. Columbus: Ohio State University Press, 1989.

————. "Narrating the PC Controversy: Thoughts on Dinesh D'Souza's *Illiberal Education*." *Narrative*, vol. 2, no. 3 (October, 1993), pp. 254–67, with reply by Dinesh D'Souza, pp. 268–69, and rejoinder, pp. 270–71.

Phelan, James, and Peter Rabinowitz, eds. *Understanding Narrative*. Columbus: Ohio State University Press, 1994.

Polanyi, Livia. *Telling the American Story: A Structural and Cultural Analysis of Conversational Storytelling*. Norwood, N.J.: Ablex, 1985.

Polkinghorne, Donald. "Narrative and Self-Concept." *Journal of Narrative and Life History*, vol. 1, no. 2–3 (1991), pp. 135–53.

————. *Narrative Knowing and the Human Sciences*. Albany: State University of New York Press, 1988.

Posner, Richard. *Law and Literature: A Misunderstood Relation*. Cambridge: Harvard University Press, 1988.

Potter, Jonathan, and Margaret Wetherell. *Discourse and Social Psychology.* Newbury Park, Calif.: Sage Publications, 1987.

Preece, Allison. "The Range of Narrative Forms Conversationally Produced by Young Children." *Journal of Child Language,* vol. 14 (1987), pp. 353–73.

Prince, Gerald. *Narratology: The Form and Functioning of Narrative.* Berlin: Mouton, 1982.

Propp, Vladimir. *Morphology of the Folktale,* trans. Lawrence Scott. Austin: University of Texas Press, 1968.

Rabinow, Paul, and William Sullivan, eds. *Interpretive Social Science: A Reader.* Berkeley: University of California Press, 1979.

———, eds. *Interpretive Social Science: A Second Look.* Berkeley: University of California Press, 1987.

Raglon, Rebecca, and Marian Scholtmeijer. "Shifting Ground: Metanarratives, Epistemology, and the Stories of Nature." *Environmental Ethics,* vol. 18, no. 1 (Spring 1996), pp. 19–38.

Randall, Frederika. "Why Scholars Become Storytellers." *New York Times Book Review* (January 29, 1984), pp. 1, 31.

Reagan, Charles, and David Stewart. *The Philosophy of Paul Ricoeur.* Boston: Beacon Press, 1978.

Reason, Peter, and Peter Hawkins. "Storytelling as Inquiry." *Human Inquiry in Action: Developments in New Paradigm Research,* ed. Peter Reason. London: Sage Publications, 1988, pp. 79–101.

Reed, John S. "On Narrative and Sociology." *Social Forces,* vol. 68 (1989), pp. 1–14.

Reid, Margaret. "Narrative Silence in America's Stories." *Journal of Narrative and Life History,* vol. 3, no. 2–3, pp. 269–82.

Richardson, Laurel. "The Collective Story: Postmodernism and the Writing of Sociology." *Sociological Focus,* vol. 21, no. 3 (August, 1988), pp. 199–208.

———. "Narrative Sociology." *Journal of Contemporary Ethnography,* vol. 19 (1990), pp. 116–25.

Ricoeur, Paul. "Action, Story, and History." *Salmagundi,* no. 60 (Spring-Summer, 1983), pp. 60–72.

———. "History as Narrative and Practice." *Philosophy Today,* vol. 29 (1985), pp. 213–22.

———. "The Human Experience of Time and Narrative." *Research in Phenomenology,* vol. 9 (1979).

———. "The Model of the Text." *Social Research,* vol. 38, no. 3 (1971), pp. 529–62.

———. "The Narrative Function." *Hermeneutics and the Human Sciences,* trans. and ed. John Thompson. Cambridge: Cambridge University Press, 1981, pp. 274–96.

———. *Time and Narrative* (3 vols.), trans. Kathleen McLaughlin and David Pellauer. Chicago: University of Chicago Press, 1984, 1985, 1988.

Riessman, Catherine. "Beyond Reductionism: Narrative Genres in Divorce Accounts." *Journal of Narrative and Life History*, vol. 1, no. 1 (1991), pp. 41–68.

———. "Strategic Uses of Narrative in the Presentation of Self and Illness." *Social Science and Medicine*, vol. 30, no. 11 (1990), pp. 1195–1200.

———. *Divorce Talk: Women and Men Make Sense of Personal Relationships*. New Brunswick: Rutgers University Press, 1990.

Rimmon-Kenan, Shlomith. *Narrative Fiction: Contemporary Poetics*. New York: Methuen, 1983.

Robbins, Wesley. "Narrative, Morality and Religion." *Journal of Religious Ethics*, vol. 8, no. 1 (Spring, 1980), pp. 161–76.

Robinson, John. "Personal Narratives Reconsidered." *Journal of American Folklore*, vol. 94 (1981), pp. 58–85.

Robinson, John, and Linda Hawpe. "Narrative Thinking as a Heuristic Process." *Narrative Psychology*, ed. Theodore Sarbin. New York: Praeger, 1986, pp. 111–25.

Roe, Emery M. *Narrative and Policy Analysis: Theory and Practice*. Durham: Duke University Press, 1994.

Roeh, Itzhak. "Journalism as Storytelling, Coverage as Narrative." *American Behavioral Scientist*, vol. 33, no. 2 (November-December 1989), pp. 162–68, with comments by Tamar Liebes (pp. 169–71) and Paolo Mancini (pp. 172–74).

Rorty, Richard. *Contingency, Irony, and Solidarity*. New York: Cambridge University Press, 1989.

Rosaldo, Renato. *Culture and Truth*. Boston: Beacon Press, 1989.

———. "Ideology, Place, and People Without Culture." *Cultural Anthropology*, vol. 3, no. 1 (1988), pp. 77–87.

Rose, Carol M. *Property and Persuasion: Essays on the History, Theory, and Rhetoric of Ownership*. Boulder: Westview Press, 1994.

Rosenau, Pauline. *Post-Modernism and the Social Sciences*. Princeton: Princeton University Press, 1992.

Rosenwald, George, and Richard Ochberg, eds. *Storied Lives: The Cultural Politics of Self-Understanding*. New Haven: Yale University Press, 1992.

Rosie, Anthony. "'He's a Liar, I'm Afraid': Truth and Lies in a Narrative Account." *Sociology*, vol. 27, no. 1 (February, 1993), pp. 144–52.

Roth, Paul. "How Narratives Explain." *Social Research*, vol. 56, no. 2 (Summer, 1989), pp. 449–78.

————. "Narrative Explanation: The Case of History." *History and Theory*, vol. 8 (1988), pp. 1–13.

Rowland-Serdar, Barbara, and Peregrine Schwartz-Shea. "Empowering Women: Self, Autonomy, and Responsibility." *Western Political Quarterly*, vol. 44, no. 3 (1991), pp. 605–24.

Rudelic, Dana. "Tragic Fiction of Identity and the Narrative Self." *Dialectic and Narrative*, ed. Thomas Flynn and Dalia Judovitz. Albany: State University of New York Press, 1993, pp. 217–23.

Runyan, William. *Life Histories and Psychobiography: Explorations in Theory and Method*. New York: Oxford University Press, 1983, pp. 61–78.

Russell, Robert. "Analyzing Narratives in Psychotherapy." *Journal of Narrative and Life History*, vol. 3, no. 4 (1993), pp. 337–60.

Ryan, Marie-Laure. "Narrative in Real Time: Chronicle, Mimesis and Plot in the Baseball Broadcast." *Narrative*, vol. 1, no. 2 (May, 1993), pp. 138–55.

————. *Possible Worlds, Artificial Intelligence, and Narrative Theory*. Bloomington: Indiana University Press, 1991.

Sabia, David, and Jerald Wallulis, eds. *Changing Social Science*. Albany: State University of New York Press, 1983.

Sacks, Oliver. *An Anthropologist on Mars*. New York: Alfred A. Knopf, 1995.

————. *The Man Who Mistook His Wife for a Hat*. New York: Harper and Row, 1987.

Saldivar, Ramon. "Lyrical Borders: Modernity, the Nation and Narratives of Chicano Subject Formation." *Narrative*, vol. 1, no. 1 (January, 1993), pp. 36–44.

Sarbin, Theodore. "A Narrative Approach to 'Repressed Memories.'" *Journal of Narrative and Life History*, vol. 5, no. 1 (1995), pp. 51–66.

————. "The Narrative as a Root Metaphor for Psychology." *Narrative Psychology: The Storied Nature of Human Conduct*. New York: Praeger, 1986, pp. 3–21.

Sarbin, Theodore, and Karl Scheibe, eds. *Studies in Social Identity*. New York: Praeger, 1983.

Sass, Louis. "Anthropology's Native Problems." *Harper's*, no. 272 (May, 1986), pp. 49–57.

Schank, Roger. *Tell Me a Story: A New Look at Real and Artificial Memory*. New York: Charles Scribner's Sons, 1990.

Schank, Roger, and Robert Abelsen. *Scripts, Plans, Goals, and Understanding*. Hillsdale, N.J.: Lawrence Erlbaum Associates, 1977.

Scheibe, Karl. "Self-Narratives and Adventure." *Narrative Psychology*, ed. Theodore Sarbin. New York: Praeger, 1986, pp. 129–31.

Scheppele, Kim Lane. "Foreward: Telling Stories." *Michigan Law Review*, vol. 87 (August, 1989), pp. 2073–98.

Schleifer, Ronald, Robert Davis, and Nancy Mergler. *Culture and Cognition: The Boundaries of Literary and Scientific Inquiry.* Ithaca, N.Y.: Cornell University Press, 1992.

Schneewind, J. B. "Virtue, Narrative, and Community: MacIntyre and Morality." *Journal of Philosophy*, vol. 79, no. 11 (1982), pp. 653–63, with reply by Alasdair MacIntyre, pp. 663–65.

Scholes, Robert, and Robert Kellogg. *The Nature of Narrative.* New York: Oxford University Press, 1966.

Schwartz, Barry, Yael Zerubavel, and Bernice Barnett, "The Recovery of Masada: A Study in Collective Memory." *Sociological Quarterly*, vol. 27 (1986), pp. 147–64.

Scott, Joan Wallach. "The Evidence of Experience." *Critical Inquiry*, vol. 17 (1991), pp. 773–97.

———. "History in Crisis? The Others' Side of the Story." *American Historical Review*, vol. 94, no. 3 (1989), pp. 680–92.

Scott, Robert. "Narrative Theory and Communication Research." *Quarterly Journal of Speech*, vol. 70 (May, 1984), pp. 197–204.

Sewell, William. "Introduction: Narratives and Social Identities." *Social Science History*, vol. 16, no. 3 (Fall, 1993), pp. 479–88.

Shafer, Ray. "The Psychoanalytic Vision of Reality." *A New Language for Psychoanalysis.* New Haven, Conn.: Yale University Press, 1976, pp. 22–56.

Shea, John. *Stories of God.* Chicago: Thomas More Press, 1978.

Sherman, Sandra. "Lady Credit No Lady: Or, the Case of Defoe's 'Coy Mistress,' Truly Stat'd." *Texas Studies in Language and Literature*, vol. 37, no. 2 (Summer, 1995), pp. 185–214.

Sherzer, Joel. "The Interplay of Structure and Function in Kuna Narrative." *Analyzing Discourse: Text and Talk*, ed. Deborah Tannen. Washington, D.C.: Georgetown University Press, 1982, pp. 306–22.

Sherwood, Stephen Jay. "Narrating the Social." *Journal of Narrative and Life History*, vol. 4, no. 1 (1994), pp. 69–88.

Shotter, John, and Kenneth Gergen. *Texts of Identity.* London: Sage, 1989.

Showalter, Elaine. "On Hysterical Narrative." *Narrative*, vol. 1, no. 1 (January, 1993), pp. 24–35.

Shuman, Amy. *Storytelling Rights.* Cambridge: Cambridge University Press, 1986.

Shweder, Richard, and Robert Levine, eds. *Culture Theory.* New York: Cambridge University Press, 1984.

Silvers, Anita. "Politics and the Production of Narrative Identities." *Philosophy and Literature*, vol. 14, no.1 (1990), pp. 99–107.

Simpkinson, Charles, and Anne Simpkinson, eds. *Sacred Stories: A Celebration of the Power of Stories to Transform and Heal*. San Francisco: Harper Collins, 1993.

Singer, Jerome, ed. *The Child's World of Make-Believe: Experimental Studies of Imaginative Play*. New York: Academic Press, 1973.

Smith, Bruce J. *Politics and Remembrance*. Princeton: Princeton University Press, 1985.

Smith, Joseph H., ed. *Telling Facts: History and Narration in Psychoanalysis*. Baltimore: Johns Hopkins University Press, 1992.

Smith, Philip. "The Semiotic Foundations of Media Narrative." *Journal of Narrative and Life History*, vol. 4, no. 1 (1994), pp. 89–118.

Snow, Catherine, and Beverly Goldfield. "Building Stories: The Emergence of Information Structures from Conversation." *Analyzing Discourse: Text and Talk*, ed. Deborah Tannen. Washington, D.C.: Georgetown University Press, 1982, pp. 127–41.

Snyder, Gary. *The Practice of the Wild*. San Francisco: North Point Press, 1990, pp. 48–77, 110–13.

Somers, Margaret. "Narrativity, Narrative Identity, and Social Action: Rethinking English Working-Class Formation." *Social Science History*, vol. 16, no. 4 (1992), pp. 591–630.

Sparshott, Francis. "This Is Not the Real Me." *Philosophy and Literature*, vol. 17, no. 1 (1993), pp. 1–15.

Spence, Donald. "Narrative Smoothing and Clinical Wisdom." *Narrative Psychology*, ed. Theodore Sarbin. New York: Praeger, 1986, pp. 211–32.

———. *Narrative Truth and Historical Truth: Meaning and Interpretation in Psychoanalysis*. New York: W. W. Norton, 1982.

Stahl, Sandra Dolby. *Literary Folkloristics and the Personal Narrative*. Bloomington: Indiana University Press, 1989.

Stanzel, Franz Karl. *A Theory of Narrative*. Cambridge: Cambridge University Press, 1984.

Steele, Robert. "Deconstructing Histories: Toward a Systematic Criticism of Psychological Narratives." *Narrative Psychology*, ed. Theodore Sarbin. New York: Praeger, 1986, pp. 256–75.

Stein, Nancy, and Christine Glenn. "An Analysis of Story Comprehension in Elementary School Children." *New Directions in Discourse Processing*, ed. Roy Freedle, vol. II. Norwood, N.J.: Ablex, 1979, pp. 53–120.

Stein, Nancy, and Susan Goldman. "Children's Knowledge about Social

Situations: From Causes to Consequences." *The Development of Children's Friendships*, ed. Steven Asher and John Gottman. Cambridge: Cambridge University Press, 1981, pp. 297–321.

Stein, Nancy, and Margaret Policastro. "The Concept of Story: A Comparison Between Children's and Teachers' Viewpoints." *Learning and Comprehension of Text*, ed. Heinz Mandl, Nancy Stein, and Tom Trabasso. Hillsdale, N.J.: Lawrence Erlbaum Associates, 1984, pp. 113–55.

Steinmetz, George. "Reflections on the Role of Social Narratives in Working-Class Formation: Narrative Theory in the Social Sciences." *Social Science History*, vol. 16, no. 3 (Fall, 1992), pp. 489–516.

Stempel, Wolf-Dieter. "Everyday Narrative as a Prototype." *Poetics*, vol. 15 (1986), pp. 203–16.

Stern, Alfred. "Fiction and Myth in History." *Diogenes*, no. 42 (Summer, 1963), pp. 98–118.

Stone, Elizabeth. *Black Sheep and Kissing Cousins: How Family Stories Shape Us.* Hammondsworth: Penguin Books, 1988.

Stone, Lawrence. *The Past and the Present.* Boston: Routledge and Kegan Paul, 1981, pp. 74–96.

———. "The Revival of Narrative: Reflections on a New Old History." *Past and Present*, vol. 85 (1979), pp. 3–25.

Stone, Robert. "The Reason for Stories: Toward a Moral Fiction." *Harper's*, no. 276 (June, 1988), pp. 71–76.

Stoneburner, Tony, ed. *Parable, Myth, and Language.* London: Church Society for College Work, 1968.

Stroup, George. *The Promise of Narrative Theology.* Atlanta: John Knox, 1981.

Sturgess, Philip. "A Logic of Narrativity." *New Literary History*, vol. 20 (Spring, 1989), pp. 763–83.

Sutton-Smith, Brian. "Children's Fiction Making." *Narrative Psychology*, ed. Theodore Sarbin. New York: Praeger, 1986, pp. 67–90.

Tanaka, Stefan. "History: Consuming Pasts." *Journal of Narrative and Life History*," vol. 4, no. 4 (1994), pp. 257–76.

Tannen, Deborah. *Analyzing Discourse: Text and Talk.* Washington, D.C.: Georgetown University Press, 1982.

Taylor, Bron, ed. *Ecological Resistance Movements: The Global Emergence of Radical and Popular Environmentalism.* Albany: State University of New York Press, 1995.

Taylor, Charles. *Sources of the Self.* Cambridge: Harvard University Press, 1989, pp. 91–107.

Thiemann, Ronald. "The Promising God: The Gospel as Narrated Promise."

Why Narrative?, ed. Stanley Hauerwas and L. Gregory Jones. Grand Rapids, Mich.: William B. Eerdmans, 1989, pp. 320–47.

Thorndyke, Perry. "Cognitive Structures in Comprehension and Memory of Narrative Discourse." *Cognitive Psychology*, vol. 9 (1977), pp. 77–110.

Tilley, Terrence W. *Story Theology.* Collegeville, Minn.: Liturgical Press, 1990.

Todd, Alexandra, and Sue Fisher, eds. *Gender and Discourse: The Power of Talk.* Norwood, N.J.: Ablex Publishing, 1988.

Todorov, Tzvetan. *The Poetics of Prose*, trans. Richard Howard. Ithaca: Cornell University Press, 1977.

Toews, John. "Perspectives on the 'Old History and the New': A Comment." *American Historical Review*, vol. 94, no. 3 (1989), pp. 693–98.

Tololyan, Khachig. "Cultural Narrative and the Motivation of the Terrorist." *Journal of Strategic Studies*, vol. 10, no. 4 (1987), pp. 217–33.

Toulan, Michael. *Narrative: A Critical Linguistic Introduction.* New York: Routledge, 1988.

Trabasso, Tom, Tom Secco, and Paul Van Den Broek. "Causal Cohesion and Story Coherence." *Learning and Comprehension of Text*, ed. Heinz Mandl, Nancy Stein, and Tom Trabasso. Hillsdale, N.J.: Lawrence Erlbaum Associates, 1984, pp. 83–111.

Trabasso, Tom, and Linda Sperry. "Causal Relatedness and the Importance of Story Events." *Journal of Memory and Language*, vol. 24 (October, 1985), pp. 599–611.

Trabasso, Tom, and Paul Van Den Broek. "Causal Thinking and the Representation of Narrative Events." *Journal of Memory and Language*, vol. 24 (October, 1985), pp. 612–30.

Trad, Paul. "Use of Developmental Principles to Decipher the Narrative of Preschool Children." *Journal of the American Academy of Child and Adolescent Psychiatry*, vol. 31, no. 4 (July, 1992), pp. 581–92.

Trumpener, Katie. "The Time of the Gypsies: A 'People Without History' in the Narratives of the West." *Critical Inquiry*, vol. 18, no. 4 (Summer, 1992), pp. 843–84.

Turner, Victor. *The Anthropology of Performance.* New York: Performing Arts Journal Publications, 1986.

———. *From Ritual to Theatre: The Human Seriousness of Play.* New York: Performing Arts Journal Publications, 1982.

Turner, Victor, and Edward Bruner, eds. *The Anthropology of Experience.* Urbana: University of Illinois Press, 1986.

Van Buren, John. "Critical Environmental Hermeneutics." *Environmental Ethics*, vol. 17, no. 4 (Fall 1995), pp. 259–75.

Van Dijk, Teun. "Action, Action Description, and Narrative." *New Literary History*, vol. 6 (1975), pp. 273–94.

Van Maanen, John. *Tales of the Field: on Writing Ethnography*. Chicago: University of Chicago Press, 1988.

Van Teeffelen, Toine. "Scripts and Projects as Modes of Understanding Political Actions: The Representation of Palestinians in Best-Selling Literature." *Journal of Narrative and Life History*, vol. 2, no. 2 (1992), pp. 163–82.

Viney, Linda, and Lynne Bousfield. "Narrative Analysis: A Method of Psychosocial Research for Aids-Affected People." *Social Science and Medicine*, vol. 32, no. 7 (1991), pp. 757–65.

Vitz, Paul. "The Use of Stories in Moral Development: New Psychological Reasons for an Old Education Method." *American Psychologist*, vol. 45 (June, 1990), pp. 709–20.

Vizenor, Gerald. "Bone Courts: The Rights and Narrative Representation of Tribal Bones." *American Indian Quarterly*, vol. 10 (Fall, 1986), pp. 319–31.

Wagner-Martin, Linda. *Telling Women's Lives: The New Biography*. New Brunswick: Rutgers University Press, 1994.

Walsh, W. H. "'Plain' and 'Significant' Narrative in History." *Journal of Philosophy*, vol. 65 (1958), pp. 479–84.

Watson, David. "Against Forgetting." *Utne Reader* (March/April 1994), pp. 112–15.

Watson, Karen Ann. "A Rhetorical and Sociolinguistic Model for the Analysis of Narrative." *American Anthropologist*, vol. 75 (1973), pp. 243–64.

Weintraub, Stanley. "Autobiography and Historical Consciousness." *Critical Inquiry*, vol. 1, no. 4 (1975), pp. 171–93.

———. *The Value of the Individual: Self and Circumstance in Autobiography*. Chicago: University of Chicago Press, 1978.

West, Barbara. "Women's Diaries as Ethnographic Resources." *Journal of Narrative and Life History*, vol. 2, no. 4 (1992), pp. 333–54.

West, Robin. "Economic Man, Literary Woman: One Contrast." *Mercer Law Review*, vol. 39 (1988), pp. 867–78.

———. *Narrative, Authority, and the Law*. Ann Arbor: University of Michigan Press, 1993.

Whaley, J. F. "Readers' Expectations for Story Structures." *Reading Research Quarterly*, vol. 17 (1981), pp. 90–114.

White, Hayden. *The Content of the Form: Narrative Discourse and Historical Representation*. Baltimore: Johns Hopkins University Press, 1987.

———. *Metahistory: The Historical Imagination in Nineteenth-Century Europe*. Baltimore: Johns Hopkins University Press, 1973.

————. "The Question of Narrative in Contemporary Historical Theory." *History and Theory*, vol. 23 (1984), pp. 1–33.

White, James Boyd. "What Can a Lawyer Learn from Literature?" *Harvard Law Review*, vol. 102 (1989), pp. 2015–47.

White, Morton. *Foundations of Historical Knowledge*. New York: Harper and Row, 1965.

White, Stephen K. *Political Theory and Postmodernism*. New York: Cambridge University Press, 1991.

Widdershoven, Guy. "The Story of Life: Hermeneutic Perspectives on the Relationship Between Narrative and Life History." *The Narrative Study of Lives*, ed. Ruthellen Josselson and Anita Liebich. Newbury Park, Calif.: Sage, 1993, pp. 1–20.

Wiggins, James, ed. *Religion as Story*. New York: Harper and Row, 1975.

Williams, Gareth. "The Genesis of Chronic Illness: Narrative Reconstruction." *Sociology of Health and Illness*, vol. 6 (1984), pp. 175–200.

Winquist, Charles. *Epiphanies of Darkness: Deconstruction in Theology*. Philadelphia: Fortress Press, 1986.

Winson, Jonathan. "The Meaning of Dreams." *Scientific American* (November, 1990), pp. 86–96.

Wyatt, Frederick. "The Narrative in Psychoanalysis: Psychoanalytic Notes on Storytelling, Listening, and Interpreting." *Narrative Psychology*, ed. Theodore Sarbin. New York: Praeger, 1986, pp. 193–210.

Yoffe, Emily. "How the Soul Is Sold." *New York Times Magazine* (April 23, 1995), pp. 44–49.

Young, Katharine. "Perspectives on Embodiment: The Uses of Narrativity in Ethnographic Writing." *Journal of Narrative and Life History*, vol. 1 (1991), pp. 213–43.

————. *Taleworlds and Storyrealms*. Boston: Martinus Nijhoff, 1987.

Zwiebach, Burton. *The Common Life: Ambiguity, Agreement, and the Structure of Morals*. Philadelphia: Temple University Press, 1988.

Contributors

PHILIP ABBOTT is Professor of Political Science at Wayne State University, where he teaches political theory. His most recent book is *Strong Presidents: A Theory of Leadership on America* (1996), which examines presidential discourse. He is currently writing a book on the role of narrative in the theory of American exceptionalism.

BARBARA (ROWLAND-SERDAR) AGLAIA, who formerly taught political science at Northern Arizona University, is a free-lance writer and poet. She is writing a book on the medical/psychiatric use of the diagnosis, "borderline personality," and how its use takes power away from women and their stories. The book offers an alternate way for borderlines and all women to view, and live with, the power of their intuition and intensity.

EDWARD M. BRUNER is Professor Emeritus of Anthropology and Professor Emeritus of Criticism and Interpretive Theory at the University of Illinois. He was past president of the American Ethnological Society and the Society of Humanistic Anthropology. He has done field work among Native Americans, and in Indonesia and Africa. He edited *Text, Play and Story* and *The Anthropology of Experience* (with Victor W. Turner).

DAVID CARR received his Ph.D. from Yale University and has taught at Yale University, Washington University, the University of Oklahoma, the New School, and the University of Ottawa. He is the author of *Phenomenology and the Problem of History; Time, Narrative and History; Interpreting Husserl;* and articles on phenomenology, narrative theory, and the philosophy of history. Since 1991, he has been Professor of Philosophy at Emory University, where he currently serves as department chair.

JIM CHENEY teaches environmental ethics and American Indian philosophy at the University of Wisconsin—Waukesha. He was the recipient of a Rockefeller Foundation Visiting Humanities Fellowship during the 1996–97 term to work with the interdiscipinary Native Philosophy Project at Lakehead University, Thunder Bay, Ontario.

STEPHEN CRITES has taught philosophy and religion at Wesleyan University, Connecticut, since 1961. He has done scholarly work on Hegel, Kierkegaard, and other nineteenth century continental thinkers. Currently, he is writing a book entitled *The Aesthetic Formation of Experience.*

WALTER S. FISHER is Director of the School of Communications, University of Southern California. He is author of *Human Communication as Narration: Toward a Philosophy of Reason, Value, and Action,* and most recently co-editor of *Rethinking Knowledge: Reflections Across the Disciplines* (with Robert F. Goodman), which includes a chapter he wrote entitled "Narration, Knowledge, and the Possibility of Wisdom."

KENNETH J. GERGEN is Gil and Frank Mustin Professor of Psychology at Swarthmore College, Pennsylvania, where he also directs the Interpretation Theory program. He has contributed to psychology by helping to introduce social constructionist ideas within various domains and is currently developing a "relational theory" approach to social psychological issues. Among his most recent writings are *Realities and Relationships: Soundings in Social Construction* (Harvard University Press, 1995), *The Saturated Self* (Basic Books, 1992), and *Therapy as Social Construction,* co-edited by Sheila McNamee (Sage, 1992). He and Mary Gergen are among the founders of the Taos Institute, a group dedicated to the practical development of social constructionist ideas, particularly in family therapy and organizations.

MARY GERGEN is Associate Professor of Psychology and Women's Studies at Pennsylvania State University, the Delaware County Campus. Her area of professional interest involves feminist theory, social constructionism, and narrative studies. Her most recent publication is *Toward a New Psychology of Gender: A Reader,* co-edited by Sara Davis (Routledge, 1996). She has also written numerous articles and chapters on gender issues, and is the editor of *Feminist Thought and the Structure of Knowledge* (New York University Press, 1988). She is currently writing a book tentatively entitled *Improvisations in Psychology: A Feminist/ Social Constructionist Practice.*

GERTRUDE HIMMELFARB is Professor Emeritus of History at the Graduate School of the City University of New York. Her most recent books are *The Demoralization of Society: From Victorian Virtues to Modern Values* (Knopf, 1995), and *On Looking into the Abyss: Untimely Thoughts on Culture and Society* (Knopf, 1994). The essay in this volume appeared in *The New History and the Old* (Harvard University Press, 1987).

LEWIS HINCHMAN is Professor of Government in the Center for Liberal Studies, Clarkson University. A Hegel specialist, he is author of *Hegel's Critique of the Enlightenment* (1984) and co-editor of *Hannah Arendt: Critical Essays* (1994). He has written articles on autonomy, individuality, human rights, the work of Alasdair MacIntyre, and the theory and practice of the environmental movement.

SANDRA HINCHMAN is Professor of Government at St. Lawrence University. Much of her scholarly work concerns the thought of Hannah Arendt, on whom she co-edited (with Lewis Hinchman) an anthology of critical essays. She has also published articles on environmental theory and public policy, and on the work of Joan Didion, whose essay, "The White Album," helped to stimulate her interest in narrative.

ANTHONY PAUL KERBY is author of *Narrative and the Self* (Indiana University Press, 1991), as well as articles on language and continental thought. A former member of the Philosophy Department at the University of Ottawa, he co-founded The Canadian Society for Hermeneutics and Postmodern Thought. He is currently writing novels and philosophical manuscripts on a full-time basis.

ALASDAIR MACINTYRE is Arts and Sciences Professor of Philosophy at Duke University, having taught previously at Oxford University, the University of Essex, Boston University, Vanderbilt University, and the University of Notre Dame. He is the author of many works of moral philosophy, including *After Virtue; Marxism and Christianity; The Unconscious; Hume's Ethical Writings; A Short History of Ethics; Against the Self-Images of the Age; Whose Justice? Which Rationality?;* and, most recently, *Three Rival Versions of Moral Enquiry.*

DAVID NOVITZ studied at Rhodes University before taking his doctorate at Oxford. He is currently Reader in Philosophy at the University of Canterbury, New Zealand, and is author of *Pictures and Their Use in Communication* (1977); *Knowledge, Fiction, and Imagination* (1986); and *The Boundaries of Art* (1992).

PEREGRINE SCHWARTZ-SHEA is Associate Professor of Political Science at the University of Utah. Her research examines the application of rational choice theory to organizations, individual-group relations, and gender inequality.

GARETH WILLIAMS is Reader in Sociology in the Institute for Social Research and Assistant Director of the Public Health Research and Resource Centre, University of Salford, England. He has published extensively in academic and professional journals on the subjects of public health, health services, disability, and the relationship between lay and biomedical knowledge. He is co-editor of *Challenging Medicine* (1994) and *Researching the People's Health* (1994), and co-author of *Understanding Rheumatoid Arthritis* (1995).

Index

Abbott, P., xv, xxv, 238
Abelson, R., 74, 84
aborigines, 343–34
abortion, 286–90
Abrahams, R., 271
Abram, D., 348
action, 18, 20, 95, 144, 323. *See also*
    behavior
    in analytic philosophy, 246
    and autonomy, 224
    central, of a story, 77–79, 81–82,
        87, 89, 93, 99
    and communication, 308, 314
    as enacted narrative, 249
    intelligibility of, 247–48
    musicality of, 27–29
    and personal narrative, 163, 176,
        243, 249
    and plot, 102
    and narrative rationality, 313
    and self-image, 151
    social, 73, 94
    structuralist view of, 107
    teleological nature of, 12–13,
        15–16
    temporal form of, 27
actor, 88, 142, 251
Addelson, K., 222
agency, 195
agriculture, 341
Aiken, C., 335, 343
Ainu, 339
alienation, 333
Allen, P. G., 334
American dream, 321–22
American Revolution, 67

Annales historians, xxii, xxvii–xxviii,
    52, 66, 68–70
annals, xv, xx, xxvi, 9, 52, 145, 147,
    156
anthropology, 4, 187, 237, 265–68,
    270–72, 275, 347
anticipation, 38–40
anti-narrativists, xxvi–xxvii
anxiety, 206, 219
Applebee, A., 181
Aquinas, T., 70
Arendt, H., ix, 70, 237
Aristotle, xxviii, 9, 17, 62–63, 68, 70,
    137, 189–90, 203, 236, 242, 251
Arnett, R., 309
Arnold, M., 104
art, xix, 31, 35, 40, 137–38, 143–44,
    157–58
Atwood, M., 346
audience, xvi, 13–14, 17, 75, 96, 106,
    131–32, 134, 270, 272, 323
Augustine, 10, 33–34, 36–39, 49, 128
Austin, J. L., 262
authenticity, 310–13, 244
author (authorship), 30, 119, 139,
    251–53
authority, 47–48, 56, 284
autobiography. *See* narrative,
    personal
autonomy, xxvii–xxviii, 122, 127, 138,
    201, 203, 213, 222–24, 226, 228

Barthes, R., ix, 2, 9, 11, 13, 127, 135,
    235, 264, 270, 274
Bateson, G., 271, 313
Beard, C., 52

Becker, C., 53
Beckett, S., 127, 136
behavior, 146, 151–52, 155, 176, 245, 270. *See also* action
Bellah, R., 282, 291–95, 302, 322
Bennett, W. L., xxi, xxviii, 3, 72–103
Bentham, J., 56, 288
Benveniste, E., 127, 132, 137–38
Berscheid, E., 184
Bettelheim, B., 162, 168
biography, 188, 209
bioregionalism, 334–35, 339, 341–44
Bird, E., 342, 346
body, 132, 137, 139–40, 144, 187, 193, 198, 201–3, 209, 289
Booth, W., 315
bourgeois society, 299–300
Braudel, F., xxii
Brewer, M., 123
Brooks, P., 136
Bruner, E., xxiv, xxix, 237, 264–80
Bruner, J., xx, xxiii
Bruss, E., 130
Buber, M., 307–11
Burke, E., xxiv, 260
Burke, K., 93–94
Burrell, D., 315
Butterfield, H., 54, 68

Calhoun, J., 67
Callicles, 321
Calvino, I., 127
Campbell, J., 164–65
Caputo, J., 329
Carr, D., xx, xxvi, 2, 7–25
Carroll, D., 139
Cartesianism, xiv, xviii, xxvii, 46, 332. *See also* Descartes
Cassirer, E., 274
cast, supporting, 178
causality, 11, 79, 116, 130, 190, 194, 200, 203–4, 206–10, 244, 266
censorship, 153
chance, 193
character (personal), 137, 174, 255, 316, 322
characters, ix, 88, 237, 251
as authors, 252–53
in cultural narratives, 235

imputed, 254
literary, 134, 142
in personal narrative, 120
relation of, to storyteller, 13–14, 16, 19
structualist views of, 106
Chatman, S., 9, 270
Cheney, J., xxv, xxvii, xxix, 238–39, 323–49
childhood, 31, 36, 76–77, 171, 217–18, 241, 341–42
Christianity, 50, 189, 285, 296, 314, 340
Christman, J., 222
chronicles, xv, xx, xxvi, 9, 35–39, 119, 145, 147, 156, 187
Cicourel, A., 183
cinema, 35
citizenship, xxviii
civility, 307, 321
Clement of Alexandria, 43–44
closure, 149
Cobb, E., 37
coherence, 120
of events, 154, 163, 169
in narratives, 3, 172, 312–16, 319
personal, 121, 136, 146, 148, 173, 223, 336
Collingwood, R. G., xxi–xxii, 189
Comaroff, J., 209
comedy, 164, 167, 171–72, 175, 248
communication, 72, 174
and cognition, 73–74
and community, 238, 307–9, 311, 313, 323–24
dialogic, 176, 220, 309–10, 320
effective, 171
and symbolic understanding, 77, 97–98, 176
communitarianism, 237, 294–95
community, ix, xviii, 213–16, 322, 334
bioregional, 238
and communication, 238, 308, 311, 313, 319
formation and maintenance of, xvii, xxv, 20, 22, 340, 343
hierarchy in, 318–19
and identity, 259, 338
and language, 311, 328, 331–32

and narrative, 237, 259, 314, 339, 344–45
   political, 257, 283
   tribal, 331
Confucianism, 347
consensus, 237, 311–12
conservatism, 227, 260
conversation, 248–49, 295, 329
Craig, G., 64
Crites, S., xvi, xx–xxi, xxix, 2, 26–50, 119
culture, 106, 158, 171–72, 247, 338
   American, 302
   changes in, 265, 268, 274
   and discourse, 133, 329, 332
   export of, 331
   forms of expression in, 26, 28, 240–41
   and narrative genres, 167, 169
   male supremacy in, 216, 218
   and selfhood, 120, 158, 243
   role in shaping narrative, 220, 236–37
   and time, 40–41
   traditional, xiii, 30, 236, 332
   utility of narrative in, 173, 184, 235

Dahrendorf, R., 242
Dante, 42
Danto, A., 14, 16
Darnton, R., 64
Darwin, C., 109–10, 114–16
death, 12, 20, 243, 250, 255, 287, 319
deconstruction, 136, 329
Degler, C., 67
Deleuze, G., 11, 129, 136, 140
Deloria, V., 331, 346
democracy, 308, 310, 323
dependency, 217, 219–21, 223, 230
Derrida, J., 127, 130, 136–38, 140, 311
Descartes, R., xviii, 130, 133. *See also* Cartesianism
desire, 139
Dewey, J., 307–11, 318
dialogue, 181, 220, 238, 272, 310–11, 320
Dillard, A., 290
Dilthey, W., 121, 128, 139
Disch, L., xxvii

discourse, 130, 308, 346. *See also* language
   contextualist, 331–34, 337
   and experience, 267, 271
   feminist, 336
   implied subject of, 127
   modernist, 328
   monologic, 309
   and narrative, 269–70
   about Native Americans, 276
   postmodernist, 334
   public, 310–11
   and rationality, 314
   of stress, 199
drama, 39–41, 131, 146, 169–70, 237, 251
dualism, xviii, 45–46, 220, 329, 333
Dunn, J., 284–85
Durkheim, E., xxiii

Eco, U., 141
ecology, 333, 337, 342
economics, 4, 121
Elliot Smith, G., 108–9
Elton, G., 57–58
Emerson, R. W., 291
empathy, 148
empiricism, 145, 255
empowerment, 213–15, 222, 224, 227, 318. *See also* power
Engels, F., 62, 251
environmentalism, xxv, 335
environmental studies, 238
epistemology, xix, 125, 138, 183, 204, 313, 329–30, 332–33
Epstein, S., 123
equality, 196, 210, 214, 216, 276, 318
Erikson, E., 173
ethics, 17, 238, 281, 320, 334–35, 339, 345. *See also* morality
ethnicity, 265
existentialism, 241, 255
experience, 18, 32, 46–47, 128, 314
   and communication, 75, 77
   and community, 338
   dramatic nature of, 40
   and identity, 38, 150
   interpretation of, 75, 77, 235
   and language, 138, 267, 345

experience *(continued)*
  and memory, 35, 37
  and narrative, 17, 24, 29, 42, 54, 48,
    131, 271–72
  past, 35, 150
  and temporality, 28, 38–39, 41, 49
explanation, xv

fairytales, 107–8, 115, 168
family, 213, 215, 220–21, 223, 226–28,
  320, 337
farce, 248
Faust, 46
Feldman, M., 102
feminism, xix, 3, 121, 123, 214,
  222–23, 227, 328–29, 336–37,
  342–43
fidelity, narrative, 314–15, 317, 319
film, 169
Filmer, R., 285
Finkelhor, D., 218
Fisher, W., xxv, 238, 307–27
folklore, 4, 83, 109
form, narrative, 106, 182
Forster, E. M., 104–5
Foucault, M., 11, 136, 140, 268, 274,
  311
fragmentation, 136, 187
Franklin, B., 291, 294–95
freedom, 68, 172, 273, 319
French Revolution, 65–66
Freud, S., 36, 68, 131, 146
Frye, N., 164
functionalism, 107, 237
Furet, F., 52, 66, 68

Gadamer, H. G., xv, 121, 307, 310–12,
  319
Garfinkel, H., 96, 101
Geertz, C., ix
genesis, 186, 189
genre, 248, 250
geography, 336–38
Gergen, K., xviii, 120–21, 161–84
Gergen, M., xviii, 120–21, 161–84
Gilligan, C., 122, 225, 227
Gnosticism, 346
God, 200, 204–7, 210, 283, 285
Goffman, E., 146, 152, 242, 259

Goodman, N., 159
Goodman, R., 318
Gorfain, P., 277
Gorz, A., 297, 299–300
Gould, C., 227
government, 57–58, 63, 65, 175, 284
Gramsci, A., 56
Greeks, ancient, 189–90, 347
Gregory, W. K., 108, 110
Grimshaw, J., 222–23
Guattari, F., 136
guilt, 180, 201–2
Guttman, A., 282, 302

Habermas, J., 238, 307–8, 310–11
happiness, 42–43
Harding, S., 329
Hardy, B., 11, 130, 249
Hare, R. M., 262
Harre, R., 183
Hauerwas, S., 313, 315, 317–18
health, 332, 342, 344–45
Hegel, G. W. F., 20–22, 58, 274, 308
Heidegger, M., 15, 139, 237, 252,
  329–30
Hempel, C., 8
Herman, J., 218
hermeneutics, xv, xviii, 106–7, 121,
  125, 237
hero, 4, 109, 111–12, 164–65
Herrnstein-Smith, B., 270
hierarchy, 319
Hillman, J., ix, 220, 340
Himmelfarb, G., xxii, xxvi–xxvii, 3,
  51–71
history, 23, 184, 244
  and action, 18, 249, 251
  Annaliste view of, xxviii, 52, 66,
    68–70
  and community, 318, 338
  consciousness of, 1
  and fiction, 7, 9, 16, 282
  narrative, xx, xvii, xxiii, xxvi, 8
  new vs. old, xx, xxii, 3, 51–54,
    65–66, 69
  and personal narrative, 171, 207,
    255, 261, 264
  reason in, xxvii, 56–59, 63, 68
  social vs. political, 51–56, 59–66, 68

and tradition, 259, 261
and truth, 7, 254
Whig interpretation of, 53–55
Hobbes, T., 290–91
Hobsbawm, E., 66
Homer, xxviii, 250
homosexuality, 155
Howard, G., xxix
human nature, 143–44
Hume, D., 148, 189–90, 212
hunter-gatherers, 341, 344
Husserl, E., 11, 15, 121, 128, 130,
    137–38
Hutton, J., 116
Huxley, A.,114
Huxley, T., 104, 114–15
hypnosis, 183

identity, ix, xxii, 17, 43, 314. *See also*
    self; narrative, personal
    anti-narrativist views of, xxviii
    and the arts, 143–44, 157–58
    and community, 20, 155, 235, 239,
        258–59, 332, 336, 338
    constructedness of, 156
    and experience, 38, 41
    and first-order narratives, xvii
    impact of illness on, 185, 199, 203,
        210
    narrative constitution of, xvii, xxii,
        235–36
    nested, 182
    politics of, xxvii, 146
    postmodern views of, , 336, 338,
        343
    pre-narrative, xix, xx
    and self-esteem, 151
    and time, xviii, 38
    traditional accounts of, 173
    unified, 148, 254–56
ideology, 253, 310, 313
illness, 121, 185–210
images, visual, 145, 147, 158
imagination, 131, 146, 151
individualism, 213–14, 228, 236–37,
    258–60, 263, 293, 295, 309, 343
intelligibility, 246–47, 251–52, 255–56,
    261, 263
intention, 243–47

interpretation, 97, 269
    of actions, 79
    conflicting, 273
    vs. description, 131
    effect of story structure on, 99
    evaluation of, 93–95
    mediating function of, 133
    of narratives, 75, 84–85, 101, 300,
        302
    in personal narrative, 189, 195
    psychotherapeutic, 120
    of texts, 115
    in trials, 79, 84–85
introspection, 145
irony, 13–14, 164

Jaggar, A., 222
James, W., 120, 126, 132, 185
Jay, T., 332–33
Jaynes, J., 346
Jefferson, T., 291, 295
Jepthah, 282–85
Johnson, S., 252
Jonas, H., 346
Jones, G., 313, 317–18
Jorgenson, J., 268–69
Joyce, J., 254
Judaeo-Christian tradition, 144
judgment, 72–74, 76–77, 82, 87, 90–91,
    93, 95–96, 99, 175, 224, 242, 263
Julliard, J., 70
Jung, C., 137
justice, xxiv, xxv, 73, 96–98, 195–96,
    225, 227, 261, 302

Kafka, F., 68, 251
Kant, I., xix, 48, 142, 222, 259, 262, 315
Karst, K., 322
Keith, A., 108–10
Kellner, H., xxix
Kellogg, R., 14
Kempe, M., 61
Kerby, A., xviii, xx, xxix, 120–22,
    125–42
Kermode, F., xix, 9, 11, 48, 50, 117
knowledge, xiv, 35, 74
Knowles, D. D., 250
Kolodny, A., 122
Krausz, M., 160

Lacan, J., 134, 137, 141
land, 331, 334, 339–40, 343
Landau, M., xxii, 4, 104–18
language, 41, 86, 131, 133, 139, 158, 312, 332–33. *See also* discourse
  as human capacity, 26, 135
  and landscape, 340, 343
  ordinary, xiii, 73, 89
  postmodernist views of, 128, 328–31
  and selfhood, 120, 125, 132, 138, 163
  and social change, 265, 269
law, xxi, xxiv, xxvi, 3, 58–59, 72, 214, 217, 297, 299, 318, 322
Leach, E., 270
Lecky, P., 173
Leibniz, G., 254–55
Leopold, A., 335
Lerner, H., 226
Levi-Strauss, C., 266, 274
Lewis, C. S., 302–3
Lewis, G., 207
liberalism, xxvi, 214, 216–17, 221–22, 225, 227–28, 260, 296, 299, 312
Linton, R., 266–67
literary criticism, xxvi, 7, 9, 105, 114, 127, 132
literature, 10, 13, 134–35, 137, 154, 164, 168, 248
Locke, J., 282–86, 291, 296, 300, 302
logic, 316–18
Lyotard, J. F., ix, xiii, xvii–xviii, xxvii, 236, 311–12

Macaulay, T. B., 53–54, 61
Machiavelli, N., 57, 146
MacIntyre, A., ix, 11–12, 140, 165, 201, 205, 238, 241–63, 281, 302, 307, 309, 313, 335
  and community, 320–23
  critique of, 17, 312
  on epistemological crises, 183
  summary of argument on narrative, xxiii–xxiv, 236–37
Maguire, P., 209
Maines, D., xiii
Mair, M., xxiii
Malinowski, B., 237

marriage, 243
Martin, B., 336, 341, 344
Marxism, xiii, 54–55, 62, 187, 252–53, 274
maturity, 173
Mead, G. H., 120–21, 133, 146, 212
meaning, 236, 269
  creation of, 220, 265
  cultural, 40, 237, 293
  of discourse, 96, 247
  and ethics, 238
  and identity, 129
  of life, 321
  loss of, in modernity, xiii
  of narratives, 119, 314
  of past events, 61–62, 116
  personal, 146, 149, 162, 199–200, 205, 238, 255, 293
  and selfhood, 125, 224
  of social action, 73, 96
  social construction of, 176, 178
  and temporality, 44, 266–67
  of texts, 106
meaninglessness, 201
medicine, 185, 208, 322
Meilander, G., 290–91
memory, ix, xvii–xviii, xx, xxvii, 1–4, 103, 236
  chronicle of, 32–40
  and identity, xix, xxiii, 129–30
  and introspection, 145
  social constructionist view of, 103
Merleau-Ponty, M., 12, 128
Merton, T., 43
metanarratives, xiii, 1, 311, 323
metaphor, 10, 202, 345
metaphysics, 46, 133, 201, 209
Mill, J. S., 229
mimesis, 9–10
mind, 126
Mink, L., xix, 8, 10, 14, 16–17, 249–50, 252
Mitterand, F., 65
modernity, 44, 241–42, 252, 260, 330, 332, 347
Mohanty, C., 336, 341, 344
Montaigne, M. de, 129
morality, xxviii, 208, 225, 242, 256, 259, 262, 307, 321, 339–41

motherhood, 202, 215, 341
Munz, P., 11
music, 26–32, 40–41, 46–47
Musil, R., 188–89
myth, 109, 157, 264, 321, 342
  and community, 340, 345
  hero in, 164–65
  and identity, 135, 254
  moral instruction through, 254,
    339
  Native American, 333–34
  and selfhood, 135, 223, 345
  and social cohesion, 236, 254
  structuralist view of, 266
  traditional, 30, 32, 44

narrative. *See also* reconstruction,
    narrative; sequence, narrrative;
    structure, narrative
  abstraction from, 45, 47, 238
  consistency in, 93–94
  co-authored, xxv, 191
  contraction of, 45, 47'
  cultural, 121
  definition of, xvi
  embedded, 171–72, 250–51, 256,
    259, 316
  first vs. second order, xvii–xviii,
    23, 129, 237
  historical vs. fictional, 7–11, 22–23,
    282
  logic of, 89
  negotiation of, 177–78, 180
  personal, xiv, xix,xxx, 120–21, 127,
    129, 132, 135, 154, 156, 162–63,
    172, 176, 179, 181, 186–87
  progressive, 166–67, 169, 174–76
  sacred vs. mundane, xxi, 2, 31–33,
    38, 41–42, 47–49
  social function of, 173–76
  stability, 165–67, 169, 175
  regressive, 166–67, 169–70, 175–76
narratology, 105–6, 128, 132, 137
nationalism, 322
Native Americans, xxiv–xxv, 49, 237,
    264–69, 272, 274, 276, 331–34,
    343, 347
naturalism, 345
naturalness, 155–56, 158

nature, 329–30, 334, 337, 339–43
Neanderthals, 104–5
Nichols, R., 70
Nieburg, H., 184
Nietzsche, F., 68, 130, 137
nihilism, 47
Nisbet, R., 189
Novitz, D., xix, xxvii, 120–21, 143–60

objectivity, 95–96, 329
Olafson, F., 11
oligarchy, 309
ontology, 328
oppression, 273
order, 187, 205
organicism, 342–43
Ortega y Gasset, J., 163, 172
Orwell, G., 189
Osborn, H. F., 108, 110
Outka, G., xxviii

Paine, T., 304
Palmer, P., 320
Parfit, D., 254
paternalism, 224–26
patriarchy, 284, 343–45
Peirce, C. S., 126–27, 133, 293
Perelman, C., 315, 318, 323
personhood, 137
persuasion, 308
phenomenology, xiv, xviii, 2, 18, 48,
    121, 126, 129
philosophy, 7, 126, 130, 151, 236, 255,
    331–32
Piltdown man, 108
Plato, xxviii, 20, 144
plot, ix, 1–2, 4, 10, 12–13, 101–2, 106,
    135, 235, 237, 248, 271–72, 303,
    323
political theory, 237–38, 281, 288, 303
politics, xxvi, 70, 174–75, 283, 311. *See
    also* power; public sphere
  and the arts, 143, 157
  Burkean, 260
  conflict in, 236, 277
  in history, xxvii, 52–53, 66, 68
  of identity, 120, 144, 146, 152–53,
    158
  and narrative, 238

politics *(continued)*
  and narrative reconstruction,
    195–97, 206
  and private sphere, 215, 227
  in scholarship, 265
political science, 237, 245
Polkinghorne, D., xxi
postmodernism, xviii, 44, 47, 307
  anti-foundationalism of, xxviii
  and discourse, 311, 328, 336, 346
  and environmental ethics, 335,
    339, 345
  feminist, 328–29, 343
  in fiction, 101
  French, 140
  and identity, , 344
  and language, 311, 328–29, 334
  and narrative, xxvi–xxvii, xxix, 1
  and selfhood, 126, 136, 138
  and the subject, 330
poststructuralism, xxv, 11, 120, 127,
    156
Potter, D., 70
Poulet, G., 49
power, 322. *See also* empowerment
  in Foucault, 311
  in Habermas, 310
  inequalities of, 196, 210
  and narrative, 235, 269
  political, 284, 299
  societal, 198
powerlessness, 216, 218–19, 223, 225,
    227, 276
practice, 257, 259, 320
pragmatism, 312
Pratt, M. B., 336
predictability, 253, 245
pride, 150
private sphere, 122, 213–17, 219–22,
    224, 226–28, 257, 297, 299, 320
Propp, V., 83, 102, 107–8, 114
protagonist, 177
Proust, M., 134, 139
psychoanalysis, 187, 270
psychology, xiv, xviii, xix, xxii, xxvii,
    12, 73–74, 120, 151, 198, 208, 333,
    336–37
psychopathology, 151, 199, 247,
    331–32, 337

public sphere, 139, 176–77, 197–98
  and autonomy, 222
  discourse in, 311
  and private sphere, 213–17,
    219–21, 224, 226–28, 257, 297,
    320
  self-expression in, 132
  virtue in, 257

quest, 205–6, 237, 256–57

Reagan, R., 316
reason (rationality), 281
  in Aristotle, 63, 68
  and community, 238
  elitist view of, 318
  in evolutionary theory, 111
  in history and politics, 3, 56–59, 63,
    68
  as human capacity, 63, 68, 310, 319,
    324
  instrumental, 330
  medical, 193, 201
  modernist view of, 312
  narrative, xxv, 313–17
  pure, 220
  and tradition, 260
rebellion, 194, 197, 201, 203
recollection, 2, 145, 150
reconstruction, narrative, xix, 186,
    188–90, 195, 200, 204, 206, 209
Reich, C., 74
relationships, 179
relativism, moral, 156
religion, 30, 42, 118, 136, 294
  export of, 331
  and illness, 190–200, 202, 207, 210
  Native American, 268
  and personal narrative, 190, 200,
    202, 207, 210
  and personal coherence, 148
  and rationality, 152
  monotheistic vs. polytheistic, 340
  as agency of socialization, 153
religious studies, 2
representation, 8–9
repression, 131, 136
republicanism, xiii, 297
resistance, 264–65, 267–69, 272–76

responsibility, 90–91, 198, 201–2, 213, 216, 222, 224–26, 228
revolution, 47
rhetoric, 319–20
Richardson, L., xxix
Ricoeur, P., ix, xx, 2, 9–10, 23–24, 50, 126, 131, 134–35, 138, 140, 159, 177, 236, 340
Ridington, R., 334
rights, 213, 215–16, 225, 228
ritual, 135, 163, 264, 334
Robbe-Grillet, A., 101
Robinson, J., 52
Rogers, C., 173
role, 18, 142, 163, 178–79, 198, 203, 242, 254, 259
Rolston, H., 335
romance, 164, 171
Romans, ancient, 189
Rorty, R., 238, 312, 330, 333
Rosaldo, M., 224
Roth, P., xxii
Rowland-Serdar, B., xix, xxvii, xxix, 122, 213–33
Rubin, S., 182

Sachs, H., 86, 89
saga, 250
Said, E., 273
Sarbin, T., 183
Sartre, J. P., 21, 125, 131, 161, 209, 242, 251–52, 259, 262
satire, 164
Schafer, R., 134, 159, 267, 270
Schapp, W., 178
Scheler, M., 137
Scheman, N., 226
Schochet, G., 285
Scholes, R., xxiv, 14
Schutz, A.,15, 96, 121
Schwartz-Shea, P., xix, xxvii, xxix, 122, 213–33
science, natural, xxi–xxii, 4, 104, 114, 196, 208
science, social, xiv–xv, xxii, xxvii, 18, 21, 56
script, 163, 237
self, xix, 137, 140. *See also* identity; personal narrative

coherence of, 20, 146, 149
and community, 340, 344–45
empowerment of, 224, 228
essentialist, xviii, 133, 338–39
knowledge of, 222
and language, 120, 125–26, 139, 332, 334, 343
loss of, 201
postmodern view of, 138, 334
narrative view of, xiv, 17, 22, 119, 128, 243, 255
and other, 134
in Sartre, 251
and social roles, 259
in sociological theory, 242, 269
in women, 220–21, 224, 228
self-determination, 273
self-esteem, 151
self-image, 151–52, 161–62, 186
self-government, 222
self-knowledge, 232
semiotics, xviii, 126, 132–34, 138–39
Seneca, 70
sequence, narrative, xv, 2, 8, 11–13, 15, 17, 19, 80, 116, 119, 146–47, 162, 252, 255, 265–67, 277, 314
setting, ix, 244–46
sexuality, 218–19
Shakespeare, W., 146, 170
Shannon, F., 298
Shepard, P., 340–42
Shklovsky, V., 102
Silko, L. M., 328
Skinner, B. F., 245
socialism, 296, 309–10, 323
socialization, 154, 171, 235, 254
sociology, xix, 121, 187, 209–10, 241, 263
Socrates, 321
solipsism, xviii
Sophocles, 170
speech-act, 248
Spence, D., xv, 141
Spranger, E., 137
Stacey, J., 215, 227
state, xxv, 153, 157
state of nature, 284
Stevens, W., 136
Stone, L., 4, 52, 64

story. *See* narrative
storyteller, 13–16, 19, 96, 254, 269, 279
Stout, J., 322
stress, 199–200, 203
Strindberg, A., 170
structuralism, xvi, 9–10, 106–8, 115, 132, 138, 187, 237, 266
structure, deep, 105
structure, narrative, 10, 80, 149, 155, 253, 267, 274–75, 277
Sturtevant, B., 274
style, 27, 29–30, 48
Swidler, A., 292
subject, collective, xvii
subjectivity, 125, 127, 130, 132, 134, 137–38, 140, 330, 332
subject/object relations, 273–74
Sunday, P. R., 347
symbol, 41–42, 84–86, 89, 91–92, 94–95, 97–98, 133, 176, 235, 274
Synge, J. M., 154

Tax, S., 271
Taylor, A. J. P., 187
Taylor, C., 121, 133–35, 139, 141, 237
telos (teleology), 236, 241, 343
 deconstruction of, 136
 and myth, 334
 personal, 119, 189–90, 199, 201, 203, 205–7, 255
 and unpredictability, 253
temporality, 19, 246, 266. *See also* time
 of action, 27
 of experience, 34, 44
 and identity, xx
 of memory, 37
 of music, 28
 of narrative, 29
 of narrative self, 162, 164
 of the subject, 33
theater, 142, 169
theme, 303
theodicy, 190, 210
theory, vs. narrative, xv, xxv, 238, 281–303
therapy, xix, 120
time, 14, 31, 41, 48, 50. *See also* temporality

 and action, 15, 83
 clock, 129
 and community narrative, 235
 experience through, 26, 38
 future, 259, 267
 identity over, 128
 order of, 200
 passage of, 11, 13
 past, 259, 261, 265, 267, 277
 and personal narrative, 170
 present, 267, 277
 in narrative, 42–43, 147–48, subjective, 130
Thomson, J., 282, 286–91, 302
Thucydides, xxviii
Tocqueville, A. de, xvi
Toulmon, S., 318
tradition, xiii, xxvii, 265
 in American society, 291, 294
 Burkean view of, 260
 and community, xxiv, 235
 constitution of, 259
 loss of, 136
 and meaning, 44
 moral, 254
 in narratology, xxiii
 and personal narrative, 132
 and virtues, 261, 263
tragedy, 164, 167, 169–72, 175, 248, 250, 261–62, 293
Trevelyan, G., 53–54
Tronto, J., 225
tribalism, 331, 334, 347
truth, 136, 261, 313, 333
 bioregional, 343
 correspondence theory of, 329
 historical vs. narrative, 1
 of narratives, 2, 7, 119, 317
 objective, 57, 59, 145, 263
 social negotiation of, 328
 transsubjective, xvi
 versions of, 312
Turgenev, N., 209
Turner, V., ix, 270

understanding, 310–13

Vico, G., 254
Vilar, P., 69

Virgil, 251
virtue, 242–43, 254, 257–59, 261, 263

Walzer, M., 237, 282, 296–300, 302
Wells, H. G., 303
Wendell, S., 214, 225
Westkott, M., 221, 224–25
White, H., ix, xix, xxvi–xxvii, xxix, 2, 8, 10–13, 24, 154
Whitman, W., 291, 295

Whorf, B., 49
Williams, G., xix, 185–212
Wilshire, B., 142
Winthrop, J., 291
Wisdom, J., 340
Wittgenstein, L., 172, 293
Wolf, D., 182
Wollheim, R., 131, 135, 146
Wood Jones, F., 108–11
workplace, 190–98